THE UNITED STATES IN A CHANGING WORLD

BOOKS BY THE AUTHOR

THE
UNITED STATES
IN A
CHANGING
WORLD

AN HISTORICAL ANALYSIS
OF AMERICAN FOREIGN POLICY

JAMES P. WARBURG

G. P. Putnam's Sons   New York

Copyright, 1954, by James P. Warburg

Library of Congress Catalog Card Number: 54-10506

MANUFACTURED IN THE UNITED STATES OF AMERICA

To Jimmy, Jennifer and Philip
in the hope that their generation
will be wiser than mine

And it shall come to pass in the last days, that the mountain of the Lord's house shall be established in the top of the mountains, and shall be exalted above the hills; and all nations shall flow unto it . . . and they shall beat their swords into plowshares, and their spears into pruninghooks: nation shall not lift up sword against nation, neither shall they learn war any more.

ISAIAH ii:2, 4; MICAH iv:1, 3.

PREFACE

HISTORICAL research ofen serves as the intellectual's escape from contemplating the anxiety-laden present. This study of the development of American foreign policy has been undertaken from the opposite point of view—that is, in the belief that insight into the sources of our past conduct is essential to an understanding of the baffling problems of the present.

We are living in what appears to be a major turning point in world history. The age of sovereign nation-states living perpetually on the brink of armed conflict is drawing to a close in what should be the dawn of a new era of supra-national world organization. Yet, at the very moment when armaments have become instruments of self-destruction, the nation-states have been driven to rely more than ever before upon military power as an instrument of self-preservation. Only a re-awakening of reason and the re-assumption of command by reason can halt the present compulsive rush toward disaster. Only faith in man as a rational being can guide the world through this somber interval in which it is apparently too soon for world government and too late for anything less.

The United States of America was founded precisely upon the belief that "Nature and Nature's God" created man as a creature endowed with reason and a capacity for infinite progress. That faith—and only that faith—denies the possibility that man may have been created merely in order that he might learn how to destroy himself in a final mushroom cloud of atomic particles.

At such a time, it is not irrelevant to re-examine past experience and, especially, the problems faced by that extraordinary group of men who shaped our early foreign policy in such

vii

a manner that it became a shield behind which the young republic could grow into strength and independence.

We are faced with the necessity of accommodating ourselves to a world of divided aims and divided power, but of an increasingly evident common interest in survival. Both we and our enemies possess vast physical power but can use it as an instrument of policy only at the risk of self-annihilation. Our problem is that of arriving at universal disarmament under enforced world law before fear and frustration drive us to destruction.

Our forefathers, however, were faced with the problem of independent survival in a world of conflicting national interests and of power divided between contenders for supremacy each greatly superior in physical strength to their young nation. Yet, without appreciable armed force or economic power of coercion, our early statesmen and diplomats made the United States into the most dynamic moral force in their world. It bears directly upon our contemporary problems to understand how this feat was accomplished—to understand that it was not merely a miracle of statesmanship and diplomacy but the product of a people dedicated to an overriding common purpose which enlisted the sympathy and allegiance of mankind.

A less pleasant but equally profitable lesson to be drawn from our own history derives from the succeeding period. Having attained a high degree of self-sufficient independence, of prosperity and of physical power, we somehow lost our wisdom, our skill in diplomacy and our moral influence in the world, permitting the ebullient pursuit of "success" to submerge the common ideal and the common purpose and to dictate a policy often far from wise and frequently executed with considerably less than adequate skill.

The key to our behavior as a nation among other nations in the latter part of our history lies in the nature of our domestic development. We have gone a long way toward proving that political democracy and what we call "free enterprise capitalism" are not fundamentally irreconcilable—toward proving that Karl Marx was wrong in maintaining that capitalism is necessarily and by its very nature a self-destructive system. What we have done, perhaps more than any other nation, is to demonstrate that capitalism can be made into a self-improving system; that its inherent anti-democratic forces can be controlled; and that its dynamic power can be harnessed to the greatest good of the greatest number in a society steadfastly dedicated to democratic principles. To say that we have gone a long way toward proving that these things can be done is not to say that we have done them. We are still far from having closed the gap between our political beliefs and our economic behavior. But the progress which has been made at definite periods in our history should fortify the conviction that the gap can eventually be closed. It is surely no accident that, during the last century, the periods of our greatest folly in foreign policy have followed or coincided with phases in our domestic development when internal conflict or runaway economic forces have submerged political principle and controlled national policy; and that periods of domestic reform have coincided with or been followed by greater sanity and restraint in dealing with foreign affairs.

External factors have, at times like the present, exercised a profound influence upon our aims and actions but, in the final analysis, it is what we are and what we wish to be, here at home, that governs our behavior as a nation.

Part of our present bafflement arises from the fact that "we" have changed. The United States began as a nation of individual free enterprisers, each knowing where his interest lay and what he expected of his government. Today, we are rapidly becoming a nation of wage and salary earners, working for Big Business or Big Government. The great masses of American men and women dependent upon the managerial elite are disoriented, unsure of where their own interests lie and of what national policies would advance or injure them. The old, pluralistic "we," composed of infinitely diverse individuals pursuing each his interest, is being supplanted by a new mass "we," composed of men and women seeking security through conformity to standards of thought and behavior set by the managerial elite. The picture of "the American" is becoming a composite of white-collar faces, from research-scientist and sales-manager down to office boy. What does this mass "we" want? What does it believe? "We," in relation to our government, were formerly like passengers in a stagecoach, each of whom knew how to handle a team of horses, knew the road and could, if necessary, take the driver's place. Today, we are more like passengers sealed up in an airliner in flight, unable to jump off if we sense danger, unable to communicate with the captain and ignorant of what to ask him to do, if we were able to speak to him. We can, to be sure, fire the captain, once we reach ground safely—but, if the captain makes a wrong move, we may not live to enjoy that privilege.

In this strange, new world, we are probably no more confused and disoriented than most other peoples, but most other peoples neither aspire to world leadership nor have they had unsought responsibility thrust upon them by history.

Whether we wish to lead or reluctantly accept the unsought responsibilities of leadership, we can no longer afford the egocentricity, the vacillation and the notional behavior which are the privilege of the very young, the weak and the dependent. The United States has come of age; and, when a nation comes of age, it behooves its people to understand the inner conflicts and contradictions which caused the ups and downs and the sudden zigzags of its youth.

As a first step in that direction, this study attempts a synthesis of domestic development and foreign policy, seeking to show wherever possible the impact of each upon the other. It aims at the limited objective of making accessible to the ordinary baffled citizen the essential outlines of the past from which derive so many of the puzzling problems of the present. In a sense, it merely provides the basic raw material for a much more exhaustive investigation of the complex motivations of national behavior.

In seeking to gain a first insight, one is compelled to choose between two methods—between making a necessarily superficial survey of the whole sweep of the American past or undertaking a microscopically close examination of perhaps a few significant years in American history. The two methods are not mutually exclusive. Indeed, the attempt to make the broad survey suggests any number of projects for the more minute study of isolated periods. In such research, a more thorough examination might be made not only of the political and economic bone structure of society but of its surrounding cultural and psychological fabric and, especially, of the irrational elements in public opinion and sentiment. Three outstanding works have broken the trail: James Harvey Robinson's *The American Mind in the Making;* Vernon L. Parrington's *Main Currents in American Thought;* and Henry Steele Commager's *The American Mind.* These studies suggest an approach which might fruitfully be employed in a more intensive exploration of the sources of American conduct.

A host of intriguing questions arise. What, for example, has been the impact of Darwinism upon American thought and behavior? What has been the influence of Freud's discoveries, or of Karl Marx's economic interpretation of history? What has been the effect of foreign criticism, or of self-criticism by American reformers and dissenters? What has been the influence of the various religious movements? More specifically—to what extent has the proselyting drive of the Protestant churches affected American foreign policy, and what motivates the missionary spirit? What psychological factors have impelled us toward isolating ourselves from Europe while being drawn toward intervention in the Orient, when both our major economic interests and our cultural ties might be expected to incline us in the opposite direction?

The limited aim of the present study is to stimulate further inquiry, to contribute toward a more widespread realization that foreign policy cannot be understood merely in terms of international relations, and to indicate a method of investigation through which the individual citizen may find his way back into a sense of direct involvement and responsible participation. Our greatest danger lies in the alienation of the ordinary citizen from the conscious processes of policy formation. Foreign policy is not—even though it often appears to be—an esoteric business conducted by experts; it is the product of a society of men and women; its effectiveness or ineffectiveness depends, in the last analysis, upon mature citizenship.

Compression necessarily has involved subjective selection and the omission of much important detail; footnote references indicate where some of the original documents may be found and where more scholarly studies are available in the works of eminent historians. Among the latter, Thomas A. Bailey and Samuel Flagg Bemis have supplied the classical texts on American diplomatic history. Other careful and competent scholars have illuminated the detail of almost every period of American history. The author does not pretend to have digested more than a small part of the great fund of available research. He has drawn liberally upon whatever sources he could discover. The result is a selective study of American history, rather than history itself.

The prudent scholar would probably have stopped this survey at the conclusion of World War II. The author has ventured beyond the limits of conscientious scholarship, partly because the more recent developments bear so heavily upon the problems of the present and partly because the postwar period happens to be the field of his own most concentrated study. The reader should, however, be explicitly warned that this period is as yet so insufficiently documented that its history cannot be written with any true sense of perspective. In the concluding chapters, the discussion is necessarily colored by personal opinion not only as to how and why things happened —which is legitimate—but also, in some cases, as to *what* happened. President Truman's memoirs have not yet been published. Of the three men who served under him as Secretaries of State, only the first has published an account of his stewardship.* Much of the available material—such as that provided by the Senate hearings occasioned by the recall from Korea of General Douglas MacArthur—still awaits impartial, expert evaluation.

Finally, the concluding section is, on balance, sharply critical of United States postwar policy. The reader may feel that such criticism would be more useful if it presented alternatives to the policies criticized. Such alternatives have been put forward by the author in a series of books and pamphlets published during the past ten years; they are not included here because they would be out of place in an analysis of history, concerned not with what might have happened but with what actually occurred.

JAMES P. WARBURG

* James F. Byrnes, *Speaking Frankly* (New York, Harper & Brothers, 1947).

CONTENTS

xiii

PART FOUR

The Imperialism of Runaway
Free Enterprise

PART FIVE

The First World War
and Its Aftermath

PART SIX

The Diplomacy of
Franklin D. Roosevelt

CONTENTS

PART SEVEN

Disenchantment and
Cold War

EPILOGUE

PART ONE

The Establishment

CHAPTER ONE

The Colonial Background
(1607 – 1688)

MANY of the ideas, prejudices and predilections which today influence the making of United States foreign policy have deep roots in the past. Some of them originated in the war-torn, semi-feudal Europe from which the early settlers emigrated. Others developed on our own soil during the century and a half which elapsed between the establishment of the first English colonies and their emergence as an independent nation.

When Captain John Smith landed at Jamestown, the poet Milton and John Locke, the philosopher of early English liberalism, were as yet unborn. Yet the first germs of liberalism had already sprouted in the Reformation. Among the early settlers there were a few who, like Roger Williams, came to these shores in revolt against religious intolerance, seeking to found a society in which "each person may at all times freely and fully enjoy his own judgment and conscience in matters of religious concernments." The majority, however, came, like the Reverend John Cotton, to acquire freedom to worship as *they* pleased and to establish a community in which only their religious beliefs might be practiced. With a few rare exceptions, the Puritans brought with them not a revolutionary belief in liberty of conscience but a bigotry more narrow and repressive than that from which they had fled. Thus, both tolerance and intolerance were included in the ideological baggage brought from Europe during the first half of the century of early settlement.

Although Adam Smith was not to provide the rationalization for free enterprise capitalism until the year of Thomas Jefferson's Declaration of Independence, most of the early settlers

3

brought with them the strong desire to acquire wealth through individual enterprise, unhampered by political interference. The tobacco planters who settled Virginia and the merchants who were soon to build up the shipping trades of New England were stout believers in the as yet unformulated law of supply and demand operating in a free competitive market. On the other hand, the Jamestown colony was originally settled with the understanding that all property would be held in common, and it was in fact so held during the earliest years. Thus, since the earliest days of an American society, there were present both the competitive and the cooperative impulses, the one leading toward a "free economy" and the other toward a planned cooperative commonwealth.

Among the men who risked the hazards of a perilous voyage and the unpredictable hardships of settling in an unknown land were patriots and pacifists. Some came to America because they loved England and, in the spirit of Drake and Raleigh, wished to help expand her empire. Others came because they were weary of the incessant wars of Europe and wished to be free of the burdens they imposed.

And, finally, there were many who came here because they loved England, but not the England of King James I. Some felt reluctantly compelled to leave their homeland because its government had become weak and vacillating. Others were driven to depart by the conviction that the rule of the first Stuart king was too harsh and too arbitrary.

The seeds of these various contradictory sentiments had germinated quite naturally in the 17th century European environment. The Reformation had unleashed a series of religious and dynastic wars which meant little to the common people except hardship and impoverishment. The continuous quarrels of kings and bishops had tended to destroy what little freedom and security had existed for the masses under the feudal system, as well as the sense of responsibility for the people which had attached itself to feudal power. For the people of England, the long reign of Queen Elizabeth had been a comparatively happy period. Pursuing an official policy of peace while her "volunteer" sea-hawks enriched English coffers with gaily hijacked Spanish gold, Queen Bess had built up English power until, in the long war of 1585-1604, it was capable of successfully challenging Spanish control of the seas. When Elizabeth died, England was a proudly independent nation, free not only from the influence of Spain but from that of Rome.

James I came to the throne when the reaction to this period of efflorescence had already set in. The Scottish Protestant sat uneasily upon the thrones of Elizabeth and Mary, Queen of Scots. With control of the seas waiting to be firmly established as against Spain and Holland, and with the French challenge yet to come, James I needed money for ships and men. Claiming his divine right to levy imposts without the consent of Parliament, he became embroiled in a long and bitter struggle with that body as a result of which government was all but paralyzed. With the king unable and Parliament unwilling to raise revenues, the treasury was soon bare and hard times descended upon the country. Not only the perennially wretched poor, but artisans, merchants, farmers and country squires felt the pinch of the depression. These conditions supplied the economic motive for emigration, especially for those who were at the same time victimized by religious persecution.

Thus corn, vegetable seeds and the native tobacco were not the only items planted in the soil wrested from the Indians and cleared of forests by the early settlers. Tolerance and intolerance, predilections toward *laissez-faire* capitalism and toward cooperative common ownership, feelings of warlike patriotism and isolationist pacifism, the belief and the disbelief in the ability of people to govern themselves through parliamentary institutions—all these seedling sentiments were implanted in our soil from the day when it was first turned by spade and primitive plow.

In a new environment wholly different from that of Europe, some of these plants grew faster than others, while others slowly withered and died. Native permutations developed and new strains were added as the colonies grew and attracted settlers from Holland, Scotland, Ireland, Germany and France. The sentiments and beliefs originally imported from Europe began to show interesting variations, arising partly from the nature of the settlers, partly from varying physical environment and partly from historical accidents affecting the development of the individual colonies.

From the outset, there were marked differences between the Southern settlements in Virginia and the Carolinas and those in New England, with the Middle Atlantic colonies sharing some of the characteristics of each but also developing certain features of their own.

The Southern English colonies were founded partly as commercial ventures and partly as outposts against northward encroachment by the earlier Spanish settlements in Florida. (St. Augustine, the oldest city in what is now the United States, was founded in 1565.) During one of the earliest English attempts at settlement made by Sir Walter Raleigh, Virginia Dare was born, in 1587, as the first child of English parents to see the light of day on the North American continent. The first permanent English settlement was made at Jamestown in 1607.

The land and the climate in Virginia and the Carolinas favored the development of a plantation economy. Virginia became a tobacco-raising colony. North Carolina originally flourished through trade in deerskins. South Carolina raised tobacco, rice and indigo. Later, cotton was to become the major crop of the southeastern section. As individual land grants took the place of the original common tenure, there soon came into being two classes of colonists—the large plantation owners, who almost at once began to employ Negro slave labor, and the small farmers, who gradually pushed their way westward into the wilderness. Between these two classes a continuing struggle developed which provided a miniature preview of the protracted conflict soon to arise between the older seaboard colonies and the expanding West.

The frontiersmen, fighting their way forward against hostile Indians, became, in effect, the defense forces of the colonies. They, too, were the first settlers to encounter a "foreign policy problem," for, as they pushed across the mountains into the Tennessee and Ohio valleys, they found their egress to the sea blocked by Spanish control of the Mississippi. The frontiersmen constantly demanded freer land grants, a voice in government and greater cooperation in holding off hostile Indians. The tidewater oligarchy, backed by the royal governments and the established church, fought off these demands. In Virginia, the conflict actually reached the point of civil war when Governor Berkeley refused for 16 years to hold elections in order to preserve the control of the plantation oligarchy. With the overthrow of the Stuarts and the accession of the more liberal William of Orange (William III), the conflict subsided, but it was not until the last decades before the American Revolution that Virginia became a representative democracy. A similar development took place in North Carolina, but South Carolina remained an essentially oligarchical society until after the Revolution.

The Southern colonies, as a whole, were more docile toward the English crown because their economies fitted naturally into the mercantilist system. The plantation owners produced what the English wanted and bought from the mother country their clothes, their household furnishings and even some of their building materials. Thus they became both a valuable source of raw material and a desirable market for English manufactures.

The New England colonies, on the other hand, tended from the beginning to become economically independent and, later, to compete with the mother country. This came about partly because the colonists who settled Plymouth and Massachusetts Bay (in 1620 and 1625) were refugees from English persecution but even more because of the physical environment in which they happened to settle. The land of New England was suitable to small farms but not to plantations. The climate, with its short growing season and harsh winters, forbade the raising of cash crops such as were produced in the southern colonies. On the other hand, the wealth of good harbors and navigable rivers led naturally to the settlement of many small towns and villages, to the exploitation of timber resources, to the building of ships and to the development of the shipping and fishing trade. Where the Southerners imported their household goods in exchange for tobacco, rice and indigo, the New Englanders began to grow the necessary food on their little farms, to make homespun clothes, to build their own furniture, and to sail their own ships.

These environmental factors produced from the outset a

more democratic structure of government than in the South.
The town quite naturally became the basic unit of representative government. The single legislative assembly was composed
of deputies elected at town meetings and magistrates were
chosen by popular ballot. On the other hand, the nature of the
original settlers was such as to introduce certain anti-democratic
elements. The franchise was limited to property owners and
members of the established Congregational church. Where the
growth of democracy was inhibited in the South by the plantation economy, it was distorted in New England by religious
bigotry. Between 1644 and 1662, the persecution of Baptists and
Quakers in Massachusetts was so severe that Charles II intervened to put a stop to it. But even this was not enough. It took
an annulment of the charter in 1684 to end the religious limitation of the franchise. A new charter granted by William III
in 1691 provided for a democratic constitution and put an end
to theocratic rule, but not until after bigotry had had its final
orgiastic paroxysm in the Salem witch-burnings of 1691-1692.

Connecticut, New Hampshire and Rhode Island were settled
largely by migration from the Massachusetts colony, inspired
by a search for new lands and by revolt against religious bigotry.
The Rhode Island settlers in particular were motivated by Puritan persecution of the religious minorities and founded their
colony at Newport with the specific purpose of establishing complete freedom of worship for all sects and denominations. From
the original settlement at Hartford, Connecticut, an interesting
statement of policy has come down to us. It reads:

> To avoid notoriety and public attitudes; to secure priv-
> ileges without attracting needless notice; to act as intensely
> and vigorously as possible when action seems necessary and
> promising; but to say as little as possible and evade as much
> as possible when open resistance is evident folly.

The development of New England was characterized by a
process which was almost the antithesis of that which took place
in the South. Whereas, in Virginia, representative democracy
developed through the conflict of the frontier communities with
the land-owning, tidewater oligarchy, in Massachusetts an oligarchy of merchants and traders backed by the reactionary

clergy grew up within the originally democratic structure. The economic interest of the Southern colonists developed in such a way as to make them loyal to the mother country, so long as the mother country accorded reasonably fair political treatment, but the economic interests of New Englanders developed along lines which were inherently hostile to the English mercantilist system.

Beginning in 1651, the English Parliament enacted a series of laws designed to increase the dependence of the colonies upon the mother country, to stimulate their consumption of English products and to reserve colonial trade to English merchants and English shipping. The first Navigation Act of 1651 was primarily a measure against Dutch competition, but it applied to the American colonies the rule that all their exports must be carried in English or English-controlled vessels manned by English crews. Beginning in 1660, Parliament imposed a list of "enumerated goods" which the American colonies were permitted to export only to the mother country. Still later, laws were enacted prohibiting the colonists from manufacturing goods which might compete with English manufacturers. These restrictions were not rigorously enforced during the Civil War in England but, after 1673, measures were adopted to stop smuggling. This mercantilist system of colonial exploitation collided with the interests of New England and, to a certain extent, with the interests of the Middle Atlantic states.

In 1700, British exports to the colonies totalled £344,343 and colonial exports to England amounted to £395,023. By far the largest English trade was with Virginia and Maryland. The most important items of colonial export were tobacco, rice, deerskins and furs, to which were soon added indigo and naval stores (resin and turpentine). Lacking the ability to raise cash crops for export, the more northerly colonies paid for their smaller imports with fish, whale-oil and lumber.

The outstanding characteristic of the Middle Atlantic colonies was that they were originally settled by a stock of people quite different from those which founded the Southern and New England settlements. Swedes and Dutch first settled the mid-Atlantic seaboard. The Dutch took over the original Swedish settlements and were, in turn, taken over by the English.

The interior of Pennsylvania and New Jersey was colonized by English and Welsh Quakers and German sects brought over by William Penn. Both the Dutch and the Quakers were eminently more humane and, therefore, more successful in making friends of the aboriginal inhabitants than the English. This turned out to be of great importance in the subsequent history of North America. From the English settler's point of view, the only good Indian was a dead Indian. The Spaniards to the south were no less brutal; they did not kill off the aborigines but set out simultaneously to save their souls and to make them into slaves. The French, unlike the English settlers, were not interested in acquiring land for permanent settlement nor in imposing Catholicism and subservience, like the Spaniards; their interest being primarily in developing the fur trade, the French did not, as a rule, regard the Indians as hostile savages but as friends. The Dutch and the Quakers, fortunately, pursued a similar course; the alliances which they formed with the powerful Six Nations brought about something like a balance of power in the French and Indian Wars. It is an interesting fact that the English, after they took Nieuw Amsterdam from the Dutch, used Peter Schuyler, the former Dutch mayor of Fort Orange (Albany), to act as an intermediary between them and the Iroquois. Of William Penn's treaty with the Indians, Voltaire later said that it was "the only treaty not sworn to and never broken."

Whereas Penn's colonies introduced the stable and peaceful elements of Quakers, Mennonites and Moravians into the American melting-pot, the neighboring colony of Maryland added the first Roman Catholic communities.

Toward the close of the seventeenth century, the total population of the twelve English colonies was about 250,000. This was to rise during the next sixty years to about 2,000,000 and to almost 4,000,000 by the time the United States became a nation. Already, at about the turn of the first colonial century, there were present in the American society many variegated elements affecting the development of divergent attitudes toward religion, property rights, the relationship of the individual to the state and the relationship of the colonies toward the mother country.

In order to gain some insight into the further development of these trends and attitudes, we must now turn briefly to the European scene which determined the course of events in North America during the remainder of the colonial period.

CHAPTER TWO

Entanglement and Revolt
(1688–1776)

WHILE Britain was wresting control of the seas from Spain, France was engaged in a struggle for Continental hegemony with the declining Hapsburg Empire. Louis XIV, the "Sun King," dominated the European scene during the latter half of the seventeenth century. His chief adviser in foreign affairs was the powerful Cardinal Fleury.

So long as the Roman Catholic Stuarts maintained their dynasty in England, Anglo-French relations were, on the whole, friendly—so friendly, in fact, that during the reign of James II the colonists feared that the two monarchs might combine to impose Catholicism upon all of North America. With the overthrow of James II and the accession of William of Orange, there began a period of Anglo-French conflict, lasting from 1688 to 1763, which involved the American colonies in a series of wars between the rival mother countries. Under William III, England became the heart and soul of the Grand Alliance against France.

The first of the series of Anglo-French wars was the War of the League of Augsburg, which we call "The Dutch War." This conflict blocked French ambitions in the Low Countries. Though the war involved sporadic fighting in North America, the Treaty of Ryswick (1697) effected no territorial gains or losses for either side in this hemisphere.

Louis next turned his attention to Spain and succeeded in obtaining the succession to the Spanish throne for his grandson, Philip of Anjou. This diplomatic stroke occasioned the long and fiercely fought War of the Spanish Succession (1700-1713), which is called "Queen Anne's War" in American history books. In this long struggle the English-led Grand Alliance successfully fought off a consolidation of the French and Spanish empires. By the terms of the Peace of Utrecht, the victors conceded Philip of Anjou's succession to the Spanish throne, but robbed this concession of its significance by imposing a balance-of-power agreement forever separating the French and Spanish empires. In addition, France was compelled to cede to England Hudson Bay, Newfoundland and Acadia (Nova Scotia), thus yielding control of the mouth of the St. Lawrence river and endangering the French hold upon all of Canada. Spain was forced to grant important trade concessions to the English, including the rights to the Negro slave trade with the Spanish colonies.

This war again involved considerable bloodshed between the English and French colonists and their Indian allies. Its major importance from the American point of view was that it prevented the English colonies from being caught in a hostile pincer between Spanish power on the south and French power on the north. Moreover, the treaty emphasized a fact important to the colonists—namely, that the European balance of power had become to a very large extent dependent upon the balance of power in North America.

The death of Louis XIV, in 1715, brought to an end both the longest reign in European history and a period of French ascendancy.

The balance of power agreement was almost immediately violated by Spain. This brought on a short war in which Austria sided with France, while England, under Sir Robert Walpole's leadership, remained more or less aloof though preserving its alliance with France. The Treaty of Madrid (1721) disposed of Spain as a violator of the compact. During this brief conflict the French captured Pensacola but returned it to Spain under the peace settlement.

It was now England's turn to challenge the Utrecht balance of power. With France and Spain involved in dispute over the Polish succession and in an Austro-Prussian quarrel over Silesia, King George II was persuaded, against the advice of Walpole, to seize the opportunity for aggression against Spain. When this unsuccessful war—the War of Jenkins' Ear—merged into the War of the Austrian Succession, France entered the conflict as Spain's ally. In America, an expedition composed largely of New Englanders captured Louisburg on Cape Breton Island. Much to the disgust of the New Englanders, the port was returned to France under the Treaty of Aix-la-Chapelle in 1748. It was of little interest to the colonists that England thereby regained possession of Madras in far-off India. In this hemisphere, the sole result of the war was the founding of Georgia; this had been one of the provocative English acts leading up to the conflict with Spain. Eight years were now to elapse before England would make another attempt to upset the Utrecht balance.

The Duc de Choiseul, foreign minister under Louis XV, was shrewd enough to understand that the future of Europe now depended to a large extent upon the struggle for America. Unsuccessfully, he endeavored to persuade his sovereign to seek a new, firm alliance with Spain. Louis, under the influence of Madame de Pompadour and her favorites, became involved, instead, in an alliance with Austria which embroiled him in a war to recover Silesia from Frederick the Great of Prussia. Choiseul tried in vain to bluff England into remaining neutral by threatening to renew the family compact with Spain, but William Pitt, the Elder (later the Earl of Chatham), had now become the dominant figure in English policy and was not to be restrained by any such empty threat. Pitt realized that Germany was not in itself the decisive theater of action. During the ensuing Seven Years' War, he pursued a policy of giving Frederick the Great of Prussia just enough subsidies and just enough military aid to enable that redoubtable warrior to keep the field against the vastly superior coalition of France, Austria, Russia,

Sweden and Saxony, while England directed her own major effort against the French empire overseas.

Had Frederick been a less indomitable character, Pitt's strategy could not have succeeded. As it was, "Old Fritz" performed the incredible feat of marching and counter-marching, fighting first one member of the coalition and then another, throughout seven successive campaigns, being saved from defeat through sheer exhaustion by the death of the Russian Empress and the willingness of the new Tsar, Peter III, to make peace. By this time (1762), British troops under Clive had conquered India, Wolfe and Amherst had overcome Montcalm in Canada, Guadaloupe and Martinique had fallen to the British fleet and France had ceased to possess an overseas empire. After long hesitation, Spain entered the Seven Years' War just in time to share in the French defeat and to lose Florida to the English.

The American colonists participated to a considerable extent in this last of the so-called French and Indian Wars. Montcalm —a brilliant leader—managed to unite most of the northwestern Indians and, with their help, to invade upper New York and to push down the Ohio valley. The establishment of Fort Duquesne at the present site of Pittsburgh posed a serious threat to the western frontier and brought about the ill-fated expedition of the British General Braddock, in which George Washington and a Virginia contingent participated. After Braddock's death, Lord Geoffrey Amherst took over the British command; the colonists participated in his recapture of Fort Ticonderoga and in Wolfe's march on Quebec, as well as in the second and this time permanent capture of Louisburg.

It is doubtful whether Montcalm could have been turned back and defeated—irrespective of the outcome of the war in Europe—had it not been for the alliance with the powerful Iroquois tribes which the British had inherited from the Dutch. Had the Iroquois not remained loyal, the American colonies might well have been overrun. Ironically enough, victory over the French soon alienated the friendly Indian tribes after they had been instrumental in saving the English settlements. Fear of losing their hunting grounds to the expanding Anglo-American colonies led to Pontiac's rebellion, suppressed only after a bloody struggle. Soon thereafter, when it became British policy to restrain the westward expansion of the American colonies, and when British traders took over the formerly French fur trade, the northwestern Indians became the allies of the British against the American colonists. The Americans had now become the threat to Indian land, while the English had become its protectors. For many years after the Revolution, this was to become an important factor in Anglo-American relations.

The Treaty of Paris, in 1763, ended the balance of power established at Utrecht fifty years earlier. To acquire Corsica and Lorraine and to restore Silesia to the Hapsburgs, Louis XV lost an empire. French claims to lands west of the Mississippi had already been ceded to Spain in order to induce Madrid to agree to a quick peace involving the loss of Florida. Now all of Canada and all French claims east of the Mississippi were abandoned to Britain.

In order to obtain these vast concessions, England returned to France the West Indian islands of Martinique and Guadaloupe.* This decision marked an important departure from past British policy, influenced perhaps by the early effects of the first stages of the industrial revolution. The beginnings of industrialization and the rising population of the British Isles may have stimulated the notion that, in the future, continental space for development would be of greater value to the Empire than the rich tropical islands over which the European powers had fought for so many years. Whatever the motivation for the decision, its effect was far-reaching upon the American future. But for the Iroquois alliance contracted by the Dutch and the English government's decision of 1763, North America might well have become a French-speaking continent.

With the French menace eliminated, the colonists no longer felt dependent upon British protection. Slowly they began to realize that, for half a century or more, they had been involved in one essentially European war after another at the will of a distant English sovereign. This gave rise to an early trend toward what was later to be called American isolationism.

* The decision was much debated in England. For a strongly dissenting view, see the letter of April 2, 1762, written by the Earl of Hardwicke to the Duke of Newcastle: Ruhl J. Bartlett, *Record of American Diplomacy* (Knopf, 1947), page 5.

At the same time, the common necessities of defense had created a feeble but nevertheless perceptible impulse toward unity. Provincialism was still a powerful centrifugal force, but even as early as 1745, when Governor Clinton's wrangling with the New York legislature had delayed essential action and endangered the Iroquois alliance, the need for united action had become apparent. Those colonies whose borders were invaded or threatened by the French and Indians responded most readily to the need for defense forces, but they also resented bearing the major burden of what was, after all, a defense of the colonies as a whole. At an Albany assembly, called by the English home government in 1754, commissioners from seven of the colonies met to discuss the problem and actually adopted a plan for union submitted by Benjamin Franklin. Neither the colonial assemblies nor the home government supported this proposal and eventually the cessation of hostilities removed the immediate need for any such action. The impulse toward unity was lost and did not re-awaken until stimulated by common resentment against the English crown.

In 1764, some years before there was any serious thought of rebellion, Choiseul and his disciple, the Comte de Vergennes, foresaw that the English colonies might revolt and that the European balance of power might thus be restored. In a remarkable memorandum, discovered in the archives of Quai d'Orsay years later, Choiseul outlined a French policy of alliance with Spain and Holland, of undermining the British financial position wherever possible and of promoting the independence of the American colonies.*

The first serious resentments against English rule were kindled at just about the time of the accession of George III, when the colonists were aroused by an act of Parliament forbidding them to settle beyond the Appalachian mountains. Many had already settled in the Kentucky and Tennessee regions, while others had their eyes on the expanding West.

A second cause of early rebellious sentiment was the British decision to leave a permanent garrison in the colonies under a

---

* Max Savelle, "The American Balance of Power and European Diplomacy," in the symposium *Era of the American Revolution,* edited by Richard B. Morris (Columbia University, 1939).

commander in chief of all the colonial forces. The ill-fated
Braddock had been named to this post in 1754 and a certain
amount of military union had been achieved in the very year
when Franklin's plan for political unification had failed of
adoption. With the end of hostilities in 1763, the surviving
overlordship of the commander in chief aroused resentment.

Economic causes of discontent also began to make themselves
felt at this time. During the wars, there had been considerable
smuggling and contraband trading, particularly by the merchants of Rhode Island and Massachusetts. This stirred up resentment in England and led to the more rigid enforcement of
controls over colonial trade. British imperialism was raised to
high pitch by victory, but Parliament was also acutely conscious of the increased national debt and the continuing costs
of maintaining adequate defenses for the greatly expanded Empire. There was a strong feeling that the American colonies had
reaped most of the advantages of victory and that they should
be made to pay at least part of the cost.

Grenville's Sugar Act of 1764 was the first step in this direction. The imposition of import duties on sugar, molasses and
certain other specified commodities upset the whole pattern of
New England trade with the British West Indies. One aspect of
this trade was the highly profitable triangular commerce in
West Indian molasses, New England rum and African Negro
slaves—a strange trade to be carried on by the righteous Puritans of Massachusetts and the Rhode Islanders whose colony
had been dedicated to religious freedom. The Sugar Act
aroused indignation not only in the directly affected New England settlements but throughout most of the colonies, because
it was rightly suspected to foreshadow "taxation without representation."

In the following year, Parliament passed the anticipated
Stamp Act. This was taxation, pure and simple. Pitt vainly objected to it on the same constitutional grounds as the colonists,
but his advice was rejected. The revolt against this measure
centered in the already aroused New England colonies, where
town meetings and colonial assemblies provided a natural
forum for the ventilation of grievances by such fiery orators
as Samuel Adams and James Otis. The sense of outrage spread

to New York, where the Sons of Liberty added a mass movement of indignation to the protests of the merchant class. The
Virginians also became incensed over the violation of constitutional principles. At the instigation of Massachusetts leaders,
a congress of nine colonies met in New York to consider what
action might be taken. As a result, there soon developed
throughout most of the colonies a tacit boycott of English
goods which, in a short time, had the English merchants pro-
testing to Parliament. Before the end of the year (1765), the
Stamp Act was repealed, but the conciliatory effect of this action was nullified by the adoption of a Declaratory Act bluntly
asserting the right of the English Parliament to legislate for and
to tax the colonies.

With the spirit of antagonism hardening on both sides of the
Atlantic, the intransigent advice of Lord North now prevailed
over the wiser counsels of such men as Pitt and Edmund Burke.
The Mutiny Act and the Townshend Act of 1767 were supported by a now angry English merchant class and served to in-
furiate the colonists still further. The new legislation was
directed at more rigid enforcement by the English military and
civil authorities of the various political and economic sanctions
imposed by Parliament, including, specifically, the quartering
of troops and the collection of customs revenues.

Historians differ as to the relative importance of the various
grievances which now accumulated, but certain primary factors
are commonly accepted as having played an important part.
The mere existence of a redcoat garrison on American soil in
times of peace was considered obnoxious. The restrictions upon
American trade were deemed unjustly injurious, although at
least one reputable historian questions whether they imposed
substantial hardship.* To have an authority obnoxious in itself used to enforce controls considered injurious and to collect
taxes held to be unjustly levied was, quite literally, to heap
insult upon injury.

To make matters worse, the laws of 1767 legalized the issuance of writs of assistance, entitling the English customs official,
behind whom stood the military, to demand help and protec-

* George L. Beer, *The Old Colonial System* (New York, 1912).

tion from the civil authorities in his search for contraband. The sense of outrage over the search of private houses and places of business spread from Massachusetts to Virginia, where the matter became a highly publicized issue in the courts.* The strong feelings engendered by this controversy later found expression in both the Virginia constitution and in the Constitution of the United States, where a separate (4th) amendment expressly forbade search without duly issued warrant.

Thus the elements which combined to foster a spirit of rebellion were many and varied. New England free enterprise, struggling to emancipate itself from mercantilistic control and combined with the innate New England spirit of independence, found an echo in other colonies, especially in the vigilant leadership group in Virginia. Along the western frontier, Scotch-Irish antagonism toward England combined with the backwoodsman's natural hatred of all authority. In the urban centers, the ever-present resentments of the ill-housed and ill-fed were readily mobilized into a spirit of revolt against the existing order.

The colonists' chief weapon of reprisal was the non-importation of British goods. From 1768 to 1769 English goods entering the ports of New York and New England declined in value from £1,363,000 to £504,000.† The boycott was the first instrument of foreign policy devised by an emerging nation and became the forerunner of one of the major policies pursued by the Republic in its early years.

The events which followed are well known to every American. The seizure of John Hancock's sloop *Liberty*, the American plundering of the grounded British revenue vessel *Gaspee* and other such incidents led to civil disorder culminating in the so-called Boston Massacre in which British troops were charged with unprovoked murder of American citizens. (John Adams successfully defended the accused and obtained their acquittal by an American jury.) With the revolt against the Tea Act in 1773, matters went rapidly from bad to worse. Designed pri-

* O. M. Dickerson, "Writs of Assistance as a Cause of the Revolution," in *Era of the American Revolution, op. cit.*

† John R. Craf, *Economic Development of the United States* (McGraw-Hill, 1952), page 83.

marily to rescue the East India Company from bankruptcy by permitting it to establish wholesale centers in the colonies, this legislation was viewed by the colonists as merely another act of oppressive taxation. Widespread refusal to permit tea to enter and the dumping of cargoes into the sea constituted the colonial reprisal.

The Virginia House of Burgesses created a Committee of Correspondence to keep in touch with other similar bodies to be established in each of the colonies. Massachusetts already had its very active committee. Within a year, nine such committees came into existence. The creation of this first, orderly intercolonial network of communication—largely the work of Thomas Jefferson of Virginia—led to the evolution of the League of Friendship, or Confederation. The central committees soon developed local branches in each of the colonies and later became the directing centers of the Revolution.

When Virginia's royal governor Dunmore dissolved the Burgesses, Jefferson moved, in a secret meeting held at Raleigh's Tavern in Williamsburg, that the Virginia Committee be instructed to invite the colonies to send delegates to a Congress to be convened at Philadelphia. This, the First Continental Congress, met shortly thereafter in a tense atmosphere created by the so-called Intolerable Acts of 1774.

These acts were: an act closing the Port of Boston; an act substituting an appointed council for the duly elected Massachusetts legislature and taking the selection of jurors out of the hands of the people; an act providing for the extradition to England of persons indicted for mutiny and for extradition to other colonies of persons indicted for offenses committed in support of British authority; and, finally, an act placing the administration of the western territories under the royal governor of Quebec, establishing the Roman Catholic church and making no provision for a popularly elected assembly.

The Continental Congress promptly supported the Massachusetts demand for repeal. Its most important action consisted in formulating the Articles of Association—a no-trade-with-Britain agreement, accompanied by resolutions encouraging the formation of local committees to enforce the boycott. Further resolutions encouraged the rapid development of home industry and agriculture. Adherence to the Association soon became the generally accepted criterion of patriot or loyalist sentiment. On April 6, 1776, Congress threw open the colonial ports to all nations, in defiance of British restrictions.

The carrying out of the Intolerable Acts in Massachusetts devolved upon General Thomas Gage, appointed to act as royal governor of Massachusetts in addition to his duties as commander in chief of the British garrison in North America. Among his responsibilities was that of preventing the accumulation of military supplies by the colonists. His sending of a detachment to seize a supply of such stores at Concord occasioned the first skirmish of the American Revolution.

During the following weeks and months, the Association changed from being a system of cooperation against British trade into a loose union for the defense of the colonies. As the revolutionary movement progressed, royal government collapsed. One by one, the colonies instructed their delegates to the Second Continental Congress to vote for a resolution of independence, submitted on June 4, 1776, by Richard Henry Lee of Virginia. Exactly one month later, the Congress adopted the full Declaration of Independence drafted by Thomas Jefferson.

"Out of decent respect to the opinions of mankind," the preamble listed the grievances against the mother country which impelled the colonies to declare their independence. Far more important than the eloquently stated case for separation, however, was the affirmative case presented for the establishment of a new government under which the people of the American colonies proposed to "assume among the powers of the earth the separate and equal station to which the laws of Nature and of Nature's God entitle them."

Two ringing sentences set forth a faith and a philosophy not new as such, but new as the foundation stone of government:

> We hold these truths to be self-evident, that all men are created equal; that they are endowed by their Creator with certain unalienable rights; that among these are Life, Liberty and the pursuit of Happiness. That, to secure these rights, governments are instituted among men, deriving their just powers from the consent of the governed. . . .

And then the clarion call to revolution against tyranny which was to echo around the world:

> That, whenever any Form of Government becomes destructive of these ends, it is the right of the people to alter or abolish it, and to institute a new Government, laying its foundations on such principles, and organizing its powers in such form as to them shall seem most likely to effect their Safety and Happiness.

What produced so extraordinary a declaration of faith, principle and purpose? What bond united Yankee traders, Virginia planters, lawyers, clergymen and the ordinary little folk of the thirteen colonies in pledging their lives, their fortunes and their sacred honor to an aspiration of such magnitude and to an adventure of such risk?

A common sense of justice, derived from the common suffering of injustice, was without doubt one powerful force; but men had suffered injustice throughout the ages without being able to formulate out of their experience either the exact nature of the justice they sought or the philosophy and system of government upon which it might be founded. What the men of 1776 possessed that others before them had lacked was a common experience of freedom in a vast, new, rich and unsettled land—an experience of both self-reliant individual independence and voluntary association for the accomplishment of common ends. They had acted together as free men, compelled to cooperation not by superior authority but by personally experienced necessities and dangers.

Thomas Paine's *Common Sense,* published in January, 1776, had spread like wildfire through the colonies working, as George Washington said, "a powerful change in many minds." Paine, a superb propagandist, stated and popularized the case for rebellion and independence. Jefferson and Franklin provided the affirmative philosophical base upon which the new republic was to be erected. These two elements, combined with Jefferson's extraordinary gift for organization of leadership in the colonies, created the climate in which the founding fathers were able to assert: "We hold these truths to be self-evident."

They had not been self-evident to many who now accepted them in the hot fire of impending revolution; later, they were to be questioned and challenged time and again after the struggle for independence had been won.

The promise of America was stated on July 4, 1776. With its enunciation began the long, arduous struggle to make the promise come true.

CHAPTER THREE

———————

The Struggles of the Confederation
(1776–1789)

THE CONFEDERATION was little more than an alliance between thirteen sovereign states, united only in a common effort to defeat the English occupying power. The Congress, lacking practically all the powers of government, depended for the execution of its policies upon the states; it could neither levy taxes, nor conscript men, nor regulate the production and trade of the colonial economy. Yet it faced the task of raising and supplying an army, of somehow finding funds at home or abroad and of gaining allies.

The magnitude of the task undertaken in going to war against the world's foremost power and universal respect for General Washington held the Confederation together, causing the state governments to meet the financial requisitions of the Congress, to supply men and to provide war matériel. But the Congress could only recommend and request; it had no power to issue orders. That the war could be won in these circumstances was something of a miracle.

At the very beginning of the Revolution, Congress assumed the right to take charge of foreign affairs. This right was never questioned, yet, throughout the thirteen years of the Confederation, Congress lacked the power to enforce the execution of the treaties which it negotiated. It was, therefore, all the more remarkable that Congress did, in fact, succeed in contracting alliances, in borrowing substantial funds abroad and in making treaties of commerce which it had no power to fulfill.

In November, 1775, Congress had created a secret committee "for the sole purpose of corresponding with our friends in Great Britain, Ireland and other parts of the world." Benjamin Franklin, John Dickinson (author of the Articles of Confederation), John Jay, Benjamin Harrison and Thomas Johnson were the original members. After the outbreak of war, this committee became a "Committee on Foreign Affairs." Its first two foreign correspondents were Arthur Lee, who had been in London as agent for Massachusetts, and Franklin's friend, Charles F.W. Dumas, at The Hague.

The Comte de Vergennes, who had succeeded Choiseul in the French foreign office, watched with interest the developing rebellion of the English colonies and had already discussed the furnishing of supplies with Arthur Lee, through the intermediary of Caron de Beaumarchais, author of *The Barber of Seville* and likewise a courtier with a flair for intrigue and international politics.

On March 3, 1776, the Congress decided to send one of its members, Silas Deane, of Connecticut, to France in the guise of a merchant to explore the possibilities of obtaining French aid in the event of war. By the time Dean arrived, Beaumarchais had already created a fictitious concern, Rodrigue Hortalez and Company, to which Deane was referred by Vergennes. Through Beaumarchais's cover company, Deane succeeded in purchasing several cargoes of war supplies which were promptly dispatched in French vessels. Their arrival made possible the important victory of the American forces over General Burgoyne's invading army at Saratoga.

Meanwhile, shortly after the Declaration of Independence, Congress decided to send a formal mission to Paris and appointed Franklin, Lee and Deane as commissioners. Before the commission left, the secret committee worked out a Plan of Treaties, to serve as a model for commercial treaties to be negotiated with the European powers. This "Plan of 1776" was, in a sense, the first formulation of United States foreign policy and laid down the doctrine of "free ships, free goods" which was to become basic to the American interpretation of neutral rights. (This doctrine, generally accepted by the Continental nations, had been repudiated by Britain during the Seven Years' War in the "Rule of 1756" and became a serious bone of contention between Britain and the United States.) Under the Plan of 1776, neutral ships were permitted to carry non-contraband to and from the ports of belligerents and contraband was carefully defined, foodstuffs and naval stores being excluded from the list. When the commission was appointed, there was no idea of seeking an alliance with France.

The news of Burgoyne's surrender caused the British government to change its policy and to decide to offer the American colonies peace on the basis of home rule within the Empire. When these plans reached Vergennes, he was filled with anxiety lest the American colonies accept peace on this basis—as, indeed, they would have in 1775. This gave Benjamin Franklin his great opportunity.

The kindly, wise and witty philosopher had already captured the affection not only of the French court but of the French people. His accomplishments as a scientist and philosopher and his intimate knowledge of the European scene impressed diplomatic circles, while his unassuming simplicity of dress and demeanor endeared him to French hearts as a living symbol of the freedom to which they themselves aspired. When Vergennes asked Franklin whether he thought the Americans would accept the sort of peace which Britain seemed about to offer, Franklin made it clear that the best insurance against such an event would be a French alliance.

Diplomacy in those days was an intricate game of subtlety and espionage. Fearful that the American commissioners might negotiate a French alliance, the British sent their ace under-cover operator, Paul Wentworth, to spy out the ground and to try to

bribe Franklin and Deane to sell out their country. Throughout this period, the British had a concealed agent, Edward
Bancroft, in the secretariat of the American commission.

Using the British pressure to good advantage in their negotiations with the French, the American emissaries succeeded, in
March 1778, in concluding first a Treaty of Amity and Commerce, and then a "conditional and defensive alliance." In the
latter treaty, both sides gave pledges against making a separate
peace and agreed not to lay down their arms until "the Independence of the United States shall have been formally established or assured by the Treaty or Treaties that shall terminate
the War."

The commercial treaty was announced, but the defensive alliance was kept secret from the British—or so it was thought.
The British promptly received a copy from Bancroft. In an effort to get its peace proposal before the Congress ahead of
Franklin's treaties, England sent a formal peace mission under
Lord Carlisle. The ship bearing the French treaties arrived
first and, two days later, on May 4, 1778, the treaties were ratified by Congress. France and Britain slipped into war with each
other without a formal declaration.

Franklin's great achievement had two other effects besides
assuring the successful outcome of the American Revolution:
the first was to send Congress off on a course of "militia diplomacy," seeking treaties of amity, recognition and commerce—
an enterprise undertaken against the advice of Franklin himself; the second was to involve the United States in a highly
complicated European conflict.

After the conclusion of the French treaties, the commission
was withdrawn and Franklin was appointed minister to France,
the first and for the time being the only American diplomat
accredited to a foreign government. In his view it was unwise
for the Congress to go hunting for recognition among the belligerent and neutral European powers. Nevertheless, Congress
sent Arthur Lee to Spain which, though at war with England,
gave the American emissary a cold shoulder. In Prussia, at war
with Austria over the Bavarian succession, Lee was ignored.
William Lee, brother of Arthur, had a similar lack of success at
Vienna. An attempt on William Lee's part to negotiate a Dutch

treaty with the wholly unauthorized mayor of Amsterdam resulted in a British declaration of war upon the Netherlands.* Finally, Francis Dana was sent by the Congress on a fatuously conceived mission to Russia to obtain recognition by asking Catherine the Great to permit the United States to join the Armed Neutrality Bloc—a curious notion, considering that the United States was a belligerent. All these rather undignified and foolish proceedings accomplished nothing.

The French alliance indirectly involved the United States in European affairs which had nothing to do with American interests. Spain came into the war against England and signed a treaty of alliance with France under which the two powers agreed not to conclude peace until Spain should have regained Gibraltar from England. Thus the French were committed to continue the war until two wholly different objectives had been attained. This, in turn, implied that the United States could not make peace until Gibraltar was captured by Spain.

Fortunately, the victory of Franco-American arms and the surrender of Cornwallis took the United States out from under this complicated entanglement. Lord North's government was overthrown and the succeeding ministry of Lord Shelburne was ready to make peace.

Having discovered that its "militia diplomacy" was none too effective, Congress created, in 1781, a Department of Foreign Affairs, with a Secretary and five assistants. (This rudimentary foreign office consisted of five men: a Secretary [$4,000]; 1st and 2nd Undersecretaries [$800 and $700]; and two clerks.) John R. Livingston was the first Secretary of Foreign Affairs, succeeded in 1784 by John Jay. The Department was an adjunct of and directly responsible to Congress, so remaining until after the adoption of the Constitution.

In the same year, Congress appointed John Adams as plenipotentiary to negotiate peace, but, when Adams showed too much independence to suit Vergennes, the French persuaded Congress to name Franklin, Jay, Henry Laurens and Thomas

* Lee's "treaty" with the Burgomaster of Amsterdam interested Congress to the point of sending Henry Laurens with powers to negotiate with the Dutch government. The ship on which he sailed was captured by the British and Laurens remained a prisoner for the rest of the war. The copy of Lee's "treaty" which Laurens carried served the British as an excuse to declare war on Holland.

Jefferson along with Adams as peace commissioners. As it turned out, Jefferson arrived too late to take part in the negotiations and Laurens played only a very minor part; the long and complicated negotiations fell to Franklin, Jay and Adams.

Because of various proposals for mediation, Congress formulated its own peace terms as early as 1779. These included recognition of independence and the fixing of boundaries: in the north, substantially the present Canadian border; in the west, the Mississippi; in the south approximately the northern boundary of the present state of Florida. Congress also expressed the desire that Nova Scotia and Canada be ceded and, should this be unattainable, insisted upon fishing rights in Canadian waters.

At first, the peace commissioners were told to place themselves completely in the hands of Vergennes in accordance with the terms of the treaty with "his most Christian Majesty." It soon developed, however, that the wily French foreign minister was playing a complicated game, being in no hurry to forward peace between Britain and the United States until Spain should have secured its objectives. Moreover, while Vergennes wished the American colonies to achieve independence in order to weaken Britain, he had no desire to see them emerge as a strong nation. The American commissioners were shocked by a French proposal to extend Spain's claim for the return of Florida northwestward, east of the Mississippi, to such an extent that the American colonies would, in effect, have been bottled up behind the Allegheny mountains. The victory of Yorktown and the overthrow of Lord North's government saved the Anglo-American peace treaty from becoming part and parcel of a complicated European settlement.

After lengthy negotiations the American commissioners signed preliminary articles of peace with Britain. The terms were almost exactly those demanded by Congress. Independence was recognized. The so-called "Nipissing Line" formed the boundary with Canada subject to later adjustment of the Maine frontier. The southern boundary was set at the St. Mary's River and 31st parallel, with a secret provision for a shift northward in the event that Britain should retain Florida. The idea of annexing Canada was dropped because John Jay was in a hurry to make sure that there would be no Spanish encroachment east of the Mississippi. Fishing privileges were obtained not as *rights* but as a *liberty,* which implied the right of revocation and led to later lengthy disputes.

These extraordinarily favorable terms were obtained because the American commissioners showed skill and determination and because Britain was anxious to make peace. The commissioners did not show the preliminary articles to Vergennes until after they had been signed. They did not, however, violate the pledge against making a separate peace, since their agreement with Britain was conditional upon an Anglo-French treaty. They did—wisely and justifiably—violate the proprieties in view of Vergennes' unwillingness to back American interests. Vergennes himself protested only mildly. Congress gladly accepted the terms and would have been content with less, making no issue of the fact that the commissioners had violated their instructions.

Actually, while Vergennes was no doubt astonished at the terms obtained by the Americans, the signing of the articles suited him rather well, since it enabled him to bring pressure upon Spain to make peace without regaining Gibraltar. On January 20, 1783, France, Spain and Britain signed preliminary articles which, to all intents and purposes, ended the war and brought the Anglo-American agreement into effect. Britain retained Gibraltar but ceded the Floridas to Spain, without defining their northern boundary. Spain was not, of course, bound by the Anglo-American treaty's definition of the southern boundary of the United States.

The Anglo-American treaty established the sovereign independence of the thirteen separate states. It made no provision for diplomatic relations with the Confederation as such and it established no commercial relations. None of the European powers were at all anxious to see the loose Confederation attain nationhood. Most of them expected that it would disintegrate.

The ensuing period from 1783 to 1789 was a trying time for the newly independent states. With the cessation of hostilities, the common bond forged by common danger no longer existed. The Confederation itself was financially bankrupt and so were

most of the thirteen states. The war had been financed largely
by the issuance of paper money, once Congressional requisitions
failed to be met by the state assemblies. The notes issued by
Congress depreciated and became almost worthless, as did most
of the paper currency issued by the states.* Congress had no
power to levy taxes or to regulate commerce. Each of the thirteen states competed with the others for trade both internally
and with foreign countries.

Loans and subsidies obtained from France and Holland during the war totaled over $8,000,000; approximately $650,000
was owed to Spain. The hoped-for foreign trade remained
mostly a trade with England which had to be conducted on
most unfavorable terms in the absence of a commercial agreement. The channels through which such an agreement might be
negotiated remained closed, because the British government
refused to send an ambassador to America and failed to recognize John Adams, whom Congress sent as minister to London.

In April, 1783, Franklin succeeded in signing a commerce
treaty with Sweden, based on the Plan of 1776. In the following year, Congress appointed Franklin, Adams and Jefferson
(presently to succeed Franklin as minister to France) as a commission to negotiate similar treaties with other countries.
Before he retired, Franklin signed a treaty with Prussia, embodying some interesting humanitarian clauses for the mitiga-
tion of the cruelty of warfare. In 1787, an agent sent by Adams
and Jefferson signed a treaty with Morocco. These three treaties,
with Sweden, Prussia and Morocco, were the sum total of what
could be achieved by the postwar diplomatic efforts of the Confederation. One of the two powers with whom treaties were
urgently needed—Great Britain—refused altogether to negotiate; the other—Spain—was willing to negotiate, but the negotiations proved fruitless.

So far as Britain was concerned, it was not only the absence

---

* Congress raised about $50,000,000 by requisition and $240,552,000 by fiat
money. The states issued $209,524,000 of their own bills. The value of the Con-
tinental currency declined to such an extent that Congress found itself compelled to declare that "any person so lost to all virtue and regard for his country
as to refuse the bills or obstruct their currency or circulation, shall be deemed,
published and treated as an enemy of the country and precluded from all
trade and intercourse with its inhabitants.".

of a commercial treaty which distressed the Congress. The peace treaty had provided for the evacuation "with all convenient speed" of any British forces remaining within the agreed boundaries of the United States. Throughout the war, the British had held seven frontier forts south of the boundary which controlled navigation on the Great Lakes, the fur trade and the military alliance with the Indians. Contrary to the treaty, the British refused to evacuate these outposts and continued to cultivate Indian tribes within the borders of the United States. In addition, there were several other matters in dispute. In its efforts to reach a settlement, the Congress appealed for help to Vergennes, but the French minister was not at all interested. His purpose of weakening Britain had been achieved; whether or not the English adhered to the terms of the peace treaty was a matter of indifference to him. With the Confederation powerless to enforce its rights, the British continued to occupy the border posts. Worse yet, they launched an intrigue to induce the people of Vermont to secede from the Union, offering trade and navigation privileges on the Great Lakes as enticement.

An equally dangerous and difficult situation confronted the Confederation in the South. Spain had valid claims not only to Florida but to the mouth of the Mississippi and, through alliance with the Creeks, Choctaws, Cherokees and Chickasaws, controlled the disputed territories of Alabama and Mississippi. The Tennessee and Kentucky settlers urgently desired navigation rights on the Mississippi and a right of deposit at New Orleans pending trans-shipment but Congress had nothing to offer in exchange for the rights it wished to acquire. The Spanish government, chiefly because it feared that the rapidly growing western settlements would some day be strong enough to take what they demanded by force, sent Diego de Gardoqui to negotiate with Jay, then Secretary of Foreign Affairs. The two men reached agreement on several important matters, including commercial reciprocity and a mutual guarantee of territorial integrity. The latter provision, which amounted to an alliance, was never submitted by Jay to the Congress, but Jay did ask to have his instructions amended so as to enable him to conclude a treaty of commerce by agreeing to an estoppel of American navigation on the Mississippi for a period of thirty years. This aroused a furor of protest from the Southern states. Realizing that a two-thirds vote of Congress would not be obtainable, Jay and Gardoqui suspended their negotiations. The Spaniards then tried to induce the Kentucky and Tennessee settlers to secede by offering them navigation rights if they would break away from the Union. The chief figure in this so-called "Spanish Conspiracy" was General James Wilkinson, who secretly entered the employ of the Spanish governor of New Orleans and later became involved in a somewhat similar venture with Aaron Burr. The practical effect of this plot was not to cause secession but to give the Kentucky and Tennessee settlers limited *de facto* rights of navigation.

Thus, the Confederation was threatened in the North by British intrigue and cultivation of the hostile Indians while, in the South, similar tactics were pursued by Spain. If a final touch was needed to show that the Union must either be strengthened or disintegrate, this was provided by Shay's Rebellion in western Massachusetts, which showed that the Confederation was as unable to provide internal security as it was helpless to defend American interests abroad. When the Congress broke up in disgust, the French minister reported to his government:

> There is now in America no general government—neither Congress nor President, nor head of any one administrative department.

When the Constitutional Convention assembled, in May, 1787, there was general agreement among the delegates that the national government should be supreme in foreign affairs and that treaties should prevail over state laws, but there was little agreement as to how this should be accomplished.

Some delegates felt that treaties should be "ratified by law," thus requiring the concurrence of both Houses. This view was motivated by the fear that, if the sole responsibility were placed with the Executive and the Senate, the Upper House might come to exercise powers of taxation through the levying of import or export duties. On the other hand, most delegates were inclined to agree that the Lower House would be unsuited to the handling of delicate matters frequently requiring confidential negotiations. Ultimately the Convention decided that treaties should be negotiated by the President "with the advice and consent of two-thirds of the Senators present." The two-thirds requirement stemmed from the recent experience with the Jay-Gardoqui negotiations. The intention of the framers of the Constitution to entrust the conduct of foreign relations to the Executive was later clarified by the Act of July 27, 1789, establishing a new Department of Foreign Affairs (changed in September to the Department of State), with a Secretary at its head who was to conduct the business of the Department "in such manner as the President of the United States shall from time to time instruct."

As to the relationship of the federal government to the states, opinions among the delegates varied widely. Alexander Hamilton represented the most extreme centralist view and proposed to vest monarchical powers in a President elected for life, to create a Senate elected for life or good behavior, and to give the President the prerogative of appointing the governors of the states. Few of the delegates shared Hamilton's dislike and distrust of democratic government or his openly expressed contempt for public opinion. His proposal was shelved without much ado; yet, in a somewhat milder form, many of the delegates shared in the widespread doubt as to the virtues of democracy resulting from the chaos existing under the Confederation. John Adams, who, in 1776, had been a fiery revolutionary leader, favored a mixture of monarchical, aristocratic and democratic elements in a Constitution. His fellow-delegate, Elbridge Gerry, held that "the evils we experience flow from an excess of democracy." The records of the Convention are full of similar expressions, suggesting a strong reaction from the spirit which had prevailed at the sessions of the Second Continental Congress.

Given the temper of the times, it is surprising that the Constitution finally adopted should have retained so much of the spirit of 1776. Considering that most of the delegates were lawyers or men of property,* it is astonishing that so many strong safeguards of the peoples' interest were erected. In the

---

* Charles Beard, *Economic Interpretation of the Constitution* (Macmillan, 1913), especially page 149.

end, it was neither the extreme nationalist view nor the extreme states-rights view which triumphed, but the middle-of-the-road doctrine of which James Madison of Virginia was the chief exponent.

Jefferson, absent in Paris, had had much to do with shaping Madison's philosophy of government and corresponded at length with his fellow Virginian during the Convention. His view of the Constitution as drafted largely by Madison was expressed in a letter to a friend, dated December 21, 1787: "I find myself nearly a Neutral," Jefferson wrote. "There is a mass of good in it, in a very desirable form; but there is also to me a bitter pill or two." * The bitter pills were that a bill of rights was omitted and that the President was made eligible for re-election during his lifetime. A little later, after having received a long explanation from Madison, Jefferson wrote that, if he were at home, he would warmly advocate the adoption of the Constitution until nine states had ratified it "& then warmly take the other side to convince the remaining four that they ought not to come into it until the declaration of rights is annexed to it." † Still later, after the bill of rights seemed assured and Jefferson had become reconciled to the perpetual eligibility of the President—at least, during the lifetime of George Washington—he felt, as he had earlier expressed himself regarding the new state constitutions, that "the worst of the American constitutions is better than the best which ever existed before in any other country." ‡

The fundamental philosophy embodied in the Declaration was not new. The belief in natural law and the rule of reason went back to the Greeks, to Cicero and to Thomas Aquinas. The "Enlightenment" of Locke and Harrington, from which Jefferson's philosophy derived, was part of the heritage of western civilization. What was new was that the belief in the dignity, the reasonableness and the rights of the human individual should serve as the foundation for a structure of government. When the Constitution became the fundamental law of

* Paul Leicester Ford, *Jefferson Papers* (Princeton University Press, 1951), Vol. IV, page 481.

† *Ibid.*, Vol. V, page 2.

‡ *Ibid.*, Vol. IV, page 403.

the United States in 1789, there came into being a form of government which, by its mere existence, challenged the "rightness" of every government based upon political or religious authoritarianism. Years later, Abraham Lincoln appraised Thomas Jefferson as "the man who, in the concrete pressure of a struggle for independence by a single people, had the coolness, the forecaste (sic) and sagacity to introduce into a merely revolutionary document an abstract truth, applicable to all men at all times, and so to embalm it there that today and in all coming days it shall be a rebuke and a stumbling-block to the very harbingers of reappearing tyranny and oppression." *

From the "abstract truth" on the one hand, and from past experience on the other, the United States derived at birth something of a split personality. The philosophy upon which it was founded gave the nation an interest in all of mankind and its people a sense of mission. Yet the background of colonial experience imbued the people with a yearning to be free of foreign entanglement, to be left alone and at peace and to avoid world responsibility. It was this latter sentiment which Thomas Paine had exploited and which John Adams expressed in a letter to Robert Livingston in which he said:

America has been long enough involved in the affairs of Europe. She has been a football of the contending nations from the beginning and it is easy to foresee that England and France will both endeavor to involve us in their future wars. It is our interest and our duty to avoid them as much as possible, to be completely independent, and to have nothing to do with either of them except in commerce.

Once the Constitutional Convention had completed its work, it took almost a year and a half before the necessary nine states ratified the fundamental law and brought it into effect. During the protracted debate, Hamilton, Madison and Jay teamed up in writing most of the famous "Federalist Papers," explaining the Constitution and arguing for its ratification. Hamilton bore the brunt of the fight in New York and Madison in Virginia. Two states—North Carolina and Rhode Island—did not ratify

* Caleb P. Patterson, *The Constitutional Principles of Thomas Jefferson* (Texas University Press, 1953), page 62.

until after the new government had come into being. With eleven ratifications in hand, Congress set the date for the elections and for the inauguration of the new government. Then it ceased to function. The long, trying period of the Confederation was at an end.

With George Washington elected as its President and John Adams becoming Vice President, the United States was now about to enter upon its existence as a nation.

Bibliographical Note

FOR the important original documents pertaining to the diplomacy of the Confederation, see Ruhl J. Bartlett; *Record of American Diplomacy;* Knopf, 1947, *op. cit.*

Instructions to Silas Deane	pages 15-16
Plan of Treaties 1776	17-19
The French Treaties	24-27
Instructions to the Peace Commissioners	31-39
Peace Treaty with Britain	39-42
Treaty with Prussia	46-47
Jay's defense and C. C. Pinckney's attack on Proposed Treaty with Spain	52-60

CHAPTER FOUR

Washington, Hamilton and Jefferson
(1789–1797)

NEW YORK CITY, the nation's first capital, was an overgrown village of some 33,000 inhabitants when George Washington took the oath of office. The population of the United States was

about 4,000,000, of whom roughly 700,000 were Negro slaves.*
Quite a few of the Southern leaders, among them Thomas Jefferson, thought slavery should be abolished. The South was not
yet as dependent upon slave labor as it became after the invention of the cotton gin, but the Southern planters' reluctance
combined with the interest of the New England "blackbirders"
to prevent abolition at the time of the nation's birth.

The whole country was still predominantly agricultural. In
Connecticut a few enterprising manufacturers were beginning
to make tinware and clocks. Iron manufacture had been stimulated throughout the colonies by the need for war matériel but
could scarcely as yet be called an industry. In Rhode Island and
Massachusetts, men were beginning to work cotton fiber on
machines surreptitiously obtained from England. (Cartwright's
power loom had only just been invented and steam power was
in the early stages of development in the British Isles.) Travel
was by saddlehorse, stagecoach or river boat.

The most pressing problems facing the new government
were:

1. The establishment of the credit of the United States

2. The assertion of the nation's territorial rights west of the
Appalachians

3. The establishment of satisfactory commercial relations
with other countries, especially with Great Britain.

President Washington's first cabinet, with Jefferson as Secretary of State and Alexander Hamilton as Secretary of the
Treasury, was the first and only true coalition cabinet in American history, in the sense that it represented the two opposing
schools of thought whose conflict was to dominate the nation's
early development. There was as yet no party alignment and
Washington expressed the hope that there would be none; yet
the essence of party conflict was there from the beginning
through the mere presence of two powerful figures holding
diametrically opposed views in both domestic and foreign affairs. Each was to make his great contribution—Jefferson in
holding firmly to the principles of the Declaration; Hamilton
in high-handed strokes of financial genius which set the young

* Of the white population in the thirteen states, about 83% were English,
7% Scottish, 5½% German, 2% Dutch and 1½% Irish.

republic solidly on its feet, but which also came very close to destroying its democratic character.

Hamilton's great service to the nation was rendered in the first year of Washington's Presidency; it consisted in devising and putting through Congress a masterful plan for the funding of the national debt and the assumption of the debts of the states, financed by the issuance of bonds secured by customs duties and by a tax on shipping. The effect of these measures was to put the United States almost overnight into a position of domestic solvency, to re-establish confidence and to enable the government soon to begin repaying the foreign loans contracted during the war.

The other side of the picture, deeply disturbing to the Jeffersonians, was that Hamilton performed this miracle by deliberately creating an alliance between the government and those moneyed interests which he openly desired to build into a ruling aristocracy. Monarchist at heart and authoritarian by deep conviction, Hamilton thoroughly distrusted popular government, believing firmly that the only way to establish a strong and stable government lay through giving the business leaders a direct interest in its management and preservation. Whether by accident or design—more likely, the latter—the funding operation and the assumption of the state debts created within a few weeks the moneyed "aristocracy" which Hamilton desired. The manner in which this came about was even more disturbing to the Jeffersonians than the business-government alliance itself.

In addition to its foreign borrowings and its now practically worthless issues of paper money, the government owed about $50,000,000 in bonds and notes, held not only by urban merchants and traders, but throughout the country by veterans, farmers and settlers in the remote frontier. These obligations had sunk to about half their face value. Many were no longer in the hands of original holders. As soon as Hamilton's proposal to redeem depreciated paper at par in new 6% bonds was placed before Congress, not only the big merchants of New York and a crowd of speculators but some of the members of Congress itself began to use their advance information to buy up the securities from innocent holders. Agents were dispatched by chaise and on horseback into the interior to persuade holders who knew nothing of the plan to part with their bills for half their value. (In those days, it took a week to travel from New York to Boston and many weeks to reach the remote frontier.) Other agents were sent off on fast ships to the southern ports to carry out the same errand. Fortunes were made and, within a few weeks, a financial "aristocracy" was created which had every reason to ally itself with a government which provided such opportunities. Hamilton himself scrupulously refrained from making any personal profit but did not hesitate to let his friends and relatives make their fortunes at the expense of the ignorant. Protest was overshadowed by the spectacular rehabilitation of the nation's credit. Nevertheless, it was only after winning Southern support by a deal to locate the nation's permanent capital on the Potomac that Hamilton was able to put through the assumption of the state debts of about $25,000,000 by a similar operation.

Hamilton's next venture was the chartering of the First United States Bank, to act as depository for the funds of the Treasury and empowered to issue currency as circulating medium. Eighty per cent of the Bank's shares were to be issued to private individuals, while 20% were to be held by the government. Jefferson fought this proposal in the cabinet on both constitutional and ethical grounds but was overruled by Washington. The effect of the Bank's creation was both good and bad. The country had suffered abominably through over-issuance of paper money, so that Tom Paine had written: "Money is money and paper is paper and all the inventions of men cannot make it otherwise." For a time, the Bank disproved Paine's allegation; it could do so, provided that its management operated soundly and did not abuse the great privilege conferred upon it. Later events were to prove that Jefferson was right in fearing that such would not always be the case.

The Hamiltonian policy was not only openly anti-democratic but also had a profound effect upon foreign policy, creating a subservience to Britain distasteful not only to the Jeffersonians but to many who agreed with Hamilton's domestic policies. The newly established national credit depended upon import duties and a tax on shipping. Since almost the entire foreign trade of the Union was with Britain and its possessions, Hamil-

ton's financial policy demanded the maintenance of close relationships with Britain at no matter what cost. This became an
extremely important factor in determining the foreign policy
of the Washington administration, running directly counter to
the still strong anti-British sentiments of the people and to popular sympathy for France.

When the news of the storming of the Bastille reached this
country, popular sentiment was almost wholly on the side of
Jefferson in welcoming the overthrow of the absolute monarchy.
Hamilton, on the other hand, viewed even the relatively mild
first stage of the French revolution with alarm and distaste.
When, shortly thereafter, King George III entered the "Coalition of Kings" against the revolutionary government, pro-
French feeling in the United States mounted to a fever pitch,
with Jacobin clubs being formed in many cities and Americans
frequently addressing each other as "Citizen Jones" and "Citi-
zeness Smith." Many felt that, if France should call for help
under the 1778 treaty, she would be entitled to it. Hamilton
vigorously argued that the mutual assistance treaty had been
invalidated by the overthrow of the government with which it
had been contracted.

As a matter of fact, France did not desire American belligerence. It suited the revolutionary government far better to have
the United States remain a friendly neutral. When the Committee on Public Safety decided to send Citizen Genêt to the
United States as an emissary, Hamilton urged the President not
to receive him, but, for once, Washington agreed with Jefferson,
holding that the envoy should be received. Unfortunately for
France—and fortunately for the preservation of American neutrality—Genêt abused his cordial welcome by tactless and over-
bearing behavior which not even the friendly Jefferson could
defend. This enabled Hamilton successfully to argue that his
recall be demanded.

In spite of the Genêt episode, popular sentiment was still
strongly pro-French and anti-British but a revulsion occurred
when the news of the execution of Louis XVI and Queen Marie
Antoinette reached these shores. The violent turn taken by
the second phase of the French revolution frightened the already hostile propertied class and moved it to an outburst of

anti-French feeling. This served to strengthen Hamilton's hold on Congress.

The turn in sentiment came just in time from Hamilton's point of view, because relations with Britain were rapidly deteriorating. The old Navigation Acts were still in force and British men-of-war were doing everything in their power to halt neutral trade with France. The seven border posts were still being held by British troops and the British authorities were openly considering the creation of a "neutral" Indian territory in the American Northwest. There was still no diplomatic channel through which negotiations might be instituted to obtain redress. While Jefferson sought to come to grips with the problem, Hamilton favored doing nothing and leaving things as they were for fear of arousing British antagonism.

One of Washington's first actions in the field of diplomacy was to send Gouverneur Morris to London for the purpose of ascertaining whether the Pitt regime might be willing to establish diplomatic relations. Morris reported that the chances were not favorable; the British preferred to leave matters as they were, with Major George Beckwith, aid to the Governor of Canada, acting as their unofficial agent and observer in the United States. (The Morris mission established the President's prerogative to send special emissaries abroad without the advice and consent of the Senate.)

The next development was a sudden Anglo-Spanish crisis, arising over disputed rights in Nootka Sound (Vancouver). For a time it looked as if the two powers might go to war. Anticipating that in such an event the British might seek permission to march across American territory to attack the Spaniards in the Southwest, Washington posed to his cabinet the question of what should be done in that case. Hamilton favored giving the permission. Vice President Adams opposed it. Jefferson thought no answer should be given at all. The question never arose because Pitt, confident that no French help would be forthcoming for Spain, forced Madrid to back down. This "Nootka Sound Incident" ended Spanish pretensions to control the Pacific coast and laid the basis for later Anglo-American contention over the Oregon Territory. The affair also had a more immediate effect upon Anglo-American relations: being informed by Hamilton of the existence of a strong pro-British faction in the cabinet, and being assured that he could get around the Secretary of State by dealing with the Secretary of the Treasury, Major Beckwith advised London not to be in any hurry about establishing diplomatic relations.

In Congress, however, James Madison was now advocating the use of the government's newly acquired control over commerce to force the British to evacuate the border posts and to establish satisfactory diplomatic and commercial relations. He succeeded in passing through the House a bill authorizing retaliatory discrimination against British goods and shipping. Hamilton managed to block this measure in the Senate, but the escape was sufficiently narrow to cause Beckwith to change his advice to the British Government. In October, 1791, George Hammond was appointed as the first British minister to the United States and Thomas Pinckney was accredited as the American minister at the Court of St. James.

Upon Hamilton's advice, Hammond now proceeded to stall for the better part of two years. With his cabinet colleague assuring the British minister that no concessions were necessary, Jefferson's negotiations failed to produce any results * and Jefferson became convinced that, if the President continued to support Hamilton's policy and to tolerate his interference in the Department of State's affairs, there was little point in his remaining in the cabinet. His decision to resign became final in December, 1793. For the next three years Jefferson lived in retirement at Monticello.

Jefferson's policy, up to the time when Britain and Spain became allies against France, had been one of "patience and persuasion" toward both London and Madrid. The coalition war against France now made it possible for the United States to reach satisfactory settlements with its two dangerous neighbors.

Shortly after the outbreak of this conflict, President Washington issued a Proclamation of Neutrality,† followed by a

* For Jefferson's exchange of notes with Hammond, see Ruhl J. Bartlett; *Record of American Diplomacy; op. cit.,* pages 62-68. For Jefferson's statement to Congress, *ibid.,* pages 74-78.

† *Ibid.,* page 89.

statement of *Rules Governing Belligerents* and an additional proclamation forbidding American citizens from participating in Genêt's ventures on land or by sea. The rules thus laid down were enacted into law by Congress in the Neutrality Act of 1794. These regulations re-asserted the right of neutrals to trade with belligerents and excluded from the contraband list both foodstuffs and naval stores.

Britain countered with a series of orders-in-council, denouncing the doctrine of "free ships, free goods" and reasserting its "Rule of 1756." Before these orders were published, British men-of-war seized several hundred American ships in the Caribbean.

When the news reached Philadelphia, now the seat of government, great excitement ensued. The functioning of the government was impaired by an epidemic of plague and many of the officials were sick or absent. The Jeffersonians, by now emerging as a definite opposition party, proposed a Non-Intercourse Act, prohibiting all trade with Britain. The Federalists sought to block this measure and proposed that Hamilton be sent to negotiate with Pitt. This, in turn, was bitterly opposed by the Jeffersonians. The Federalists succeeded in substituting a temporary embargo and persuaded the President to send John Jay, now Chief Justice, as an emissary to negotiate a treaty at London. Madison wrote to Jefferson at Monticello that "Jay's appointment is the most powerful blow ever suffered by the popularity of the President." In the public debate over retaliation against Britain, Madison, writing as *Helvidius,* and Hamilton, as *Pacificus,* were the protagonists.

Edmund Randolph, a lukewarm Republican who had succeeded Jefferson as Secretary of State, was reluctantly compelled to adopt Hamilton's draft of instructions to Jay, but succeeded in adding an injunction to consult with the Swedish and Danish ministers at London concerning the possible formation of an armed neutrality bloc, in the event that the British government should prove intractable.* Fear that such a bloc might be formed was, as a matter of fact, the chief reason why Britain was at this time ready to negotiate. (France had just inflicted a

---

* For text, see *ibid.,* pages 77-79. For text of Jay's treaty, *ibid.,* pages 77-79.

major defeat upon the coalition at Toulon and the blockade had become Britain's major weapon.)

Hamilton, anxious to avoid putting any sort of pressure upon Britain, proceeded to cut the ground from under Jay's negotiating position by informing Hammond that the United States would in no circumstances join an armed neutrality alliance. Thus, when Jay left on his mission, he carried with him not only the ill will of the Republicans but less than whole-hearted support from the Federalists.

The protracted secret negotiations aroused all sorts of suspicions. At Paris, Monroe was hard pressed to deny that Jay was negotiating an Anglo-American alliance. (Jay refused to keep Monroe posted.) At home, the Jeffersonians suspected that Jay was truckling to the British. This was unjust, but it turned out to be true that Jay was unable to carry out his instructions in the face of British obduracy. He obtained no redress as to neutral rights, impressment or the return of abducted slaves. A nominal concession as to West Indian trade was more of an insult than a concession. On the other hand, he obtained agreement to evacuate the border posts by 1796 and an arrangement whereby joint *ad-hoc* commissions would settle the exact Maine-Nova Scotia boundary, spoliation claims and offsetting debts.

Washington, far from pleased with the treaty, sought Hamilton's advice, though the latter had by now retired from office. Hamilton recommended accepting the treaty, except for the West Indian article. The Federalist-controlled Senate voted "not to countenance the publication of the document," seeking to push through ratification before public opposition could be aroused. When Senator S. T. Mason of Virginia defied his colleagues and gave the treaty to *Aurora,* chief organ of the Jeffersonians, there followed an outburst of popular indignation in which marching mobs burned Jay in effigy all over the country. Hamilton leaped to the defense of the treaty in a series of papers, signed *Camillus,* arguing that the treaty must be ratified on the grounds of supporting the President. The Senate ratified, but even then, Washington hesitated for seven weeks before affixing his signature to the treaty. When he finally did so, he lost the respect of many former admirers and incurred venomous abuse from the Republican press.

During the public furor, Jefferson was constantly urging Madison to reply to the *Camillus* papers, but Madison, for once, was preoccupied with personal affairs. (This was the time of his courtship and marriage.) What Madison's sharp pen failed to accomplish was, however, more than compensated by continuing British depredations at sea. Even Hamilton was moved to private anger.

The Senate's action did not dispose of the matter of Jay's Treaty. In the House, where the Jeffersonians were gaining control, Edward Livingston and Albert Gallatin led a movement to refuse the appropriations required for setting up the *ad-hoc* commissions. This set an important constitutional precedent. A further precedent was established when Congress demanded that the President supply it with the papers concerning the negotiations and Washington, again acting on Hamilton's advice, refused. Before the final roll-call, every available Federalist vote was mustered under the slogan: "Stand by the President." Fisher Ames, the outstanding Federalist spokesman in the House, rose from a sickbed in Boston and undertook the week's journey to Philadelphia to make the final, impassioned plea. His ultimate argument was: "Accept the treaty or face war, with the Indians scalping your families." The appropriation passed by the narrow margin of three votes.

Meanwhile, with Jay in London, Thomas Pinckney had been sent from his post there to negotiate a treaty with Spain. Godoy, the Spanish minister and Queen's favorite, was receptive, fearing that, unless he came to some understanding with the United States, a hostile Anglo-American alliance might result. Godoy renewed Gardoqui's earlier suggestion of a mutual defense pact but Pinckney was not to be drawn into any entangling alliance. His highly successful negotiations produced the Treaty of San Lorenzo, which settled the Florida boundary at the St. Mary's River and the 31st parallel, gave the Americans free navigation of the Mississippi and a right of deposit at New Orleans, and provided for a mutual agreement to restrain the Indians from hostile action. Pinckney's treaty was unanimously ratified by the Senate in October, 1795. While satisfactory to the Jeffersonian Westerners, it did not offset the hostile sentiments engendered

by Jay's Treaty and the Whiskey Rebellion.* Popular sympathies were still strongly anti-British and pro-French. The Federalists were in a precarious position. They were to be rescued, ironically enough, by the incredibly stupid behavior of the French.

Jean Fauchet, Genêt's successor as French minister, worked
desperately to prevent the ratification of Jay's treaty and to
stimulate hostility to Britain. His attempted intervention in
domestic American politics was disastrous both to the cause of
France and to the Francophile Jeffersonians. The disclosure of
certain mysterious conversations between the French minister
and Edmund Randolph at the time of the Whiskey Rebellion
had led to the latter's dismissal as Secretary of State and the
appointment of Timothy Pickering—an extreme Massachusetts
Federalist of pro-British leanings and a Hamilton henchman.
When Robespierre went to the gallows and the *Directoire* took
over, Fauchet was succeeded by P. Adet, an equally unfortunate
choice, who not only continued the intrigues of his predecessor
but launched an overt campaign against the Washington administration. This embarrassed the Jeffersonians more than it
hurt the Federalists. In July, 1796, as the American election was
approaching, the *Directoire* announced that henceforth France
would adopt British tactics at sea, in spite of the provisions of
the French-American treaty of 1778. (As a matter of fact, the
French had been steadily harassing American shipping, expecting the United States to ignore the infraction of the treaty.)
As if this were not provocation enough, the *Directoire's* foreign
minister, Delacroix, took it upon himself to announce that
"Washington must go."

Long before this, Washington had made up his mind to refuse a third term. His health was broken and his spirit wounded
by personal attack. In his Farewell Address of September 19,
1796, composed to a large extent by Hamilton, Washington
spoke out against the spirit of partisanship and made good use
of the French intrigues to bolster the case for his policy of
neutrality. Warning against "foreign entanglements," the retiring President pointed out the danger of permitting either
hostile or friendly feelings for other nations to grow over-strong.

* An uprising in Western Pennsylvania against Hamilton's excise tax.

The elections of 1796 marked the emergence of the Jeffersonian Republicans as a definite opposition party. Foreign policy was the chief issue, but pro-French and pro-British feelings were inextricably involved in the struggle between two conflicting theories of American government. Jefferson, though conducting no sort of personal campaign for the Presidency, was the accepted Republican leader and became the major target for Federalist abuse. Accused not only of atheism and dangerous radicalism, he was charged with pro-French leanings amounting to disloyalty, but the French minister had no illusions as to Jefferson's attitude. "Jefferson," Adet wrote to his government, "is an American and, as such, he cannot be sincerely our friend. An American is the enemy of all the peoples of Europe."

John Adams carried Washington's endorsement as the candidate of the Federalists, but Hamilton worked behind the scenes for Thomas Pinckney, in the belief that Pinckney would be more amenable to his guidance than the crotchety Massachusetts veteran. Hamilton's intrigue very nearly resulted in Jefferson's becoming the second President. When the votes were counted in the Electoral College, Adams led with 71, followed by Jefferson with 68; Pinckney ran third with 60. Under the then existing Constitutional procedure, altered by the 12th amendment in 1804, Jefferson became Vice President.

The miscarriage of Hamilton's plans marked the beginning of the end for the powerful Federalist machine which he had built and dedicated to the creation of an oligarchical government; but the end was not yet. It would take four more years before democracy would emerge triumphant—four more years of war crisis, hysteria and reign of terror, before the nation would stand securely under a government deriving its just powers from the consent of the governed.

The Treaty of Paris, in 1763, had ended the threat of encirclement by France and Spain. The Treaty of Peace, in 1783, had established independence but had left the nation exposed to containment within the Appalachians by Spain and Britain. The Jay and Pinckney treaties had now firmly established American sovereignty over all the territory east of the Mississippi from the Great Lakes to Florida, but Spain still controlled the vast, unknown regions beyond the great river. There was still the danger that the United States might become entangled in the European power struggle—that Washington's policy of neutrality might not be carried on by his successors. There was also the possibility that the United States might profit from the never-ending wars of Europe to extend its domain to the shores of the Pacific Ocean.

CHAPTER FIVE

Adams, Hamilton and Jefferson
(1797–1801)

JOHN ADAMS, of Braintree (now Quincy), Massachusetts, was a strange mixture of wisdom and vanity, of apathy and energy, and of belief and disbelief in democracy. During the fight for the Declaration of Independence, Jefferson had called him "the Colossus of the Debate." Yet this staunch advocate of independence had a lingering fondness for the trappings and even for some of the substance of monarchy and no great belief in the principles enunciated by the Declaration for which he had fought so well. His distrust of popular government grew during the chaotic period of the Confederation and his sympathies in the fight between Jefferson and Hamilton had been more often than not with the latter. Nor did Adams' anti-democratic sentiments mellow with the years; fourteen years after his retirement, he wrote to John Taylor: *

Remember, democracy never lasts long. It soon wastes, exhausts and murders itself. There never was a democracy that did not commit suicide.

* James Truslow Adams, *The Adams Family* (Little, Brown, 1930), Vol. I, page 404.

In spite of the jealous vanity with which he guarded his pre-
rogatives as President, John Adams was of a singularly trusting
nature, at least until his suspicions were aroused. For a sur-
prisingly long time he ignored the intrigue which Hamilton
had carried on against his election and seemed unaware of the
disloyalty of the cabinet officers whom he inherited and took
no action to replace. His Secretary of State, Timothy Pickering,
had been Hamilton's choice to succeed Randolph in Washington's cabinet. James McHenry, Secretary of War, was a devoted
Hamilton henchman; so was the slippery, ever-smiling Oliver
Wolcott who took over the Treasury. It was not until the end
of his term in office that Adams rid himself of the men who
steadily betrayed him, reporting to Hamilton every secret of
the cabinet discussions.

When Adams became President, the scene was already set
for a violent partisan struggle, needing only a crisis in the
steadily worsening relations with France to touch off the final
conflict. The Federalists hated the French revolution and all
Americans who sympathized with it. To them, "democracy" had
become a hate-word and its advocates objects of suspicion. Jefferson, on the other hand, had pronounced a doctrine which
was anathema to the Federalists, when he held: *

> We certainly cannot deny to other nations that principle
> whereon our government is founded, that every nation has
> a right to govern itself internally under what form it pleases
> and to change these forms at its own will.

Both Britain and France were ruthlessly violating American
neutral rights. The Federalists applauded all efforts to insist
upon French observance of obligations but denounced as pro-
French any attempt to restrain British depredations. This attitude stemmed primarily from antipathy toward France and
"Jeffersonian Jacobinism," but it also derived from Hamilton's
deliberately pro-British policy, adopted for financial reasons.

The French intrigues against Washington, plus the acts of
spoliation which the French navy now proceeded to commit,

* Letter to Edward Rutledge, 1792.

quickly produced the crisis. James Monroe * was recalled from
Paris by Pickering and Charles C. Pinckney was sent to replace
him, only to be rudely rejected by Foreign Minister Talleyrand. Pickering and the extreme Federalists wanted war, but
Hamilton counseled moderation, suggesting to Adams that he
appoint either Jefferson or Madison to a three-man commission
with Pinckney in order to involve the Republicans in what he
expected to be an unsuccessful attempt at conciliation. Adams,
rejecting this advice, named John Marshall and Elbridge Gerry
to act with Pinckney, but Talleyrand once more played into
Pickering's hands by withholding approval of the commission.
French depredations continued and the Federalists worked
themselves into a fury of warlike sentiment. Their newspapers
warned of a French invasion, hinted at a slave revolt instigated
by seditious Jacobin sympathizers and French refugees, and
denounced any further negotiation as appeasement.

For months nothing was heard from the envoys at Paris.
Finally, Marshall and then Pinckney came home, reporting not
only failure but treatment which aroused nation-wide resentment. (Gerry had remained in Paris.) Indignation reached its
climax when it was revealed that Talleyrand had dealt with the
commissioners through third parties, asking not only for a large
"loan" to France as a *douceur* to insure French respect for the
1778 treaties but also a bribe for himself of $250,000. When the
sordid details were disclosed by the publication of the famous
"XYZ Papers," the slogan became "Millions for defense but not
one cent for tribute." The Jeffersonians were stunned. Many of
them absented themselves from Congress. Adams urged the
rapid building of a navy and the raising of an army, declaring
that he would never send another minister to France without
being assured that he would be "received, respected and hon-

---

* Although he had been successful in calming French resentment over Jay's
Treaty, Monroe had indulged in rather extreme pro-French statements on a
number of occasions. Also, he had obtained the release from French prison of
Thomas Paine, by this time an advanced alcoholic who, while living with Monroe, wrote a violent attack upon the Federalist administration. Accused of disloyalty, Monroe published a defense after his return entitled: *A View of the
Conduct of the Executive in the Foreign Affairs of the United States.* This
pamphlet infuriated Washington and incurred his lasting enmity.

ored as the representative of a great, free, powerful and independent nation."

Riding the crest of a wave of patriotic anger, the Federalists were triumphant in the Congressional elections of 1798. Abandoning all pretense of non-partisanship, Washington came out of retirement to assume command of the armed forces, stipulating that Hamilton be named as his second in command. Adams resisted this condition, finally accepting it only with extreme reluctance and with unconcealed resentment.

The Republicans vainly opposed these warlike preparations and were particularly alarmed over Hamilton's appointment, fearing—not without reason—that Hamilton might use the army not merely for defense but for domestic purposes. Hamilton, at this time, seems to have had certain plans for seizing the French and Spanish possessions in North America. Relying upon the British navy to prevent a French invasion of the United States, he apparently planned an overland attack upon Louisiana and Florida in conjunction with insurgent forces to be raised by the Venezuelan conspirator, Francisco Miranda. Meanwhile, Britain was to seize Santo Domingo and the French West Indies.

Although Adams knew nothing of this plot, he undoubtedly suspected that Hamilton now wanted war; and he was certain that Pickering and the Essex Junto of New England Federalists desired war, not because they feared a French invasion but because they wished to destroy the Jeffersonian Democrats. The President, however, was determined to declare war only as a last resort and then not in reliance upon the British fleet but with an independent American navy. Following his lead, Congress authorized the building of a nuclear navy, abrogated all treaties with France, and passed a Non-Intercourse Act from which Santo Domingo was explicitly exempted. (This amounted to recognition of the slave rebellion against France led by Toussaint l'Ouverture.)

For the next two years, the United States fought an undeclared naval war with France, in which some 85 armed French vessels were captured. The success of the infant navy, particularly the victories of Commodore Truxtun in the *Constellation* over the *Insurgente* and *Vengeance,* inspired the country with confidence and caused the French to reconsider their American policy. Victor DuPont, returning from the United States, warned Talleyrand that he was driving the United States into the arms of Britain. Gerry returned and reported a favorable change in the French attitude, only to be denounced by Pickering. Dr. George Logan, an American Quaker, visited Paris and made a similar report. (Logan's unauthorized exploration, deeply resented by the Federalists, brought about the passage of the Logan Act, which still stands as a prohibition against such private ventures.)

Sensing the growing danger of an Anglo-American alliance and with Napoleon in Egypt, Talleyrand made an approach to William Vans Murray, American minister at the Hague, through the secretary of the French legation, Pichon. After consulting John Quincy Adams, then minister to Prussia, Murray reported this approach to the elder Adams and received permission to follow up the conversations. Again through Pichon, Talleyrand wrote a letter, destined for the President, in which he declared that he would welcome an American mission and that it would be "received, respected and honored as the representative of a great, free, powerful and independent nation."

On January 15, 1799, Adams sent a message to Congress transmitting Talleyrand's letter and nominating Murray as Minister to France. In taking this step without consulting his disloyal cabinet, Adams knew that he would outrage the Federalists and probably ruin his chances of renomination, but he knew that the national interest demanded peace, if peace could be obtained on honorable terms. He knew also that Congress did not share the Essexmen's desire for a British alliance in a war against France, because the following resolution already stood on the record: *

> Disdaining reliance on foreign protection, wanting no foreign guarantee of our liberties, resolving to maintain our independence against any attempt to despoil us of this inestimable resource, we confide, under Providence, in the patriotism and energies of the people of these United States for defeating the hostile enterprises of any foreign power.

* *Annals of 3rd Session of the 5th Congress,* Vol. III, pages 39-42.

The Essexmen were dumfounded but the most they could do was to insist that Murray be accompanied by two other commissioners. Adams cheerfully complied, appointing Chief Justice Ellsworth, an outspoken Federalist, and the somewhat neutral ex-governor Davie of North Carolina. With Washington and Jay backing the President, Pickering could no longer resist openly, but managed to stall the departure of the commission for several months.

Thoroughly alarmed and utterly disgusted with Adams, Hamilton apparently entertained the hope of inducing Washington to run for a third term in order to save the Federalist cause from disaster. Washington's death, in December, 1799, extinguished whatever slim prospects there may have been of that development and left the Federalists without their strongest popular appeal.

On the domestic front, the Essexmen used the crisis to good advantage. Exploiting the wave of popular indignation over the "XYZ Papers," they directed suspicion against the foreign-born —particularly against the Irish and the French—and against any and all citizens who expressed disagreement with Federalist policies. Backed by the reactionary clergy, they introduced the notorious Alien and Sedition Acts, modeled in part on similar legislation passed by the English Parliament. The Alien Act permitted the President to deport all aliens considered to be "dangerous." (Many of the Jeffersonian editors were foreign-born and so, of course, was a large part of the working population.) The Sedition Act, as originally drawn, made it an act of treason to question the justice or constitutionality of any act of the administration. Even as amended, it was clearly aimed at suppressing all criticism of the Federalist policies. Both measures were so extreme that even Hamilton worked to soften them.

Hampered by the indefensible behavior of the French *Directoire*, the Jeffersonians fought a brilliant but losing battle against the legislation, with Gallatin, Madison and Livingston leading the opposition. A part of Livingston's speech, delivered on the last day of the debate, will serve to state the major issues raised by the Jeffersonians.*

* *Annals of Congress,* June 21, 1798.

If we are to violate the Constitution, will the people submit to our unauthorized acts? Sir, they ought not to submit; they would deserve the chains that these measures are forging for them . . .

The country will swarm with informers, spies, delators and all the odious reptile tribe that breed in the sunshine of despotic power . . . The hours of the most unsuspected confidence, the intimacies of friendship, or the recesses of domestic retirement afford no security. The companion whom you must trust, the friend in whom you must confide, the domestic who waits in your chamber, all are tempted to betray your imprudent or unguarded follies; to misrepresent your words; to convey them, distorted by calumny, to the secret tribunal where jealousy presides—where fear officiates as accuser and suspicion is the only evidence that is heard . . .

Livingston did not know how strangely applicable his words would be a century and a half later, when another wave of irrational suspicion and fear would sweep the land. Nor could he foresee how history would repeat itself when he said:

Do not let us be told that we are to excite a fervor against a foreign aggression to establish tyranny here at home . . . that we are absurd enough to call ourselves free and enlightened, while we advocate principles that would have disgraced the age of Gothic barbarity.

Even more prophetic was the observation of James Madison:

Perhaps it is a universal truth that the loss of liberty at home is to be charged to provisions against danger, real or pretended, from abroad.

The bills were passed and signed by President Adams. George Washington "went full length, finding nothing objectionable" in the legislation.* Against the more moderate advice of Hamilton, he insisted that no officers' commissions be given to Republicans, refusing to commission even so sound a patriot as

* Claude Bowers, *Jefferson and Hamilton* (Houghton Mifflin, 1925), page 382.

former Speaker Muhlenberg and thereby driving the German vote into the camp of the Jeffersonians.

In the disgraceful reign of terror which followed the enactment of the Alien and Sedition Acts, "all legal safeguards laboriously erected by the common law and the Constitution were disregarded by the Federalist judges; and packed juries, under their threats and brutal charges, almost invariably brought in verdicts of guilty." * Far from accomplishing its purpose of destroying the Republican party, the reign of terror strengthened its position. Sentiment as to the unconstitutionality of the acts was crystallized by resolutions adopted by the Virginia and Kentucky legislatures. These were stimulated, if not drafted, by Jefferson at Monticello and introduced by Madison and Breckenridge. (Later, these resolutions were to serve as the foundation for the dangerous doctrine of nullification.)

Meanwhile, Pickering's stalling tactics in midsummer of 1799 were aided by what appeared to be a turn of events in Europe against the all-conquering French. Hamilton rushed down to Trenton, where the American government was temporarily seated, and informed Adams that before Christmas Louis XVIII would be restored to the throne of France. The wise veteran of European diplomacy thought this as unlikely "as that the sun, moon and stars will fall from their orbits." † Knowing his action would definitely end his own political future, Adams peremptorily cut short Pickering's arguments for further delay and ordered the commission to sail for France. The split in the Federalist party was now irreparable.

By the time the American commissioners had crossed the Atlantic, the military situation had again changed completely. Napoleon returned from Egypt. The 18th *Brumaire* ended the regime of the *Directoire* and made Bonaparte First Consul for ten years. While the commissioners waited at Paris, Bonaparte crossed the Alps and won the decisive victory of Marengo (June 14, 1800). With his hold over the heart of Europe assured, Napoleon now wanted peace with the United States and a new empire beyond the Mississippi. Talleyrand, back in office after

* Nathan Schachner, *The Founding Fathers* (Putnam, 1954), pages 476-485.

† Stewart Mitchell, *New Letters of Abigail Adams* (Houghton Mifflin, 1947), page 224.

a short interval, treated the American representatives with the utmost courtesy. There was no longer any question of blackmail or bribery. On September 29, 1800, at the secret treaty of San Ildefonso, Napoleon obtained from Spain the retrocession of all Spanish claims to Louisiana. A day later, a treaty was signed with the American commissioners.

Under the Convention of Morfontaine, the United States finally became free of the French alliance which, though a life-saver in 1778, had since become a serious entanglement. The American commissioners had been instructed to obtain payment for the French spoliations at sea, but this demand had to be dropped because its legitimacy depended upon the old treaty which the United States desired to abrogate. Talleyrand insisted upon re-instituting the "free ships, free goods" clause in the commercial treaty; the Americans accepted this in order to obtain the repeal of the obnoxious French maritime decrees, but with some misgivings because of the established British refusal to recognize the Franco-American doctrine of neutrality.

At first, the Federalists blocked the ratification of the treaty but, when Adams resubmitted it, the necessary two-thirds vote was obtained. At the probable cost of his own political future, John Adams had saved the country from becoming a British pawn in the Napoleonic Wars.

Now, at long last, John Adams proceeded to rid himself of Pickering and McHenry, retaining the third Hamilton henchman, Oliver Wolcott, whose treachery he apparently never suspected. John Marshall, one of the few Federalist leaders who had opposed the Alien and Sedition Acts, became Secretary of State and was shortly thereafter to be appointed Chief Justice as well. (John Jay preferred to seek the governorship of New York—a decision which profoundly affected the development of the Republic.)

With the top Federalist leadership openly hostile to Adams while the lower echelons remained faithful to him, Hamilton gloomily foresaw a Republican victory. Everything depended upon the pivotal states of New York and Pennsylvania. Having first failed in an effort to manipulate the Federalist nomination for C. C. Pinckney, Hamilton engaged in an open campaign on his behalf. A journey through New England, ostensibly undertaken to dissolve the army over which Hamilton now held command, turned into an anti-Adams crusade. On one occasion, Hamilton recklessly declared that, if Pinckney failed to be elected, "I shall either lose my head or lead a triumphant army." This frantic effort served only to widen the split in the Federalist party. Worse yet, in his own stronghold of New York, Hamilton was outmaneuvered and defeated by Aaron Burr's skillful management of the Republican campaign. Confronted with this disaster, Hamilton went so far as to propose to Governor Jay a wholly outrageous scheme for stealing the New York electors. "In times like these," Hamilton said, "it will not do to be overscrupulous." * Jay, shocked and amazed, pigeonholed the proposal.

This was Hamilton at his desperate worst. To cap the climax, he wrote a violent personal attack upon John Adams, utilizing confidential information from Pickering and McHenry, now exiled from the cabinet. The pamphlet, intended only for private circulation, fell into Burr's hands and was given to the press.

Hamilton had now reached the point at which he preferred to see Jefferson, his ancient enemy, elected President rather than Adams; but Hamilton no longer controlled the Federalist machine which he had created. As it became more and more evident that Pinckney had no chance, some of the Federalists began talking about secession in the event of Jefferson's election. Others began to flirt with the strange expedient of defeating Jefferson by electing his fellow-Republican, Aaron Burr. Intrigue and counter-intrigue marked an election in which both sides resorted to every known political maneuver. After Pinckney had declined to participate in a fraud which might have made him President, the ballot-count showed Jefferson and Burr tied, with Adams and Pinckney eliminated. The election was thus thrown into the House, where a protracted deadlock ensued, with the Federalists voting for Burr and the Republicans for Jefferson. The Federalists hoped to prolong the deadlock and then to demand a new election which would leave the old Congress in power for another year. Federalist

* Claude Bowers, *op. cit.,* page 454.

leaders approached both Burr and Jefferson, seeking to make some sort of deal. Burr remained at Albany and apparently rejected all overtures. Whether Jefferson also rejected the making of any promises is still a matter of debate. His word that he had asserted that he "would not receive the government on capitulation, that I would not go into it with my hands tied" seems more to be trusted than the contrary assertions of some historians. In any event, the Federalists finally capitulated and the danger of "usurpation" passed.

For John Adams, there was little comfort, whichever way the House might decide. When Jefferson called upon him at the new Executive Mansion during the week of deadlock, he was barely civil. After Jefferson's election, he sent him no friendly message. The night before the inauguration of his successor, Adams spent in filling with Federalist appointees the vacancies created in the Federal Judiciary by a last-minute act of the expiring Federalist-controlled Congress. Since the judges so appointed had life tenure, Adams' "midnight appointments" preserved Federalist control of the Judiciary long after the Federalist party had ceased to exist.

Early in the morning of the day of Jefferson's inauguration, John and Abigail Adams boarded their coach and, almost surreptitiously, began their homeward journey to Braintree.

As for Hamilton, the bitterness of the Federalist defeat was mitigated by the fact that Jefferson, with whom he profoundly disagreed, had become President, rather than Burr whom he deeply hated and distrusted.

The first two Presidents had established the United States on a firm footing, assured its territorial integrity and laid the foundations for its emergence as "a great, free, powerful and independent nation." They had accomplished this in large measure because Europe's wars had provided the opportunity; but that opportunity would have been lost, had not both Washington and Adams steered a determined course of vigilant neutrality.

The success of the neutrality policy was, to a large extent, the product of the battle between the Titans—Hamilton and Jefferson. But for Hamilton's determination to remain on good terms with England, the War of 1812 might have been fought twenty years earlier and brought the United States into alliance with Napoleon. But for Jefferson's persistent patience and sympathy for France, Adams might not have been able to avoid open war with France and an entangling British alliance.

In domestic affairs, both Washington and Adams were by nature inclined toward belief in rule by the elite. During Washington's two terms, Hamilton clearly had the advantage over Jefferson; his firm authoritarianism and his military proclivities attracted the soldierly side of the first President, while his financial genius and skill in political controversy won Washington's confidence and esteem. Adams, while sharing Hamilton's predilection for oligarchy, never accepted—as Washington had —the Hamiltonian insistence upon maintaining friendly relations with Britain, no matter what concessions this might require. Adams remained essentially anti-British from the time when he signed the Declaration of Independence, though this did not make him in any sense pro-French. The New Englander's Puritan morality rejected Hamilton's unscrupulous methods, and his vanity caused him to resent Hamilton's all-too-ready advice and intervention. Yet Adams subscribed on the whole to Federalist aims and to Federalist antipathy toward Jeffersonian democracy.

Thus, in a sense, the Jeffersonians triumphed not only over Hamilton and the ideas which he represented but over both of the two first Presidents. They triumphed primarily because the decision rested with the people and because the Federalist party had never put down roots among the people. In a sense, the Republican victory of 1800 was a sectional victory of the agricultural South and West over the mercantile Northeast, but in its deeper meaning, it was a victory of the people. It is true that, because of property qualifications, only about one sixth of the white population had a vote and that in many states the electors were chosen by the legislatures. This stacked the odds, but did not alter the fact that the Jeffersonians won because they believed in the people, understood their changing needs and tried to serve them. Where Hamilton had relied upon the power and intelligence of the "wise and well-born few," Jefferson placed his faith in the common sense and integrity of the many. Where Hamilton had catered to Eastern privilege and wealth, Jefferson

—himself a frontiersman—remained in step with the needs and aspirations of the rapidly expanding West.

With the triumph of the Republicans, the battle for political democracy was won. The election of 1800 decided that the country belonged to the people. It remained to be seen whether the people were, as Jefferson and Madison believed, capable of governing themselves wisely and well, and whether they would be able to preserve their sovereignty against such challenges as the future might hold in store.

NOTE: The two foregoing chapters do scant justice to a decade which shaped the fundamental nature of the Republic. They also frankly reveal the author's Jeffersonian bias, for which no apology is offered. Detailed support for the Jeffersonian interpretation is perhaps most interestingly supplied by Claude Bowers' *Hamilton and Jefferson*. Nathan Schachner's more recent work, *The Founding Fathers,* presents a well-documented history of the period, written from a point of view which reveals considerable scepticism as to Jefferson and presents Hamilton and the Federalists in a somewhat more favorable light. The more one studies the early years of the Republic, the more one is impressed with the interlocking nature of the contributions made by the towering figures of the times. In one's fascination with the antithesis between Jefferson and Hamilton, one is apt to overlook the fact that each saved the other from disaster and that James Madison probably did more to make the antithesis productive than either of the two protagonists. It was Madison's cool constitutional reasoning which checked Hamilton, and Madison's judgment which often restrained Jefferson. Yet, without Hamilton's financial genius, democracy would have floundered, and without the fiery flame of Jefferson's spirit, it would have been lost.

PART TWO

Continental Expansion

CHAPTER SIX

Diplomatic Expansion
(1801 – 1825)

THE PERIOD of continental expansion, during which the United States extended its domain to the Pacific Ocean, can best be divided into three phases. The first phase, of *diplomatic expansion*, begins with Jefferson's purchase of the Louisiana Territory, is interrupted by the War of 1812, and culminates in the Transcontinental Treaty with Spain, negotiated by John Quincy Adams, as Secretary of State under James Monroe. The second phase, of *interrupted expansion*, begins with the Presidency of John Quincy Adams, during which the Jacksonian revolution got under way, and ends with John Tyler's accession to the Presidency. The third phase, of *aggressive expansion*, begins with the annexation of Texas and ends with the accomplishment of "Manifest Destiny" through the War with Mexico and Nicholas Trist's strange Treaty of Guadalupe Hidalgo, in 1848.

This chapter deals with the first of these three stages of continental expansion, covering the Presidential terms of the three great Virginians—Jefferson, Madison and Monroe. This period, running from 1801 to 1824, carries American diplomacy to its high water mark, from which it then receded both in wisdom and in competence.

1. Jefferson, President;
Madison, Secretary of State.

The keynote of the new era of tolerance and belief in the common man was struck on the raw, March morning when a tall, plainly dressed citizen walked along the unpaved, muddy street from Conrad's boarding house to the unfinished Capitol Building in Washington, in order to take the oath of office as the third President of the United States.

"We are all Republicans," Jefferson said in his first inaugural; "we are all Federalists. If there be any among us who would wish to dissolve this union or to change its Republican form, let them stand undisturbed as monuments to the safety with which error of opinion may be tolerated where reason is left free to combat it."

Having uttered this challenge to the spirit of suspicion and fear which had produced the Alien and Sedition Acts and expressed his unshakable faith in the rule of reason, Jefferson proceeded to carry out the purpose which he himself described as follows in a contemporary letter: "Believing that all our citizens (excepting the ardent monarchists) agreed in ancient Whig principles, I thought it advisable to define and declare them, and let them see the ground on which we can rally." Thus, in a spirit of conciliation, the nation was rededicated to the principles of the Declaration which it had come so perilously near to abandoning.

Jefferson's election gave him the opportunity to test his conviction that the people were capable of governing themselves wisely and well and that the strongest government would always be that in which every man "would meet invasions of the public order as his own personal concern." Jefferson's case still remains to be proved, but it is doubtful whether, without him, the United States would ever have become the great proving ground.

Both background and experience gave Thomas Jefferson exceptional qualifications for the Presidency at this time.

Born in the frontier wilderness of the Blue Ridge Mountains in 1743, Jefferson was the son of a surveyor, who became a Virginia Burgess and a colonel of militia. His mother was a Randolph—one of the oldest and most aristocratic of the Virginia families. At 26, Jefferson was elected to the House of Burgesses. At 36, he succeeded Patrick Henry as governor of Virginia. In the intervening period, he had transformed his native state from a plantation oligarchy to a democracy,* had participated in the organization of the First Continental Congress and had written the Declaration of Independence.

In the Congress, he had headed the Committee to consider the terms of peace, had helped to draw the first plan for the government of the western territories and had fathered the provision which prohibited slavery in the Northwest Territory after 1800—a decision which is considered by many historians to have saved the Union in the Civil War. He had assisted Franklin and Adams in negotiating treaties for the Confederation and, from 1785 to 1789, had served as minister to France.

As Secretary of State under Washington, Jefferson had profited from the insight gained into the true nature of the French revolution. No less concerned than Washington with the preservation of neutral rights, he never lost sight of the fact that the revolution, in spite of its violence and later brutal imperialism under Napoleon, nevertheless represented an historical process of evolution from absolute monarchy toward what he hoped and believed would be a system of constitutional government based upon the rights of man. The early violence seemed to Jefferson the outcome of previous tyranny, rather than evidence of the inherent weakness of democracy. The perversion of the revolution by Napoleon seemed to him to prove the danger of militarism rather than the weakness of a republican form of government. Where Jefferson's humanitarianism and belief in the essential decency of all men made him slower than others to realize the nature of the Napoleonic threat to the very future in which he placed his hopes, his faith in the ultimate outcome of the French revolution provided a much-needed antidote to the hysterical fears prevalent at the time.

The most important men in the Jefferson administration were James Madison, Secretary of State; Albert Gallatin, Secretary of the Treasury; John Marshall, Chief Justice of the Su-

* Himself an eldest son, Jefferson had sponsored and seen enacted into law the repeal of entail and the abolition of primogeniture. He had fought for the guarantee of absolute religious freedom and the repeal of taxation to support an established church and laid the foundations for a humanitarian revision of the Virginia penal code and the abolition of capital punishment except for murder and treason. He had sought unsuccessfully to abolish slavery and to create a state-supported system of general education.

preme Court; and James Monroe, who served as envoy
plenipotentiary on several important foreign missions. Madison
and Monroe were Jeffersonian disciples. Gallatin, a native of
Switzerland, had won his spurs in Congress as the only Republican able to hold his own against the brilliant Hamilton in
matters of finance and had later become one of the most powerful Jeffersonians in debate.

Aaron Burr had little in common with Jeffersonianism, although he had contributed in no small measure to the
Republican victory by winning the electoral votes of New
York. In a sense, Burr was the prototype of the urban political
boss interested primarily in building a personal machine of
political power. While Vice President, Burr openly engaged in
a campaign to wrest the governorship of New York from Governor Clinton. Here he was frustrated by the active and determined opposition of Hamilton whose vituperations against
"this unscrupulous Catiline" led to the duel in which Burr inflicted a mortal wound. The killing of Hamilton ended Burr's
political career and, for a number of years, he disappeared from
view.

In domestic affairs, the story of the two Jefferson administrations became very largely the story of the struggle between
Jefferson and Marshall—between a President who believed that
the government of the United States possessed only the powers
explicitly given to it by the Constitution and a Chief Justice
who as firmly believed in what came to be known as the doctrine of implied powers. This conflict was crystallized in four
great decisions of the Marshall Court.

In *Marbury versus Madison*, Marshall affirmed that it was
the duty of the Court to disregard any act of Congress and,
therefore, any act of a state legislature, which the Court thought
in conflict with the Constitution.

In *Cohens versus Virginia*, Marshall held that the Congress
could lawfully pass an act permitting a person convicted in a
state court to appeal to the United States Supreme Court, if he
alleged that the state law under which he was convicted con-
flicted with the Constitution or with an act of Congress.

In *McCulloch versus Maryland*, Marshall laid down the rule
that Congress, in the exercise of a power delegated under the

Constitution, has a wide latitude in the choice of means: "Let the end be legitimate, let it be within the scope of the Constitution, and all means which are appropriate, which are plainly adapted to that end, which are not prohibited but consist with the letter and spirit of the Constitution, are Constitutional." This was the heart of the doctrine of implied power, opposed by Jefferson, but without which the Federal government could never have become firmly established.

Finally, in *Gibbons versus Ogden,* Marshall held that the power to regulate commerce, conveyed by the Constitution, included the power to regulate or license the carrying of goods and passengers between the states as well as between the United States and foreign countries. This decision finally made the United States an economic unit.

To understand Jefferson's objection to these decisions in the light of some of his own actions, such as the extension of the Federal power over the western territories, one must take into account two major considerations: first, his aversion to concentrated power in any form, magnified by the experience of combatting Hamiltonian oligarchy; and, second, his conviction that the Constitution should, whenever necessary, be amended by Constitutional process, rather than interpreted by the Supreme Court. It was not so much the substance of Marshall's decisions to which he took exception as Marshall's conception of the Court's function, which gave it, in Jefferson's opinion, a dangerous amount of power. For precisely the opposite reasons, the die-hard Federalists for a time saw in Chief Justice Marshall their one hope for the future, not realizing that Marshall had little in common with their oligarchical ambitions. On the other hand, the extreme States-rights Jeffersonians now saw in the Chief Justice the danger of authoritarian centralization which, until the election of 1800, had been spear-headed by Hamilton's mercantile aristocracy and the reactionary clergy.

When Jefferson became President, he did not know about the secret treaty of San Ildefonso under which Spain had ceded Louisiana to France. He knew only that an honorable peace with France had been obtained by the United States and that negotiations for peace were under way between the British and Napoleon. With the cessation of hostilities, after the Peace of

Amiens, in 1802, the whole vexing problem of neutral rights
seemed to have disappeared.

Suddenly the news came that France had acquired all or part
of the Spanish possessions in North America and that a powerful imperialism might soon supplant a weak Spain as the western neighbor of the United States. It was generally assumed that
Spain had ceded not only Louisiana but also West Florida
(Alabama and Mississippi). The Spanish Intendant of Louisiana revoked the American right of deposit at New Orleans,
giving rise to the belief, never actually proved correct, that this
action had been taken in collusion with Bonaparte. It was correctly surmised that Napoleon was preparing some sort of expedition to North America. Actually, he was preparing two
major expeditions: the first, to put down the Negro rebellion
in Santo Domingo, and the second, to occupy New Orleans.

When the news of the Spanish cession was confirmed after
Talleyrand had first denied it to the American minister, Jefferson made use of Pierre S. DuPont, a private citizen about to
visit France, to warn Minister Livingston that a French occupation of New Orleans might drive the United States into an
alliance with Britain. DuPont suggested that possibly it might
suit France to sell New Orleans; later, after his arrival in
France, he wrote Jefferson suggesting that the United States
might buy New Orleans and the Floridas for something like
$6,000,000.* Jefferson promptly obtained an appropriation of
$2,000,000 for "expenses for foreign intercourse" and sent James
Monroe to assist Livingston in exploring the situation. Monroe
carried instructions to offer up to 10,000,000 francs for the island of New Orleans and the Floridas. If this proved impossible
he was to obtain some sort of right of deposit on the Mississippi,
and, if certain that France would make no deal and intended
war, he and Livingston were to proceed to London to negotiate
an Anglo-American alliance.

Before Monroe ever reached France, on April 12, 1803, the
situation had changed. Napoleon's plans for an American empire had fallen through, and Livingston had already had certain
revealing conversations. General Leclerc had encountered un-

* Gilbert Chinard, *Correspondence of Jefferson and DuPont de Nemours*
(Johns Hopkins, 1931).

expectedly strong resistance from Toussaint l'Ouverture in Santo Domingo; his expeditionary force had been all but wiped out by war and yellow fever. General Victor's second force, due to have sailed for New Orleans from Helvoet-Sluys, in Holland, was ice-bound by an unprecedentedly severe winter. Meanwhile, Napoleon's aggressions in Holland, Italy and Switzerland had caused the British to refuse to carry out the evacuation of Malta, provided for in the treaty of Amiens. With resumption of war imminent, Bonaparte decided that any further effort to establish an empire in North America would probably lead to an Anglo-American alliance. Hence, before Monroe reached Paris, Livingston had already learned that not Florida but the whole of Louisiana might be purchased by the United States.

No news could have been more thrilling to Thomas Jefferson. The unexplored lands beyond the great river had long excited his interest and kindled his imagination. Before he had any intimation of the Spanish retrocession to France, Jefferson had often talked with his secretary, Meriwether Lewis, about an exploratory expedition. These conversations led to obtaining permission from Spain for the famous Lewis and Clark expedition, sent to discover the headwaters of the Mississippi and Missouri rivers and, ultimately, to penetrate to the Columbia River.* The unexpected opportunity to acquire this vast unknown area came as a veritable gift from heaven. Jefferson's reaction was swift and unhesitating.

On April 30, 1803, Monroe and Livingston signed the treaty under which the United States acquired New Orleans and all the vast trans-Mississippi Louisiana Territory for the sum of $11,250,000. Under two conventions, signed the same day, the United States agreed to set aside an additional $3,750,000 to pay the claims of its own citizens against France and agreed to place France and Spain on an equal commercial footing with respect to the acquired territory for a period of twelve years.

The treaty conveyed Louisiana "with the same extent that it now has in the hands of Spain"—France had not yet taken physical possession—"and that it had when France possessed it; and

---

* For a fascinating account of the Lewis and Clark Expedition and a unique study of the Indian tribes of the West, see Bernard de Voto, *The Course of Empire* (Houghton Mifflin, 1952).

such as it should be after the treaties subsequently entered into between Spain and other States." This was an exact quotation of the language employed in the secret treaty of San Ildefonso. When the American emissaries sought a clearer definition of what they had purchased, Napoleon is said to have remarked to Talleyrand that "if an obscurity did not already exist, it would perhaps be good policy to put one there." The lack of precise boundary definition created the West Florida and Texas disputes and affected the later Anglo-American conflict over the Oregon Territory.

Napoleon's action directly violated his pledge to Spain never to dispose of Louisiana to a third party. Spain protested, but did nothing to enforce its protest.

In the United States, grave doubt existed not only in the minds of hostile critics, but in Thomas Jefferson's own mind as to the constitutionality of the purchase. There was no clause among the enumerated powers granted by the Constitution which authorized the acquisition of foreign territory or the promise of the wholesale admission of foreigners to American citizenship. Jefferson's single most important action as President was also the most inconsistent act of his entire career. He, the champion of a strict interpretation of the Constitution, now extended the powers of the Federal government far beyond any previous limits. Ironically enough, once Jefferson laid aside his own scruples in what he rightly conceived to be the vital national interest, the only serious objections were raised by the die-hard Federalists under Pickering's leadership. The Federalist senators voted against ratification—all but the newly-elected Senator from Massachusetts, John Quincy Adams.

The Louisiana Purchase also constituted a departure from Jefferson's principles of fiscal policy. He had fought Hamilton's creation of a national debt and had been a consistent advocate of limited Federal expenditure. Now, on his own Executive authority, Jefferson had entered into a commitment which amounted to more than a fifth of the figure at which the national debt had stood at the time of his inauguration.*

* According to J. P. Craf, *Economic Development of the United States, op. cit.*, the national debt stood, in 1800, at $82,900,000. By 1812, it had been reduced to $45,200,000.

Out of the acquisition of Louisiana arose another frequently cited Jeffersonian inconsistency. This had to do with the steps undertaken to remove the Indians from east of the Mississippi to the new western domains. Jefferson had never shared the frontiersman's brutal attitude which denied that the "savages" had any rights whatever to the lands they sought to hold. Yet he himself now adopted methods of extinguishing Indian land titles east of the Mississippi which could scarcely be considered less than ruthless, though the harsh judgment of Henry Adams in calling "his greed for land equal to that of any settler on the border," seems a little exaggerated. Jefferson made no contemporary explanations or excuses, yet he must have been uncomfortably aware that, under his own doctrine of human equality, men of copper-colored skin were no less entitled to "life, liberty and the pursuit of happiness" than were their white brothers.

In an attempt to settle the northwest boundary with Britain, Jefferson was saved from a mistake of far-reaching consequences by John Quincy Adams. A treaty with Britain, negotiated by the American minister Rufus King, would have fixed the boundary along a line running westward from the Lake of the Woods to the Rocky Mountains. This would have left in Canada the then undiscovered iron deposits in the Mesabi range as well as large parts of North Dakota, Montana, Idaho and probably—if the line had been extended to the Pacific—the northern part of what is now the state of Washington. When Jefferson submitted this treaty to the Senate, Adams was instrumental in bringing about its rejection, thereby saving the United States a strip of territory 152 miles wide running from the headwaters of the Mississippi westward to the Rocky Mountains and, very likely, to the Pacific.

By 1804, the once-powerful Federalist party had melted away and Jefferson was re-elected with 162 out of the 176 votes in the Electoral College. Under the revision of the electoral system brought about by the 12th Amendment to the Constitution, George Clinton was elected Vice President.

Three major themes dominate the four years of Jefferson's second term: the unsuccessful attempt to acquire the Floridas; the struggle to maintain neutral rights while again profiting from the renewed Napoleonic Wars; and the treason trial of Aaron Burr. The period of 1804-1808 added no particular luster to the already illustrious record of the third President.

Owing to the vagueness of the Louisiana Purchase, Jefferson thought he had a case for claiming that West Florida had been a part of the acquisition. This rested upon Livingston's contention that West Florida had been a part of Spanish Louisiana when ceded to France at San Ildefonso. Henry Adams' barbed comment on Livingston's construction was: "He discovered that France had actually bought West Florida without knowing it, and had sold it to the United States without being paid for it." The Spanish ambassador, Yrujo, violently protested any such claim and became incensed when Jefferson persuaded Congress to pass the Mobile Act of February 24, 1804, giving him power, when he deemed it expedient, to annex "all the navigable waters, rivers, creeks, bays and inlets lying within the United States, which empty into the Gulf of Mexico." Jefferson, cautiously avoiding an explicit occupation, declared a new "customs district" along the Gulf coast. Negotiations with Spain at Madrid led to no result, but, when Spain once more became involved in the Napoleonic War, Jefferson sent Monroe to assist Charles Pinckney * in another attempt. This, too, was unsuccessful. At this time, Jefferson apparently contemplated a forcible seizure of West Florida under cover of a British alliance, but the beginning of a protracted and bitter disagreement with Britain over the impressment of seamen and neutral rights put an end to that possibility.

There then followed what most historians consider a rather disreputable episode. Although Napoleon had earlier refused to lend aid to the American claim of having purchased West Florida, Talleyrand now hinted that, for certain monetary considerations, it might be possible to arrange for the United States to purchase this territory. The suggestion was that the United States should offer $7,000,000, ostensibly to Spain but actually at least in part to the treasury of Napoleon. In spite of having maintained that he had already purchased West Florida, Jefferson was apparently willing to explore this dubious suggestion.

* Not to be confused with C. C. Pinckney.

He obtained a preliminary appropriation of $2,000,000 from Congress, as he had done in the case of the Louisiana Purchase. However, before the negotiation could be carried any further, Talleyrand changed his mind, because the military situation in Europe had so shifted in Bonaparte's favor that the Emperor of France now had his own eye upon the Spanish possessions. This ended the Florida question for the time being.

Napoleon resumed the war against England in 1803, with Spain as an ally, Holland and Italy in his control and a newly-built French fleet at his command. Nelson's victory at Trafalgar, in 1805, destroyed the Emperor's hope of conquering the British Isles, but his own victories over Austria (at Ulm and Austerlitz in 1805), over Prussia (at Jena and Auerstaedt in 1806) and over Russia (at Friedland, resulting in the Peace of Tilsit in 1807) sealed up the Continent against British trade. With Russia and North Germany included in his "Continental System," Napoleon now sought to bring the Mistress of the Seas to terms by strangling her commerce. The war became a war of blockade and counter-blockade, in which freedom of the seas and neutral trading rights again became a major issue. Britain sought to pierce the boycott by forcing the European neutrals to leave the Continental System and, for a time, by stimulating American trade with the Continent. In 1805-1807 the United States profited handsomely from neutral trade with the blockaded countries of Europe. Exports of domestic products rose to almost $50,000,000 a year, while foreign goods imported and re-exported rose to about $60,000,000. Insofar as the latter came from the British West Indies and were carried in American bottoms through the Continental blockade, this was a welcome aid to Britain. There was also, however a considerable volume of American import from the French West Indies which, under the British rule of 1756, could be re-exported legitimately provided that the goods were not carried from the French possessions to Europe in a continuous voyage.

Resentment of the British shipping interests over the growing American trade, as well as the exigencies of a life-and-death struggle, caused the British government to revise its traditional attitude toward neutral shipping; it proceeded to do this in two

ways, both exasperating to the American shippers. Under the
Essex decision, a British court held that a neutral voyage could
not be considered broken, unless the goods were actually imported into the neutral country and import duty paid, not to
be refunded when the goods were re-exported. Second, the
British began trying by various means to force neutral carriers
to take their goods to British ports and there to obtain a license to carry their cargoes to enemy or blockaded ports. In this
manner, the British tried not only to control neutral trade but
to force it to pay a toll which would help defray the costs of
war. The new orders-in-council of November 11, 1807, nailed
down the rules which made it mandatory for American vessels
to stop en route to Europe and purchase a British license.

In the same year, the anger and humiliation aroused by the
long-standing British practice of impressment came to a head,
when a British man-of-war, the *Leopard,* halted the American
frigate *Chesapeake* and fired a broadside into the unsuspecting
vessel, forcing submission to a search of its crew and to seizure
of four alleged British deserters. The inhuman conditions of
service in the Royal Navy had long discouraged voluntary en-
listment and the established practice had been to recruit crews
through forcible seizure by press-gangs operating not only in
British but in foreign ports, and by search and seizure at sea.
In response to repeated protests, the British pleaded necessity. The barbarous conditions of the British service led thousands of British seamen to transfer to American ships; many of
them had by this time become naturalized American citizens.
The British refused to recognize naturalization. Not only did
they seize from American ships and impress great numbers of
naturalized American seamen with families established in the
United States, but also thousands of native-born Americans on
the pretext that they had been born in Britain or had deserted
from the Royal Navy.

In an attempt to deal with these issues, Jefferson had sent
Monroe and Charles Pinckney to London in 1806. The treaty
which they negotiated failed to deal with impressment and Jefferson did not even submit it for ratification. A repetition of
Washington's methods (Jay's Treaty) having failed, Jefferson

now once more resorted to his favorite device of commercial reprisal. His Embargo and Non-Importation Acts of 1807 were, in essence, nothing more than a self-imposed blockade, technically impartial as against the belligerents, but actually aimed solely at Britain. While damaging to that country, the measures proved even more harmful to the trade of the United States and resulted in a considerable amount of smuggling. Shortly before Jefferson's retirement from the Presidency, both acts were repealed and a new Non-Intercourse Act, limited to the embargo of trade with Britain and France, was substituted. When Madison succeeded Jefferson, the crisis with Britain was unsolved and unmitigated by Jefferson's policy.

Many historians, especially Admiral Mahan, have dealt harshly with Jefferson's failure to build a strong navy and to resort to more forceful measures. Yet, in many ways, Jefferson's attitude toward the problem was similar to that of Washington and Hamilton in 1794. Short of going to war, it is difficult to see what Jefferson could have done to achieve redress. Had the War of 1812 been fought five years earlier, the United States might have been spared considerable humiliation, but it would almost certainly have become involved on the side of Napoleon and found itself supporting the Corsican's schemes for world conquest.

The final unhappy episode in Jefferson's second term, the treason trial of Aaron Burr, had its roots in an appointment made by Jefferson in his first administration. Burr, then Vice President, was about to preside over the Senate's impeachment proceedings against Supreme Court Justice Samuel Chase, for whom Jefferson felt a strong antipathy because of his implacable enforcement of the Alien and Sedition laws. Chase, a die-hard Federalist, had laid himself open to impeachment by indulging in highly unjudicial comments from the bench concerning Jefferson's administration. Whether to win Burr's aid in the impeachment proceedings, as alleged by some historians, or simply because he had refused the Vice President's other requests for patronage, Jefferson acceded to Burr's request that the already notorious General Wilkinson, mentioned earlier in connection with the Kentucky conspiracy, be appointed as Inspector General of the military forces to be stationed in the Louisiana Territory.

To this day it is not clearly established what Burr actually did when he disappeared from view after the duel with Hamilton. It is known that he purchased a tract of land in the new western territory; whether he did so in order to develop a new state or to create the nucleus for a new nation is uncertain. He apparently had a plan for conquering Mexico, either for the United States or for a new empire of his own. Wilkinson, already for some years in Spanish pay, may have thought at first that Burr's plan was one of collusion with Spain. Whatever the facts and whatever Wilkinson's motivation for betraying the conspiracy, he denounced Burr to Jefferson as a traitor plotting to seize part of the territory of the United States.

Learning of Wilkinson's betrayal, Burr fled from Blennerhasset Island where his force was assembled and made his way back into Mississippi Territory before he was captured. He was then brought to trial before the United States Circuit Court at Richmond, with Chief Justice Marshall presiding as Circuit Judge. The trial took place in an atmosphere of great public indignation, inspired by Jefferson's unqualified denunciation, and it was generally hoped and taken for granted that Burr would be convicted. Burr, however, conducted his own defense with consummate skill, tripping up and embarrassing the prosecution, particularly with respect to its star witness, General Wilkinson.

In his charge to the jury, Justice Marshall so defined "treason" and "levying war" that the jury found itself unable to convict. Marshall rejected the English definition of "constructive treason," holding that, while treason might have been plotted, no act of treason had been committed; and that the only evidence of intent to levy war had been the force on Blennerhasset Island discovered when Burr was miles away from the scene.

The acquittal was a bitter blow to Jefferson, who had unnecessarily involved his own prestige in the matter. Yet his prestige and popularity did not actually suffer, because the public on the whole resented the verdict of acquittal, believing that Burr had escaped conviction on a technicality. Public indignation turned, quite unfairly, against Marshall who was denounced and burned in effigy.*

If Thomas Jefferson, as President, seems a somewhat less inspiring figure than he had been as the spiritual leader of the Revolution and the champion of democracy in the days when the issue of democracy and oligarchy hung in the balance, several factors should be taken into consideration. First: It is easier to be a distinguished leader of an opposition than a distinguished chief of state. Second: Jefferson's fight against Hamiltonian centralism pushed him into a more extreme decentralist position than was actually consistent with his own nature and philosophy. He did not *become* a nationalist when he assumed the responsibilities of the chief executive; he had always been a nationalist as to foreign relations, but his nationalism had been obscured by the necessity to combat oligarchy. Third, and perhaps most important: Jefferson's outlook was essentially agricultural. His dream was of an ever-expanding nation of people owning their own homes and farms. Cities were to him "sores upon the body politic." As early as 1775, he wished to exclude from buying public land any man who already owned fifty acres. In 1785, he wrote: "The small landowners are the most precious portion of the state." The availability of cheap public land was to Jefferson the essential basis of democracy. This accounts for his readiness to jettison his constitutional scruples in purchasing Louisiana, for his none too humanitarian eviction of the Indians and for his continental isolationism. He had no vision of an industrial future and but little sympathy for the manufacturer, the middleman and the trader. Here again, his originally limited outlook was exaggerated by the Hamiltonian threat of oligarchical rule by the very elements which he most distrusted and least understood. Finally, Thomas Jefferson was not a man of great personal ambition who could take naturally to a position of power. He was by nature a student, a philosopher, a farmer—almost a recluse by inclination. It was a sense of duty, rather than ambition, which made him forsake private for public life. When he

* It is interesting to speculate whether Jefferson, were he a witness of events in 1950-1954, would not support Marshall's refusal to stretch the definition of treason.

declined a third term as President, he did so out of deep conviction that the Constitution should have limited the eligibility of any one man to hold that office and in the hope that his action would firmly establish a precedent—but he also declined re-election with joy rather than regret, looking forward with pleasure to a life of retirement.

Jefferson's own evaluation of his services to his country and his fellow men makes no mention of his ever having been President of the United States. The epitaph, which he himself wrote for his tombstone, reads:

> Here was buried Thomas Jefferson, author of the Declaration of American Independence, of the statute of Virginia for religious freedom, and father of the University of Virginia.

2. Madison, President;
Monroe, Secretary of State.

James Madison was so closely associated with Thomas Jefferson in thought and through a long period of common effort that his administration was, in essence, a continuation of that of his predecessor. Eight years younger than his great fellow Virginian, Madison was coolly practical where Jefferson was visionary, ready and effective in debate where Jefferson was reluctant to enter controversy, and an accurate, specialized scholar where Jefferson was a philosopher of widely scattered interests. Beginning with his service in the Continental Congress in 1778, and continuing through the succeeding years of the Confederation and the administrations of Washington and Adams, Madison was in effect Jefferson's chief of staff, assuming that position even more completely as Secretary of State during Jefferson's Presidency.

The earliest political association of the two men was in working for the establishment of religious freedom in Virginia. In the Continental Congress, Madison helped Jefferson to formulate the solution for the problem of governing the western territories. He was one of the first to insist that the Federal government must have direct power over the individual and that it must have a legislature elected by the people, rather than merely by the states. Conscious of the weakness of the

Confederation, Madison fought for giving the Congress the power to lay import duties and to stop the issuance of paper money. In 1787, Madison's paper on *The Vices of the Political System of the United States* laid bare the need for strengthening the Confederation and became the basis of the Virginia Plan for the Constitution. Madison, more than any other single man, was the father of the Constitution.

Elected to the first House of Representatives in 1789, it was Madison who wrote and fought through the Bill of Rights for which Jefferson had pleaded from Paris. If it was Jefferson who directed the long and successful fight against Hamiltonian oligarchy, it was Madison, along with Albert Gallatin, who led the Jeffersonian forces in Congress.

Gallatin, as Secretary of the Treasury, Monroe in the State Department and John Quincy Adams, whom Madison called back into the public service and sent to St. Petersburg, turned out to be the stalwarts of the Madison administration.

The issues with Britain—impressment, neutral rights and boundary disputes—which Jefferson had been unable to settle, became the inheritance of his successor. It was during Madison's first term, however, that Congress for the first time seized the initiative in foreign policy from the Executive. Henry Clay, the youthful and popular Speaker of the House, was the spearhead of a group of western Congressmen who cherished the ambition of clearing the European powers out of the North American continent, seizing the Floridas from Spain and all of Canada from Great Britain. The continued depredations of the British played into the hands of this group of "Warhawks" and eventually forced Madison into war, although he, like his predecessor, believed in the patient exploitation of the European conflict and the protection of neutral rights by economic sanctions, rather than by resort to arms. Madison's restraining influence over the Congress was severely damaged by two episodes in each of which the intransigents claimed, with a certain amount of justification, that he allowed himself to be hoodwinked—first by Britain and then by France.

Shortly after Madison's inauguration, David Erskine, the British minister to Washington, negotiated an agreement for the unconditional repeal of the obnoxious British orders-in-council of November 11, 1807. Madison thereupon promptly lifted the restrictions of the Non-Intercourse Act with respect to Britain and several hundred American vessels left, laden with supplies sorely needed in the British Isles. Immediately thereafter, Britain's foreign minister, George Canning, repudiated the Erskine Agreement, announcing the repeal of the orders-in-council but declaring a new paper blockade of the European coast which made the repeal meaningless.

A year later, by an equally spurious revocation of the French maritime decrees. Talleyrand persuaded Madison to reinstate the restrictions against British trade. These two episodes brought popular resentment to a fever pitch and strengthened the hand of the "War-hawks."

During this period Napoleon had reached the zenith of his power. Having won control of Italy and the Adriatic, thus gaining a causeway to the Near East, the French Emperor stood astride Europe. To cement his hold, he divorced the Empress Josephine and married Maria Louisa of Austria.

From his new post in St. Petersburg, John Quincy Adams watched developments, much as he had observed them for his father in 1794-1795 as minister at The Hague and, later, at Berlin. Within a year, having established most friendly personal relations with Tsar Alexander and his Chancellor, Count Rumiantzov, Adams succeeded in obtaining the release of a number of Danish and American ships which had been seized as blockade runners. Both Adams and his adversary, the French minister, de Coulaincourt, were fully aware of the significance of this action; neither was surprised when Alexander issued his December 1810 *ukase* declaring Russia independent of Napoleon's Continental System. Having switched sides, the Tsar now earnestly hoped that the United States would not become involved in war with England. Adams shared this hope; he was in the midst of negotiations concerning the Russian-American boundaries in Alaska. These conversations ended when the American Congress declared war on England, now Russia's ally. Fortunately, Adams was able to assure Rumiantzov that the American war with Britain would not involve an alliance with Napoleon.

If ever there was a thoroughly unnecessary war, this might

be said of the War of 1812. Throughout 1811, the weak Perceval ministry in Britain allowed matters to drift along. The continued harassment of American shipping and the unabated practice of impressment combined with the expansionist pressure of the "War-hawks" to take matters out of the control of President Madison. Reluctantly, knowing that the country was wholly unprepared for war, Madison summoned Congress in November and recommended that the nation be placed in a state of preparedness. Instead of taking the recommended action, Congress spent seven months debating whether or not to declare war.

Clay's war party profited from Indian unrest on the northwest frontier believed to be instigated by the British. The Shawnee chief, Tecumseh's defeat of General William Henry Harrison, at Tippecanoe, plus expansionist ambition and British obduracy at sea led Congress to declare war on June 18, 1812.

Had there then been a transatlantic cable, or even fast steamships, there might have been no war. Congress was unaware that, on May 11, Prime Minister Perceval had been assassinated and that Lord Liverpool, with the conciliatory Lord Castlereagh as foreign minister, had come into power, pledged to a more moderate policy. On June 25, ignorant of the American declaration of war, the new British government unconditionally repealed the obnoxious orders-in-council as well as Canning's paper blockade. Thus, as John Quincy Adams observed at St. Petersburg, "the principal cause and justification [of the war] was removed precisely at the moment when it occurred." *

If England's hands had not been tied in Europe, the war would have ended in a disastrous defeat for the United States. Its first year saw the surrender of General Hull at Detroit, defeat at the foot of Lake Champlain and failure of the Niagara expedition. Only Perry's extraordinary feats on Lake Erie prevented utter disaster. In 1813, the failure of the campaign against Montreal and the British burning of Buffalo were somewhat offset by the recapture of Detroit and the defeat of a British force at the Thames. In 1814, the northern front was stabilized but, by now, British veterans of the Napoleonic wars

* Samuel Flagg Bemis, *John Quincy Adams* (Knopf, 1949), page 183.

were becoming available. One invading army was halted at Plattsburg, but another landed in Chesapeake Bay and burned the nation's capitol.

Meanwhile, 1812-1814 witnessed Napoleon's fatal attack upon Russia, his march to Moscow and the retreat which reduced his Grand Army from 650,000 men to 50,000. A new quadruple alliance of Britain, Russia, Austria and Prussia gained control of Europe and restored Louis XVIII to the throne of France. Napoleon was exiled to Elba. Wellington's victorious veterans were embarking at Bordeaux for the invasion of New Orleans.

Such was the state of affairs when, on August 8, 1814, Anglo-American peace negotiations began at the Belgian town of Ghent.*

Through Adams, the Tsar had offered to mediate the Anglo-American conflict almost as soon as it began. Madison eagerly accepted the offer. Britain, knowing that the peace of Europe was not yet secure, was not averse to liquidating the conflict in order to concentrate its efforts upon the Congress of Vienna. However, Castlereagh let it be known that direct negotiations would be preferable to the use of an intermediary. Madison accepted the suggestion and nominated a five-man commission, consisting of Adams, Gallatin, Clay, James A. Bayard, a Federalist senator from Delaware, and Jonathan Russell, a Clay henchman stationed at Stockholm. The three negotiators named by Britain were little more than messengers for Britain's Big Three—Liverpool, Wellington and Castlereagh.

The British held all the cards at the beginning of the negotiations. The war had so far gone in their favor. The Essex Junto was planning a Hartford Convention to bring about the secession of New England; British troops were preparing to sever New England from the rest of the states. One British force was approaching the Chesapeake and another was embarking for New Orleans.

The Americans were instructed to deal with neutral rights and impressment. In the existing circumstances, the most they could do was to seek a restoration of the *status quo ante bellum*. The British were in no hurry. Castlereagh's instructions were

* For a full account of the negotiations at Ghent see Bemis, *op. cit.*, Chapter 10. Also, for subsequent relations with Britain, Chapter 11.

to make peace on the basis of *uti possidetis* (each side to keep what it held at the end of hostilities). In addition, the British were told to insist upon the abolition of American fishing rights off Canada, the modification of the Canadian frontier, and the establishment of an English-protected, Indian neutral territory in the Northwest. Meanwhile, delay might increase their holdings of American territory.

In spite of the high grade of diplomacy exhibited by Gallatin, Adams and Clay, it is difficult to see how the United States could have escaped from an extremely disadvantageous and humiliating treaty had it not been for Castlereagh's sincere desire to make peace because of a new danger arising in Europe. Gallatin's tact, Adams' proud insistence upon the maintenance of American rights (especially upon the New England fisheries so dear to the heart of his father) and Clay's optimism managed to persuade the British to agree to a peace on the basis of the prewar status. Neutral rights and impressment were not mentioned. (With the establishment of peace between Britain and France these matters soon ceased to be an issue.) The fishing rights were left to subsequent negotiations. So were the boundary gaps in the Northeast and Northwest. The Treaty of Ghent, signed the day before Christmas, 1814, left the United States undamaged by a bungled war for which it had been insufficiently prepared.

On January 8, 1815, before the news of the treaty reached the United States, General Andrew Jackson redeemed the prestige of the American army by his smashing victory over General Pakenham's invading forces at New Orleans. Madison lost no time in sending the treaty to the Senate and that body ratified with enthusiasm, even the chastened "War-hawks" voting for ratification. Madison had shown wisdom in making the leader of the "War-hawks" a member of the peace commission.

The die-hard remnants of the once-powerful Essex Junto slunk home from Hartford in disgrace. The Federalist party ceased to exist.

During the famous Hundred Days between Napoleon's return from Elba and his final defeat at Waterloo, the American commissioners remained at London to conclude a commercial treaty, establishing the mutual non-discrimination policy which has stood throughout all subsequent Anglo-American agreements.

When the Spanish colonies revolted against the mother country during Jefferson's administration, Jefferson had declared that the United States would not wish to see Mexico or Cuba annexed by either Britain or France. In 1811, Congress had passed a similar resolution with respect to Florida. (Both declarations foreshadowed the Monroe Doctrine.) During the war, Madison took over West Florida as far as the Pearl River but was careful not to disturb the Spanish settlements at Mobile and Pensacola. These two cities were taken by Andrew Jackson without Madison's authority just before the end of the war and Congress then annexed the entire Florida strip along the Gulf coast. This was the one territorial gain resulting from the war which the Congressional leaders had started in the hope of driving Britain and Spain from the North American continent. Napoleon's defeat, the restoration of Ferdinand VII to the throne usurped by Joseph Bonaparte and the temporary subsidence of the colonial revolt against Spain once more removed the Florida question from the immediate agenda.

Two other foreign policy efforts of the Madison administration require mention.

In 1815, Madison declared war on the Barbary States and sent Stephen Decatur with an American fleet strong enough to end, once and for all, the depredations so long committed against American merchant vessels.

The final accomplishment of Madison's administration, actually not completed until after James Monroe had become President, was the Rush-Bagot Agreement with Britain, limiting naval armaments on the Great Lakes to vessels sufficient for the collection of customs duties. This treaty, negotiated by Adams in London, was the first disarmament treaty entered into by the United States.

One might summarize the Madison period as that during which Congress, for the first time taking the expansionist bit in its teeth, would have run the nation into a disastrous defeat, had it not been for British preoccupation with the European scene and the firm diplomacy by which the Executive retrieved American fortunes. The war settled none of the outstanding issues with Britain. Canada remained in British hands with the two frontier gaps unsettled. The issues of impressment and neutral rights were not settled by the Treaty of Ghent; they were removed as issues by the end of the long European conflict.

With the treaties of Ghent and Vienna, one period of American foreign policy ended and another began. The world now entered upon what was to be almost a century of relative peace. The European balance of power, which Britain had fought so stubbornly to establish, was finally an accomplished fact. During the ensuing years of the *Pax Britannica*, the United States would face no danger of involvement in European quarrels and no problems of maintaining neutral rights. For the next hundred years, the nation became involved only in conflicts of its own making.

The impact of the war in Europe and of our own war with Britain accelerated certain domestic developments which were probably in any case inevitable. Essentially, these were the growth of domestic manufacturing and the consequent need for capital and "protection."

The Jeffersonian dream of an agricultural democracy had already received a few shocks in Jefferson's own administration. Eli Whitney's cotton gin (1793) and Cartwright's power loom (1785) had revolutionized the cotton industry. The South was on its way toward becoming a one-crop economy, its agriculture headed toward something very different from that of Jefferson's dream. Meanwhile, home industries were beginning to make cloth in competition with British manufacturers, even though the Lancashire textile industry was growing by leaps and bounds.* Enforced self-sufficiency from 1807 to 1815 stimulated the growth of domestic manufacture. The demand for capital was supplied chiefly by state-chartered banks whose currency issues were less and less controlled by the First United States Bank. After 1811, when Hamilton's charter expired, Congress declined to sanction a renewal and the issuance of paper money became altogether an affair of the states.

When the end of hostilities once more permitted the impor-

* In 1764 Britain imported 4,000,000 pounds of cotton. In 1833, it imported 300,000,000 pounds.

tation of foreign manufactures, a depression set in. This occasioned a demand by the manufacturers for protection against ruinous foreign competition and also caused a rising clamor for "cheap money." Faced with this situation, Madison departed —apparently with Jefferson's concurrence—from two major tenets of Jeffersonianism. He agreed to the chartering of the Second United States Bank and to the Tariff Act of 1816, which imposed a 20% duty on imported woolens and cotton cloth.

This apostasy aroused angry protest from such states-rights Jeffersonians as John Randolph, John Taylor and Nathaniel Macon. To these men, Madison had always been somewhat suspect because of his cooperation with Hamilton and Jay in writing the Federalist Papers. Suspicion was enhanced by the appointment of the Federalist outcast, John Quincy Adams, to an important diplomatic post and became conviction by reason of the tariff of 1816 and the chartering of the new bank. The so-called "Tertium Quids" were now certain that both Madison and Jefferson had deserted the principles of the Republican Party.

On the other extreme, the Westerners, led by Henry Clay, were beginning to push the Republican Party much further into Neo-Federalism than either Madison or Jefferson wished to go, advocating the use of customs revenues and the proceeds of land sales to build roads, canals and other "improvements." Clay was soon to call this policy "The American System."

Between these two extremes, Jefferson and Madison wavered unhappily, recognizing the inevitable death of their vision of an agricultural Utopia and yet unable to apply their democratic principles to the changing nature of American society. The dream of unlimited land for agricultural expansion had been realized. The threat of Hamiltonian oligarchy had been overcome. And yet, a new threat to democracy seemed to be arising. That new, mysterious, anti-democratic force was the inherent tendency of the emerging mercantilist capitalism to concentrate wealth and power in the hands of a few.

3. Monroe, President;
Adams, Secretary of State.

James Monroe, last of the Virginia dynasty, enjoyed the confidence of both Jefferson and Madison; at the same time, his early Jacobinism made him acceptable to the "Tertium Quid" orthodoxy while his good relations with Clay and Adams made him equally acceptable to the emerging Neo-Federalist, nationalist wing of the Republican party. In the election of 1816, Monroe received 183 votes in the Electoral College to 34 for Rufus King, his nearest rival.

Monroe's cabinet, with John Quincy Adams as Secretary of State, William H. Crawford as Secretary of the Treasury and John C. Calhoun as Secretary of War, was selected primarily from the point of view of composing the sectional and political differences which were beginning to split the old Jeffersonian party. The orthodox states-rights wing was appeased by the appointment of Crawford, while Calhoun at this time represented a Southern point of view rather similar to that of Clay and the ambitious Westerners. Both men entertained Presidential ambitions. Clay had strongly desired to become Secretary of State, but Monroe knew that his appointment to the accepted stepping-stone to the Presidency would cause sectional jealousy. He offered Clay the Treasury, but Clay declined, preferring to bide his time as Speaker of the House. Gallatin was aging and preferred to remain in Paris. This made Adams the logical choice for Secretary of State, even though the orthodox Jeffersonians considered him still a Federalist and a monarchist at heart.

With the "Era of Good Feeling" successfully established at home through skillful compromise, with Monroe in the White House, Adams presiding over the State Department, Gallatin in Paris and Richard Rush in London, the continuity of American foreign policy was assured. The extraordinary chain of able diplomats which had begun with Benjamin Franklin remained unbroken.

In 1820, Monroe was all but unanimously re-elected, the single electoral vote of Senator Plumer, of New Hampshire, being cast against him either out of personal spite or because

Plumer—as he later claimed—did not wish any other President to share with George Washington the honor of having been unanimously chosen.

From the first days of the Monroe administration, one major change was noticeable. Jefferson had made a point of abolishing the rather rigorous formality of his predecessors, doing away with formal dinners and receptions as well as all titles and protocol of rank and seniority. Under him the Executive Mansion had ceased to be a palace and had become simply the home of the first citizen. Madison had adhered to what the foreign diplomats were in the habit of calling *"la pêle mêle de* Jefferson." Monroe, however, re-established diplomatic formality as it existed in most of the European countries, though not the almost monarchical formality of Washington and John Adams. It fell to the lot of the naturally unsociable son of John Adams to provide the less formal and more intimate opportunities of diplomatic intercourse.

The new Secretary of State threw himself at once into the unfinished business of continental expansion. While Adams himself took up with the Spanish ambassador the question of Florida and other Spanish claims in North America, Gallatin and Rush discussed with Lord Castlereagh the unsettled leftovers with Britain. The Rush-Gallatin Treaty renewed the commercial agreements of 1815, referred the matter of compensation for carried-off slaves to neutral arbitration and affirmed the fishing "liberty" as perpetual as to certain specified coasts of the Canadian maritime provinces while the United States renounced any further claims. The most important aspect of the Rush-Gallatin Treaty, however, concerned the gap in the northwest boundary. The British had endeavored at Ghent to obtain access to the headwaters of the Mississippi and navigation rights on that river. They now tried once more to obtain these objectives in exchange for the granting of permanent fishing rights off Newfoundland and Labrador. Adams and his emissaries held firm, insisting that the boundary should not descend from the Lake of the Woods southward to the Mississippi but should run due west along the 49th parallel to the Pacific coast. They did, in fact, obtain this boundary in the

1818 Treaty—but only as far west as the "Stony" Mountains. Thus the disputed 152-mile strip became American, but, for the time being, only as far as the Rockies. Beyond the mountain barrier the British were not yet ready to relinquish their claims to territory south of the 49th parallel.

Meanwhile Adams was engaged in active negotiations with the Spanish ambassador. Ferdinand VII vainly endeavored to obtain support for Spanish retention of Florida from Britain and the Holy Alliance. Failing in this, he instructed his ambassador Onís y Gonzalez to offer Florida in return for American recognition of the East Texas border and American agreement not to recognize or support the revolting Spanish colonies. At this point the negotiations were interrupted by Andrew Jackson's invasion of Florida to "pacify" the Seminole Indians. Jackson destroyed the Negro fort at Appalachicola and captured St. Marks, where two English adventurers fell into his hands and were hung for supplying arms to the Indians and inciting trouble. Once more, Spain tried to involve Britain, but Castlereagh declined to be drawn in. Onís y Gonzalez was now instructed to make the best deal he could with Adams.

The Transcontinental Treaty of 1819 was Adams' major achievement as Secretary of State. It involved not only the final cession of Florida but the clear definition of the southwestern boundary of the Louisiana Territory purchased by Jefferson. The Treaty left in Spanish possession only the southwestern corner of what is now the United States: that is, California, Nevada, Utah, Arizona, New Mexico, Texas, about half of Colorado and parts of Oklahoma and Kansas. By extending the boundary to the Pacific Ocean along the northern boundaries of the present states of Utah, Nevada and California, Adams immeasurably strengthened American claims to the Oregon Territory between the 42nd and 49th parallels. Exulting over his achievement, Adams wrote in his diary:

> The acknowledgement of a definite line of boundary to the South Seas [this was the term used for the Pacific Ocean since the earliest colonial grants to the settlers of Virginia and Massachusetts Bay] forms a great epocha in our history.

The first proposal of it in this negotiation was my own and I trust it is now assured beyond the reach of revocation. It was not even among our claims by the Treaty of Independence with Great Britain. It was not among our pretensions under the purchase of Louisiana—for that gave us only the range of the Mississippi and its waters.*

Adams' treaty with Spain was the last act of the era of continental expansion by peaceful diplomacy. It is true that the later boundary settlements with Britain were achieved by similar means, as was also the purchase of Alaska, but by this time the use of force or the threat of force had entered into American diplomacy. Monroe and John Quincy Adams were the last of the great nation-builders who relied almost exclusively upon peaceful persuasion and diplomatic skill. They were also the last of the diplomatists who took and held the initiative in the shaping of foreign policy as against conflicting internal pressures.

Adams' success in negotiating the Transcontinental Treaty was in large measure due to the fact that the Spanish bargaining position was impaired by the growing revolt of the Spanish colonies. The question of recognizing their independence had already been raised in Madison's time, but the restoration of Ferdinand VII had postponed the issue. Nevertheless, Madison's proclamation of neutrality, which recognized the belligerent status of the colonies, had constituted an implied recognition of their independence. In 1817, and again in the following year, Monroe strengthened the neutrality provisions in order to prevent any action by private American citizens on behalf of the Spanish colonies from interfering with Adams' negotiations with Onís y Gonzalez. Congress, however, clamored for recognition, with Clay leading the pro-colonial forces. Monroe held back recognition until the Transcontinental Treaty had finally been ratified in February, 1821.†

With the treaty assured, Monroe yielded to Congressional sentiment and, on May 4, 1822, signed an act appropriating $100,000 for the establishment of missions to "the independent

---

* John Quincy Adams, *Memoirs* (Lippincott, 1874-77) Vol. IV, page 274.

† The Spanish Cortés ratified in late 1820. The six months' time limit after American ratification having expired, Monroe had to re-submit the Treaty to the Senate, which re-ratified in February 1821.

nations of the American continent." Neither Great Britain nor the Holy Alliance was prepared to do anything to hold the crumbling Spanish empire together. Austria, Russia and Prussia were far more interested in suppressing revolts against absolute monarchism in Italy and Spain. By the end of 1824, the independence of Latin America from Spain and Portugal was an accomplished fact. Brazil separated peacefully from Portugal under an independent Emperor.

Meanwhile, the United States was faced with grave decisions as to its future policy. In 1821, the Tsar of Russia had asserted Russia's ownership of the Alaskan coast as far south as the 51st parallel. Both Britain and the United States protested and a lengthy negotiation ensued between Adams and the Russian minister, Baron Tuyll. During these conversations, Adams formulated the doctrine of non-colonization. Believing that colonial empires were inconsistent with just government, Adams was the father of that trend in United States foreign policy which was to make this country friendly to all peoples seeking emancipation from colonial status, until the cold-war alliances against Russia after World War II threw the trend into reverse. On the other hand, Adams also believed firmly in the abstentionist policy of Washington, John Adams, Jefferson and Madison and in keeping the "American System" free from entanglement in the "European system." To these two beliefs was soon to be added the principle of non-toleration of European intervention in the affairs of the Western Hemisphere. Before that principle was to find expression in the Monroe Doctrine, Adams had already stated flatly to the Russian minister that "the American continents are no longer subjects for any new European colonial establishments." The Russian settlements in Alaska were not, of course "new"; Adams himself had begun negotiations to define their boundaries at St. Petersburg in 1812. Hence, it was idle to attempt to force Russia to withdraw altogether, but Adams succeeded in establishing the southern boundary of Russia's Alaskan colony at 54° 40', instead of at the 51st parallel. The Treaty of 1824 formalized this agreement.

Simultaneously with the Alaskan boundary problem, there

arose the question of Europe's attitude toward the newly-independent nations of Latin America. Castlereagh, the great peacemaker, died in 1822, before he had carried out British recognition, and was succeeded by his enemy, George Canning. France, with the backing of the Holy Alliance, was engaged in putting down a revolt against the absolute monarchy of Ferdinand VII. The reactionary policies of the Holy Alliance ran counter to the British purpose of preserving a balance of power on the continent. Suspicious of France and its backers, Canning sought to draw the United States into partnership with Britain. In strict confidence, he proposed to Richard Rush a joint Anglo-American declaration stating that neither country aimed at possession of the former Spanish colonies, nor would either "see any portion of them transferred to any other Power with indifference."

Rush immediately reported this interesting proposal to Adams, hoping that it might open the door to an agreement with the obdurate Tory government on impressment, on the northwest frontier and on the abolition of the slave trade. Before his dispatches had time to reach Washington, Canning had changed his mind and decided on unilateral action. This may have been because Rush had intimated that Canning's proposal would be more likely to receive favorable consideration if Britain were first to recognize the independence of the colonies. More probably, Canning's action was precipitated by the rapidity of the French occupation of Spain.* In any case, the British foreign minister summoned Prince Polignac, the French ambassador, and handed him a brusque memorandum declaring that Britain would not tolerate any French or European interference with the trade or the political status of the Spanish colonies.

The existence of this "Polignac Memorandum" was not known to Monroe and Adams when they received and deliberated over Rush's report of Canning's proposal. Monroe sought

* For this episode and the whole background of the Monroe Doctrine, see Dexter Perkins, *The Monroe Doctrine 1823-26;* John Quincy Adams, *Memoirs,* Vol. VI; and the account as well of the voluminous scholarly references in Bemis, *John Quincy Adams,* Chapters XVIII and IX.

advice from both Jefferson and Madison. Both supported Calhoun's view that Canning's proposal should be accepted. Neither apparently saw in the proposition the danger of an entangling alliance. Jefferson, as already noted, had been determined not to let Cuba fall into the hands of any other power and Madison had taken the same position with respect to Florida. Adams, certainly no less anxious than either of the elder statesmen to keep Spain's former possessions from falling into the hands of any other European power, nevertheless felt equally convinced that the affairs of this hemisphere were no more a concern for Britain than they were for France. According to his diary, he alone persuaded Monroe not to accept the British proposal, but some doubt is cast upon this claim by other sources. The decision to make a unilateral declaration of policy seems to have been Monroe's alone, though the pronouncement which he delivered on December 2, 1823, was the work of many hands.

In the original draft of the annual message to Congress, which covered many domestic matters as well, the part which has since become known as the Monroe Doctrine was several times revised. Originally more belligerent in asserting the no-transfer doctrine, it was toned down when Monroe was asked whether it was intended to involve a commitment to go to war with any trespasser. As delivered, the address stated three major principles of American policy:

1. . . . the American Continents, by the free and independent condition which they have assumed and maintain, are henceforth not to be considered as subjects for future colonization by any European Power . . .

2. In the wars of the European Powers, in matters relating to themselves, we have never taken any part, nor does it comport with our policy so to do. It is only when our rights are invaded or seriously menaced, that we resent injuries, or make preparation for our defense . . .

3. With the movements in this Hemisphere we are of necessity more immediately connected, and by causes which must be obvious to all enlightened and impartial observ-

ers . . . We owe it, therefore, to candor, and to the amicable relations existing between the United States and those powers, to declare that we should consider any attempt on their part to extend their system to any portions of this Hemisphere, as dangerous to our peace and safety. With the existing Colonies or dependencies of any European power, we have not interfered and shall not interfere. But with the Governments who have declared their Independence we have, on great consideration and on just principles, acknowledged we could not view any interposition for the purpose of oppressing them, or controuling in any other manner, their destiny, by any European power, in any other light than as the manifestation of an unfriendly disposition toward the United States . . .

Abstention from involvement in the affairs of Europe was an old principle, established by Washington and adhered to by every succeeding President. *Non-Colonization* was a new principle contributed by John Quincy Adams. *Non-Interference,* generally regarded as Monroe's contribution, actually had been foreshadowed by Jefferson's pronouncement on Cuba, and by the 1811 resolution passed by Congress with relation to Florida.

Up to the declaration of the Monroe Doctrine, American foreign policy had been realistically cut to fit the cloth of American power. The policy of abstention—or of isolationism except in commerce—had been compatible with the relatively small military or naval forces at the young nation's disposal. Under Washington, Adams, and Jefferson, the United States had insisted upon and protected its neutral rights against belligerents to the extent possible without actually going to war, even though Adams had used force against France. Madison had been compelled by popular sentiment to make an attempt to assert American rights by resorting to open war. The resulting conflict had proved the futility of such action against a superior naval power. The logical conclusion would have been to revert to the policy of abstention and enforcement of rights by diplomacy, especially since Europe was now at peace, or to recognize that any commitments beyond such a policy required the creation of a commensurate military and naval establishment.

*The Monroe Doctrine fell in between these two logical alter-
natives. It undertook what amounted to a commitment to resist
by force any new colonization or intervention by European
powers in the Americas, without any accompanying recommendation to create the physical power required to make the commitment effective.*

Some historians have contended that Monroe acted in concert
with Britain and that the commitment was undertaken in tacit
alliance with that great naval power, thus making it unnecessary
for the United States to create a fleet of its own. That there was
no such tacit alliance is clear from Canning's decision to act
unilaterally before he could possibly have received an answer
to his proposal for joint action. Even though Monroe probably
knew nothing of the Polignac Memorandum when he made his
declaration, he did know of the Canning-Rush proposal and,
knowing it, decided to act unilaterally rather than in concert
with Britain. Monroe and Adams shared the responsibility for
launching the nation upon a new phase in its foreign policy—
the phase of commitment without power. This phase of expansion was to carry American interests across the Pacific and to
pile up vast commitments before Theodore Roosevelt was to
think of providing the nation with commensurate power.

In domestic affairs, the Monroe administrations witnessed
the beginnings of the great struggle over Negro slavery which
was soon to tear the union apart. In 1819, when Missouri applied for admission, there were an equal number of states in
which slavery existed and states in which it had been abolished.
The House authorized the admission of Missouri with a no-
slavery amendment. This Tallmadge amendment was rejected
by the Senate. By the time Congress reconvened, Maine had
applied for admission as a free state. The House passed an act
admitting Maine, but the Senate joined this measure to one
admitting Missouri without mentioning any prohibition of
slavery. Senator Thomas of Illinois offered an amendment admitting Missouri as a slave state but with the proviso that in the
remainder of the Louisiana Purchase slavery should be prohibited north of the 36°-30′ line. This "Missouri Compromise"
was ultimately adopted, but only after a debate which startled

the nation by its fury. Sectional feelings were aroused not so much over the moral issue of slavery as over the conflicting economic interests of the two sections. With the South rapidly becoming a one-crop country, dependent upon slaves for the raising of cotton and upon free trade for selling it abroad, the tariff imposed for the benefit of northern manufacturers became as much of an issue as slavery. The Union was rapidly being split apart into two sections of directly conflicting interests, each seeking to dominate national policy by obtaining preponderant representation in the Federal government. Hence the allocation of the new states to be formed out of the recently-acquired western lands as between slave and free became of crucial importance.

CHAPTER SEVEN

Interrupted Expansion
(1824 – 1841)

THE "Era of Good Feeling" had ended by the time Monroe's second term expired. Although sectional differences had, for the time being, been smoothed over by the Missouri Compromise and no formal opposition to the Republican party had as yet developed, there were personal issues of great bitterness among the contending rivals for the succession. To a large extent, these centered about the figure of Andrew Jackson. The hero of New Orleans had acquired a great popular following, not only because of his military achievements but because he personified the hopes and ambitions of the western frontier. Clay, a hot rival for western leadership and for the Presidency, was Jackson's bitter enemy. In addition, three other members of Monroe's cabinet were avowed candidates: Calhoun, who subsequently withdrew in order to accept the Vice Presidency and, as he hoped, the ultimate succession; Crawford, representing the discontented South; and Adams, with no political following but with the greatest amount of experience and prestige.

Martin Van Buren and other Jackson organizers had built up a powerful political machine, especially in New York, Pennsylvania and the West. In the Electoral College, Jackson had 99 votes, Adams 84, Crawford 41 and Clay 37. The choice among the three leading candidates was thus thrown into the House. Clay, himself eliminated, threw his support to Adams, thereby ensuring Adams' election on the first ballot. Adams' subsequent appointment of Clay as Secretary of State gave rise to the charge of "bargain and corruption," sustained throughout the succeeding years by the Jacksonians. While Adams undoubtedly discharged a political debt, such as is frequently incurred in public life, no one ever discovered the slightest evidence of corruption. Nevertheless the accusation was hurled again and again, contributing to the ruin of Adams as President and to the destruction of Clay's chances of attaining the Presidency.

In large measure, Adams' failure as President was due to circumstances over which he had no control. The careers of many men have been blasted by their unsuccessful attempts to attain the highest office in the land, but to Adams fell the unhappy distinction of having a hitherto brilliant career of public service blighted by the attainment of the Presidency. The period of 1825-1829 was notable for the absence of major issues in dealing with which a statesman might have achieved distinction. The great diplomatic objectives to which Adams had devoted most of his career had been accomplished; and the time was not yet ripe for picking up the remaining loose ends. The great questions of domestic policy which were soon to divide the nation had not yet come to the surface. It was a time made to order for a politician rather than for a statesman; and Adams was a poor politician. Not only his lack of political talent but his contempt for any seeking of popularity, his Puritan self-righteousness and his almost masochistic tendency toward lonely martyrdom rendered Adams ill-suited for the American Presidency and utterly incapable of dealing with a ruthless opponent like Andrew Jackson. Henry Clay as President, with Adams as Secretary of State, would have made a happier and more successful combination.

Jackson and his highly skillful lieutenants accepted defeat with ill grace and only as a temporary setback. They were determined to wreck both Adams and Clay as possible contenders in 1828. The orthodox southern states-righters, whose candidate had been Crawford—now out of the running because of broken health—were equally hostile. John Randolph of Roanoke spoke of the Adams-Clay alliance as a "combination of the Puritan with the blackleg" and denounced Adams' appointment of Rush to the Treasury by declaring that "never were abilities so much below mediocrity so well rewarded—no, not when Caligula's horse was made consul." Calhoun, whose position with relation to the contending factions was not yet clearly established, began as an uncertain ally of the Adams administration and ended as its bitter enemy.

Having sought the Presidency primarily as a fitting capstone to a career modeled upon that of his father, Adams found it both painful and difficult to deal with an opposition based not upon policy but upon personal antagonisms and ambitions.

He made the fatal mistake of not discharging even his most flagrant enemies in the public service. Crawford had filled the Treasury and the Revenue offices with his henchmen, many of them openly hostile to the new administration. The Postmaster General, McLane, was an enthusiastic and active Jacksonian. In spite of Clay's urgent advice to the contrary, Adams flatly refused to replace any such openly hostile civil servants, except on grounds of established incompetence. This was a matter of deeply felt principle, admirable in itself, but fatal to the President's political fortunes, since it soon became apparent that political intrigues against the administration entailed no risk. This played directly into the hands of the wholly unscrupulous Jacksonians. Shrewd as he had proved himself to be as a diplomat, John Quincy Adams was a helpless innocent in the rough-and-tumble of domestic politics.

Adams' first major experience with the as yet rather shapeless opposition in the Congress came about as the result of a natural sequel to the Monroe Doctrine. The newly independent nations of Latin America organized what was intended to be a first step toward hemispheric solidarity, in which they hoped to interest the United States. In extending an invitation to send representatives to the Congress of Panama, to be held in the summer of 1825, they hoped to see the Monroe Doctrine implemented by more definite political and commercial treaties. Adams and Clay made it clear that the United States would not be drawn into any military commitments or alliances, but were interested to discuss concerted action toward safeguarding neutral rights and establishing freedom of the seas. At the back of Adams' mind were, of course, Cuba and Puerto Rico; these two islands were now all that remained of the Spanish empire in North America and, so long as their future remained unsettled, would constitute a danger. Adams knew that Britain was at this time close to war with Spain over Portuguese independence and that Canning, too, had received an invitation to send delegates to the Panama Congress. In the circumstances, either Britain or France might be expected to take advantage of whatever opportunities might present themselves in Cuba and Puerto Rico.

Clay, always eager to help the Latin republics, was even more enthusiastic than Adams. He, too, opposed any departure from the traditional policy of neutrality, but he envisaged and partially drafted a series of "good-neighbor treaties" which anticipated a policy not to be realized for over a century.

When Adams nominated two commissioners and asked for an appropriation to defray their expenses, Congress rebelled. The Senate objected to the "new departure in foreign policy." The House opposed the appropriation for various alleged reasons, among which only one was clear: the Southerners were hostile to the Panama Congress because of two items on its proposed agenda—the establishment of relations with the Negro republic in Haiti, and the abolition of the slave trade by the nations of the Western Hemisphere. The administration's arguments finally prevailed over the still unorganized opposition. This was to be Adams' one victory over Congress. It cost him the undying hatred of the Southern slave-owners.

The Panama Congress itself came to nothing. One of the Commissioners died on the way to the Isthmus and the other arrived too late for the first session. At an attempted second meeting only a small number of nations attended and nothing was accomplished. This was about the only foreign policy matter of importance which came up during the uneventful four years of Adams' administration. Oregon, the Maine boundary and other items of unfinished business with Britain were left to the future, except for Adams' institution of certain countervailing restrictions designed to force the British to abandon their mercantilistic control of trade with the West Indies.

In domestic affairs, the Adams administration was marked by an apparent tranquillity, except for the political activity of the ambitious Jacksonians. The depression had been overcome. Manufacturers were once again prosperous. Exports flourished. Land seemed available without limit. The "American System" seemed to have brought an era of prosperity which, together with the establishment of peace in the world, made the clamorous criticisms of the Jacksonians appear baseless and irrelevant. To a very large extent they were irrelevant, because the Jacksonians had no program or policy; their one aim was to take over power; they understood as little as the administration the undercurrent of conflict which was flowing beneath the serene surface of prosperity.

The "American System" had evolved by an almost unconscious process within the Republican party, beginning with Madison's tariff and the use of revenues to retire the public debt, and then growing into a system of using the revenues derived from the sale of western lands to build roads, bridges and canals. The theory, clearly articulated by Clay, was that a protective tariff on manufactures would not only foster industrial growth but would also provide a wider domestic market for agricultural products, particularly if transportation and other improvements helped to open up the West.

This "American System" ran into two obstacles.

The first and more easily recognized arose from the inevitable competition for tariff protection. The Monroe Tariff of 1824 had raised the Madison rates on woolens and cotton goods and had initiated protective duties on iron, hemp, glass, silk, linens and cutlery. This stimulated demands for similar protection for other industries and gave impetus to sectional "log-rolling"— an evil which has cursed American tariff legislation from the beginning. If the New England textile manufacturers were to be protected, then the Kentucky hemp growers wanted similar protection; if Kentucky hemp was favored, the Pennsylvania iron manufacturers wanted their bit of subsidy; and so on, with each special sectional interest saying: "I'll vote for yours, if you'll vote for mine." In 1828, the various interests seeking tariff protection met at a convention in Harrisburg and presented their new demands to Congress. The resulting act was properly called "The Tariff of Abominations." The Adams administration fought the excessive imposts and would normally have had the support of the representatives of the free-trade South. The Southerners, however, adopted the strange tactics of seeking to demonstrate the iniquity of all tariffs by voting *for* the "abominations" which were thus enacted by an unnatural alliance of eastern manufacturers and southern free-traders. The backfiring of their tactics enraged the southern leadership and gave the first serious impetus to the dangerous doctrine of "Nullification."

The second difficulty arose out of certain contradictions in the "American System" and was less clearly visible, because it involved new and unfamiliar economic forces. The high-tariff policy was consciously designed to develop industry and to hold the necessary labor supply in the East, since tariff protection made possible the payment of relatively high wages. This was in conflict with the land policy of selling western land at $2.00 an acre on long-term credit which tended to draw off the eastern labor supply to the West.* Furthermore, the land policy en-

* Actually, it was not the eastern factory worker who tended to be drawn West but the farm population in the East from which the labor supply was recruited. The factory worker rarely became a frontier settler; in times of unemployment, he tended to migrate to another city or perhaps even to another country in search of work. But the factory workers were recruited to a large extent from the rural population surrounding the cities and it was this reservoir of labor which Clay sought to protect against drainage through westward migration. For a full discussion of the land policy of this time, see William Graham Sumner, *Life of Andrew Jackson* (Houghton Mifflin, 1894), Chapter IX.

couraged speculative purchases which created a great demand for borrowed capital.

These contradictions were not fully realized by the proponents of the "American System"; much less were they understood by its opponents, who merely exploited the resulting tensions and discontents.

In the East, a vicious circle of tariffs, wages and prices came into operation. The greater the pull of the West, the less the eastern labor supply and the greater the pressure for raising wages; the higher the wages paid, the greater the need for protection against foreign competition; the higher the costs of manufacture, the higher rose prices to the consumer; and, the higher the price level, the greater the demand for higher wages. Thus, in the manufacturing East, the "American System" supported both a high scale of American wages as against those paid in Europe and a relatively inefficient American production. Eventually, American ingenuity was to invent its way out of this vicious circle by developing the techniques of mass production but, for the time being, rising *money* wages did not mean rising *real* wages; they were merely part of an unhealthy inflationary spiral. In political terms, this meant that the hard-pressed eastern wage-earner, unhappy in new conditions of factory work and uneasy because of rising living-costs, became a target for Jacksonian manipulation of discontent.

With the South already alienated from the administration and from the "American System" by the tariff, and with the eastern working class beginning to realize that the machine was creating a new kind of industrial slavery, it remained only for the Jacksonians to capture the sentiments of Clay's western stronghold. This turned out to be the easiest political task of all.

In Kentucky and Tennessee, land speculation created an urgent demand for capital, which was supplied by the state banks through the granting of credit and the issuance of paper money out of all proportion to the banks' capital assets. A runaway boom resulted, until the Second United States Bank—as was its proper function—called a halt by demanding specie redemption of the state banks' paper currency. This caused a violent contraction of credit, numerous foreclosures, bankruptcies and a resort to the courts by the defrauded creditors. The courts—by their very nature upholders of contract fulfilment —thus became, along with the "Big Bank," the targets of popular indignation. Relief of debtors became the dominant issue in western politics and a state of open conflict developed between those who sought some orderly and constitutional way out of the difficulty and those who wished to abolish whatever laws and institutions stood in the way of immediate relief. The Supreme Court of the United States became the ultimate obstacle to anarchy and another link in the chain by which the resentment of the debtor class attached itself to the administration. This was all that the Jacksonians needed.

During the entire period of Adams' Presidency, the Jacksonian opposition never had an affirmative program of its own. Calling itself for the first time the "Democratic Party"—while the administration supporters officially adopted the name of "National Republicans"—the opposition devoted its efforts solely to fostering the discontent of the southern free-traders, the eastern workers and the western debtors. The Democrats offered no alternative land policy, no tariff policy and no answer to the rising demand for capital.

Faced with this sort of opposition, Clay—had he been in Adams' position—might have put up a strong political fight; he had the temperament for it as well as the politician's ability to avoid fundamental issues and to deal in vote-catching generalities. Adams' peculiar makeup did not permit him even to cultivate the by no means inconsiderable groups who respected his integrity and whose economic interests made them his natural allies. He was unwilling to do more than stand upon his principles, his integrity and his record of patriotic service. He had no illusions as to what the outcome would be. The popular vote in the election of 1828 was 648,273 for the Jacksonian Democrats and 508,064 for the National Republicans. Like his father before him, John Quincy Adams left the White House an embittered and disappointed man, but, unlike his father, he was destined to a second and, in some respects, an even more remarkable political career.

Jackson's victory ended the era of great American diplomacy and the leadership of that extraordinary group of men who had guided the American Revolution, established the Union, and assured the nation of continental security. The new era had its roots in the American frontier society: the military hero would now replace the diplomat; the politician would supplant the statesman; the self-educated frontier lawyer would take the place of the classical scholar. The Jacksonian revolution was a conscious revolt of the West against the East—of a new, wholly indigenous and somewhat raw Americanism against the Americanized Europeanism of the New Englanders and the Virginians. The fact that the tariff and the rising issue of slavery had thrown the conservative South temporarily on the side of the revolution was a political accident without which the revolution could not have succeeded; but the unnatural alliance contained from its beginning the seeds of dissolution. When the Jacksonian coalition was formed the West was still strongly linked to the South by the natural flow of transportation. Trade from most of the region west of the Appalachian Mountains moved southward along the great water routes of the Mississippi and its tributaries. In addition, there was the bond created by the fact that much of the territory beyond the mountains had been settled by migration from Virginia and the Carolinas. With the building of the Erie Canal and the Cumberland Road, the West obtained a transportation link with the East which rapidly changed its sectional orientation. Trade from the West began to flow east rather than southward, and new settlers came more and more from the East or from Europe, rather than from the southern states. Thus the Jacksonian coalition was based not only upon an unnatural marriage of northern radicalism and southern conservatism but also upon a physical relationship between the West and the South which was soon no longer to exist.

Triumphant in 1800, the party founded by Thomas Jefferson had, by 1828, proven itself incapable of meeting the challenge to political democracy of economic forces which lay to a large extent beyond its comprehension. Almost unconsciously, it had drifted into sectional conflict and class struggle, in which its essentially idealistic conservatism had thrown it on the side of the emerging anti-democratic forces. The resulting split was far from a clean cleavage. The Jacksonian Democrats reverted to Jeffersonian aims but were soon to pursue them by Hamiltonian methods.

Interestingly enough, the Jacksonians attracted the support of a new group of intellectuals, many of them working journalists. This group included not only such men as Amos Kendall and Frank Blair, but writers like William Cullen Bryant, James Fenimore Cooper, Nathaniel Hawthorne and Walt Whitman. These men were not merely poets and storytellers; they represented the vanguard of a new, native intelligentsia which allied itself to the crude political power of the Jacksonian coalition. Political scientists, like William M. Gouge, helped to convert destructive opposition into something like a program of reform. Jurists, like Roger B. Taney, brought the Federal courts into closer step with the popular demand for control of the economic forces threatening democracy. Around the somewhat enigmatic figure of a western military hero, the temper of the times coalesced various constructive forces which had been scarcely visible before the sixty-one-year-old general entered the White House.

There is probably no figure in American history more controversial than that of Andrew Jackson. Among his contemporaries, the seventh President of the United States was loved and hated, praised and reviled, as were only Lincoln and Franklin D. Roosevelt in succeeding generations; but Lincoln and Roosevelt ended their careers as great war leaders—a fact which tended to dim the controversies over their domestic policies. Jackson, on the other hand, came to the White House as a war hero and left it in the full tide of domestic controversy. Hence, to this day, historians are sharply divided in their judgments.

In part, this was no doubt due to Jackson's peculiar personality.* In part, the controversy persists because so much of it was engendered over an issue which has remained a matter of debate down to the present day. That issue, which in Jackson's time centered upon the question of the currency, was actually the much broader and still unresolved question of the extent to which what we call a "free enterprise economy" can be made compatible with the principles and practices of political democ-

* A. M. Schlesinger, Jr., *The Age of Jackson* (Little, Brown, 1946); and Wm. G. Sumner, *op. cit.*

racy. In the age of Jackson and Van Buren, the conflict appeared to be between the "money power"—meaning the banks which issued currency—and the people. Actually, it was a conflict between the few whom the industrial revolution, primitive finance capitalism and the "American System" had raised to power, and the many who felt themselves increasingly dispossessed.

The Age of Jackson was as much the age of Clay, Webster, Calhoun and Biddle as it was the age of Jackson and his successor, Martin Van Buren. It was not only a time in which American radicalism rose to a new high-water mark and then receded, but also the period during which American conservatism passed through a highly significant reformation—from the Neo-Federalism of Clay and John Quincy Adams to the Whiggery of William H. Seward and Thurlow Weed. It was the phase in our history which determined that the typical class struggle generated by capitalism in other countries was to assume a different and altogether American form in the United States. Finally, it was a period of internal convulsion which preceded a renewed outburst of nationalism and increasingly reckless expansionism, held in check only by the fact that expansion meant facing the fearful problem of the extension or elimination of the slave interest.

This study is concerned only with so much of the Jacksonian revolution as directly affected the dramatic change in United States foreign policy which began with Jackson himself and continued, though interrupted by the Civil War, throughout the remainder of the nineteenth century. The details of Jackson's long fight with the Second United States Bank and of the various measures of banking and currency reform tried or advocated during the Jackson-Van Buren administrations are fascinating to the student of monetary and banking history, but only the broader implications of this struggle are relevant to this discussion.

The "American System" had marked the birth of mercantilist capitalism in this country—of the "money power" which came to be concentrated in banks licensed to issue currency and in corporations which attracted concentrated wealth. It marked the emergence of a double standard of morality, resulting from the gradual depersonalization of capitalistic enterprise. The corporation made it possible for individuals to combine their resources while limiting their individual liabilities; the corporation was given the rights and immunities of the individual entrepreneur, but it did not—and by its nature could not—assume the obligations of individual conscience. The larger the corporation became, the less could its management reflect the religious or ethical restraints which had affected the sole proprietor's conduct of his business. The manager tended to become the hireling of absentee owners and his mandate became more and more simply the making of profit. Thus business became infected with a dog-eat-dog morality which ran counter to the principles of democratic justice and also counter to the articles of the Christian faith. This led to several consequences.

The corporate manager began to seek relief from a guilty conscience in the church or in the law courts. The church gave him absolution as an individual. The courts gave him justification for his dealings as a businessman by telling him that his conduct was within the law and therefore irreproachable.

On the other hand, the depersonalization of business management and the increasing concentration of wealth and power gave rise to a new radicalism on the part of those who felt themselves unjustly treated or dispossessed. The tendency of the new radical movement was to identify both the church and the courts with the oppressive "money power." Thus, seen from the conservative side, the Jacksonian revolution acquired the attributes of "atheism" and "lawlessness," while, as seen from the side of those seeking redress, both the church and the courts appeared as tools of the privileged few, designed to protect property and the status quo.

Andrew Jackson came upon this scene almost wholly ignorant of its fundamental causes but aware of the widespread discontent and with a political obligation to take action. The action he took in eliminating the Second United States Bank did not cure the problem of "money power." It eliminated an institution which deserved its fate because it had fallen into the hands of a selfish, vain and irresponsible manager, Nicholas Biddle. This, in itself, did not solve the problem of providing a sound and dependable currency; it merely took power away from the largest and most potent bank and scattered it among a large number of smaller banks. Had Biddle been a wise and responsible manager of the "Big Bank," instead of the opposite, this would not have brought about any substantial improvement. The value of the long Bank War was psychological, rather than economic. It produced an alignment of forces in which, over the symbol of the Bank, the property interests and the people locked horns in a contest for political power. In this struggle, the people won, and this was the major significance of the protracted controversy. (This highly oversimplified statement does injustice to the serious and constructive thought given to currency and banking problems by such men as William Gouge, Albert Gallatin and Senator Thomas Hart Benton.*)

So far as this study is concerned, the basic fact is that the Jacksonian revolution, for the time being at least, took political power away from the relatively small group in whose hands it had been accumulating under the Neo-Federalists and transferred it—if not to the people—at least to a greatly strengthened government responsive to the popular will. The Jacksonian revolution was the first major skirmish between the contradictory forces of political democracy and a rapidly evolving *laissez faire* economy. To accomplish their victory, the Jacksonian Democrats abandoned the Jeffersonian belief that the best government is that which governs least. They became, in a sense, Hamiltonians, using a strong central government to accomplish Jeffersonian purposes. This brought forth cries of "tyranny" and "usurpation" from the Neo-Federalists, who had believed in a strong government as long as they controlled it.

In the elections of 1832, most of the press and—as de Tocqueville reported—"all the enlightened classes" opposed Jackson and supported Clay. But, when the ballots were counted, Jackson had 219 electoral votes to Clay's 49.

An overwhelming proportion of the material power was against him [Jackson]. The great media of the dissemination of information and the molding of opinion fought him.

* Wm. M. Gouge, *Short History of Paper Money and Banking in the United States* (London, 1833), and *Inquiry into the Expediency of Dispensing with Bank Agency and Bank Paper in the Fiscal Concerns of the United States* (Stavely, 1837). Both have been widely read and are still rewarding to the student.

Haughty and sterile intellectualism opposed him. Musty reaction disapproved him. Hollow and outworn traditionalism shook a trembling finger at him. It seemed sometimes that all were against him—all but the people of the United States.

Thus Franklin D. Roosevelt described the election of 1832, one hundred and four years later. All that Jackson had done up to this point was to declare war on the "money power." He had not even succeeded in destroying Biddle's Bank, but the mere fact of his clear determination to do so was enough. Soon after his re-election, however, Jackson was presented with an issue which won him the support of many who had been his enemies.

An almost silly, minor matter, the marriage of Jackson's Secretary of War, John H. Eaton, to the daughter of a Washington tavernkeeper, caused a "social crisis" in Washington and the reorganization of Jackson's official family. Along with most of Washington's high society, Mrs. Calhoun, wife of the Vice President and heir presumptive, declined to receive Polly Eaton, while Martin Van Buren, the widowed Secretary of State, espoused her cause. This brought about a break between Calhoun and Jackson which widened into an unbridgeable chasm when Calhoun's casting vote blocked the nomination of Van Buren as minister to London. Calhoun resigned as Vice President and accepted a seat in the Senate, thereafter becoming Jackson's implacable enemy. Van Buren became the President's choice as a successor.

A tariff act, passed by Congress and signed by Jackson in the summer of 1832, had reduced the "abominations" but still continued the principle of protection. In November, Calhoun's state of South Carolina declared the tariff act null and void within the state after February 1, 1833. This act of nullification, based upon Calhoun's extrapolation of the Virginia and Kentucky Resolutions against the Alien and Sedition Acts, was the first Southern move in the direction of secession.

Jackson countered with a powerful proclamation on the nature of the Union and the introduction of a "Force Act," authorizing the President forcibly to compel the execution of laws enacted by the Congress. His prompt and decisive action instantly won nation-wide acclaim, except, of course, in the South. Even Webster, Adams and other Clay supporters enthusiastically praised the President's action. His popularity rose to new heights. Rejecting Van Buren's proposals for a drastic tariff reduction, Clay offered a compromise sufficient to appease the South and to bring about rescission of the act of nullification. However, in order to uphold Calhoun's doctrine, the South Carolina legislature nullified the "Force Act," which had now become academic. The net result was to establish that, in future, nullification would mean secession, if not war.

Both the defeat of the propertied interests and the split between Calhoun and Jackson had important bearings upon the development of the nation's foreign policy. The first greatly enhanced the power of public opinion in the making of foreign policy; the second raised an issue which the Democratic Party would sooner or later have to face—namely, whether to remain a party of radical liberalism (which would entail an alienation of the Southern planters) or whether to attempt to maintain itself in power by alliance with the slave-interests.

Characteristically, Jackson's foreign policy, announced in his first message to Congress, was "to ask nothing that is not clearly right and to submit to nothing that is wrong."

The question of spoliation claims arising from the Napoleonic wars engaged his immediate attention and demonstrated a new, consciously "tough" policy. Minor claims against the Two Sicilies, Denmark and Sweden were quickly settled, but the major claims were against France. Aided by the internal disturbances of the revolution which placed Louis-Philippe of Orleans upon the French throne in 1830, Jackson's ambassador, W. L. Rives, was able to negotiate a treaty, under which France ultimately paid about 60% of the American claims of $9,362,-193.27. This brought considerable credit to the Jacksonian administration.

The next matter concerned trade with the British West Indies. Adams' countervailing restrictions had forced Britain to soften its mercantilist controls, but they had also inflicted hardship upon the South. Jackson repudiated Adams' policy and effected a compromise which ended the traditional British system of colonial trade monopoly.

A less creditable phase of Jacksonian foreign policy related to the Indian tribes in the Southeast which the state of Georgia sought to displace. Georgia's policy consisted of a more or less continuous making and breaking of successive treaties, each of which pushed the Indians further westward. The state disposed of the lands so acquired by lottery, thus stimulating the avarice of the frontier settlers. In one of the cases where Georgia flagrantly violated Indian rights, the Supreme Court of the United States held its action to be unconstitutional and ordered redress for the Indian tribes. Jackson, however, took no action to compel compliance with the Court's decision and tacitly permitted the expulsion of most of the remaining Indians to lands west of the Mississippi. When it came to a question like this, the old, lawless Indian-fighter's instincts and prejudices overcame Jackson's sense of responsibility as Chief of State.

The expulsion of the southeastern Indians brought the question of Texas to the forefront. Under the Transcontinental Treaty of 1819, the United States had promised to respect the Texas-Louisiana boundary established at the Sabine River. This obligation carried over to Mexico, when that country declared its independence of Spain in 1821. Various attempts by Jackson to push the boundary westward by purchasing Texan land from Mexico were unsuccessful. This, however, did not prevent American citizens from settling in Texas, nor did the Mexican government at first object to immigration. The result was inevitable. When the Mexican government recognized the danger of American colonization, it was already too late. The American settlers revolted and declared their independence. If Jackson cannot justly be accused of having fomented the revolt, it is certainly true that he did nothing to prevent it or to prevent Americans from enlisting in the Texan army. Led by Sam Houston, with whom Jackson maintained intimate relations, the Texans met and defeated Santa Anna's Mexican army at the battle of San Jacinto, in April 1836.

Both Houses of Congress demanded recognition of the new republic. Jackson temporized, insisting that this was a matter for Executive decision. A year later, Congress again took the initiative, this time passing a bill providing funds for a diplomatic mission to Texas whenever the President might deem it expedient. Jackson signed this bill and shortly thereafter extended recognition. By this time the Texans were asking for admission to the Union. There can be no doubt that Jackson desired annexation, but this act would involve the politically explosive issue of the extension or non-extension of slave territory—a matter which Jackson did not wish to precipitate at this time. The succeeding Van Buren administration declined to consider annexation for the same reason.

Jackson's moves in the direction of "hard money" and his distribution to the states of a $28,000,000 Federal surplus produced a boom which aided Van Buren's election but which collapsed in a serious depression shortly after Jackson's successor entered the White House. Van Buren's refusal to intervene resulted in a bitter struggle between the administration and the banks, which culminated in the creation of the "Independent Treasury" and the divorce of the government from the private banking system. This ended the second skirmish between the government and the "money power" with a victory for the people against property more apparent than real. It was not to be long before the "money power" would find an escape from the shackles which had been placed upon it.

In a broader sense, however, this second encounter had an important effect upon the future. The extent to which the conservative interests identified themselves with the private banks in their losing struggle to retain the government deposits, and the betrayal of the conservative interests by the utterly unscrupulous and irresponsible behavior of Nicholas Biddle in the last stages of the fight, deprived the Neo-Federalists, once and for all, of a moral rationalization for their basic tenet: that property *had a right* to control political power. No one since Hamilton had affirmed this doctrine in more resounding phrases than Daniel Webster, whose talents were retained by the Biddle management.

The political scene from 1836 to 1840 deserves at least brief comment because of its impact upon later developments in the field of foreign policy. Having failed to unseat Jackson in 1832 by running their most distinguished leader, Henry Clay, the Whigs tried a new tactic against Van Buren in the electoral contest of 1836. By running three regional favorites, they endeavored to throw the final election into the House of Representatives, where the widening cleavages in the Jacksonian coalition might best be exploited. The favorite sons were Hugh L. White of Tennessee for the Southwest; William Henry (Tippecanoe) Harrison for the Northwest; and Daniel Webster for New England. Of these, Harrison made the best showing, but Van Buren gathered 170 electoral votes against a combined total of only 124 for his opponents. Failure to throw the election into the House temporarily saved Calhoun from having to make an agonizingly difficult decision. Having fought Clay and broken with Jackson, Calhoun was tortured by the unhappy choice between making an alliance with the Whigs, the banks and the tariff, which he abhorred, or supporting the egalitarian radicalism of Van Buren which he distrusted and feared. A Southern planter by marriage, but a man of the people at heart, Calhoun remained neutral throughout the campaign. So, on the whole, did the South; the majority of the planters were Whigs, while popular sentiment favored the Democrats.

By 1840, the political picture changed, due primarily to three factors. The depression of 1837 operated against the party in power. Even without the depression, however, a decline of radical impetus had set in and the Jacksonian coalition had begun to disintegrate. This was not surprising, considering the disparate elements of which the coalition had been composed; as so often in history, it had proved easier to unite various interests and groups in opposition to a regime which had incurred widely varying resentments than to hold a coalition together behind an alternative program of reform. Finally, there was the Whig reformation.

Defeat had taught the conservatives a valuable lesson: whether they liked or disliked, trusted or distrusted the people, universal suffrage meant that the people had power. No matter how ignorant or stupid the masses might be, they had the votes without which the conservative interests could not hope to control the government. Under the leadership of such younger men as William H. Seward and Thurlow Weed, the Whigs proceeded, in 1840, to meet the Jacksonians on Jacksonian ground. Turning from class-conscious aristocracy to a new, homespun, backwoods conservatism, they dropped the forthright doctrine of Federalism and Neo-Federalism that property was entitled to power. They carefully refrained from expressing contempt for the propertyless masses, wooing them instead, endeavoring to show them that conservatism served their interests, and animating their desire to escape from the ranks of the propertyless into the always open society of the propertied. Conservatism went into buckskins and overalls, located its home in the log cabin and preached for the first time the gospel later to be popularized by Horatio Alger. The new Whig leaders asked: "What is all this talk about the dispossessed? Who is dispossessed? Surely not the workers, happy in their beautiful new factories and mills—surely not the farmers, glorying in their independence and their honest toil beneath the healthy sun. Tyranny of wealth? What tyranny of wealth? The only tyranny oppressing Americans and hampering their progress is the tyranny of Executive despotism with its ever-more-grasping bureaucracy."

This was something new in American politics. It was, in fact, the first real "public relations" campaign. And it worked; it worked so well that it became clear before the conventions of 1840 that almost any Whig candidate would be elected, provided that he said nothing to remind the people of the forthright doctrines of Henry Clay or the massive thunderings of Daniel Webster. Clay, wanting the nomination more than before, went into a black rage when the Whigs nominated William Henry Harrison and John Tyler.

The Democrats renominated Van Buren. ("Old Kinderhook," they called him, after his birthplace in the Hudson valley, and coined the slogan "O.K. You can stay in the White House," thus adding the expression O.K. to the vernacular.) The Whigs roared back: "Poor Old Van is a worn-out man"— "Tippecanoe and Tyler Too." The log cabin and cider barrel became the symbols of the new conservatism. The frontispiece was the picture of a somewhat musty military hero. The Whigs brought out something like a million new voters who had never before been to the polls. Harrison won, with 234 votes in the Electoral College to Van Buren's 60.

Perhaps the most spectacular effect of the Jacksonian revolution was its impact upon American conservatism. The Age of

Jackson did, to be sure, mark the emergence of new radical forces which were from then on to wage a continuing struggle for the preservation of the rights of the many in an economic order which tended to concentrate power in the hands of a few. But, even more dramatically, the Age of Jackson marked the passing of the old order of conservatism. The property interest was permanently driven out of a basically anti-democratic position into the open field of competition for popular support, where advocacy of reform or defense of the status quo would in future win or lose according to popular decision.

In the shaping of the nation's foreign policy, the effect of the Jacksonian revolution was to transfer initiative from Executive leadership to popular sentiment or opinion. Henceforward, the conduct of foreign relations would be less a matter for experienced diplomats working behind closed doors and more a concern of politicians swayed by prevailing moods and internal conflicts. Up to this point, one might say that, with the exception of the War of 1812, American foreign policy had been the product of leadership planning. With Jackson and his successors it became more the product of individual ambitions, group pressures and popular emotion.

The Whig victory in 1840 might, if Harrison had lived, have caused a slowing down in the tempo of expansion. Clay, the dominant figure in the Whig party, was no longer the young "War-hawk" of 1812. But the death of President Harrison, a month after his inauguration, brought to the Presidency a man who would follow popular sentiment rather than seek to lead it.

CHAPTER EIGHT

Aggressive Expansion
(1841–1848)

JOHN TYLER's nomination for the Vice Presidency had come about through the desire of the Whig leadership to attract as many as possible of Calhoun's followers. A Virginia aristocrat by birth, Tyler had served in the state legislature and as governor of the state, as well as in both Houses of Congress. He had consistently opposed the tariff, held strong states-rights convictions, but had condemned South Carolina's nullification ordinance. Opposed on the whole to Clay's "American System," he had nevertheless been on the side of the "Big Bank" in the fight over the withdrawal of the government's deposits. Tyler was about as lukewarm a Whig as Calhoun was a lukewarm Democrat.

As President, Tyler endeavored to steer a middle course between the two parties. He submitted to Clay's demand for a repeal of the Independent Treasury and a modified tariff, but when Clay tried to put through a new Bank charter, Tyler vetoed the Bill. This led to an open break with Clay and the Whig majority in the Congress. The Whigs lacked the power to override Tyler's veto; the whole cabinet resigned, except Webster who remained as Secretary of State. Clay, convinced that Whig control of the government was hopelessly lost just when, at last, it seemed to have been won, resigned his seat in the Senate in utter disgust, hoping that the next elections would at length bring him to the Presidency.

The resulting deadlock over domestic policy did not interfere with two important foreign policy developments during President Tyler's single term of office. The first of these was the final settlement of the old Northeast boundary dispute with

Britain under the Webster-Ashburton Treaty of 1842. The second was the annexation of Texas, completed just before Tyler left office, in March 1845.

Daniel Webster had stayed on in Tyler's cabinet primarily in order to carry on the negotiations with Britain. A particularly favorable opportunity for a settlement had been created at the time of Harrison's becoming President by the fall of the British Melbourne-Palmerston government and the coming to power of Sir Robert Peel as prime minister, with the conciliatory Lord Aberdeen as foreign secretary. Prior to this time feeling in both countries had been running high as the result of two Canadian border incidents, both more spectacular than important.* With the truculent elements in eclipse on both sides of the Atlantic, Webster was able to settle these minor affairs and to open negotiations concerning the Maine-New Brunswick frontier. Aberdeen sent Alexander Baring (Lord Ashburton), a member of the banking firm of Baring Brothers, as his emissary.

The treaty negotiated by Webster just about split the difference between the American and British boundary claims and resulted in the present American-Canadian border of Maine, Vermont and New York. The British obtained the desired overland connection between St. John and Montreal. The United States obtained Rouse's Point and the fort commanding the outlet of Lake Champlain. On the question of Oregon and the northwest frontier, the negotiators were unable to make any headway.

The amicable settlement arrived at by Webster with Lord Ashburton helped considerably to set the stage for the annexation of Texas. The Palmerston policy had been to keep Texas independent and, therefore, available as a second source of cotton, envisaging the possibility that a new independent, southwestern empire might limit the growth of the United States as a world power and as a competitor in world trade.

Both British and French diplomacy were directed at this

---

* The so-called *Caroline* case arose over Canadian seizure of an American ship which had carried supplies to insurrectionists. The McLeod affair arose over the arrest in New York of the Canadian accused of having killed an American during the seizure of the *Caroline*.

time toward mediating Mexican recognition of Texan independence on condition that Texas would not join the United States.

Seeking some means of dramatically recouping his drooping political fortunes, Tyler revived the issue of annexation in 1843. Jackson emerged from retirement to take a hand in strongly urging Tyler forward and in seeking to influence his old friend, President Sam Houston. The latter was still smarting over Van Buren's rejection of annexation in 1837. However, largely because of Jackson's efforts, he swallowed his pride and wrote to Jackson:*

> Now, my venerated friend, you will perceive that Texas is presented to the United States as a bride adorned for her espousal . . . Were she to be spurned she would seek some other friend.

Webster having retired after concluding the treaty with Britain (this was Webster's one concrete contribution in an otherwise frustrated career), the task of negotiating the annexation fell to Abel P. Upshur, the new Secretary of State. With the affair well advanced, Upshur was accidentally killed by a gun explosion on board a warship and John C. Calhoun was appointed by Tyler to take his place. Calhoun signed the treaty of annexation on April 12, 1844 and Tyler sent it to the Senate for ratification. Clay, in retirement, but just nominated for the Presidency by the Whig convention, came out in opposition to annexation because he feared that it would mean war with Mexico. Calhoun further complicated the matter by telling Sir Richard Pakenham, the British minister, that British abolitionism was the main reason for annexation. This was, of course, not true, even though the extension of slavery was uppermost in Calhoun's own mind, but Calhoun's tactlessness and Clay's opposition were enough to kill the treaty in the Senate.

The question of annexation split the Democratic Party no less than it divided the Whigs. The Southern wing, under Calhoun's leadership, was solidly for annexation. Tyler, now back in the Democratic Party, was nominated at a rump convention

* Quoted without source by S. F. Bemis, *Diplomatic History of the United States, op. cit.,* page 227.

in Baltimore, held in May; this was little more than an office-holders' caucus, but it served notice of the Tyler-Calhoun alliance. Van Buren was the leading candidate of the party, but flung a bombshell into the proceedings with a statement opposing annexation. This left the Democrats in much the same position as that created for the Whigs by Clay's anti-annexation pronouncement. Popular sentiment was strong for annexation. People were on fire with the vision of a nation which stretched from ocean to ocean. The phrase "Manifest Destiny" was yet to be coined, but the idea, born long ago in the mind of John Quincy Adams, had caught the popular imagination. And yet, here were Clay, the Whig nominee, and Van Buren, the probable Democratic candidate, both announcing their opposition.

The matter was complicated not only by the question of extending slavery but by the fact that Oregon loomed at least as large in the popular mind as Texas. To oppose the one implied opposition to the other; yet Oregon involved no question of slavery at all.

Van Buren's anti-annexation position did not shock the radical (Barnburner) wing of the Northern Democratic Party, although radical thinking on the slavery question was by no means uniform. The Barnburners, while opposed to slavery, had little or no sympathy with the abolitionists, many of whom were either clerical or political conservatives. Some radicals, like Theophilus Fisk, contended that the abolitionists of the North had mistaken the color of American slaves and that there were more slaves with pale faces in the Northern textile mills than black slaves below the Potomac. On the other hand, many northern capitalists opposed annexation precisely because it would open up more free land and reduce the eastern labor supply.

The real issue, which most thinking men recognized and few except John Quincy Adams would openly admit, was that ultimately the question of slavery could not be settled without either abolition or a dissolution of the Union. Sooner or later the terrible question would have to be faced. Clay, the great compromiser, and Calhoun, the anguished philosopher who sought to reconcile national majority rule with the preservation of sectional majority rights, had come up against this dreaded question in 1820 and turned away from it. Jackson had turned away from it in 1837. Neither Clay nor Van Buren were ready to face it in 1844; but whereas Van Buren, so often accused of equivocation, took his stand uncompromisingly against annexation, Clay—the man who had once said that he would "rather be right than be President"—now proceeded to straddle the question of annexing Texas. He was not against it, he said, if it could be done peacefully and "upon fair and just terms."

Van Buren's anti-annexation stand cost him Jackson's support and the Democratic nomination. He obtained a majority vote in the convention but Calhoun's Southern delegates insisted upon maintaining the two-thirds rule. When it became apparent that their candidate could not be nominated the Van Buren forces reluctantly decided to throw their votes to the man whom they had originally decided to run as Vice President—the dark horse whom Andrew Jackson had carefully groomed for the Presidency—James K. Polk.

The Whig press at once took up the chant: "Who is James K. Polk?" Clay's supporters acted as if they had never heard of this "little Jimmy Polk of Tennessee," but, as a matter of fact, they should have had good reason to remember him. It was Polk who had led the Jackson forces in the House in the Bank War. Later he had recaptured his state from the Whigs and served two terms as its governor.

The campaign of 1844 was the first election since that of 1796 in which foreign policy was the major issue. The Democratic slogan "Fifty-four-forty or fight" was, if anything, more popular than Texas. The lure of the Pacific coast was greater than that of the Lone Star Republic.

The election was extremely close, with a remarkable absence of clear sectional division, largely because of the appeal which Oregon held for the North. A change of only a few votes in New York would have given Clay the victory which he had so long and so desperately sought. Nevertheless, the outcome was decisive.

Taking the result of the election as a mandate for annexation, Tyler proposed and obtained Congressional approval by means of a joint resolution, which required only a majority vote in both Houses. This new device had two advantages: it avoided the possibility of having the annexation blocked by a Senate minority; and it enlisted the cooperation of the House, which had shown that it could block diplomatic action by withholding appropriations required for the execution of Senate-approved treaties. Tyler signed the annexation resolution on March 1, 1845, just before turning over the White House to his successor. He had accomplished his purpose, and so had that most ardent of the annexationists, Andrew Jackson.

Tyler's administration is noteworthy for the first move of American diplomacy in the Far East; this was inspired by a sectional commercial interest. New England traders engaged in importing tea from China had developed a small but highly profitable triangular trade, in some respects like the triangular trade in molasses, rum and Negro slaves. The Chinese had little or no use for New England hatchets, tools and utensils, but the shrewd Yankee traders soon discovered a ready market for these articles in the vicinity of Vancouver, where they could be profitably exchanged for sealskins. The sealskins, in turn, were highy prized by the Chinese mandarins and could be exchanged at another good profit for tea, which was then brought back around the Horn and sold at a third profit in the United States. A single voyage would net as much as 200% profit. When Britain defeated China in the Opium War of 1839-1842 and forced the opening of China to the opium traffic, the New England traders were concerned to make sure that the British merchants had obtained no special advantages. This caused Tyler to send Caleb Cushing to China to negotiate the first Chinese-American Treaty. Cushing's Wanghia Treaty of 1844 obtained what we would now call "most favored nation rights." In essence it was a "me too" treaty, setting the pattern to develop later into the "Open Door Policy."

James K. Polk came into office with the unique determination to serve only one term and with the avowed purpose of accomplishing the annexation of Oregon and Texas, of re-establishing the Independent Treasury and of reducing the tariff. His attitude toward the various factions in the Democratic Party was dispassionate and essentially neutral. This pleased none of the contending elements. Polk's appointment of James Buchanan as Secretary of State was unpopular in the

North. His choice for Secretary of the Treasury, Robert J. Walker, was disliked by the South and distrusted by the radical, Northern Jacksonians. George Bancroft, as Secretary of the Navy, pleased Van Buren but not Calhoun. The New Yorker, William L. Marcy, as Secretary of War, satisfied neither the radical Barnburners nor the conservative Hunker faction.

Under the firm leadership of Robert J. Walker, Congress quickly re-established the Independent Treasury and reduced the tariff. This disposed of Polk's domestic program. The administration now turned its attention to Texas and Oregon.

When President Tyler signed the annexation resolution just before leaving office, the Mexican government declared that it would break off diplomatic relations and declare war. Confronted with this declaration, Polk sent American troops into Texas to protect its territory from attack during the completion of the annexation proceedings. He also sent naval squadrons into the Gulf of Mexico and to the coast of California. Simultaneously, on the same ship with the returning Mexican ambassador, Polk dispatched an agent (William S. Parrott) to find out whether the Mexican government would be disposed to receive a minister from the United States and to discuss a peaceful settlement of disputes other than the annexation of Texas. (These consisted primarily of fixing the Texas boundaries and settling certain already adjudicated claims.) Parrott reported that the Herrera government would be prepared to receive a "minister," provided that the United States would withdraw its naval forces from the Vera Cruz area. The fleet was withdrawn and Polk sent John Slidell to Mexico as a "special *ad hoc* commissioner." Whether or not Polk misunderstood the difference between this sort of special envoy and the "minister" whom Mexico had been reportedly willing to receive, or whether he purposely drew the distinction is not very important. The instructions to Slidell clearly showed that Polk intended to give the Mexican government a fair chance to reach a peaceful settlement, although Polk actually preferred war, since a peaceful settlement would not give him California. Slidell's instructions were to offer to release Mexico from payment of the adjudicated claims if it would agree to fix the

Texas-Mexican boundary at the Rio Grande, thus yielding the disputed area between the Nueces and Rio Grande rivers.

There were in Mexico at this time two factions contending for power. Popular opinion was inflamed and inclined to the belief that the Mexican army could hold its own in war and that help might be expected from England or France. Both the Herrera government and the succeeding Paredes regime were afraid to agree to the annexation of Texas; both made use of the technical excuse that Slidell was not a "minister."

When the news of the Mexican refusal reached Washington, Polk ordered General Zachary Taylor to move from Corpus Christi across the disputed territory to the Rio Grande. This was in late March, 1846. Meanwhile, in his annual message of December 2, 1845, Polk had already warned Britain to keep hands off, reiterating Monroe's declaration that the United States would not tolerate any new European settlements or colonies on the North American continent. The presence of an American fleet off the coast of California reinforced this statement. It also served notice upon the Californians that, if they should revolt from Mexico, they could expect to be taken into the Union.

There can be no doubt that, having made his effort to obtain Texas and the disputed area by peaceful means, Polk now wanted war. His action in sending Taylor into the disputed territory was deliberately provocative. From March 26, when Taylor reached the Rio Grande, until May 9, Polk waited impatiently for news of a Mexican attack upon Taylor's forces. Then he called in his cabinet and proposed a message to Congress asking for authority to use armed force to collect the adjudicated claims. This proposal would doubtless have been carried out, had not the news reached Washington on the same day that Mexican troops had crossed the Rio Grande on April 24 and attacked Taylor's forces.

Congress, following the President's lead, declared, on May 13, 1846, that "by the act of the Republic of Mexico, a state of war exists between that Government and the United States."

We must turn now to the dispute with Britain over the Oregon Territory. This dated back to the conflicting claims staked out by the early explorers. The earliest claim was that of Spain, arising from the voyage of Cabrillo in 1542. In 1579, Sir Francis Drake landed in the San Francisco Bay area and staked out a claim in the name of Queen Elizabeth. No permanent settlements were made until the Spaniards settled California in 1769-1776. Russia's claim in the Northwest dated from the voyage to Alaska of Vitus Bering, in 1741. Both British and American explorers and fur traders visited the Columbia River region in the late eighteenth century. The first official American overland expedition was that of Lewis and Clark sent by Jefferson in 1805. A fur company founded by John Jacob Astor established Astoria in 1811, at the mouth of the Columbia River.

In 1818, Adams' treaty with the British had carried the boundary along the 49th parallel to the Rocky Mountains. A year later, the Transcontinental Treaty with Spain had extinguished the Spanish claims north of the 42nd parallel. The American (1824) and British (1825) treaties with Russia had fixed the southern boundary of Alaska at 54° 40'. At various times since then, the United States had proposed, and Britain had almost accepted, an extension of the 49th parallel to the Pacific.

The difficulties had regularly arisen over control of the mouth of the Columbia River and the islands off Puget Sound. The Treaty of 1818, renewed in 1827 and again in 1842, left the disputed territory open to the citizens of both countries without prejudice to the claims of either. This was not, as sometimes described, a condominium; it was an arrangement to permit both sides to trade and settle without affecting the ultimate disposition of the territory.

The delay in reaching a settlement actually favored the United States, because of its easier overland access to the region and its more rapidly growing population. By 1846, a substantial overland migration created a popular demand for annexation and made the matter a political issue. Since most of the covered wagons moved into the Willamette valley or into the Columbia River region, the demand for annexing all the territory up to the Alaskan border (54° 40') was absurd—all the more so since the United States had always been willing to settle for the extension of the 49th parallel. Polk had no desire to live up to the slogan which had been created for him. He was willing and eager to fight for Texas, the Southwest and California, but not for 54° 40'—certainly not at one and the same time. Moreover, the debates in the British Parliament made it quite clear that Britain would not submit to being pushed out of the whole Northwest Territory. On the other hand, Canning, too, had once made a proposal which accepted the principle of the 49th degree boundary, and Britain was no more willing to go to war for lands below that line than Polk was willing to fight for territory above it. This was the atmosphere in which Secretary of State Buchanan took up negotiations with Lord Pakenham in 1846.

Both sides were in a hurry to get the matter settled. Britain was in haste because its fleet was at the River Plate, engaged in blocking a French attempt to acquire predominant influence in that area. Also Lord Aberdeen no doubt feared that a victorious war with Mexico might make the United States more intransigent. Polk was in a hurry because he wanted to get the dispute with Britain out of the way before he became too deeply involved in the Mexican War. Moreover, he knew that the weak Peel government might at any moment fall and be replaced by a ministry in which the difficult Palmerston would again become foreign secretary. The draft treaty, sent over by Aberdeen in May, was hastily accepted by Polk and ratified by the Senate on June 15, by a vote of 41 to 14.

Except for relatively minor adjustments left to subsequent arbitration, the Treaty of 1846 finally closed the northwestern gap in the American frontier, fixing the boundary as it stands today. Like the Webster-Ashburton Treaty of 1842, it was a fair compromise, if anything, slightly favoring the United States. Polk's moderation and decisiveness had won a great diplomatic success.

The friendly settlement of the Oregon dispute was all the more of an accomplishment because, during the negotiations, Great Britain and the United States were engaged in stiff competition for control of possible canal sites in Central America.

Polk's emissary to New Granada (now Colombia) negotiated a treaty upon which Theodore Roosevelt based the building of the Panama Canal.* At the same time, Britain and the United States were each trying to block off the other from obtaining control over a route across Nicaragua. This contest was later liquidated by the Clayton-Bulwer Treaty of 1850.

With Oregon settled, Polk was now free to prosecute the war with Mexico and the acquisition of California. But there was trouble for the President on the domestic front. Following the tradition set by Jefferson in such matters, Polk asked Congress for an appropriation of $2,000,000 to finance negotiations with Mexico. (The amount of $2,000,000 seems to have acquired a magic significance in major land acquisitions.) David Wilmot, a radical Democrat from Pennsylvania, proposed an amendment providing that slavery should be excluded from all lands acquired from Mexico. In the debate over this "Wilmot Proviso," the long-smoldering conflict over the slavery issue came to a head, with feelings on both sides rapidly mounting to fever pitch. Polk considered, and told Wilmot, that this was a tempest over "an abstract question," since slavery already existed in Texas and would in any case never exist in New Mexico and California. Polk's posthumously-published *Diary* makes it clear that his attitude was quite evidently one of "a plague on both your houses" in a dispute which threatened the successful accomplishment of expansion to the Pacific. He thought Calhoun had become "desperate in his aspirations for the Presidency," using the issue of slavery extension to bolster his sagging fortunes. Similarly he thought the Northern Free Soilers and Abolitionists were making political capital out of the issue in order to reinstate Martin Van Buren in the Presidency. With his own attention focused upon foreign affairs, Polk undoubtedly underestimated the importance of a question which was to rend both major parties asunder and carry the nation to the abyss of civil war, but there appears to be little justification for the frequently made allegation that his "neutrality" con-

---

* For the interesting details of Benjamin Bidlack's negotiations at Bogota, see R. R. MacGregor, "Treaty of 1846," *Clark University Thesis Abstracts 1929* (Clark University, Worcester, 1930).

cealed a sympathy for the cause of slavery.* Polk's mistake was the antithesis of the mistake made by Martin Van Buren in 1840: Van Buren overlooked the importance of expansionist sentiment when he made anti-annexation the issue; Polk overlooked the importance of anti-slavery sentiment when he made expansion the sole issue.

Patriotism, aroused by the war, got Polk his appropriation, but the dangerously divisive question remained unsolved.

The military campaign against Mexico consisted of three parts: an invasion of northern Mexico by Taylor, an overland march from Missouri to Santa Fe and California by Stephen Kearney, and a drive at the Mexican capital launched from Vera Cruz under the command of Winfield Scott. The main thrust was Scott's seaborne expedition which landed at Vera Cruz on March 9 and reached the gates of Mexico City by September, 1847.

Polk, though not himself a candidate for re-election, did not desire either of his generals to become a national hero. He wished, if possible, to achieve victory by diplomatic, rather than by purely military means. Also, he wished to make the peace his own personal achievement. For these reasons he adopted the rather curious expedient of sending the Chief Clerk of the State Department—one Nicholas P. Trist—along with Scott, endowed with plenipotentiary powers to make certain peace proposals. Scott and Trist promptly fell into such bad relations that they were not even on speaking terms. Trist refused to show Scott his instructions, and the General refused to transmit Trist's peace proposal unseen.

The special agent had been authorized to offer the Mexican government these minimum terms: Mexico to cede the disputed territory in West Texas, permit Texan annexation and agree to a boundary running along the Rio Grande to El Paso and from there due west to the Pacific. This meant a cession of all lands north of what is now the southern boundary of New Mexico, Arizona and California. For this settlement Trist was

* See James K. Polk, *Diary* (Longmans, Green, 1952), Volume II, pages 309-348. The assertion that Polk was in secret alliance with the Calhoun pro-slavery forces was made by a number of contemporary writers, especially by Thomas Parker in the *Massachusetts Quarterly Review* and by James Russell Lowell in the *Biglow Papers*.

authorized to offer $15,000,000, plus the assumption by the United States of $3,000,000 of adjudicated claims of its citizens against the Mexican government. In addition, if he could get Lower California and a right of way for a canal or railroad across the Isthmus of Tehuantepec, Trist was authorized to pay up to a total amount of $30,000,000.

Unable to deal with Scott, Trist managed to convey his minimum proposal to the Mexican government through the intermediary of the British minister. The latter reported that Santa Anna might be willing to accept, if he were given a personal bribe big enough to enable him to entrench himself in power. Scott, by this time reconciled to Trist's activities, arranged an armistice and was prepared to provide the bribe money out of his secret service funds. Mexican sentiment against yielding any territory to the hated *gringo* imperialists was, however, so strong that Santa Anna did not dare to consummate the deal. The short armistice ended; Scott entered Mexico City on September 14; and Santa Anna fled the country.

Disappointed with Trist's failure, Polk recalled his envoy and decided to let Mexico sue for peace in its own time. Buchanan and Walker, with considerable popular and Congressional sentiment on their side, demanded the annexation of all of Mexico. Polk wisely opposed this, but, before any conclusion could be reached as to the terms to be imposed, there developed one of the strangest episodes in American history.

Under recall and with his authority canceled, Nicholas Trist —with the approval of General Scott—proceeded, at the request of the now desperate Mexican government, to sign the Treaty of Guadalupe Hidalgo, in which Mexico accepted precisely those minimum terms which Trist had originally been authorized to offer. Trist performed this incredible act on February 2, 1848, and was promptly dismissed in disgrace. But, while Polk was justifiably incensed at Trist's procedure, the illegally-signed treaty gave him exactly what he wanted; to wit—the present states of New Mexico, Arizona, Nevada, California and Utah, plus the western half of Colorado and a corner of Wyoming. And all this for the paltry sum of $18,000,000!

Polk wasted little time in approving the treaty and sending it to the Senate. On March 10, 1848, that body ratified by a vote of 38 to 14. The fantasy expressed in the original charters of the seaboard colonies, granting them borders extending to the "South Sea," had become a reality.

More than twenty years were to elapse before the disgraced Chief Clerk of the State Department was to receive from Congress the payment of his salary and expenses incurred in performing his strange but real service to the country.

"Manifest destiny"—the belief that God or nature had intended the United States to become an ocean-to-ocean nation of English-speaking people—had narcotized the American conscience into eagerly endorsing a war of aggressive expansionism and joyfully accepting its result as a just reward. What resistance there had been to the enterprise had arisen out of political rather than moral considerations. Few Americans considered that a neighboring republic had been deliberately provoked into war because it refused to cede or sell lands to which it held title acknowledged by the United States in the Transcontinental Treaty of 1819. What right had the Mexicans to California? Why, no more right than the Indians had had to their sacred Hickory Grounds in Alabama. (What right did the French have, in 1871, to Alsace-Lorraine, when Bismarck "needed" it? What right had Hitler to the Sudetenland, in 1938, or Russia, in 1939, to Latvia, Estonia and Lithuania? What right had Poland to Pomerania, or France to the Saar, in 1945?)

In Polk's justification it must be said that few Americans, even today, would wish to undo his actions while, at the time, Polk was actually a moderate executant of existing sentiment. Some of Polk's contemporaries would have wanted to go to war for 54° 40'. Others, including the two top members of his own cabinet, would have annexed all of Mexico. James K. Polk represented a wholly immoral cupidity for land which, at one time or another, has taken possession of most of the occidental peoples. He was elected President because he represented that phenomenon in our own history; but at least, by his moderation and common sense, he performed a service in limiting the bounds of national avarice. Moreover, he kept a wise balance between commitment and power—a matter which later American statesmen were to ignore to their cost.

The acquisition of Oregon and California, the Isthmian

negotiations and the rapid development of the steamship were already bringing Asia closer to the United States. Coaling stations were becoming important. The Yankee traders were soon to be joined by merchants on the Pacific coast demanding equal rights with other nations in exploiting trade with the Far East. Hawaii began to attract attention and pressures were beginning to accumulate for opening up Japan and Korea. Even as the dreams of "Manifest destiny" were fulfilled, the impetus to carry on across the Pacific was already gathering strength.

The last fateful years of appeasing the slave interest and the convulsion of the Civil War were about to impose a halt, but the tide of American imperialism was rising. From 1848 until 1861, that imperialism was to become distorted into a strange form, representing not the will of the people as a whole but the desperate twisting and turning of the Southern slave-interest. In the House of Representatives, crusty old John Quincy Adams set his face resolutely toward the rising storm. His dream of a transcontinental nation had come true, but history had yet to prove the truth of his premonition that the Union must either dissolve or else purify itself of "the great and foul stain" upon its conscience.

PART THREE

Internal Conflict Rules Diplomacy

CHAPTER NINE

Prelude to Tragedy
(1849–1861)

IN THE PERIOD which followed the era of continental expansion, American foreign policy was dominated first by the imminence of the conflict between the Union and the Southern slave states and then by the conflict itself. The last twelve years before the Civil War were marked by two phases: the first, a Whig Interlude of cautious restraint; and the second, an eight-year period of unbridled Slave-Interest Imperialism.

The Whig Interlude came about chiefly as the result of a split in the Democratic Party which began in New York State and widened into a national cleavage. The issue was that raised by the Wilmot Proviso. The radical (Barnburner) wing of the Democratic Party was determined to keep slavery out of the new Western territories. The conservative (Hunker) faction favored the doctrine of "Squatter Sovereignty"—that is, letting the people of each territory settle the question of slavery for themselves. When the National Democratic Convention of 1848 seated both of the rival New York delegations, the Barnburners walked out, joining with the Ohio Liberty Party to form a new national organization which took the name of the Free Soilers. This new party nominated Martin Van Buren as its candidate, while the regular Democrats nominated Lewis Cass of Michigan.

As a result of the Democratic split, the Whigs should have won an easy victory, but they, too, were divided. The Northern "Conscience Whigs" were at loggerheads with the "Cotton Whig" Southern planters. The Convention rejected the old party leadership of Clay and Webster, putting up General Zachary Taylor with the comparatively unknown Millard Fillmore of New York as his running mate.

Taylor carried New York by a narrow margin and this was decisive.

President Taylor, with John S. Clayton as his Secretary of State, tried to keep the question of slavery from dominating foreign policy. The Whig tradition had been anti-expansionist, but there was not much to be done about an expansion which had already taken place. The Whigs made one move in the direction of withdrawal; this was in the Isthmian area. Clayton negotiated a treaty with Britain designed to end Anglo-American competition in Central America. Under this Clayton-Bulwer Treaty, the United States agreed to neutralize an eventual Isthmian canal, to forego fortification and to grant Britain equal rights in its use. Though ratified by the Senate, the treaty was extremely unpopular and led to Clayton's resignation.

Daniel Webster, succeeding Clayton, pursued an essentionally negative policy. Events abroad, however, provided the great orator with a last opportunity to play for popular acclaim. 1848 was the year of widespread liberal revolution in Europe. The popular risings against absolutism evoked the traditional American sentiments of sympathy. When the Austrian envoy protested against official American encouragement of the Hungarian revolt, Webster cut loose with a spread-eagle fulmination, hurling defiance and insult across the Atlantic at a regime which could only squirm in angry impotence. (This was the last of Webster; he died in 1852, within a few months of the death of the equally tragic and equally frustrated Henry Clay.)

The European revolutions affected the United States chiefly through their failure, which caused the first great flood of European immigration. Up to 1820, new arrivals in the United States had not exceeded 8,000 a year. In 1842, the figure had risen to 100,000 but had then dropped off sharply. In 1849, it rose to 300,000; and, in 1850, to 428,000. This great influx of disappointed liberals, preponderantly German, settled almost exclusively in the free states, thus adding to the growing discrepancy in sectional growth and development.

Texas was the last slave state to be admitted to the Union. Up to 1850 it had been possible to balance the admission of a free state by the admission of another in which slavery would be permitted; this had enabled the South to hold its own in the

Senate, even though its power in the House was dwindling. The
more the South found itself threatened with falling into a hope-
less minority position, the more desperate its efforts to maintain
a balance. The rapid settlement of California after the Gold
Rush brought the question to the immediate forefront. While
Congress wavered indecisively over the basis for admitting the
richest prize of the Mexican conquest, the people of California
took the matter into their own hands, adopting a constitution
prohibiting slavery. The resulting crisis was temporarily overcome through another compromise; California was admitted as
a free state, but it was agreed that the remaining once-Mexican
territory would be organized in two units—Utah and New
Mexico—in which "Squatter Sovereignty" would determine the
slavery issue. The South was further appeased by the enactment
of a Fugitive Slave Law providing for the Federal enforcement
of extradition. The brutal application of this act inflamed
Northern resentment against the California Compromise, but
the Southern slave-interest was still not satisfied. It now saw that
it needed either outright Congressional protection of slavery or
an expansion of slave territory by the annexation of Latin
American states.

Even before President Taylor's death (and before the California Compromise), there had been signs of this new slave-
interest imperialism. A number of filibustering expeditions had
been launched from the South to assist Cuban insurgents
against Spanish rule. President Taylor took a firm stand against
American participation in such ventures and, since the excuse
for them was that Britain might take over the island, he considered a joint declaration with Britain, renouncing any annexationist ambitions in the event that Cuba should declare
itself independent. After Taylor's death, President Fillmore
considered it inadvisable to carry out this plan, largely for reasons of domestic politics. At his request Edward Everett—
Webster's successor as Secretary of State—issued a unilateral
declaration preserving complete freedom of action for the
United States. This "Everett Memorandum," phrased in the
Websterian tradition, was aimed more at attracting Southern
votes in the forthcoming elections of 1852 than at annexation.

In the campaign of 1852, both parties competed for Southern

favor—the Whigs by claiming credit for the California Compromise, and the Democrats by promising to go even further in extending the doctrine of "Squatter Sovereignty." The Whigs, having been successful with one of Polk's generals, now nominated the other—Winfield Scott. The Democrats, after a protracted deadlock between Stephen Douglas, Lewis Cass and James Buchanan, came up with the comparatively unknown Franklin Pierce, of New Hampshire, who turned out to be a stalking horse for the Southern slave-interest. The Democrats won primarily by reason of the Southern vote. The fact that they had sold out to the slave-interest was quickly to become apparent in the field of foreign policy.

In his Inaugural Address, Franklin Pierce set the stage for the ensuing period of slave-interest imperialism:

> The policy of my administration will not be controlled by any timid forebodings of evil from expansion. Indeed, it is not to be disguised that our attitude as a nation and our position on the globe render the acquisition of certain possessions not within our jurisdiction eminently important for our protection.

One can scarcely conceive of a more barefaced attempt to identify the national interest with the interest of a slave-owning minority.

Pierce lost no time in surrounding himself with the most ardent expansionists; the leading slave-interest imperialists were sent abroad—James Buchanan as minister to London, John Y. Mason to Paris, and the notorious Pierre Soulé—already involved in several filibustering conspiracies against Cuba—was selected as minister to Spain. James Gadsden, a South Carolinian with a personal interest in a transcontinental railway project running through Mexican territory, was sent as envoy to the neighboring republic.

In the cabinet, Jefferson Davis occupied the post of Secretary of War and became the President's closest adviser. William L. Marcy became Secretary of State. The dominant group was determined to annex Cuba, Santo Domingo, parts of Mexico and, if possible, other Central American territory. Some of them thought in the traditional terms of increasing the slave-interest's

political power within the Union. Others were beginning to
think of secession and the building of a new slave empire dominated by the Old South.

Soulé was authorized to offer up to $130,000,000 for Cuba
and, if Spain refused to sell, he was instructed to pursue the
"next most desirable object . . . to detach that island from
Spanish domination and from all dependence upon any European power." * When Spain did, in fact, reject the offer of
purchase, Soulé not only blustered and threatened in a most
unseemly manner but actually conspired with insurgent groups.

While the envoy to Spain was indulging in this behavior,
Marcy heard from Buchanan that the British government might
conceivably favor a Spanish sale of Cuba for the reason that it
would replenish the depleted Spanish treasury and enable the
Spanish government to take care of bonds held by British in-
vestors. Marcy thereupon ordered Buchanan, Taylor and Soulé
to consult with each other and to prepare a recommendation.
At a meeting at Aix-la-Chapelle, the three American diplomats
produced a most extraordinary document—the notorious
Ostend Memorandum—which declared that if, having received
an offer for Cuba "far beyond its present value," the Spanish
government should refuse to sell the island, it would be "time
to consider the question, does Cuba in the possession of Spain
seriously endanger our internal peace and the existence of our
cherished Union?" This naked threat of aggressive war aroused
such public indignation in the United States that Marcy was
compelled to repudiate the declaration. The episode showed
not only the lengths to which the slave-interest was prepared to
go but also the consolidation of majority opinion against it.
Even so, the Democratic platform on which Buchanan was
shortly to be elected President, held firmly to the avowed
determination to acquire the "Pearl of the Antilles."

Through an agent, William L. Cazneau, Marcy next negotiated a treaty with Santo Domingo for the cession of an important harbor, but British and French intercession persuaded
the Dominican Republic to hold off.

A partial success was achieved in the consummation of Jeffer-

* For the full text of these almost incredible instructions, see Department of
State Archives, *Instructions—Spain*, Vol. XV.

son Davis' pet project when Gadsden succeeded in purchasing from Mexico the 19,000,000 acres of desert land needed for the transcontinental railway. This "Gadsden Purchase" was the bare minimum of what the annexationists had desired. Filibusters against Mexico continued well into Buchanan's administration.

The most ambitious filibuster, led by William Walker, was launched against the republic of Nicaragua and resulted in Walker establishing himself as an actual dictator in the Central American republic from 1855 to 1857. Marcy opposed and sought to repudiate this outrageous adventure, but not so President Pierce. When the neighboring state of Costa Rica declared war on Nicaragua and obtained arms from Britain, Pierce promptly recognized the Walker regime. The Democratic platform on which Buchanan was elected gave implied approval to the Nicaraguan adventure but, shortly after Buchanan took office, the Walker regime collapsed and Walker himself was executed by a firing squad. It was not until 1858 that President Buchanan took a belated stand against filibustering.

Apart from the relatively minor acquisition of land under the Gadsden Treaty, the whole slavery-annexationist drive into Latin America accomplished nothing except to impair the prestige of the United States.

Slave-interest imperialism was not, however, the only force impelling Pierce and Marcy toward expansion. The Far Eastern trading interest played a part, but perhaps even more important was the fact that the Mexican War had brought about a revival of the United States Navy. (The Mexican War, the Civil War, the Spanish-American War and the two World Wars all produced rapid naval expansion and, after each conflict, the United States found itself in possession of naval power which, in itself, provided an expansionist influence upon foreign policy.)

It was probably a combination of trading interest and the availability of naval power which prompted the two Pacific adventures of the Pierce-Buchanan period. The first of these was the negotiation of a treaty with Hawaii leading toward annexation. Here again, Marcy was frustrated by clever British diplomacy. Hearing of the negotiations, the British Foreign Office persuaded the Hawaiian government to demand statehood as a condition of annexation. Since Hawaii was most unlikely to become a slave state, this demand caused President Pierce to let Marcy's treaty die without even submitting it to the Senate for ratification.

The second and far more important Pacific adventure was the opening up of the hitherto secluded island empire of Japan. Pierce sent Commodore Matthew Perry with a squadron of American warships to protest the cruel treatment of American sailors occasionally shipwrecked on Japanese shores and, if possible, to negotiate a trade treaty. After two years of intermittent negotiations, backed by the presence of his "black ships of war," Perry successfully accomplished his mission. The result was more far-reaching than anyone could foresee at the time, leading as it did to the emergence of Japan as a powerful competitor for influence on the mainland of Asia.

An important diplomatic opportunity was lost when the United States declined to sign the Declaration of Paris, adopted by the European powers in 1856, at the conclusion of the Crimean War. This declaration established almost precisely that definition of neutral rights and freedom of the seas for which the United States had so long contended. Actually, Marcy's failure to seize this opportunity worked out, as we shall see presently, to the advantage of the North in the Civil War.

A treaty negotiated with the Argentine, opening the River Plate to American commerce after similar rights had been given to Britain and France, completes the foreign policy record of this period except for one minor but also characteristic matter. Among the initiated in the United States foreign service, Marcy is remembered chiefly as the author of the famous *Dress Circular,* ordaining that American diplomats abroad must attend court functions in attire which, for many years thereafter, frequently caused them to be mistaken for butlers and waiters.

Back of this dismal period in American diplomacy lay the tragic events which led to secession and war. The Kansas-Nebraska Act ripped the coverings from the dreaded issue so long submerged by appeasement. In disgust, Free Soil Democrats and Conscience Whigs flocked in droves into the new "Republican Party," finding that the magic of that ancient Jeffersonian name was still powerful. Another new party, the

Know-Nothings, sprang into existence on a platform of xeno-
phobic nationalism, inspired by recent heavy immigration. The
Whig Party practically disappeared from the national scene.

On top of "Bleeding Kansas" came the Dred Scott Decision
of the Supreme Court, which amounted to an assault upon the
entire Free Soil-Republican position by affirming that slavery
could constitutionally exist anywhere in the Union. The South
received a corresponding shock when John Brown's raid upon
the arsenal at Harpers Ferry raised the dreaded specter of a
slave revolt instigated by Northern abolitionists.

When the Democratic Party held its convention at Charleston in 1860, the last strands holding together the Northern and
Southern elements were severed. The Southern delegates demanded affirmative protection of slavery under the Constitution, as interpreted by the Supreme Court. Stephen Douglas,
leader of the Northern wing who had gone to the limit of appeasement in sponsoring the Kansas-Nebraska Act, knew that
accepting the Southern demand for explicit protection of the
slave-interest would utterly destroy the Democratic Party in
the North. The convention split apart. The Southerners, meeting at Richmond, nominated John C. Breckinridge. The Northerners, meeting at Baltimore, named Stephen Douglas as their
candidate.

With the Democrats split, and with remnants of the conservative Whigs uniting with the Know-Nothings in an obviously
futile "Constitutional Union Party," the problem of the Republicans was not how to win the election but how to win it
without disrupting the Union.

The story of how an anguished nation discovered, in the
backwoods of Illinois, the great and humble man who bore its
terrible burden has been told and retold by historians and—
most beautifully of all—by one of the nation's great poets. If
Washington had been, quite literally, the father of his country
—the "good king," who replaced the tyrant—if Jefferson had
personified the ideal of political democracy—if Jackson had
been the incarnation of democracy's struggle against distortion
by economic forces—Abraham Lincoln was all these things and
more. He was more, because, at one and the same time, he was
the father who bore the nation's burden while yet he personi-

fied the nation itself. Lincoln *was* America. He rose to fatherhood not as a benevolent, paternal figure but as the oldest
brother of the people, growing beyond, but never rising above
them. This was his greatness. The people's anguish was his
anguish; he bore it for them, because he bore it with them. The
people's vision was his vision. The people's doubts were his
doubts. His wisdom was no greater than the people's wisdom—
only more steadfast, more patient, more enduring in adversity.
Lincoln's voice was the voice of the people, speaking not so
much to them as for them—using words that the people knew,
to say what the people wanted to say and could not. Lincoln
was East and West, North and South, radical and conservative
and—because he was neither sectional nor partisan—he was both
loved and hated in just that measure which enabled him to become the guardian of the rights of all the people and to save
them from self-destruction.

It was natural that the true greatness of Lincoln should become apparent only after his untimely death. The people sensed
it during his lifetime, but the so-called leaders were, for the
most part, dissatisfied with him. The Southern leaders hated
him because he held human slavery to be a wrong. The Northern abolitionists hated him because he hesitated to coerce the
South into abolishing the evil. The conservatives feared Lincoln's Jeffersonian egalitarianism. The radicals were impatient
with his patience, contemptuous of his forbearing and distrustful of his caution. The timid thought him too bold. The hotheads thought him pusillanimous. Only the men who worked
closely with Lincoln—and not even all of these—gained insight,
during Lincoln's lifetime, into his greatness. Only they learned
to understand the fortitude that lay beneath the humility, the
steadfast purpose that directed his caution, the burning impatience that was held in check by wisdom and human understanding.

It was no accident that the two-hour oration of Edward
Everett on the battlefield of Gettysburg seemed to most newspaper editors more worthy of attention than the 268 words
which Lincoln spoke after the great Massachusetts orator had
finished. The ears of Republican editors were attuned to the
resounding periods of the Websterian tradition. Most Demo-

crats were blinded by partisanship. The Chicago *Times* produced this comment: *

> The cheek of every American must tingle with shame as he reads the silly, flat and dishwatery utterances of the man who has to be pointed out to intelligent foreigners as the President of the United States.

It was no accident either that, in 1864, even Lincoln's most devoted supporters should despair of his re-election. Practically all the political leaders were against him. But the people were for Lincoln, and the people knew—far better than the leaders of either North or South—what their spokesman meant when, a year later, he defined their task: "to bind up the nation's wounds . . . and to do all which may achieve and cherish a just and lasting peace among ourselves and with all nations."

When—with victory for freedom won on the battlefield, but with a peace of justice not yet assured—the assassin's bullet struck Lincoln down, it seemed as if the central pillar of the edifice of the people's hopes had been toppled and broken. Where would the nation find "charity for all," with Lincoln dead? Where would it find "firmness in the right, as God gives us to see the right," without the firmness and the vision which God had given to that homely and deeply melancholy figure— to that "man who had to be pointed out to intelligent foreigners as the President of the United States?"

* Benjamin P. Thomas, *Abraham Lincoln* (Knopf, 1952), page 403.

CHAPTER TEN

Lincoln's Civil War Diplomacy
(1861 – 1865)

THE HISTORY of the war between North and South has been written and rewritten. From the first Battle of Manassas to Appomattox it is a household saga. The heroes and the miscreants on both sides are familiar figures; the campaigns and battles are living stories; even the tintype photographs of the time, the battlegrounds and the trails of marching armies are a part of our national lares and penates. Less well known to us are those aspects of the Civil War period which influenced the making of Lincoln's foreign policy and those events abroad which burdened him with cares shared by only a few of his associates.

When Lincoln took office, in March, 1861, the war had not begun, but secession was already an accomplished fact. Between the elections, in November, 1860, and the inauguration of the new administration, South Carolina, Mississippi, Florida, Alabama, Georgia, Louisiana and Texas had withdrawn from the Union and formed a provisional Confederate government, with Jefferson Davis as President and the capital at Montgomery, Alabama. The immediate problem was not only how to deal with the seceded states but how to keep as many as possible of the border states from joining in the secession. Opinion in the North was singularly unformed and divided. Few favored the use of force to coerce the seceding states back into the Union. Some favored "letting the erring sisters go." Others, like Senator John J. Crittenden of Kentucky, proposed constitutional amendments which would have enacted something like the Missouri Compromise into basic law. The United States Army was a tiny force, greatly reduced by Southern captures of detachments stationed in the seceding states and by resignations of competent officers. The Navy had only two vessels in commission to defend the Atlantic coast. The coastal forts in the South had been taken over by the secessionists with the exception of Fort Sumter, at Charleston, and Fort Pickens, off Pensacola. The United States Treasury had been left all but bankrupt by the Buchanan administration.

Such was the problem faced by Lincoln and his group of almost wholly inexperienced advisers. After some hesitation, William H. Seward accepted the post of Secretary of State under the man whom he had hoped to outrun for the Presidency. An ambitious and avowed expansionist, Seward thought for a short time that he could dominate Lincoln in the shaping of foreign policy. Rather than face civil war, he preferred to pick a quarrel with some foreign power, seeking thus to reunite the country by war against a common enemy. In an extraordinary document, entitled *Some Thoughts for the President's Consideration,* he said:

> I would demand explanations from Spain and France, categorically, at once. I would seek explanations from Great Britain and Russia, and send agents into Canada, Mexico and Central America, to rouse a vigorous continental spirit of independence on this continent against European intervention. And, if satisfactory explanations were not received from Spain and France, would convene Congress and declare war against them.

Lincoln quietly placed this document with his private papers, where it was not discovered until years later. He knew that not even a victorious foreign war would settle the internal problem of slavery. Moreover, Seward's policy might well lead to another general war whose outcome would be wholly unpredictable. To understand Seward's astonishing proposal as well as the very different policy which he subsequently pursued with the utmost loyalty under Lincoln's direction, it is necessary to review briefly the state of world affairs in 1861.

The "explanations" which Seward proposed to demand from France, Britain, and Spain related to the interest which these three powers had been showing in Latin America.

Soulé's activities at Madrid and the outrageous Ostend

Memorandum with respect to Cuba had aroused great resentment and had given the Spanish government every reason to take advantage of whatever opportunities for recouping its dwindling fortunes might develop as a result of civil conflict in the United States.

France was now the aggressive France of the Second Empire. While the British had recognized the independence of the former Spanish colonies and busied themselves making favorable commercial treaties with them, France under the Bourbons had refused to recognize the revolt against the Spanish crown. This attitude of disinterest in Latin America had changed with the accession of Louis Philippe in 1830. In 1838, a French fleet had suddenly appeared off Vera Cruz to enforce French demands of payment of claims against Mexico, but withdrew when Congress demanded an explanation. There had then followed a series of Anglo-French interventions in the River Plate area, during which France at first sought to break into the British trade concessions and both nations finally undertook a joint intervention to force additional concessions from the stoutly resisting Rosas government of the Argentine. This was in 1845-1848, while the United States was preoccupied with the Mexican War and the negotiations with Britain over the Oregon Territory. Partly for this reason, and partly because President Polk interpreted the Monroe Doctrine as applying only to North and Central America, the United States had raised no objection to these interventions in the Argentine. The French revolution of 1848, establishing the Second Republic, temporarily ended French intrusion into the hemisphere.

The overthrow of the Second Republic and the establishment of Louis Napoleon as Emperor Napoleon III, in 1852, again radically changed French foreign policy. Napoleon proceeded to carve out a new empire, first in Europe and then overseas. Having first joined Britain in waging the Crimean War against Russia to prevent Russian domination of Turkey and the Black Sea, Napoleon sought to eliminate Austria as a threat to French hegemony. The defeat of Austria resulted in the liberation of Lombardy but not in the promised "liberation of Italy from the Alps to the Adriatic," for which Napoleon had exacted the price of Nice and Savoy. A wiser statesman than Napoleon would have sensed that the industrial revolution was about to make Prussia, with its great coal deposits, into a more dangerous threat than Austria, but Prussia's meteoric rise under Bismarck's leadership had not yet begun. By 1861, Napoleon III was ready for overseas adventure in order to divert attention from the rather unsatisfactory results of an Italian intervention which had alienated the Vatican without satisfying the liberal forces trying to unify Italy under the leadership of di Cavour.

Britain had other reasons for viewing the imminent civil conflict in the United States with satisfaction. Some 4,000,000 people in Lancashire had become dependent, through the industrial revolution, upon imports of Southern cotton. An independent South would, in addition, remove the protective tariff from a large potential market for English manufactures. Finally, there were some circles in England which viewed the breakup of the Union with favor because it would eliminate a formidable barrier to British Empire expansion. The more liberal groups sympathized with the Union because the United States represented the great experiment in democracy, but this feeling had little effect upon government policy. The only strong sentiment favorable to the North was that of anti-slavery humanitarianism, but this could not come into play so long as Lincoln felt compelled to delay emancipation for the sake of holding the border states.

Thus, in looking around the world in March, 1861, Lincoln and Seward could see several potential enemies who might aid the Confederacy and practically no foreign friends who might assist the Union. Russia was friendly for the traditional reason of wanting to see a strong United States as a counter-balance to the British Empire. Moreover, under the liberal Tsar Alexander II, Russia was at this time freeing the serfs and was, therefore, sympathetic to the anti-slavery position of the North. But Russia was too far away to be effective as an ally, except in the event of a general war. Most of the German states, too, were friendly, but they were not yet in a position to affect the European balance of power.

In the impending war between the states, the Union fortunately had no outlying possessions to defend and no weak frontiers exposed to a powerful foreign neighbor. On the other hand, it had two points of vulnerability: the Monroe Doctrine would be impossible to enforce during a major civil conflict; and the large Northern merchant fleet would become an easy prey to depredation, if the Confederacy should be able to construct or acquire men-of-war.

The primary aim of Lincoln's foreign policy was, therefore, to prevent any foreign power from recognizing or giving aid to the Confederacy. With the difficult mission of accomplishing this purpose as to Great Britain, he sent Charles Francis Adams to the post in London which had been occupied by his father and his grandfather.

For the first two years of the war, Adams' task was extremely onerous. When hostilities began with the firing of the first shots at Fort Sumter,* Jefferson Davis issued letters of marque to privateers. This action was immediately followed by Lincoln's proclamation of a blockade of all Southern ports. This ended the Northern hope of treating the conflict as an insurrection, rather than as a war. Blockade meant visit and search; but there could be no visit and search, except in time of war. The immediate effect of the naval blockade was to cause Britain, France and other European powers to declare their neutrality. Recognition of Confederate belligerency constituted an ominous step in the direction of recognizing the Confederacy's independence. It was Adams' assignment to prevent the second step from being taken and to see that British neutrality was strictly observed. To accomplish this during the two years when Lee's Confederates were outmaneuvering and often outfighting the numerically superior Union forces was no mean task.

The Confederate leadership was well aware of the crucial importance of Britain's position, operating throughout the war a highly skillful propaganda agency in London. Henry Hotze published *The Index,* currently setting forth the Confederate

* The North claimed that the South, by firing the first shots, brought on the war and, for many years, attributed this action to a conspiracy of Southern leaders. The South claimed that Lincoln had deliberately provoked the attack and forced the South to assume the role of the aggressor by attempting to re-provision Fort Sumter. These superficial views of the causes of the conflict were later revised by both sides. For an admirable analysis of the various historical interpretations of the origin and meaning of the conflict, see Thomas J. Pressly's *Americans Interpret Their Civil War* (Princeton, 1954).

position, while James Williams wrote and published a contemporary history of the conflict. To back up propaganda with diplomacy, Davis sent the veteran, John Slidell, and John M. Mason of Virginia through the blockade to Nassau, where they embarked for England on the British ship *Trent*. Having learned of this mission, a Union warship ran down the *Trent*, halted it and took off the two diplomats. This produced a crisis which might readily have resulted in a British declaration of war. Britain delivered an ultimatum, demanding the return of the two diplomats and actually prepared troops for embarkation. In spite of the public enthusiasm over the capture, Seward, even before the receipt of the British ultimatum, came to the conclusion that a mistake had been made and so advised Lincoln. He replied to the British note with a somewhat farfetched argument, holding that the persons of the emissaries were contraband but, having thus saved face, agreed to their return.*

A second and even more serious crisis arose over the construction in British shipyards of Confederate cruisers. A former officer of the United States Navy, Captain James D. Bulloch, managed to get to England and to arrange, with the advice of British legal authorities, for the construction of two Confederate cruisers. The British legal officers held that, while the building *and equipping* of Confederate warships in Britain would constitute a breach of neutrality, there was nothing to prevent such ships from being constructed in British shipyards, provided that they were equipped for war elsewhere than in Great Britain and by others than the ship constructors. Following this plan, Bulloch had the *Florida* built as the *Oreto*. When completed, she slipped away to Nassau and was there fitted out as a Confederate war vessel.†

Adams, learning of the procedure used with regard to the *Florida* and being appraised of the fact that a second vessel was being built, protested to Lord Russell. The reply was evasive and, shortly thereafter, the *Enrica* slipped away to the Azores

---

* Charles F. Adams, *The Trent Affair* (Boston, 1912); also H. W. Temple, "Seward," in *American Secretaries of State*, Vol. VI (Knopf, 1928).

† J. D. Bulloch, *Secret Service—How the Confederate Cruisers Were Equipped*, 1884.

where she became the Confederate cruiser *Alabama*. Both vessels did great damage to Union shipping. Worse than the damage, however, was the intimidating effect of Confederate privateering upon the American carrying trade. In 1860, 66.5% of 2,379,396 tons of American trade was carried in American bottoms; whereas, in 1865, only 27.2% of 1,518,350 tons was carried in vessels flying the American flag.*

The most critical part of the British ship-building affair concerned the construction of two iron-clad vessels equipped with rams. It was not until after the tide of war had turned at Gettysburg, in 1863, that Adams was finally able to force the British government to seize these two vessels. The danger they represented to the wooden ships of the United States Navy was very serious. The first such ironclad, the *Merrimac,* built by the Confederates, had struck terror into Northern hearts at the beginning of the Peninsula Campaign, when Union shot bounced harmlessly off her plated sides, and when only the fortunate existence of the *Monitor*—a much smaller, coast-defense Union ironclad—had saved McClellan's transports from disaster. It was not until Adams made his famous statement to Lord Russell, threatening war if the two ironclads were permitted to escape, that the Palmerston government took action.†

Although the British government was far from friendly to the Union, it did pursue a policy of neutrality which was, in one respect at least, helpful to the Union cause. The Union blockade was far from effective. Under the rules of war adopted by the European nations in the Paris Declaration of 1856 (which the United States had refused to sign), a belligerent blockade must be effectively imposed in order to be respected by neutrals. The United States itself had frequently protested the various "paper blockades" of the Napoleonic wars. During the Civil War, the Union discovered a vital interest in having its blockade recognized, no matter how ineffective it might be. In respecting the paper blockade, Britain pursued a typically far-sighted policy, realizing that the precedent thereby estab-

* Figures cited by Samuel F. Bemis, *History of American Diplomacy, op. cit.,* page 381. See also W. L. Marvin, *The American Merchant Marine,* 1902, pages 284, 353.

† "It would be superfluous to point out to your Lordship that this is war."

lished might some day serve her own vital interests (as, indeed, it did in 1914.)*

One other factor may have helped the Union to prevent British recognition of the Confederacy during the first two years of the struggle. Had it not been for the accident that British warehouses were overstocked with American cotton in 1860, the desperate need for that raw material might have exercised a disastrous influence. As it turned out, the South's huge exports during the period immediately preceding the outbreak of hostilities deprived it of its most powerful diplomatic weapon.† By the time the existing stocks had been used up, cotton planting had begun in India and Egypt and the tide of war had turned in favor of the North. Even so, there was an almost complete stoppage and mass unemployment in Lancashire, which—had it come earlier—might have changed the course of events.

So far as relations with Great Britain were concerned, the Lincoln-Seward policy, ably assisted by Charles Francis Adams, was about as successful as might have been hoped. The only serious loss was to American shipping. Recognition of the Confederacy was avoided and, with it, the danger of foreign intervention.

The fate of the Monroe Doctrine during the Civil War was another story.

Polk's war and the aggressive filibustering of the Pierce and Buchanan administrations had alienated Mexican sentiment. The country was in a state of anarchy which invited intervention, even if no Mexican faction had existed which was actually prepared to welcome foreign assistance in restoring law and order. The fact was, however, that the eyes of Mexican conservatives had turned to Europe for protection and that José de Hidalgo, leader of the conservatives, was eager for intervention and the establishment of a Catholic monarchy. The situation presented an almost irresistible opportunity for Napoleon III.

---

* James P. Baxter, 3rd, *Some British Opinions as to Neutral Rights, 1861-1865* (American Historical Society, 1928-1929).

† There is some question whether, by 1861, the importance of Northern wheat to England had not already reached proportions which might have offset the pull of Southern cotton. The available figures do not shed much light upon this subject.

French relations with Britain had been cemented through the successful joint venture in the Crimea. Spain would be only too glad of an excuse to attempt the re-establishment of a foothold in Central America. Napoleon dallied with the idea of placing a Spanish prince upon the throne of a new Central American empire.

The murder of the English consul in Taxco provided the excuse for what began as joint Anglo-French intervention. Spain lost interest in the affair when Napoleon decided, contrary to his implied promise, to make Maximilian, brother of the Austrian Emperor Franz Josef, the ruler of the new empire. Instead of participating in the Mexican adventure, the Spanish government decided to concentrate upon the reconquest of Santo Domingo and Peru. When the Mexican government of President Juárez refused to be intimidated by the Hidalgo conspiracy, and the French moved to conquer the country by force, the British withdrew from the enterprise. Some 28,000 French troops plus an Austro-Belgian legion (Maximilian's wife was the daughter of King Leopold I of Belgium) fought their way to the Mexican capital. There the French commander convened a hand-picked "Council of Notables" and, without even the semblance of popular approval, caused this body to invite the Archduke Maximilian and the Archduchess Carlotta to become Emperor and Empress of Mexico.

Before leaving for his new empire in 1864, Maximilian signed with Napoleon III the Convention of Miramar, obligating the Mexican empire to repay to France 270,000,000 francs to cover the cost of the conquest and, in addition, to defray the costs of maintaining a permanent French garrison, to be reduced gradually to 20,000 men. In a secret treaty, as deceitful as his earlier promise to Spain, Napoleon undertook to sustain Maximilian in power, no matter what might transpire in Europe.

Maximilian apparently entertained dreams of an empire vastly exceeding the confines of the former Mexican republic. He hoped not only to extend his domain through Central America but to acquire a dominant position in the southern continent. One of his projects was to contract a dynastic alliance with the Emperor of Brazil.

Meanwhile, Spain sent one expeditionary force to recapture

Santo Domingo and another to re-establish Spanish control in Peru. The latter effort brought the Spaniards into war with Peru, Chile, Ecuador and Bolivia.

The end of the Civil War found the Monroe Doctrine torn to shreds, with a European-sponsored monarchy established on the very doorstep of the United States, supported by French bayonets and recognized as legitimate by Britain and the other major European powers. With their hands tied by the internal conflict, Lincoln and Seward could do nothing more than issue a series of protests, while the Congress passed resolutions demanding explanations from the European intruders.

This was the situation, until Lee's surrender at Appomattox Courthouse on April 9, 1865. A week later, Lincoln was assassinated. The decision whether to enforce the Monroe Doctrine, if necessary by war, or to abandon it altogether was left to the administration of President Andrew Johnson. Fortunately for the United States, events in Europe were once more to rescue the American government from a difficult dilemma.

CHAPTER ELEVEN

"Reconstruction" and Postwar Diplomacy (1865 – 1869)

THE DETAILS of the postwar "reconstruction" of the South are not strictly relevant to this study, but some understanding of this tragedy is necessary to a comprehension of its effects upon the position of the United States in the world. The fact that "reconstruction" resulted in a one-party, white-supremacy rule in the South—that the Negro slaves became "free," but free only as second-class citizens—and that the difficult problem of race relations remained unsolved within the United States—left the nation burdened with a handicap which retarded its development as a great democracy and impaired its prestige and influence abroad.

It is difficult to say whether this unhappy outcome was due primarily to Southern habits of mind which had, by 1865, become ineradicable, or to the lack of understanding, impatience and economic rapacity of Northern leadership. A good case can be made for either side of the argument. The one thing which is clear is that Lincoln's leadership was sadly missed during the crucial years when his patience and broad sympathy would, without doubt, have exercised a restraining influence upon the extremists in both sections of the country.

In many respects, a fratricidal war leaves deeper psychological scars than a war against a foreign nation. It was precisely in the healing of such wounds—in the reconversion of sibling hatred into brotherly love—that Lincoln's fatherly compassion was most sorely missed. But, apart from this aspect of the postwar problem, and even had there existed the best of goodwill on both sides, the re-unification of the nation presented political and economic difficulties which could scarcely be surmounted without long-lasting strains and tensions.

Apart from the psychological trauma inflicted upon the whole nation by the experience of fratricidal conflict, the Civil War also affected the orientation of sentiment in both North and South toward foreign policy.

The South, with its clear economic interest in free trade, its population descended chiefly from the original English-speaking settlers and its tradition of being less anti-British than the North, even in colonial days, came out of the war with its pro-British leanings greatly strengthened. In future, so long as American foreign policy marched hand in hand with British policy, the South would be internationalist- and even interventionist-minded. Moreover, perhaps because of its gallant record in defeat—and perhaps for other reasons *—the South would be less pacifist and more war-minded than the North.

* It is tempting to speculate whether the warlike proclivities of the Old South derived in part from the fact that the postwar Southern leadership re-established itself by violent and extra-legal means and that Southern minds were therefore conditioned to accepting and even welcoming the use of force as an instrument of national policy.

In the Northeast, the Civil War strengthened the traditional anti-British sentiments. The Germans in the Middle West were a potential anti-British element, whenever Anglo-American policy might be hostile to Germany. The Irish in the big cities were passionately anti-British in all circumstances. In addition, the many nationality groups introduced by immigration produced a less homogeneous picture than that of the South. All in all, the North came out of the war with an orientation toward pacifism (having achieved what it wanted) and anti-British sentiments which combined—especially in the Middle West— to make it tend toward isolationism.

Since the stronghold of the Democratic Party was destined to lie in the South and Republican strength to center in the Middle West, the Democratic Party was weighted toward internationalism and the Republican Party toward isolationism.

The end of the war left the nation's political unity preserved, but with its two parts in such wholly different circumstances that practical unification presented almost insuperable difficulties. It was not just that one part was war-ravaged, exhausted and impoverished while the other had actually grown stronger during the conflict. On both sides the cost in casualties and material sacrifice had been stupendous,* but the two separate economies which had borne the costs were qualitatively as well as quantitatively as disparate as, let us say, the economies of Canada and Cuba are today.

The war temporarily deprived the South of one of the two essentials to its existence—namely, a market for its cotton, rice, sugar and tobacco. The peace deprived it permanently of the slave labor by means of which its cash crops had been produced. Emancipation destroyed the property and the social status of the ruling group and left some 4,000,000 suddenly-freed slaves homeless and without a place in society. What were the freedmen to do? Were they to go on picking cotton and cultivating the fields for wages? Were they to be given land of their own? Or were they to be exported back to Africa or resettled in other countries or on western land belonging to the United States?

* Total casualties were between 750,000 and 1,000,000 killed. The cost to the South is estimated at about $3,000,000,000; that of the North, including reconstruction, at about $5,000,000,000.

If the South was to do without Negroes, could and would Southern whites work the fields? And—if the Negroes were to remain in the South—what if some of the former field hands wished to acquire farms of their own, or to become carpenters or bricklayers or storekeepers? Would Negroes and white men work side by side in the fields or in the building of houses or in the corner store? Were freed Negroes and whites to become members of the same community, or were they to live in separate communities, each with its own schools, churches, courts and civic organization?

Few Southerners and, for that matter, few Northerners believed in their hearts that all men, irrespective of race and color, had been created equal. The belief that white men were racially and biologically superior to Negroes and Indians was deeply rooted in the past. In the South, this belief had served as the moral rationalization for a whole system of status and property rights based upon the institution of Negro slavery. The racial issue had become as important as the issue of slavery itself. Abolition, imposed by military defeat, left the Southern leadership disinherited and, to a large extent, discredited, transferring political power from the former elite to the masses, where Negroes, wholly unprepared for the responsibilities of citizenship, held the potential balance of power.

The South came to the end of the war bankrupt, exhausted, without either the tools or the capital required for reconstruction, and with a racial problem which seemed all but insoluble. It was to be expected that, in these circumstances, the remains of the Southern aristocracy would be sullenly resentful and anxious to repossess itself of political power; that the suddenly freed Negroes would present an unstable and unpredictable element; and that fear of being politically overpowered by the Negroes would make the "poor whites" susceptible to reactionary leadership exploiting racial prejudice to regain power. In addition, a people fresh from a fratricidal war which had sanctioned and exalted violence—as all wars do—was perhaps preconditioned to seek its ends by taking the law into its own hands.

In the North, the same basic factors which, before the war, had pushed the free states ahead of the South continued to operate and were, in some respects, magnified by the conflict. With the decline of ocean commerce, New England capital went into manufacturing. Throughout the North, old and new factories were working full time not only to supply uniforms, arms and munitions to a million men in the field but also to meet the demands of a fully employed civilian population. Machines and labor-saving devices were rapidly developed. Strategic needs stimulated the construction or reconstruction of roads and railroads. Farmers were prosperous, with women and children working in the fields in place of the men serving in the armed forces. Harvesting machinery vastly increased the productivity of farm labor and enabled the Middle West to raise an ever-increasing surplus crop of grain for export. Whereas, before the war, much of the trade of the Middle West had flowed south to New Orleans, all of this traffic now ran east and west over the new railroads which supplemented the Erie Canal. Immigrant labor was rapidly absorbed and full employment steadily increased consumer purchasing power.

The only serious offset to Northern prosperity during the war was the unstable currency produced by the huge government expenditures. The Treasury was forced to suspend specie redemption of legal tender notes which then became fiat money without metallic backing. The $449,000,000 "greenbacks" issued during the war depreciated at an increasing rate in terms of gold and in purchasing power, at one time reaching a low of less than forty cents to the dollar. In spite of increased tariffs and heavy internal taxation, the interest-bearing public debt rose from about $65,000,000 in 1860 to $2,332,000,000 in 1866.*

The problem of reintegrating the North and the South in a single economic entity was like that of merging a bankrupt

* After the war, the debt was rapidly reduced by the retention of wartime taxes and tariff duties so that, by 1888, it stood at less than $1,000,000,000. The "greenbacks" remained outstanding, not because it was impossible to retire them, but because their retirement became a political issue. During the war, a major step toward the creation of a sound currency had been taken through the enactment of the National Bank Act of 1863, authorizing the establishment of banks under Federal charter and giving them the right to issue their bank-notes against holdings of government securities. State-bank paper money was, to all intents and purposes, taxed out of existence.

enterprise in need of total reorganization with a prosperous, going concern.

What would be the proper function of the Federal government in this complicated undertaking? To what extent would it be able to act "with malice toward none, with charity for all?" Who would determine the nature of Southern reconstruction? Would the people as a whole, acting through the Federal government, help the South to find its own way toward a better future, or would a Northern-controlled Federal government seek to impose a dictated social and economic reorganization?

Before his assassination, Lincoln had gone far toward restraining the Northern Congress from vengeful or dictatorial action. After the passage of the 13th Amendment, abolishing slavery, he had said: "If we are wise and discreet, we shall reanimate the states and get their governments in successful operation, with order prevailing and the Union re-established before Congress comes together in December" (1865). Had Lincoln lived, his prediction might well have come true.

Unhappily, Andrew Johnson was a man peculiarly ill-suited to inherit the burden of Lincoln's unfinished task. Until he had entered Tennessee politics as a Jacksonian Democrat in 1828, Johnson had been a tailor. His burning resentment against wealth and privilege had made him an effective vote-getter in local, state and national politics. In Congress from 1843 to 1853, he had served in the same House with Lincoln, supporting the Mexican War, which Lincoln opposed, and differing with Lincoln also over western land policy. Later in the Senate—at the time of the Lincoln-Douglas debates over the extension of slavery—he had stood with Douglas for "Squatter Sovereignty" but, when secession became an issue, he—like Douglas—fought valiantly to hold his state of Tennessee for the Union. Douglas' death left him as the leading "War Democrat." As such, he was nominated on the "Union ticket" of 1864.

Johnson's neurotic self-consciousness of his lowly origin and his grudge against society made his behavior compulsive and irrational. Ordinarily courteous, he would occasionally burst into fits of brutal personal invective which lost him the respect of his friends and incurred the vicious hatred of his enemies.

His Inaugural Address was a sad exhibition of drunken mor-
bidity. His Proclamation of Amnesty, based upon Lincoln's
general ideas of conciliation, excluded "all persons who have
voluntarily participated in said rebellion and the estimated
value of whose taxable property is over twenty thousand dollars." This clause, inspired by Johnson's hatred of the aristocracy, infuriated the Southern leadership. Where Lincoln would
have restrained the hot-heads on both sides, Johnson inflamed
extremist sentiments both in the South and in the Northern
Republican leadership.

The Congress with which Johnson had to deal was controlled
by radical Republicans who wished to treat the South as a
conquered enemy, using the power of military government to
insure the enfranchisement of the Negroes, the disenfranchise-
ment of the Southern leadership and the election of Republican-controlled state legislatures. Johnson shared Lincoln's view
that the seceded states had never lawfully left the Union and
were not to be considered as conquered enemy territory. The
demands he made upon those states which had not already
complied with Lincoln's requirements for re-admission were
essentially the same as those set by Lincoln. These included
ratification of the 13th Amendment, the adoption of state constitutions prohibiting slavery and the repudiation of all debts
contracted in support of the movement for secession.

Congress, however, refused to admit the states which had
complied with these requirements, setting up a joint committee
on reconstruction to determine the conditions of re-admission.
In June, 1866, the committee declared that the Southern states
must ratify the 14th Amendment providing for the enfranchisement of freed slaves with the full rights of citizenship. Johnson
had vetoed the Civil Rights Act, which preceded the 14th
Amendment, on the grounds that its provisions invaded the
rights of the individual states, but his veto had been overridden.
The whole issue was put up to the electorate in the Congressional elections of 1866.

In seeking to draw the Democrats to his side and to bring
about the election of a more moderate Congress, Johnson took
an active part in the campaign; his speeches, however, were so

intemperate and his attacks upon his enemies so vituperative that his intervention backfired. The new Congress was even more firmly controlled by the radical Republicans than its predecessor.

The radical control was strengthened by events in the South. Companies of white militia were formed to keep the restless Negroes in order. "Black Codes" and peonage laws were passed and put into effect which limited the rights of Negroes and treated them as a special dependent class in the population. Mississippi denied them the right to own land. South Carolina restricted them to husbandry or service in homes or on farms.

In 1867, Congress repudiated Johnson's moderate program and adopted a plan of its own which provided for the re-institution of military government, the forced enfranchisement of the Negroes, the election of Republican-Negro-controlled legislatures and the ratification of the 14th Amendment. By the end of 1868, the Southern states had by these coercive means been restored to the Union.

Johnson's opposition to this extremist program was vain but so irritating to the radicals that they sought to deprive him of power over the civil service and the armed forces. When Johnson, in violation of the new Tenure Act, dismissed his disloyal Secretary of War without obtaining the advice and consent of the Senate, the House launched impeachment proceedings and Johnson narrowly escaped conviction by a two-thirds vote of the Senate. For the rest of his term, Johnson was to all intents and purposes impotent. Whatever his shortcomings, it was an ironical twist of history that permitted a President noteworthy for his strict devotion to the Constitution to be threatened with impeachment by a Congress distinguished for its disregard of constitutional procedures.

The price paid for victory by the Republican extremists was the ultimate creation of a "Solid South" in which, for generations, the Republican party would exist in name only—in which the Constitution would be flouted by poll-tax and intimidation and in which "white supremacy" would be enforced by hooded night-riders and lynch law. Not only the Negroes but the whole Southern population would pay the price of arrested democratic development; and not only the South but the whole nation would be polluted by the foul stain of racial discrimination. Almost a century was to elapse before the full impact of the tragic failure of reconstruction would make itself felt by crippling United States foreign policy at a time of great crisis —the crisis of emerging nationalism among the submerged colored peoples of Asia, Africa and the Middle East.

The Civil War preserved the Union, abolished slavery and disestablished Southern planter control of Congress; but the failure of reconstruction left the racial issue unsolved, while postwar developments in the victorious North and West changed what might have been the victory of free farmers and free workers into the victory of Northern monopoly capitalism.*

Nation-wide preoccupation with domestic affairs during the immediate postwar period left foreign policy almost entirely in the hands of Secretary Seward, whose expansionist aims were left-overs from the era of Manifest Destiny and found little popular support, once the hemisphere was cleared of foreign intervention.

The first and most important matter to get straightened out was that of Mexico. After the Confederate surrender, Seward's remonstrances took on an entirely different tone. On November 6, 1865, he declared that "the presence and operations of a French army in Mexico, and its maintenance of an authority there, resting upon force and not the free will of the Mexican people" was "a cause of serious concern to the United States." A month later, in his annual message to Congress, President Johnson gave additional force to this pronouncement by stating: "We should regard it as a great calamity to ourselves, to the cause of good government and to the peace of the world, should any European power challenge the American people, as it were, to the defense of republicanism against

* Thos. J. Pressly, in *op. cit.*, gives an excellent summary of the many interpretations of the Civil War formulated by historians of North and South and Middle West. Some consider the conflict irrepressible; others conclude that it might have been avoided. Some consider its basic causes moral, some incline toward a political interpretation, and still others—notably Charles A. Beard—see the conflict as motivated primarily by economic factors.

foreign interference." Seward followed this up with increasingly sharp notes, finally demanding, in February, 1866, that a time limit be set for the evacuation of French forces.

Meanwhile, American army leaders, with considerable popular support, were demanding permission to drive the French out by force. Grant had General Sheridan with 50,000 veterans in Texas; General Schofield was on leave in Mexico, helping the Juárez government to reorganize its forces. Seward, however, realized that such measures would probably not be necessary. Bismarck had hoodwinked Napoleon III into remaining neutral while he fought successful wars first against Denmark and then against Austria. After crushing Franz Josef's forces at Sadowa, he was welding "in blood and iron" the North German Confederation which would soon make Prussia an ominously rising power. Seeking to slow down the militarists and to accelerate a diplomatic victory, Seward sent General Schofield to Paris to inform Napoleon that the United States had reached the end of its forbearance. The Empress Carlotta went on a frantic mission to seek help from Napoleon and from the Vatican, but in the face of the Prussian threat, the treacherous French ruler had already decided to abandon Maximilian to his fate. Maximilian's attempt to recruit an Austrian legion was nipped in the bud by Seward's prompt and forcible protest. In the spring of 1867, the last French contingents left Mexico, the empire collapsed and Maximilian went to his death before a firing squad at Querétaro.

The Spanish attempt to reconquer Santo Domingo had already ended in failure. Impressed by the firmness of Seward's diplomacy in the Mexican affair, Spain heeded the warning and gradually withdrew from its war with Peru. The integrity of the Monroe Doctrine was restored—in part by Seward's firm diplomacy, in part by events in Europe, but most of all by the sacrifices which the American people had made to preserve the Union.

Seward was now free to pursue his dreams of expansion, provided that he could find backing from Congress and the people. The only items on his ambitious program for which he obtained support were the seizure of Midway Island, and the purchase of Alaska.

Russia had for some time been willing, if not anxious, to dispose of Alaska to the United States, primarily in order to prevent this distant and indefensible possession from falling into the hands of Britain. The Crimean War had intensified Russian apprehensions and strengthened the traditional Russian policy of making the United States a counterweight to Britain as a world power. When the Civil War began, the preliminary negotiations had to be abandoned but, early in 1867, the Russian minister was instructed to ascertain whether the United States would be interested in reviving the discussion. Seward eagerly seized upon the opportunity to purchase Alaska for $7,200,000. The treaty, signed on March 30, 1867, was promptly ratified by the Senate but the House took some time to vote the necessary funds. Russia did not wait for payment to be made; Alaska was transferred to American ownership on October 18, 1867, although the appropriation bill did not pass the House until the following July. The purchase was of little interest to the people as a whole but was backed by those leaders in Congress who viewed the acquisition of Alaska as a step toward driving Britain from the North American continent. This was especially the attitude of Charles Sumner, the increasingly powerful chairman of the Senate Foreign Relations Committee. Seward himself did not share this view; he saw Alaska as a gateway to Asia and followed up the purchase with the seizure of the uninhabited Midway Islands and a proposal to annex Hawaii. Here again, as in the Pierce-Buchanan period, the existence of a powerful navy left over from the war provided an added impulse to overseas expansion. The Senate, however, balked Seward's plans for Hawaii, refusing to ratify the reciprocity treaty which he had negotiated as a first step toward annexation.

In the Caribbean, none of Seward's plans came to fruition. Congress displayed no interest in acquiring the Virgin Islands, the Dominican Republic, or even the harbor of Samaná Bay. Seward's treaties, though ratified by the counter-parties, were allowed to lapse. The House expressed widespread feeling against further expansion in a resolution stating that "in the present financial condition of the country, any further purchases of territory are inexpedient, and this House will hold itself under no obligation to vote money to pay for any such purchases unless there is greater necessity for them than now exists."

The country was in no mood for further expansion; it had troubles enough at home. The pressures for gaining control of the Caribbean and for pushing westward across the Pacific had not yet accumulated.

PART FOUR

The Imperialism of Runaway Free Enterprise

CHAPTER TWELVE

Build-up for Aggression
(1869–1884)

THE CIVIL WAR had submerged most of the issues which had been at stake in the Jacksonian revolution. By the time the war was over, most of the old leaders, both radical and conservative, were dead. The old conflict between people and property—between political democracy and the anti-democratic trends inherent in capitalism and in the dawning age of the machine—had become obscured by the issue of slavery, and had then been forgotten altogether in the struggle to break or preserve the Union. The lines between the "haves" and the "have-nots" became blurred in both North and South. The workingman and the banker stood shoulder to shoulder in defense of the Union. The "poor white" and the rich planter fought side by side for Southern independence.

Yet the problems raised by the industrial revolution, by the growth of monopoly and by the concentration of wealth and power had not been solved; on the contrary, most of them had become more acute during the conflict. It had become more than ever necessary to devise fiscal and monetary policies which would provide adequate and sound credit for the healthy expansion of agriculture and small business; to create a satisfactory method of issuing and controlling the issue of paper money in such a manner as to keep its value stable in terms of gold; and to handle the public debt in such a way as to work off the cost of the war without creating too violent a contraction of the credit structure. The victory of the North had permanently locked the South into a tariff-protected economy; it was more than ever necessary to re-examine the basic premises of the high-tariff policy, not only in justice to the South and the agrarian West, but in view of the rapidly changing nature of American industry.

The basic problems raised by the industrial revolution, and by the development of transportation and of rapid means of communication were world-wide, becoming acute, as might be expected, in those parts of the world where technology developed most rapidly. In Europe, the earlier and more concentrated development of industry and monopoly capitalism, taking place in a thickly settled area without open frontiers for expansion, brought about a drive for colonial expansion and an internal class conflict. The degradation of the working class into an industrial proletariat by the machine age and by the rise of mercantilist capitalism gave birth to socialist theory. Karl Marx and Friedrich Engels were busily translating the earlier Utopian forms of socialist thought into a doctrine of economic determinism. A serious doubt had been raised in European minds as to whether an economic system based upon the pursuit of private profit was actually compatible with a social system based upon a concept of justice and the equal rights of all individuals.

In the United States, the open frontier and the reformation of conservatism prevented the development of a conscious class conflict; American society was fluid by comparison with that of Europe. On the other hand, the relatively vast amount of room available for expansion and development within the United States postponed—though it did not prevent—the accumulation of expansionist pressures.

To understand how these internal pressures accumulated to the point of external explosion, it is necessary to consider the purely internal and characteristically American developments which took place in the latter part of the nineteenth century. The period which began with the end of the Civil War was one in which the great American experiment in democracy was subjected to severe strains.

The establishment of one-party, white-supremacy rule throughout the Old South imposed one such strain. Another was created by the influx of Europeans which brought to this country large numbers of people unfamiliar with the democratic processes and accustomed to playing a passive role in a more or less static society. Those who settled in the large cities tended to become an easy prey for demagogues and corrupt politicians; their votes became exceedingly important but were easily captured wholesale. Those who settled in the Middle West tended to form voting blocs according to their national origins; these, too, were susceptible to wholesale capture. The belief that the people were capable of governing themselves wisely and well rested upon the assumption that "the people" meant the aggregate of thinking individuals—not majority decision by floating blocs whose votes could easily be swung by mass appeal.

Even the principles of Jeffersonian democracy became obscured during this period. The states-rights principle, deriving from the painful achievement of freedom through long struggle against monarchical tyranny, had lost its relevance in the face of new and wholly different threats to freedom. It had become an anachronism in the face of an interlocking, nation-wide economy. Calhoun, in his later days, had perceived that regions rather than states had become significant. Even Jefferson himself had recognized that, where the national interest was involved, the national government must be paramount.

Slavery and the Civil War had obscured the need for restating the nation's philosophy in terms of the newly arisen conditions. Instead of attempting a conscious re-interpretation of Jeffersonianism, the political leaders of the post-Civil War period used it as politicians have frequently used the Bible— to prove by quoting one passage or another that whatever they did or sought to do had the sanction of accepted authority. The cross currents of the sectional conflict interrupted the sequence of rational thought which had begun with the Declaration of Independence, breaking up the philosophy upon which the nation had been founded into a series of separate dogmas or doctrines, to be quoted as support for interests and actions wholly out of key with the Jeffersonian concept of a good society.

Thus, the Republican Party—because it had freed the slaves —was able to wrap itself in the mantle of Jeffersonianism, even though it rapidly became the party of the propertied interests. With the Democratic Party impotent on the national scene, the rapidly rising forces of monopoly capitalism had the field almost entirely to themselves. At intervals reform movements would get under way in protest against the increasing selfishness and corruption of the dominant party, but most of the time, because the Democrats were saddled with the reactionary South, the Republican leaders needed only to wave the bloody shirt of 1861-1865 to recapture their position as the "party of freedom."

To a very large extent the pause in the philosophical development of American society was due to the fabulous material progress of the post-Civil War era. Money could be made so easily and so fast by so many that, to most Americans, there seemed little reason to question the validity of the premises upon which this vast growth was predicated. Those who were left behind had the hope of catching up; penniless prospectors could, and did, suddenly hit pay-dirt. Political ward-heelers could, and did, rise to extraordinary power.

This was the era of railroad building, of the discovery of the vast mineral wealth which lay beneath the soil, of unheard-of industrial growth and agricultural development.* It was also the era of wild speculation in stock promotions, of the building of the great fortunes of the American dynasties of wealth—and the era of recurring financial panics.

During this incredible expansion the average citizen was almost unaware of the threat of monopoly, very largely because this was also the era of the wildest cut-throat competition. Subsidized by land-grants and financed largely by foreign loans, the railways proliferated in competitive systems for many of which, later on, there would prove to be no economic justification. To some extent the same thing was true of industry;

---

* In 1860 there were about 30,000 miles of railroad track in the United States. In 1880 there were 90,000 miles.

In 1860 the value of manufactures produced in the United States was just under $2,000,000,000. In 1894 it was almost $9,500,000,000. During this period the number of manufacturing establishments tripled, the number of wage-earners quadrupled and capital invested in manufacturing multiplied about ninefold.

Before the Civil War it took four and a half hours of human labor to produce one bushel of corn. In 1895 the same four and a half hours produced seven bushels. From 1860 to 1863 wheat exports rose from 17,000,000 bushels to 58,000,000.

competition was so keen in almost every part of the expanding economy that it was scarcely noticeable that most of the competition was actually *for monopoly position,* rather than for the favor of the consumer.

Looking back at this period with the benefit of hindsight, it is easy to perceive why all this feverish and essentially predatory activity could hide under the cloak of Jeffersonian principles. The nation had become predominantly a nation of big businessmen and little businessmen hoping to become big. The businessman wanted only two things from government: to be let alone and to get his share of subsidy or protection. The business community, originally nourished by a strong central government, had now switched to the belief that Jefferson had been right in holding that that government was best which governed least. On the other hand, "the people," who had learned in Jackson's time that a strong government represented their only defense against the concentration of property ownership and power, now tended for the most part to identify their interests with property. While all went well, the propertyless were almost as well satisfied with *laissez-faire* government as the propertied class.

The post-Civil War period was the period of runaway capitalism, of unashamed buccaneering, of dog-eat-dog and devil-take-the-hindmost, and of acquisitiveness unrestrained by moral principle which—had it not been for the extraordinary wealth and space at our disposal—might easily have culminated in violent revolution and counter-revolution. What it did produce was an accumulation of pressures which were soon to drive the nation into a foreign policy of expansion bearing no relation to its true interests and involving commitments out of all proportion to its power.

Measured solely by the economic yardstick, there could be no doubt that the latter part of the nineteenth century was an era of unheard-of progress. But, while the wealth and the productivity of the country grew by leaps and bounds, by far the greatest benefit of this growth accrued to a comparatively small part of the ever-increasing population.

With an abundant supply of unskilled and semi-skilled labor provided by immigration—with women and children as well as men employed in factories—the factory worker was increasingly at the mercy of the employer. Usually, in this era of cut-throat competition, the employer was struggling to stay in business against an encroaching monopoly or else trying to acquire a monopoly position for his own business. In either case, he was likely to give little thought to his employees; his idea would be to hire them as cheaply as possible and to get as much work out of them as possible.

In the face of these conditions, American labor was singularly slow to organize its defense. Mechanics' unions had, to be sure, existed since 1817, but these were not so much unions formed to protect labor from exploitation as guilds organized to maintain craft monopolies for a small number of highly skilled mechanics. During the Jacksonian era there had been a stirring of labor revolt against the new conditions imposed by the industrial revolution. The first mass organization was formed by the Knights of Labor, a somewhat Utopian movement of skilled and unskilled workers with a definite program of reform and a dedication to political action, but without local organizations through which workers might bargain collectively with their employers. It was not until 1886 that modern trade unionism was inaugurated by the American Federation of Labor. Under the leadership of Samuel Gompers, the American Federation of Labor pursued a policy of sticking strictly to the remedying of workers' grievances by collective bargaining, refraining from broad political action other than "backing labor's friends for election and seeking to defeat its enemies."

The farmers of America were far more politically minded, generating most of the movements of political protest during this period. By nature more independent as individual enterprisers and with a more developed sense of proprietorship in land and in the government, the farmers were the ones who suffered the most continual and the most identifiable injustices during the post-Civil War era. Droughts and storms could at any time destroy the fruits of their labors. This was taken for granted. But the men who tilled the soil now found themselves even more at the mercy of a number of other arbitrary and unpredictable forces which infuriated them and spurred them to demand redress from their government.

The post-Civil War farmer was no longer the self-sufficient individual of the earlier days, raising what his family required in the way of fruit, grain and vegetables, with a few cows, pigs and chickens and a wife who made homespun clothes for the family. The farmer had become a specialist, raising a crop which he sold for cash and buying his family's necessities at the country store. Simple tools were no longer sufficient for this kind of farming. The specialized farmer had to buy expensive equipment. In the new get-rich-quick economy, the farmer was left behind. The tariff and internal taxation made the things he had to buy more and more expensive; while the grain elevators or the packing-houses controlled the prices he obtained for his products. If the elevator man said that a farmer's wheat was second-grade and paid for it on that basis, the farmer had no recourse, even though he knew that the elevator man might turn around and sell it as first-grade wheat the next day. This was the double-barreled pinch which kept the farmer poor, no matter how hard he worked; but there were other troubles as well.

Money was unstable. If the farmer borrowed from the bank to buy more land when times were "normal," the bottom was likely to drop out of business leaving him with a debt in dollars that represented many more bushels of wheat than it had when the debt was contracted. If he could not keep up his payments, the interest mounted year by year and eventually the bank's mortgage on his farm would be foreclosed. Freight rates, which so largely determined the value of the farmer's crop, were wholly unpredictable. One year they might go down because the railroad was trying to drive a competitor out of business. The next year they might skyrocket because competition had been eliminated from that particular district and the railroad company was charging "what the traffic would bear" in order to be able to cut rates in some other more competitive area.

The farmers began to get together in local societies, or granges, through which they cooperated in using their votes to obtain redress from the various state legislatures. For a time this procedure was quite successful, until the Supreme Court of the United States held that the Federal courts had the right to decide whether such state laws and regulations were reasonable. This action by the Court turned the agrarian protest into a reform movement. Finding it impossible to obtain redress for their grievances under the existing system, the farmers began to demand public ownership of the railroads, a graduated income tax and a reform of the currency and banking system.

Neither the Republicans in power nor the Democrats in opposition paid much attention to these demands until about 1884. National politics consisted almost entirely of quarrels within the dominant Republican Party.

That there was little change in the mood of the country, so far as foreign expansion was concerned, can be seen from the fate which befell Seward's left-over projects during the Grant administration.

The first item of unfinished business was the treaty with Denmark for the purchase of the Virgin Islands. This had been approved by the Danish Parliament and awaited action by the American Congress. The Senate Foreign Relations Committee recommended the rejection of the project and the treaty failed to be brought up for a Senate vote before the time limit for its ratification expired.

A similar reception was in store for the Dominican projects, even though, in this case, President Grant took a personal interest in bringing them to a successful conclusion. Orville E. Babcock, the President's private secretary, was sent to reopen Seward's negotiations. (This was another instance of a President sending a special emissary to conduct a negotiation without having his appointment confirmed by the Senate, the precedent for which dated back to Washington's administration.) Babcock promptly worked out with President Baez two alternative treaties for consideration; the first provided for outright annexation and the assumption of the Dominican debt of $1,500,000; the second contemplated the purchase of Samaná Bay for the sum of $2,000,000. These tentative Babcock-Baez agreements contained an unusual clause, providing for an undertaking by the President to use his personal influence to carry through one or the other treaty. Grant did his utmost. He sent a naval squadron to protect the Baez government against revolutionary overthrow during the negotiations and then set about winning the support of the key men in the Senate. Here he ran into the unyielding opposition of Charles Sumner, whose Foreign Relations Committee had already killed the Virgin Islands project.

Sumner had risen to ever greater power in the Senate, and to all intents and purposes dominated that body's position on foreign affairs. He had supported Seward's purchase of Alaska as a step toward the acquisition of Canada, but he had consistently opposed any expansion in the Caribbean. Motley, the United States minister at London, had become more an agent for Sumner than for the President and the Department of State, acting as the Senator's mouthpiece in demanding the cession of Canada to extinguish Civil War claims against Britain. When Sumner blocked the Dominican negotiations, Grant decided not to put up with Sumner's domination any longer. First he recalled Motley; then he persuaded the Senate to remove Sumner from the committee chairmanship which he had held since 1861. This did not save the Dominican treaty, but it cleared the decks for Secretary of State Hamilton Fish to negotiate a settlement with Britain.

Sumner had frustrated Secretary Seward's earlier attempts to reach agreement with the British. In a speech before the Senate (in April, 1869) he had built up a case for the cession of Canada by claiming that Britain owed the United States not only $15,-000,000 for the depredations of the British-built Confederate cruisers, but $110,000,000 for damage to the American merchant marine and something like $2,000,000,000 more for the cost of prolonging the war. Such a sum could, so Sumner reasoned, be paid only by ceding Canada. Fish adopted a more reasonable position, seeking only the payment of the direct claims of about $15,000,000 and an expression of regret for having permitted the construction of the cruisers. In addition, he sought final adjudication of the ownership of the San Juan Islands in Puget Sound.

A Joint High Commission settled all these matters in the spring of 1871. The comprehensive Treaty of Washington, thanks to good preparation and careful discussion with the Senate, was promptly ratified by a vote of 50 to 12. Together with the previously ratified Naturalization Treaty of 1870, it provided for amicable adjustment of all outstanding issues between the two countries, completely clearing the decks for the first time in the ninety-five years of American independence.

The most important section of the treaty was that which dealt with the *Alabama* claims. The claims themselves were left to adjudication by a mixed commission, but the treaty laid down a set of rules which were to govern the arbitration. Expressing regret for the "escape" of the Confederate cruisers and the depredations they had committed, the British government agreed that, while the rules now laid down had not existed at the time, nevertheless they should govern the arbitration and the future conduct of both countries as neutrals. These rules provided that a neutral must use due diligence to prevent the construction or equipment within its jurisdiction of vessels which might reasonably be expected to carry on warfare against a friendly power; to prevent the departure of any such vessels from its ports; and to forbid the belligerents to use its ports or waters as a base for naval operations, for the acquisition of military supplies or for the recruitment of manpower.

The ultimate adjudication of all claims resulted in payment by Britain to the United States of $15,500,000, and payment by the United States to Britain of $7,429,819, of which $5,500,-000 constituted payment for a ten-year extension of the fishing rights.

The dispute over the maritime boundary in Puget Sound was referred for arbitration to the German Emperor who ultimately awarded the San Juan Islands to the United States.

In addition, the Washington Treaty provided for reciprocal transit in bond of goods shipped across the territory of either country, for American navigation rights on the St. Lawrence and for British navigation rights on the Yukon, Porcupine and Stikine rivers flowing from Canada through American territory to the Pacific.

The conciliatory attitude of the British government was largely influenced by developments in Europe. Prussia's quick and decisive victory over France, in 1870-1871, the overthrow of Napoleon III, the establishment of the somewhat uncertain Third French Republic and the consolidation of the German states in Bismarck's first *Reich* created an unpredictable European future. In these circumstances, it was important for Brittain to eliminate all causes of friction with the United States.

President Grant's only other foreign policy problem arose out of the Cuban insurrection which began in 1868 and lasted throughout the next ten years. Congress pressed for recognition of Cuban belligerency, but Fish, anxious not to undermine his case against Britain for over-hasty recognition of Confederate belligerency, persuaded Grant to hold off. In 1873, a crisis arose when the Spaniards seized the *Virginius,* a filibustering vessel fraudulently flying the American flag, and executed fifty-three of the passengers and crew. After a sharp ultimatum from the United States, Spain restored the ship, paid an indemnity and promised to punish the responsible officers. Fish was sharply criticized for being satisfied with this arrangement, especially when the promise to punish the guilty officers was not carried out. Considering that the incident occurred in the midst of the severe panic of 1873, when a foreign war might have been politically expedient, Grant and his Secretary of State showed praiseworthy restraint. There was as much justification for war against Spain in 1873 as there was twenty-five years later when that war occurred. Fortunately, internal pressures had not yet accumulated to the point of creating warlike sentiment and there was, as yet, no jingoistic press.

The next move made by Fish in regard to the Cuban affair showed less wisdom. Irked by embargoes, confiscations and the arrest of American citizens accused of participation in the rebellion, Fish instructed the American envoy at London, Caleb Cushing, to obtain British agreement to a joint effort at imposing peace upon Spain and the rebellious island. The British Foreign Secretary, Lord Derby, thought the time "ill-chosen" and the move "premature." This was fortunate, because the American suggestion invited Britain to take an interest in the Western Hemisphere directly conflicting with the Monroe Doctrine.

The Cuban struggle terminated suddenly with the end of the civil war in Spain and the accession to the throne of Alfonso XII. This enabled the new Spanish government to mobilize sufficient force to subdue the exhausted Cubans for another twenty years.

During the administration of President Hayes, westward expansionism began to show itself as an active force. Secretary of State William M. Evarts negotiated a treaty with Samoa resulting in the establishment of a three-power protectorate over the Samoan Islands by the United States, Great Britain and Germany.

More significantly, during the Garfield-Arthur administration, the United States unwittingly reached out to touch the most sensitive nerve in the Far Eastern political complex. For generations, China and Japan had contested control of Korea. More recently, Russia had begun to cast covetous eyes at the warm water harbors of the Korean peninsula, but, under a tacit Chinese protectorate, the "hermit kingdom" had managed to keep itself sealed off and independent. It remained for the United States to disturb this tranquil state of affairs. In 1880, Commodore Schufeldt took an American squadron of warships to Korea and demanded the opening of the country to American trade. At first unsuccessful, Schufeldt managed after two years to obtain a treaty granting access to American traders. The European powers at once sought like concessions, as they had after Perry's opening up of Japan twenty-five years earlier. Although unaware of the implications of its action at the time, the United States set off a chain of events in the Far East which was to lead first to war between China and Japan and then to the Russo-Japanese conflict.

In the same year (1882), President Arthur signed the first anti-immigration legislation enacted by the United States. This resulted from the demands of organized labor in California and marked the first occasion upon which pressure from the labor movement directly influenced foreign policy.

Up to about this time, the United States had shown no interest in the scramble for African colonies which had resulted in the carving up of that vast continent by England, France, Belgium, Portugal and Spain. In 1884, Germany asserted its claim to be considered on equal terms in the partitioning of any remaining free territory, calling a conference at Berlin to determine the disputed future status of the Congo basin. President Arthur and Secretary Frelinghuysen, departing from past American policy, instructed the American minister to Berlin to attend and later authorized him to sign the Berlin Act of 1885, establishing the Congo as a free "International Association." President Arthur's term expired before he had time to submit the Act to the Senate for ratification. Cleveland promptly withdrew the treaty, refusing to let the United States become party to an agreement to preserve "the territorial integrity of distant regions where we have no established interest or control."

CHAPTER THIRTEEN

Reform Derailed
(1885 – 1896)

THE PERIOD OF 1884 to 1896 might have marked the beginning of domestic reform and thus arrested the build-up of explosive pressures, if Grover Cleveland—the first Democrat since James Buchanan to win a national election—had been able to win the allegiance of the radical Western wing of his party. Cleveland's ideas, however, were closer to those of the liberal wing of the Republican Party than to the more radical sentiments of the Western Democrats. In the conduct of foreign relations, Cleveland was opposed to expansion and to any sort of aggressive behavior. At the same time, he possessed courage and exhibited firmness in asserting the just rights of the United States.

On the other hand, Benjamin Harrison, whose single term intervened between the two Cleveland administrations, was an Ohio Republican with traditional conservative views in domestic affairs and an expansionist leaning in foreign policy; he was about as moderate a Republican as Cleveland was a moderate Democrat. Hence the twelve-year period, which might have

arrested runaway free enterprise and the accumulation of explosive pressures, became one of sideways movement, during
which the pressures toward aggression alternately diminished
and re-accumulated.

Fiscal policy, silver and the tariff were the issues which dominated the domestic scene. The Venezuelan dispute, Hawaii and
the Cuban revolt produced the major issues of foreign policy.

The immediate problem faced by Cleveland, when he first
took office in 1885, was how to deal with the mounting annual
surplus of revenues over expenditures. Under the influence of
the business interests, Congress inclined toward keeping the
high tariff and toward making large expenditures for river and
harbor developments and pensions. The western farmers and
some of the workingmen were clamoring for lower excise taxes
and tariffs, a graduated income tax and "cheaper" money.
Cleveland took a firm stand against extravagance and vetoed
several pension bills. (Harrison, then in the Senate, opposed
these vetoes.)

Rejecting the various "cheap money" panaceas, Cleveland
proposed that a Labor Commission be appointed to look into
the workingman's problems. This was rejected by Congress. In
1887, Cleveland succeeded in obtaining passage of the Interstate
Commerce Act creating a Commission empowered to regulate
railroad rates in the public interest and to abolish discrimination and wasteful competition. Although for many years the
Supreme Court failed to interpret this act in such a way as to
make it fully effective, its passage denoted a major landmark in
the struggle to make free enterprise capitalism conform to the
principles of a democratic society, breaking the trail of reform
which was eventually to lead to government regulation of public services and utilities.

Toward the end of his term, Cleveland decided to grapple
with the politically explosive issue of the tariff. The administra-
tion-sponsored Mills Bill was deliberately designed to let in
more foreign goods and to reduce government revenues by approximately $50,000,000 per annum. The Republicans coun-
tered this proposal with a bill which provided for only a
nominal downward revision. The elections of 1888 were fought

chiefly on the issue of these two conflicting tariff proposals and resulted in Cleveland's defeat by Benjamin Harrison.

In foreign affairs, Cleveland's first term was uneventful. Cleveland expressed misgivings over the three-power entanglement in which the United States had become involved in Samoa and repudiated President Arthur's intervention in the affairs of the Congo. When a dispute broke out between Great Britain and Venezuela over the boundary between Venezuela and the old British colony of Guiana, Cleveland offered to mediate. Venezuela was prepared to accept arbitration but the British government rejected the suggestion. Cleveland's defeat in the elections of 1888 left the matter in abeyance during the four years of Harrison's Presidency.

The Harrison administration was notable in the domestic field for three major enactments completed in 1890. These were:

1. The Sherman Anti-Trust Act, aimed at suppressing monopoly. With the Supreme Court more often than not favoring the monopolies, this legislation remained largely ineffective, but, like the Interstate Commerce Act, it marked a milestone in the attempt to curb anti-democratic forces.

2. The Sherman Silver Purchase Act, a makeshift, designed to gain Western votes by raising the price of silver and meeting the agrarian demand for "cheap money." *

3. The McKinley Tariff Act, sponsored by William McKinley, of Ohio, raised the protective tariff rates on goods that could be manufactured in the United States to an all-time high and, for the first time, added protective tariffs on agricultural products. It eliminated the import duty on sugar, offsetting this action by a new subsidy to American sugar producers.

The immediate result of the new tariff was a sharp rise in prices which caused a Democratic landslide in the Congressional elections of 1890. The Democrats, now in control of the House, tried once again to reduce the tariff but were blocked by the Republican-controlled Senate.

---

* The question of silver is somewhat technical but, since it played such an important part in derailing the reform movement, *A Note on the Relation of Silver to the Causes of Discontent in the Latter Part of the 19th Century* has been appended at the end of this chapter.

In foreign affairs, the Presidency of Benjamin Harrison was notable chiefly for a resumption of expansion in the Pacific. Ever since the Reciprocity Treaty negotiated by Secretary of State Fish in 1875, Hawaii had become more and more under American influence. The American business community dominated the legislature and the island economy had become increasingly dependent upon the mainland. When Queen Liliuokalani came to the throne in 1891, she attempted to oust the "outlanders" from control of the legislature and to restore the rapidly dwindling independence of the native kingdom. This brought on a revolt of the "outlanders" and the organization of a rival government with the declared purpose of preparing the islands for annexation by the United States.

The setting was rather similar to that which had led to the annexation of Texas, except that in this case not only American citizens but the United States government openly fostered the annexationist movement. With the full knowledge of Harrison's Secretary of State, John Foster,* the American minister landed Marines, hoisted the American flag and assumed protection of the "outlanders'" insurrectionist government. He reported to Foster: "The Hawaiian pear is now fully ripe and this is the golden hour for the United States to pluck it." The American-protected "outlander" government sent a commission to Washington with which Secretary Foster promptly signed a treaty of annexation. This was on February 14, 1893; before President Harrison was able to rush the treaty through the Senate his term expired.

While the Hawaiian adventure was the outstanding feature of Harrison's foreign policy, his administration also conducted a number of other negotiations. The controversy with Britain over seal fishing in the Bering Sea was satisfactorily settled, as was a minor dispute with Chile. Relations with Germany in Samoa were improved. A number of reciprocity treaties were signed and a Pan-American conference was held at Washington.

A considerable amount of surplus revenue was devoted to naval expansion.

In the elections of 1892, Harrison ran on the Republican

---

* John Foster was the maternal grandfather of John Foster Dulles who, in 1953, became Secretary of State under President Eisenhower.

record and the explicitly stated Republican doctrine that, if legislation made the rich prosperous, prosperity would trickle down to all levels of American society.* Cleveland, nominated by the Democrats on a platform which sought to make tariff reduction the main issue, toned down the tariff plank in his letter of acceptance. Both parties quibbled over the question of "cheap money." The Western and Middle Western farmers, disgusted with the equivocation of the two parties, organized the "People's Party," soon to become known as the Populist, and nominated James Weaver for the Presidency. In many of the farming states, the Populists succeeded in putting their local candidates into office. Weaver polled over one million votes for the Presidency, but not enough in any one state to carry it. The national election returned Cleveland to the White House and gave the Democrats control of both Houses of Congress.

One of Cleveland's first acts upon returning to the Presidency was to withdraw Foster's Hawaiian treaty from the Senate. At first, Cleveland endeavored to undo the "outlanders'" revolution and to restore the Queen to power, provided that she would grant amnesty to the conspirators. This the Queen refused to do. The "outlanders," on their part, refused to permit a return of native rule and set up a republic with a constitution expressly authorizing annexation to the United States at the proper moment. Embarrassed by the obvious intention of the "outlanders" to await the return of a Republican to the White House, Cleveland turned the whole matter over to Congress.†

During his second term, Cleveland renewed his efforts to mediate the Venezuelan dispute. Cleveland held that, while the British colony had existed prior to the declaration of the Monroe Doctrine, Britain was now seeking to increase its territory by about 40% at the expense of the neighboring republic. Secretary Olney—in July, 1895—demanded to know whether Britain would or would not arbitrate a matter which, he said, involved principles which had become "a doctrine of American

---

* The survival of this philosophy in the next century was illustrated by Defense Secretary Wilson's statement, in 1952, that "What's good for General Motors is good for the country."

† *Foreign Relations of the United States 1894*, Appendix II, House Executive Document 1, 53d Congress, 3d Session (Government Printing Office, 1895).

public law." He went on to say: "Today the United States is practically sovereign on this continent, and its fiat is law upon the subjects to which it confines its interposition." Lord Salisbury, the British foreign minister, took his time in replying to this rather arrogant message, eventually declaring, in November, 1895, that, while Britain accepted the non-colonization principle of the Monroe Doctrine, the principle did not apply in the Venezuelan dispute and that the United States had no right in law or reason to impose arbitration.

Cleveland refused to accept this definition of American rights by a foreign power. In a special message to Congress, he requested authorization to appoint an investigatory commission and declared, in rather carefully qualified language, that it would be the duty of the United States to resist, by every means in its power, the appropriation by Great Britain of any rights or lands which due investigation might establish as rightfully belonging to Venezuela. Unfriendly critics have expressed the opinion that this departure from Cleveland's conciliatory and non-aggressive foreign policy was inspired by domestic considerations. On the other hand, Cleveland's authoritative biographer, Professor A. Nevins, accepts Cleveland's own privately given explanation that he was concerned solely about the Monroe Doctrine and felt sure that Britain would eventually accept arbitration.

There was good reason for Cleveland's confidence. The situation in Europe had grown increasingly tense ever since Germany had become a united and militarily powerful nation. So long as William II retained Bismarck as his Chancellor, the new Germany pursued a cautious policy, following the Iron Chancellor's dictum that colonies were not worth the blood of one Prussian grenadier. When the Kaiser dropped Bismarck and went in for colonial and naval expansion, the threat to British supremacy quickly became apparent.

An incident in South Africa supplied evidence that Britain would not risk a serious falling out with the United States. After the collapse of an attempt by British subjects to stir up revolt against the Boer government (the "Jameson Raid"), the Kaiser committed the deliberately offensive act of congratulating President Kruger on "maintaining the independence of your country against foreign aggression." The effect upon British policy was instant and permanent. From January 3, 1896—the date of the "Kruger Telegram"—the British recognized the German Kaiser as a potential enemy. From that time on, it became a principle of British policy not to permit any issue, no matter what it might be, from causing a rift in Anglo-American relations. Within a few weeks, Britain and Venezuela agreed to arbitrate their dispute.

The Cuban revolt, which had subsided in 1878, again flared up during the last two years of Cleveland's second administration, causing much the same problems and irritations as in the days of President Grant. In contrast to the firm and uncompromising manner with which Cleveland had dealt with the powerful United Kingdom, his policy toward a relatively impotent Spain was marked by patience, restraint and extreme consideration. Following much the same course as that upon which Fish had successfully insisted during the previous Cuban troubles, Cleveland did his best to prevent American citizens from aiding or participating in the insurrection, to protect legitimate American interests in Cuba and to mediate a settlement. Even though his offer of mediation explicitly stated that the United States deemed the continuation of Spanish sovereignty essential to Cuba's "stability," the Spanish government stubbornly declined the offer.

Congress did not share Cleveland's restraint. There was a rising sentiment for recognizing Cuban belligerency and for fostering the island's independence. In April, 1896, the two Houses passed a resolution authorizing the President to proceed along these lines. Cleveland nevertheless quietly renewed his offer to mediate a settlement on the basis of Cuban home rule under Spanish sovereignty, suggesting what we would now call a dominion status for the island. When the Spanish government foolishly declined this offer, Olney warned the Spanish ambassador that a new administration might not be able or willing to restrain the growing American sentiment in favor of Cuban independence.

The signs were already pointing in that direction. At its convention in 1896, the Republican Party—largely at the instigation of a rising young Senator from Massachusetts, Henry

Cabot Lodge—flatly declared in its platform that it favored Cuban independence.

In his last annual message to Congress—in December, 1896, after his party had lost the election—Cleveland himself declared that matters in Cuba might well develop in such a way that "our obligations to the sovereignty of Spain will be superseded by higher obligations which we can hardly hesitate to recognize and discharge." What he meant was that both the Cuban people and the land were being destroyed by the brutal methods employed by both sides in the conflict. The Spanish Captain General Weyler had been pursuing the inhuman policy of reconcentrado, forcing the population to concentrate in the overcrowded and unsanitary cities and towns. The insurrectionists replied with a scorched-earth policy which, if continued, would soon devastate the rich land of the strife-torn island. Had Cleveland remained in office, he might well have succeeded in convincing the Spanish government that its sovereignty over the island was irredeemably lost. The Republican victory of 1896 resulted in the election of a weak President and of a Congress difficult to restrain.

Three major causes contributed to Cleveland's defeat and the derailment of reform. The first, already mentioned, was Cleveland's failure to win the allegiance of the Populist movement. The second was Bryan's obsession with "free silver" as a panacea, which distorted the reform movement over which Cleveland had lost control. The third, and perhaps the most decisive factor, was the incidence of the panic of 1893 and the depression which lasted through the remainder of Cleveland's term in office.

Over-investment and over-production in the 1880's produced a downward price trend. The unsettled conditions of the English investment market, culminating in the panic occasioned by the failure of Baring Brothers in 1890, stopped the flow of European capital into the United States and caused the sale of European-held American securities. This caused a collapse of the American security market and a substantial export of gold, which, in turn, caused anxiety as to the soundness of the currency. Big crops and huge agricultural exports maintained an uneasy equilibrium until the winter of 1892-1893, but Federal revenues continued to fall and the Treasury was depleted by the mandatory silver purchases required by the Sherman Silver Act of 1890. In February, 1893, the Philadelphia and Reading Railroad Company failed and, simultaneously, the Treasury's gold stocks dropped below the accepted minimum reserve of $100,000,000. A stock-market panic was touched off by the failure of the National Cordage Company; banks began to suspend payment. In June, India went on a gold standard and this caused the United States silver dollar to fall to 60 cents. As commercial failures and bank suspensions increased, currency rose to a premium and people rushed to convert their currency into gold.

Repeal of the Sherman Silver Act was widely considered to be the cure for the panic and Cleveland succeeded in getting repeal through both Houses of Congress in late October. Meanwhile, imports of gold from the sale of crops had already somewhat stabilized the situation and the panic settled down into a protracted depression. Widespread unemployment resulted in labor unrest; strikes were often met with violence; Coxey's Army marched on Washington to demand the issuance of fiat money. In the great Pullman Strike, organized labor for the first time successfully banded together against the unfair practices of a large employer, with the railwaymen joining the Pullman employees to create an almost complete stoppage of transportation in the Chicago area. Governor Altgeld of Illinois refused to suppress the strike by calling out the state militia, but Federal troops were sent to Illinois "to insure delivery of the mails" and the Federal government obtained an injunction against the strikers on the grounds that their action was in violation of the Sherman Anti-Trust Act. Thus, the attempt to regulate or prevent monopoly resulted, for the time being, in giving to business monopoly a new and powerful weapon against labor. Between 1892 and 1896, only one out of five cases brought against the trusts under the Sherman Act was decided against the trust in question. Out of five cases brought against labor, all but one were decided against labor.

Cleveland's renewed attempt to reduce the excessive rates imposed by the McKinley Tariff Act was essentially unsuccessful, but the Wilson-Gorman compromise tariff included a graduated income tax of 2% on incomes of over $4,000. This, however, was promptly declared unconstitutional by the Supreme Court.

In 1895, the Treasury once more faced an acute crisis. Its gold reserve had again been drained by both foreign and domestic withdrawals. Confidence in the government's credit was all but destroyed. At this juncture, J. Pierpont Morgan, the leading Wall Street financier, came to the rescue with an offer to sell the government $64,000,000 of much-needed gold, taking payment in government bonds.* By accepting this offer Cleveland was able to arrest a second incipient panic but, in permitting the Treasury to be rescued by Wall Street, he disrupted the Democratic Party.

On the one hand, Cleveland had now enraged the Republicans by vetoing a large number of special-interest, log-rolling expenditures, by eliminating some 10,000 civil service positions from the vicissitudes of the spoils system, by sponsoring an income tax and by endeavoring to reduce the tariff. On the other hand, he had alienated what was by now the majority of his own party north of the Mason and Dixon Line by repealing the Silver Purchase Act, by refusing to issue paper money and—insofar as labor was concerned—by breaking the Pullman Strike. This enabled William Jennings Bryan—a hitherto little-known Nebraska Congressman and newspaper editor—to capture the leadership of the Democratic Party and to obtain both the Democratic and the Populist nominations for the Presidency.

Bryan stampeded the Democratic convention of 1896 with his famous "Cross of Gold" plea for the free coinage of silver. Thereafter, he chose to make "free silver" the central issue in the campaign. Actually, apart from his amazing gift for oratory, Bryan's great popular appeal derived from his natural affinity for the interests and sentiments of the underprivileged and from the fact that he explicitly challenged the prevailing theory that, if the rich were permitted to get richer, their prosperity would trickle down to the masses. Unfortunately for the cause

---

* The Morgan transaction was later severely criticized when the government bonds rose to a considerable premium, as they naturally would after the corner in the crisis was turned. Bad European crops, causing greater purchases of American agricultural exports, added to the speed of recovery in 1896-1897.

of reform, Bryan became obsessed with "free silver" as the instrument of creating greater social justice when, actually, the free coinage of silver could not possibly achieve the results which he expected.* This detracted not only from the basic merit of his position but from its political effectiveness, causing the "Gold Standard Democrats" to desert the party and to nominate their own candidate.

Thus the reform movement, instead of being guided into constructive channels by middle-of-the-road leadership, became distorted into a crusade for a meaningless objective; the Democratic Party passed into the hands of a brilliant and magnetic leader of undoubted goodwill but of little true understanding; and the field was left open to ultra-conservative and ultra-nationalist Republican reaction.

The Republican Party nominated the outstanding symbol of its policy, the author of the McKinley Tariff Act. McKinley made few speeches, running his "back-porch campaign" on a high-tariff, gold-standard platform and making his appeal directly to the business community without any attempt to conciliate the agricultural West. Mark Hanna, Great Lakes ore magnate and shipmaster, raised and supervised the spending of some $4,000,000—a hitherto unheard-of sum for such purposes—to insure McKinley's election.

Bryan, with almost no campaign funds and very little party organization to help him, waged a remarkable, single-handed fight, speaking from one end of the country to the other and eventually coming within 500,000 votes of his rival. (One may wonder what would have been the outcome of the election had radio and television existed in those days and had their facilities been equally available to both candidates.)

The election of William McKinley upon the most outspokenly pro-business platform yet placed before the American people produced a brief period which marked the culmination of materialistic irresponsibility. With Big Business in control of the White House, the Congress and—in a sense—of the Judiciary, the rule of tooth and claw pervaded American society to a greater extent than ever before. "Success" was the watch-

* For evidence to support this statement, see Note at end of chapter.

word and the ostentatious display of wealth the measure of "success." California mining multi-millionaires vied with their Midwestern counterparts and with the Eastern magnates in flaunting their great estates, their yachts and their private railway cars before the eyes of the envious. The ever-growing monopolies ruthlessly choked competition, fighting each other for the right to plunder the forests, the land and the mineral wealth of the country. More went to waste than would have supported many a less fortunate country. The gap between the beliefs upon which the nation had been founded and the behavior of its people widened into a chasm. It was not so much prosperity which trickled down through the pyramid of a business-dominated society as the morality of the robber-barons. Conscience, humanitarian principles and democratic ideals were submerged in the crass materialism of an age in which the poor aped the rich, no longer dreaming of the day when there would be no poverty but of the day when they might hope to join the glittering ranks of the privileged few.

The foreign policy of a nation so dedicated to the pursuit of profit almost inevitably came to reflect its internal development. The same state of mind which had dictated the stripping of the great forests of the Northwest, the extermination of beaver, buffalo and Indian, and the exhaustion of the fertile soil of the South—all in the name of impatient and unrestrained acquisitiveness—now burst through the confinement of a national frontier. In an economy deliberately run in the interest of quick profit, little or no thought was given to the possibility of creating a wider market by expanding the purchasing power of the domestic consumer. In an era of charging the consumer "what the traffic would bear" and of hiring labor as cheaply as possible, it was to be expected that the search for new outlets for the rapidly rising American production would be sought overseas rather than at home. The increasingly anachronistic high tariff had already placed a limit upon Europe's ability to buy American goods, and the relatively high cost of American manufactures made them incapable of competing in the European markets. Mass production techniques had not yet been invented. Thus the "great untapped markets of the Far East, with its teeming millions" and the markets of near-by

Latin America quite naturally attracted the attention of the eager expansionists.

The ground was well prepared for the events which were soon to follow. Physically and, above all, psychologically, the United States had grown "too big for its britches."

Actually, the visible mood of the people was one of bewilderment and discontent, rather than chip-on-the-shoulder belligerence. Americans were accustomed to economic change. They were unprepared for the philosophical change which came with the end of the century and which seemed to attack the very roots of their ethical structure. Darwinism, even as sugar-coated by John Fiske, and the new determinist theories of human existence challenged the fundamental moral and religious tenets of the American society. Doubt supplanted certainty and scepticism replaced firm belief. Panic and depression had shaken confidence in the economic order. Urbanization had altered the social focus of American life. The linking together of a continent into a single, great nation had imposed the need for reexamining the federal principle of decentralized political power. It was a time in which, from every point of view, the firm ground seemed to have been taken out from under the American mind and spirit. At the very moment when the pressures of popular discontent had accumulated almost to the flash-point, the moral brakes of the American society were disabled by new and unfamiliar doubt.*

A Note on the Relation of Silver to the Causes of Discontent in the Latter Part of the 19th Century.

The causes of discontent which the agrarian Populists sought to counteract through the free coinage of silver were only in part monetary. Among the non-monetary basic factors were:

1. The growth of monopolies and the monopolistic practices of business in general.
2. The growing power of concentrated wealth over government and the abuse of that power for purposes of greater aggrandizement.

* See Henry Steele Commager's admirable chapter, "The Watershed of the Nineties," in The American Mind (Yale, 1954), pages 41-54.

3. The tariff, which favored manufacturers at the expense of the raw material producers, especially the farmers.
4. The coincidence of the closing down of the frontier with a great population increase, part of it through immigration.
5. The absence of social legislation designed to put a floor under human misery, if not a ceiling over wealth and privilege.

In addition to these wholly non-monetary causes of discontent, upon which silver could have absolutely no impact, there actually was, throughout much of this period of expansion, something which could be called—though somewhat inaccurately—a "scarcity of money." Silver had something to do with this, but was by no means fundamental to the difficulty. The fundamental monetary factors were:

1. A deflationary policy consistently pursued after the inflation of the Civil War.
2. The fluctuations of an unsoundly issued paper currency in terms of gold or in terms of commodity prices.
3. The fact that gold production during most of this period failed to keep pace with population growth and the expansion of other production. (Actually, it declined from a world output of about $130,000,000 in 1865 to less than $120,000,000 in 1890.)

These factors, taken together, would have produced most of the trouble which the bimetallists attributed to a lack of free silver coinage, even if there had been no silver problem at all.

However, in addition to these basic factors which bimetallism could not alter, there was a silver problem as well. Originally the United States had coined both gold and silver, 16 silver dollars being valued at one dollar of coined gold. Due to the scarcity of silver and its use for commercial purposes, the metal in the silver dollar became worth more than the dollar itself. This led to the melting down into bullion of the silver coinage and its gradual disappearance, so that any provision for the coinage of silver dollars was actually omitted from the Act of 1873.

The silver problem arose when, all of a sudden, the world production of silver—and especially United States production—rose by leaps and bounds through new discoveries of ore bodies. In 1860, silver production in the United States totaled only $156,800. In 1865, it rose to $11,642,200. By 1890, it reached $57,242,100. When the commercial demand for silver no longer exceeded the supply, the price declined below a ratio of sixteen to one to gold and the silver producers began to demand that the government buy their output and coin it into silver dollars. That was when the silver question began to become a political issue and the Act of 1873 was denounced as the "Crime of 1873."

The silver producers alone would not have been able to make free coinage into a major issue in national politics, had not the debt-ridden farmers been misled into joining forces with them in the belief that "free silver" would produce a more plentiful supply of money and raise the prices of agricultural products. The combined pressure of these two groups brought about the Silver Purchase Act of 1890, which directed the government to purchase 4,500,000 ounces of silver each month and either to coin it or to issue silver certificates against it. This measure did not take enough silver off the market to restore the sixteen to one ratio but, in the existing circumstances of the depression which began in 1893, the expenditure created a dangerous drain upon the Treasury. At the same time, the low price of silver caused people to distrust silver certificates and the demand for their redemption in gold added to the Treasury's difficulties.

It was this experience which caused Cleveland to demand the repeal of the Sherman Silver Purchase Act and which demonstrated the danger inherent in a bimetallic standard.

Had Bryan understood all this, he might well have become President and the reform movement might not have become distorted. Ironically enough, the only monetary factor which had been operative in creating "hard times"—namely, the scarcity of gold—ceased to operate at just about the time when Bryan made silver the great issue. Insofar as hardship had actually been created by the scarcity of gold, the cure came about through science, rather than through politics. The discovery of the cyanide separation process made possible the extraction of gold from low-grade ore and the shift from placer mining to lode mining vastly increased the production of the precious metal, ending the scarcity and making bimetallism a dead issue.

CHAPTER FOURTEEN

The Years of Folly
(1897–1901)

SOON AFTER his inauguration, President McKinley turned his attention to completing the annexation of Hawaii which had been stalled off by his predecessor. A new treaty was sent to the Senate for ratification in June, 1897. Japan, previously acquiescent, protested the annexation, ostensibly out of concern for some 25,000 Japanese citizens who had recently settled in the islands. A more important reason for Japan's changed attitude was that she had just won a war against China and had now emerged as a contender for a dominant position on the mainland.

In spite of the Japanese threat to American ambitions, there were a sufficient number of Democrats and anti-annexationist Republicans in the Senate to endanger ratification. The debate lagged to such an extent that McKinley, taking a leaf out of President Tyler's notebook, attempted to push the matter through by a concurrent resolution requiring only a simple majority in both Houses. Even this effort stalled, from March 1898 to the following July. By this time the United States was at war with Spain. With an American fleet in Philippine waters, the strategic arguments of the annexationist leaders won Congressional approval. McKinley signed the resolution of annexation on July 7 and, on August 12, 1898, the Hawaiian Islands became a Territory of the United States.

For the first year of the McKinley administration, Cleveland's sane policy with respect to Cuba remained in force, in spite of the inflammatory activities of the "Young Republicans." Led by Henry Cabot Lodge in the Senate and Assistant Secretary of the Navy Theodore Roosevelt, the interventionists ardently followed the gospel of Admiral Alfred Thayer Mahan, whose writings had popularized power politics, emphasizing the importance of sea-power and the need for naval bases in the Pacific and the Caribbean.

In September, 1897, McKinley repeated Cleveland's offer of mediation. The new liberal Spanish goverment promised reforms in Cuba but once more rejected American mediation, declaring that the most useful thing President McKinley could do would be to take stronger action in preventing American support of insurrectionist juntas. Nevertheless, in his first annual message to Congress, McKinley recommended suspending any decisions until it should become clear whether the promised reforms would materialize. The obnoxious General Weyler had already been recalled and a series of measures had been announced which, if carried out, would give Cuba a large measure of autonomy. As it turned out, the conciliatory moves came too late. The insurrectionists were by this time in a mood to accept nothing less than full independence.

Although the Spanish proposals were not acceptable to the Cubans, the reforms did momentarily reduce tension, and a period of relative quiet ensued. This did not in the least suit the newly powerful "yellow press" in the United States; its sensational stories of Spanish atrocities in Cuba had become a highly profitable medium for expanding circulation.*

* Two authors, Walter Millis and J. K. Winkler, have thrown a searching light into the psychological background of this time. Millis in *The Martial Spirit*, a study of the Spanish-American War, has analyzed the various factors which built up the jingo spirit. Winkler's *W. R. Hearst, An American Phenomenon* emphasizes the utterly unscrupulous exploitation of the Cuban affair by the competing yellow journalists. *The Cuban Crisis as Reflected in the New York Press*, by Joseph E. Wisan, provides detailed documentation.

A well-known story of the time concerns the artist, Frederic Remington, whom Hearst sent to Cuba to draw illustrations of Spanish atrocities. Winkler reports that Remington, after arriving in Cuba, wired to Hearst: "Everything

While the influence of the yellow press can hardly be over-estimated, the sensation-mongering newspapers could not have whipped up a war fever if the country had not been "ready, economically and psychologically, for a glamorous for-eign policy." * Even then, war might have been avoided had it not been for two strange incidents, both capitalized to the ut-most by the yellow journals.

On February 9, 1898, the *New York Journal* (Hearst) pub-lished an exceedingly indiscreet letter written to a personal friend in Cuba by the Spanish ambassador to the United States. In this letter Senor de Lome not only made some highly un-flattering comments about the American President but also in-dicated that the Spanish promises to grant Cuban autonomy were not wholly sincere. De Lome resigned without waiting for his recall and a public clamor ensued. This, however, was noth-ing to the furor which arose when the American battleship *Maine* blew up in Havana harbor with a loss of 266 lives.†

Spain promptly expressed condolences and proposed a joint investigation of the cause of the disaster. The United States refused this offer and each nation appointed an investigatory commission. The Spanish findings indicated an internal explo-sion. The American investigators found evidence of an outside explosion which thrust the ship's bottom plates upward. Whether it was an accident or whether the disaster was caused by some irresponsible individual, it is almost impossible to believe that the Spanish government was in any way involved.‡

The yellow press held Spain responsible and whipped up a frenzy. On March 9, 1898, Congress unanimously approved McKinley's request for $50,000,000 "for national defense and each and every purpose connected therewith." The American ambassador at Madrid was instructed not to present an ulti-matum but to demand an immediate armistice of six months

---

is quiet. There is no trouble here. There will be no war. I wish to return." Hearst, according to Winkler, replied: "Please remain. You furnish the pictures and I'll furnish the war."

   * This extremely apt phrase is quoted from S. F. Bemis, *op. cit.,* page 442.

   † The exact cause of the explosion has never been ascertained. *Ibid.,* page 445.

   ‡ The *Maine* was raised in 1911. For the inconclusive findings of the in-vestigation, see *Final Report;* 63rd Congress, 2nd session; House Document 480.

during which peace negotiations were to be conducted through the friendly offices of the American President; the immediate revocation of the *reconcentrado;* and an agreement that, if peace were not agreed to by October 1, the arbitral decision of the President should be final. The Spanish government revoked the *reconcentrado* and ordered Captain-General Blanco to "grant a suspension of hostilities for such time as he might think prudent and facilitate peace negotiations," but McKinley had already made up his mind to turn the whole affair over to Congress, knowing perfectly well that this would mean war.

McKinley's message to Congress of April 11, 1898, had been prepared prior to the receipt of the Spanish reply. It ended with two newly appended paragraphs referring to Queen Cristina's order to Blanco to grant an armistice "the duration and details of which have not yet been communicated to me" and concluded: "This fact, with every other pertinent consideration, will, I am sure, have your just and careful attention in the solemn deliberations upon which you are about to enter. If this measure attains a successful result, then our aspirations as a Christian, peace-loving people will be realized. If it fails, it will be only another justification for our contemplated action."

The last two words of the message reveal the state of mind of the Chief Executive. He knew that Congress wanted war and he was not a man who would stand out resolutely for a little more patience when a peaceful and honorable settlement was in sight. It is true that, had McKinley insisted—as Cleveland almost certainly would have insisted—upon waiting a few days to see the effect of the Queen's orders, he might have been overridden. The Congressional resolution of April 20, which served as the basis for an ultimatum dispatched on the same day by the President, passed the Senate by a vote of 68 to 21 and the House by a vote of 311 to 6. McKinley undoubtedly acted in accordance with prevailing sentiment, but he acted as a follower—not a leader.

Faced with the choice of outright capitulation or war, Spain chose disaster rather than a sacrifice of national honor. The disaster was chiefly of her own making. She had waited too long and refused too many offers of friendly mediation.

Whether or not McKinley himself would have preferred a

peaceful settlement and merely lacked the strength of character to stand out against public sentiment, the Assistant Secretary of the Navy not only wanted war but had, with great foresight, prepared for it. It was due to Theodore Roosevelt—now about to emerge as the dominant figure in the Republican Party—that a fleet under Commodore Dewey had been carefully assembled, provisioned and dispatched to Hong Kong, there to await developments. Congress declared war on April 25, 1898. Within a week, Dewey sought out and destroyed the small Spanish Far Eastern fleet at the battle of Manila Bay. This disposed of Spanish power in the Pacific.

As for the Caribbean, a Spanish fleet under Admiral Cervera crossed the Atlantic and foolishly took refuge in the narrow-necked harbor of Santiago, Cuba, where it was promptly bottled up by Admiral Sampson. Meanwhile, an expeditionary force of 16,000 men, including the famous Rough Riders commanded by Colonel Leonard Wood and Lieutenant Colonel Theodore Roosevelt (who had resigned his civilian office), landed near Santiago and laid siege to the city. On July 3, 1898, Cervera made a brave attempt to battle his way out of the harbor in the course of which his entire squadron was destroyed. Santiago surrendered. Puerto Rico was taken by another expeditionary force. The war was over. On August 12, Spain signed an armistice agreement giving up all claim to sovereignty over Cuba and ceding to the United States Puerto Rico and one island in the Ladrones to be selected later. The fate of the Philippines was left to the decision of a peace conference to be held at Paris.

So far as the American people were concerned, there had been no demand for annexation of the Philippines. But, in the minds of the Mahan school of Young Republicans, the idea had for some time been cherished. Events in China after its defeat at the hands of Japan provided an economic rationalization for the American imperialists. Japan had conquered Formosa. She had also attempted to obtain a foothold in Southern Manchuria. Germany had obtained a naval base at Tsingtao and a sphere of influence in Shantung. Russia secured a lease on the Liaotung peninsula and a base at Port Arthur. Britain expanded its colony at Hong Kong and established a hold on the Yangtze valley. France obtained a sphere of influence in

South China, and Japan acquired a similar concession opposite Formosa in Fukien province. With China thus on the way to partition it appeared that American rights to equal trade opportunities would soon be extinguished. The idea that the United States might trade very profitably with the European protectorates did not seem to occur to the Young Republicans. To them, the possession of the Philippines presented the desired offset to the concessions obtained by the European powers.

After destroying the Spanish fleet, Dewey remained off Manila while, at his invitation, Filipino insurrectionists led by Emilio Aguinaldo besieged the city. On June 17, a strong German squadron appeared at Manila, followed shortly by three British warships and single French and Japanese war vessels. The German Emperor's hope was to bring about a neutralization and eventual partition of the islands. His Admiral, von Diedrichs, proceeded to violate Dewey's blockade and to enter into communication with the Spanish authorities, hoping to obtain an invitation to intervene. The British commander made it clear that he would stand on the side of the United States in the event of trouble. When Manila surrendered, on August 13, the German squadron disappeared. In the following month Germany signed a secret treaty with Spain for the purchase of the Caroline Islands of Yap, Ponape and Kusaie, later augmented by a treaty transferring to the Kaiser all the Carolines, Pellews and Ladrones, except for Guam, which Spain had ceded to the United States.

The strategic considerations of Mahan and his followers, rationalized by events in China, gained support from American business groups which had opposed the war but had now become anxious to make the most out of victory. To them, the Philippines seemed to assure American access to the presumably great market of China. This turned out to be the decisive consideration which led McKinley into the two greatest blunders of American diplomatic history: the annexation of the Philippines and the extension of the Open Door policy into what would later amount to a guarantee of China's territorial integrity.

Almost without giving thought to the consequences of so vast a commitment, McKinley came to the conclusion that the

United States had no choice but to annex the Philippines. To give them back to Spain would be "cowardly and dishonorable." To turn them over to our commercial rivals in the Far East would be "bad business." To leave them to themselves would mean "anarchy and misrule worse than Spain's was." Thus, "there was nothing left for us to do but to take them all, and to educate the Filipinos, and uplift and civilize and Christianize them, and by God's grace to do the very best we could for them, as our fellow men for whom Christ also had died." *

The Senate was by no means certain to ratify annexation. A strong opposition, led by Senator George F. Hoar, of Massachusetts, argued against annexation on both moral and practical grounds. The Anti-Imperialist League endeavored to mobilize public resistance. It was not until William J. Bryan, himself an anti-expansionist, went to Washington and urged the Democratic Senators to vote for the treaty, in order to remove the question from the coming campaign, that ratification was accomplished by the narrow margin of two votes over the necessary two-thirds majority. A subsequent resolution promising independence to the Philippines was rejected by the casting vote of Vice President Garret A. Hobart.

While the question of annexation was under consideration, the Japanese government made a suggestion of placing the Philippines under a joint protectorate. This idea was politely declined. It does not seem to have occurred to the McKinley administration that annexation of the Philippines without a Japanese alliance meant one of two things: either the establishment and maintenance of naval supremacy in the Pacific, or the handing over to Japan of a hostage by means of which it would be in a position to dominate United States policy in the Far East.

Building a huge naval establishment was contrary to the moral pacifism of the American people. Contracting an alliance with Japan was in conflict with established American policy. Unwilling to accept either alternative, but unwilling also to deny itself possession of the islands, the United States govern-

* C. S. Olcott, in his *Life of William McKinley*, Vol. II, pages 108-111, so quotes McKinley's own explanation of his decision as reported in the *Christian Advocate*, January 22, 1903.

ment acted in a manner which can best be characterized as adolescent. It persuaded itself that it had a duty to do what it wanted to do—a duty to take over, "uplift and civilize and Christianize" the Filipino people. That the Filipinos would have preferred independence—even if it meant "anarchy and misrule"—was evident from the fact that it took 50,000 United States troops some two years to subdue their rebellion.

Rudyard Kipling's "white man's burden"—the moral rationalization for imperialist expansion—fitted American policy as aptly as it suited the aims of Victorian England.

William Howard Taft—now Governor of the Philippines—referred to the Filipinos as our "little brown brothers," but Robert F. Morrison, writing in the Manila *Sunday Sun*, countered with a doggerel which expressed the sentiments of the American troops fighting in the jungle:

> I'm only a common soldier-man in the blasted
> Philippines.
> They say I've got brown brothers here, but I
> dunno what it means.
> I like the word, Fraternity, but still I draw the
> line—
> He may be a brother of Big Bill Taft, but he
> ain't no brother of mine!

The more one studies this period of aberration, the more difficult it is to reach any clear conclusions as to the cause of the war with Spain. McKinley, whom history records as the perpetrator of the great follies of 1898, was actually anything but an aggressive leader. A kindly and tolerant man, he became the instrument of explosive forces beyond his control. Theodore Roosevelt, Henry Cabot Lodge and their cohorts were the conscious promoters of aggression. The yellow press climbed aboard their bandwagon for reasons of its own self-advancement. There was a business interest in Cuba as a profitable market and a not inconsiderable American investment in the island, but Big Business in general did not want the war, although it was ready enough to exploit the spoils of victory. Big Business was not in an aggressive mood; it had every reason to be satisfied with the existing state of affairs; but Big Business government had created a mood of pent-up resentment and a frustrated demand for reform among great masses of the American people. It was among the dissatisfied and underprivileged that frustration could readily be converted into aggression against a foreign power and war made into a safety-valve for accumulated pressures. The man in the street or the country lane, who felt put-upon and neglected, supplied the tinder ready to be ignited into flame by the cry: "Remember the *Maine!*" It was not without significance that the South and the agrarian Middle West supplied the most eager enlistments.

Interesting, too, was the fact that it was not the stand-pat Old Guard in the Republican Party which promoted the war in the traditional manner of a reactionary, oppressive regime seeking to divert popular discontent by military adventure abroad. It was the progressive wing of the Republican Party that supplied the warlike leadership—to a large extent the very group which wished to unhorse the Old Guard and to remedy some of the abuses which had built up the explosive pressures.

CHAPTER FIFTEEN

"T. R."–Trust Busting–and the Big Stick
(1901 – 1909)

IN THE ELECTIONS of 1900, Bryan, again nominated by the Democrats, still stubbornly continued to flog the dead horse of free silver. The brutal suppression of the Filipino insurrection might have proved a more profitable issue, but Bryan's own position was stultified by his support of the annexation treaty. The real issues out of which the Great Commoner might have made capital where neither silver nor anti-imperialism, but the continuing oppression of the people by the monopolies and by the power of organized wealth over government. These issues were soon to be stolen from Bryan by Theodore Roosevelt who, in 1900, was carefully sidetracked by the Republican bosses and chosen as the Vice Presidential running mate of McKinley, in order to get him out of the governorship of New York, where he had shocked the Old Guard by his "altruistic, if not communistic" tendencies.

McKinley, standing pat on his record and his victories, was overwhelmingly re-elected. With the dangerous "radical," Theodore Roosevelt, safely ensconced in the Vice Presidency, the Old Guard looked forward to another four years of happy tenure. And then, at the Pan American Exposition at Buffalo, McKinley was shot by an anarchist and Theodore Roosevelt succeeded to the Presidency.

For the first decade of the twentieth century, Theodore Roosevelt dominated the American scene. Where neither Cleveland nor McKinley had understood the deep causes of popular discontent, and where Bryan—though understanding them better—lacked the intelligence and perhaps the integrity to see the true answer, Roosevelt possessed a peculiar mixture of political shrewdness and sense of justice which made him both a successful politician and an effective reformer. Himself a member of the privileged class, Roosevelt felt nothing but contempt for those who sought to use privilege and power for their own selfish aggrandizement. Ostentatious display of wealth offended his sensibilities, not just because it was vulgar but because it seemed to him effete and a sign of moral decay. Into an era of complacency, he injected a new spirit which reveled in "the strenuous life" of hard work, hard play and adventure.

In domestic affairs, these characteristics made Roosevelt into something of a crusader against entrenched economic power, the forerunner of Woodrow Wilson and of his cousin, Franklin D. Roosevelt.

In the conduct of foreign affairs, the same qualities made "T. R." a somewhat dangerous and over-exuberant leader, full of energy and self-confidence. Where McKinley had slithered into far-reaching commitments, Roosevelt consciously undertook them. Where McKinley had blithely ignored the fact that an overseas empire required vast military and naval power, Roosevelt joyfully undertook the building of power to keep pace with the commitments. Where McKinley had shrunk from war, Roosevelt had a tendency to welcome a test of national strength, much as he welcomed any challenge to his own personal courage or endurance. It was a curious paradox that Roosevelt combined in his nature the strong desire to unhorse the domestic robber-barons with an inclination to give the nation as a whole something of a buccaneering character.

The state of the nation at the turn of the century had much to do with both sides of Theodore Roosevelt's nature. It was prosperous but uneasy. It rejoiced in its wealth and strength and yet a vaguely defined feeling that something was wrong made the majority of Americans restless and discontented. In 1900, the population of the United States—exclusive of dependencies—was 76,000,000. Money in circulation had increased from $21.94 per capita in 1896 to $26.94. In the five years between 1893 and 1898, the wheat crop had risen from 400,000,000 to 675,000,000 bushels and the price of wheat from 52 cents to 57 cents per bushel. Wheat growing had moved west and the central states had become a prosperous corn-hog and dairy farming region. Farms were gradually being freed from mortgages. The South, too, was sharing in the prosperity.

Industry continued its phenomenal growth, spurred on by such new inventions as the telephone, the steam turbine, and the internal combustion engine. It was still the great age of the bicycle and the horse and buggy, but the "horseless carriage" was already a plaything of the wealthy. Gasoline, still a mere by-product of kerosene, was selling at one cent a gallon. Santos Dumont had flown a dirigible balloon around the Eiffel Tower. The Air Age was about to begin. Electric streetcars were replacing horsecars and people were talking about an underground railway in New York City. For most Americans, electric light and a private telephone were just around the corner. Magic lanterns were giving way in nickelodeons to the first gruesome attempts at producing a "moving picture."

And yet, with all the rather exciting "progress," there was a spirit of discontent. Some of it arose from the sense of guilt inspired by the war against the Filipinos. Some of it grew out of the fearful slum conditions in the big cities, the sweatshops and the factories where little children labored instead of going to school. Some people thought that alcohol was ruining the country and went to Carrie Nation's temperance meetings. Others were beginning to demand woman suffrage and equal rights for women. Beneath all these various manifestations of discontent lurked the feeling that, while Bryan was probably wrong about free silver, he was right in saying that the country was being run by the wealthy few for their own benefit.

The wealthy few had, indeed, reached the apogee of their insolent abuse of opportunity and power. This was the age of high finance; the new device of the holding company enabled the great monopolies to add horizontal trusts to the vertical combines they had already created. Rockefeller's Standard Oil, not content with its petroleum monopoly, was spreading out into ownership of banks, Great Lakes shipping, and iron ore. Interlocking railroad and bank directorates concentrated power in the hands of an ever smaller group of men in Wall Street. Morgan was forming the giant United States Steel Corporation. Hill, Morgan and Harriman were fighting for control of the Northern Pacific and driving its securities sky-high, from $110 per share to over $1,000. In the ensuing "Rich Man's Panic" all sorts of people got hurt. Yet the government did nothing, the courts in almost every instance held that it would be unconstitutional to interfere with such matters, and, each year, the fortunes of the wealthy few grew greater.

The attitude of the man in the street toward the charitable donations of the business magnates was expressed in a poem which appeared in the Chicago *Times-Herald*, in June, 1901, shortly after Andrew Carnegie (incidentally one of the most truly public-spirited of the multi-millionaires) had given $10,-000,000 to Scottish universities:

> Let us then be up and doing,
> All becoming money kings;
> Some day we may be endowing
> Universities and things.

> Lives of billionaires remind us
> That we've got to own the stock
> If we want to leave behind us
> Libraries on every block.*

It was this sort of feeling which Theodore Roosevelt understood much more accurately than William Jennings Bryan. Roosevelt also understood another thing about the American people; namely, that they wanted reform but not drastic reform amounting to revolution. He sensed that the majority of Americans wanted the abuses of capitalism to be curbed—wanted the small businessman to be given a chance—wanted a limit placed upon the political power of wealth—wanted, in other words, rules of fair play established to govern the competitive system —but that they did not want to abolish or drastically alter that system. Roosevelt's mastery over Bryan at what was essentially Bryan's own game derived from the fact that he was practical where Bryan was Utopian—a referee among conflicting interests where Bryan was essentially a partisan.

Proceeding along practical lines, Roosevelt first of all emancipated his administration from the control of the Old Guard. With men like Elihu Root and William Howard Taft in his cabinet, he set about creating a wholly different atmosphere from that which had prevailed under McKinley. One of the first things he did was to bring suit against the Northern Securities Company† under the Sherman Anti-Trust Law. Then he moved, through the Elkins Act of 1903, to strengthen the powers of the Interstate Commerce Commission. These actions served notice that an era of "trust-busting" had begun. A Department of Commerce and Labor was set up, a land reclamation service created and a study made of agricultural conservation.

In the 1904 elections, Roosevelt won decisively over the colorless Alton B. Parker, the Democratic nominee. His victory carried into power a number of reform state governments— some of them Democratic. In his second term, Roosevelt continued along the same course. Further restrictions were enacted

---

* Mark Sullivan; *Our Times;* Scribner's, 1927, pages 558-559.

† This was the holding company in which the competing interests in the Northern Pacific fight had pooled their holdings.

against unfair competitive practices by the railroads. The Pure Food and Drug Act of 1906 enforced proper grading and labeling. The big life insurance companies were scrutinized, much to the alarm of Wall Street, but the panic of 1907—beginning with the failure of the Knickerbocker Trust Company of New York—undermined Wall Street's authority.*

The "Square Deal" reforms encountered strong Old Guard opposition, led by the Senator Nelson Aldrich in the Senate and by Speaker Joe Cannon in the House. The final straw was Roosevelt's declaration in favor of a downward revision of the tariff. Nevertheless, Roosevelt succeeded in getting Taft nominated in 1908 as a candidate pledged to tariff reduction.

The outstanding characteristic of Theodore Roosevelt's conduct of foreign relations was the manner in which he practiced naked power politics in the name of "righteousness." His motto, "Speak softly and carry a big stick," rather aptly expressed his method of operation. Contrary to most of the American Presidents, Roosevelt did not feel that there was something inherently evil about the use of power, either by the United States or by other nations, so long as power was used in what he liked to call "the cause of righteousness," reserving for himself the privilege of defining its meaning. When the Japanese or the Germans practiced *Machtpolitik,* Theodore Roosevelt rather admired them; they became "evil" only when their *Machtpolitik* interfered or threatened to interfere with his own.

Caribbean Policy

Roosevelt's Caribbean policy centered upon building an interocean canal, which would make American naval power quickly transferable, and upon obtaining firm control of that waterway.

The first question was that of dealing with Cuba. The "Teller Amendment" to the resolutions passed by Congress just prior to the declaration of war had pledged the United States not to

---

* The panic of 1907 was the last of the strictly financial panics and led to the reform of the currency and banking structure in 1913. The panic of 1929-1933 arose from a different combination of causes, only some of which resembled those of the earlier recurring disasters.

seek control over the island and to foster Cuban independence. This undertaking had been confirmed by the Army Appropriation Act of 1899. The self-denying pledge with respect to an island of great strategic importance to the United States stood in strange contrast to the Senate's refusal to promise independence to the distant Philippines, possession of which constituted a strategic liability.

From 1898 to 1902, Cuba was under United States military government, the objectives of which were to assist in reconstruction, to undertake the sanitation of the disease-ridden island and to prepare the Cubans for self-government. The work of the Medical Corps under Major Gorgas led to discoveries in the field of yellow-fever and malaria control which directly affected the successful building of the Panama Canal.

In March, 1901, Secretary of War Root submitted to the Cuban constitutional convention a proposal for the future relations between Cuba and the United States, designed to make certain that no foreign power, other than the United States, should ever interfere in the affairs of the republic. In essence this was a proposal for a protectorate.

Cuba was to agree: not to enter into any treaty or compact with a foreign power which would impair its independence, permit colonization or the establishment of military or naval bases; not to contract any public debt beyond its reasonably considered resources; to ratify all acts of American military government; and to carry out the sanitation measures launched by the military government.

The United States was to be granted the right to intervene in Cuba "for the preservation of Cuban independence, the maintenance of a government adequate for the protection of life, property and individual liberty" and to discharge the obligations imposed by the Paris Peace Treaty with Spain. The United States was to have the right to purchase or lease two naval bases.

These provisions were approved by Congress in the Platt Amendment to the Army Appropriation Act of March, 1901. At first rejected by the Cuban assembly, they were accepted when it became evident that these were the conditions for the withdrawal of military government.* The agreement was then embodied in the Cuban constitution and in the Cuban-American Treaty of May 22, 1903. The protectorate thus established lasted until it was superseded by the "Good Neighbor Treaty" of 1934, signed during the administration of another Roosevelt.

The status of the inhabitants of the annexed islands raised a difficult question. Were the Puerto Ricans now citizens of the United States, or did they enjoy some peculiar and hitherto unknown status? The same questions arose with respect to the Philippines. Should "alien peoples" have a voice in governing the United States?—should they have the right of self-government?—should they enjoy tariff protection from foreign imports and free trade with the United States? In other words, did the Constitution automatically follow the flag, or could the United States annex foreign territory and hold it under some sort of dependent status? These questions were put to the Supreme Court, which delivered itself of the famous "Insular Decisions of 1901." The Court held that the islands were neither part of the United States nor yet foreign. The ambiguity remained until 1922, but meanwhile served the purpose of permitting Congress to legislate as it pleased. An apt contemporary comment came from Mr. Finley Peter Dunne's famous character, the philosophical Irish bartender "Mr. Dooley," whose conversations with his friend, "Mr. Hennessy," provided steady amusement to American newspaper readers. Dooley described the decision handed down by the nine Justices "dissenting fr'm me an' each other" in these terms:

> "Some say it laves the flag up in th' air an' some say that's where it laves the Constitution. Annyhow, something's in the air. But there's wan thing I'm sure about."
>
> "What's that?" asked Mr. Hennessy.
>
> "That is," said Mr. Dooley, "no matter whether the Constitution follows the flag or not, th' Supreme Court follows th' illiction returns."

* In a letter dated October 29, 1901, published in 1933 by the American Historical Association at Urbana, Illinois, General Leonard Wood, then military governor of Cuba, wrote to Theodore Roosevelt that the Platt Amendment would, in effect, annex Cuba. Whether the President shared the view of his old companion in arms is not clear.

We come now to the Isthmian canal. The question had long lain dormant because the Clayton-Bulwer Treaty of 1850 meant that, if the United States constructed a canal, it would be compelled to internationalize and neutralize the waterway and would not be permitted to fortify it. The dramatic dash of the U.S.S. *Oregon* around the Horn from Manila to Santiago had made Americans aware of the need for full American control of any link connecting the two oceans. In March, 1899, Congress authorized an investigation of the matter.

John Hay, Lincoln's former private secretary, had, in the years since Lincoln's death, risen through various diplomatic posts to become American envoy to London and was then promoted by McKinley to Secretary of State; this office he retained during Roosevelt's first term. It devolved upon him to seek a modification of the inhibitory treaty. Hay's first efforts were unfortunate. The first Hay-Pauncefote Treaty, signed in 1900 and rejected by the Senate, would again not have permitted the United States to fortify the canal or blockade it in time of war. When Great Britain refused to agree to the changes demanded by the Senate, Hay resigned in disgust but was persuaded by McKinley to remain and make another effort. The second Hay-Pauncefote Treaty, signed in November, 1901, and ratified by the Senate three months later, omitted any prohibition against fortifying the canal, superseded the Clayton-Bulwer Treaty and incorporated the essence of the neutralization provisions applied to the Suez Canal by the Constantinople Convention of 1888.

With the roadblock of the old treaty removed, there now followed another one of those episodes in our diplomatic history of which few Americans could be proud but which practically no American would wish to undo.

A choice had to be made between two sites—one in Panama, the other in Nicaragua. After investigation the Walker Commission recommended Nicaragua and the House passed a bill authorizing construction to be started there. This, however, would have meant complete ruin for a French company, organized by de Lesseps—builder of the Suez Canal—which had already spent almost $300,000,000 in starting to dig a canal across

Panama. The decision of Congress against completing the French project—which was estimated to be about $45,000,000 cheaper than the Nicaraguan project—had been reached because the French company demanded over $100,000,000 for a cession of its property and rights. The French company promptly reduced its price to $40,000,000 and lobbied the Senate into amending the House bill so as to switch the site to Panama, if the President could reach an understanding with the Republic of Colombia or alternatively authorizing him to proceed with the Nicaraguan project.

After nine months of negotiation, Hay signed with the Colombian foreign minister the Hay-Herrán Treaty of January 22, 1903, giving permission to the French company to sell to the United States and granting the United States full control over a six-mile-wide strip across the Isthmus. Colombia was to receive $10,000,000 plus an annuity, beginning after nine years, of $250,000 gold. The Colombian Senate foolishly rejected this treaty in the hope of driving an even more profitable bargain.

President Roosevelt was now in a quandary whether to take up negotiations with Nicaragua or to proceed with the purchase of the French rights and the completion of the old project without Colombian consent. The latter course seemed possible under a very broad construction of Bidlack's 1846 treaty.* In a message drafted but not delivered to Congress, Roosevelt recommended the second course, but at this point the French again took over.

A curious character, P. Bunau-Varilla, former chief engineer for de Lesseps, arrived in haste and proceeded to organize a revolution in the Colombian state of Panama, using the employees of the Panama Railroad, a subsidiary of the de Lesseps company. It is known that Bunau-Varilla had conversations with John Bassett Moore, then Assistant Secretary of State, and with President Roosevelt. There is no evidence that either the President or the Department directly participated in fomenting the revolution, but they certainly did nothing to stop it. On November 2, American warships were sent to both sides of the

* See chapter 8, page 126.

Isthmus and ordered to "maintain free and uninterrupted transit." The revolution broke out a day later. On November 6, the United States recognized the revolutionary government and, on November 11, it informed the Colombian government that it would oppose the landing of Colombian troops to suppress the insurrection. On November 18, the United States signed a treaty with the Republic of Panama—with Bunau-Varilla acting as the Panamanian plenipotentiary!—and obtained control of a ten-mile-wide strip from Colon to Panama, to be held as if the United States "were sovereign." For this concession, Panama received the same payment which had been offered to Colombia. In addition, the treaty established a United States protectorate over the Panamanian republic.

The shortest—though not the sweetest—version of the story of our acquisition of a great strategic asset is that stated in Theodore Roosevelt's autobiography: "I took the Canal Zone."

That there was at least some sense of guilt at the time may be inferred from the efforts of Secretary of State Root to satisfy Colombian grievances during Roosevelt's second administration. It remained for Bryan, as President Wilson's Secretary of State in 1914, to try to appease Bogota by an apology and an indemnity of $25,000,000. (Roosevelt, then in retirement, bitterly opposed this "blackmail treaty" and the Senate failed to ratify it until after his death.)

The Panamanian acquisition re-awakened interest in the Danish Virgin Islands and Hay negotiated a new treaty providing for the purchase of these possessions for $5,000,000. This time it was the Danish Parliament which rejected the treaty, probably in the hope of getting a better price since Germany was now keenly interested in acquiring the islands.*

In the same eventful year, 1902, another German threat to Roosevelt's Caribbean policy arose over the defaulted debts of Venezuela. The Castro dictatorship had over-borrowed and flouted its creditors. Under the leadership of Germany, the European powers sent warships to Venezuela to enforce collection. Britain joined, probably in order to prevent Germany

---

* Alfred Vagts' *Weltpolitik* reveals the pressure which Admiral von Tirpitz was exercising on the Kaiser to acquire naval bases; among others, the Virgin Islands in the Caribbean and the Galapagos Islands off the coast of Ecuador.

from acting as the dominant element in the affair. The European powers informed the United States of their planned action and disavowed any intention of undertaking more than a "temporary occupation" of Venezuelan territory. Roosevelt told both Britain and Germany that he expected a peaceful solution and, by way of hint, concentrated Dewey's fleet off Puerto Rico.* The European powers accepted arbitration, after some hesitation by Germany. The Kaiser was feeling out how far the United States would go in enforcing the Monroe Doctrine.

The Venezuelan crisis produced the "Drago Doctrine," which later became an article of international law adopted by The Hague Conference of 1907. The Argentine foreign minister, Luis Drago, suggested an agreement that no nation should use armed force to recover debts. The Hague Conference made this agreement subject to the proviso that a debtor government should not have refused arbitration or rejected an arbitral verdict.

In order to prevent a repetition of the Venezuelan affair when the Dominican government found itself in similar trouble, Roosevelt established what amounted to a United States custodianship of Dominican revenues and a protectorate against foreign intervention. After a year of Executive operation, the President decided to embody this arrangement in a treaty, submitted to the Senate in 1905, stating that:

> Those who profit by the Monroe Doctrine must accept certain responsibilities along with the rights which it confers, and that same statement applies to those who uphold the doctrine . . .
>
> It is incompatible with international equity for the United States to refuse to allow other powers to take the only means at their disposal of satisfying the claims of their creditors and yet to refuse, itself, to take any such steps.

The Senate took two years to ratify the Dominican treaty embodying this so-called "Roosevelt Corollary" to the Monroe Doctrine which amounted to the extension of a semi-guardian-

* Roosevelt later claimed that he had actually told the German ambassador that he would send the fleet to Venezuela if arbitration were not accepted. Some historians have doubted, while others have accepted this statement as true.

ship over the entire area. Thereafter, for some thirty years, the Corollary governed our Latin-American policy, until its implicit imperialism was repudiated by the second Roosevelt.

"T.R.'s" Caribbean policy—whatever else may be said of it —was successful in securing and safeguarding a vital national interest. By assuring the United States of full control of a canal linking the two oceans and of the approaches to it, Theodore Roosevelt took the first important step toward bringing American naval power into balance with the far-flung commitments entered into at the conclusion of the Spanish-American War. The price paid for this gain was the further alienation of Latin-American sentiment. Originally looked upon as a guide toward freedom and independence, the United States came to be regarded more and more as the "Colossus of the North," whose "Yankee Imperialism" and "Dollar Diplomacy" constituted a threat to Latin-American self-respect and independence.

Far Eastern Policy

Prior to 1898, it had been the established policy of the United States to keep out of Europe's quarrels and to assert its own predominant interest in the Americas. It was, in fact, only *by* keeping out of Europe's quarrels and by profiting from Europe's preoccupation that the United States had been able to establish a great, continental empire in North America and to assert its paramount interest over the Western Hemisphere. This wise and highly successful policy was abandoned when the United States reached out into the western Pacific to become involved in the Far Eastern back yard of Europe's quarrelsome diplomacy. If the annexation of the Philippines had been an irresponsible blunder, the next steps, taken as a consequence of that blunder, were even more unfortunate.

The original American policy in China had been little more than a "Me too" policy, seeking nothing more than a fair share in whatever advantages might be granted to foreign powers. Britain, on the other hand, was concerned with more than most-favored-nation treatment; from the British point of view, it was essential to maintain a Far Eastern balance of power between the European nations, much as it had been essential at an earlier date to maintain such a balance in America. In 1898, Britain was over-engaged; she was quarreling with France over Africa, with Russia over the Near East and fighting an actual war with the Boers in South Africa; moreover, she was acutely aware of the rising German threat to British naval and commercial supremacy. Beset with these manifold problems and faced, in addition, with the apparently imminent partition of China, Britain needed an ally in the Far East. The United States, with which all outstanding differences had been composed, seemed, after its annexation of the Philippines, to have become the logical partner who might help to preserve the European balance of power in the Far East. In March, 1898, for substantially the same reasons as those which had motivated George Canning's approach to Benjamin Rush in Monroe's time, the British government had sounded out the McKinley administration. McKinley, preoccupied with Cuba, had instructed his Secretary of State, John Sherman, to decline the suggestion. A year later, John Hay, recently returned from London and now Secretary of State, thought that cooperation in Asia might help his efforts to void the Clayton-Bulwer Treaty. He knew that "the unspeakable Senate" would not stand for an Anglo-American alliance, but concluded that the same ends could be accomplished by unilateral American action.

In the autumn of 1899, Hay sent notes to Britain, Russia, France, Germany and Japan, suggesting that all the powers interested in China grant each other equal commercial rights as to tariffs, railroad rates and port dues. This very limited proposal did not, as the British had suggested, provide any guarantee of China's territorial or administrative integrity, nor did it even provide for equal opportunity of investment.* By a considerable stretch of the imagination, Hay interpreted the equivocal answers of France, Germany, Russia and Japan as "final and definitive acceptance." Undoubtedly Hay's *démarche* suited

---

* In formulating his Chinese policy Hay was apparently influenced by a group of American exporters to Manchuria and by a somewhat mysterious British subject, formerly in the Chinese Customs Service—one Alfred E. Hippisley. He appears also to have been advised by W. W. Rockhill, an American with some diplomatic experience in China.

England and also Japan, both being primarily concerned to stop any further Russian or German encroachment, but it meant very little, unless the Open Door idea were to be carried much further. It was obvious that the Chinese door would remain open only so long as China did not fall under the domination of any one predominant power—in other words, only so long as the then existing, precarious balance of power might be maintained. If Chinese independence were threatened, the United States would have to retreat from its tentative intervention or else be willing to assert and enforce a much more far-reaching guarantee.

In the summer of 1900, a patriotic society, known as "The Boxers," stirred up a popular revolt in China against foreign encroachment and against the Manchu dynasty which had granted foreign concessions. This led to armed intervention by the foreign powers for the purpose of protecting nationals and concessions. More than 5,000 United States troops participated in quelling the disorders. For a time, there was danger that the rebellion might lead to the partition of China. Britain and the United States worked hand in hand to limit the intervention to the protection of existing concessions. At this point Hay again undertook a unilateral move, issuing a circular, dated July 3, 1900, in which he declared that the policy of the United States was "to seek a solution which may bring about permanent safety and peace to China, *preserve Chinese territorial and administrative entity,* protect all rights guaranteed to friendly powers by treaty and international law, and safeguard for the world the principle of equal and impartial trade with all parts of the Chinese empire. (Italics added.)

Hay's declaration meant that the United States had now placed itself in a position of having either to "put up" or "shut up" in the event that any foreign power should attempt to invade Chinese sovereignty. The absurdity of getting into this position is revealed by a glance at the approximate value of American investments in China compared to that of the other interested powers. The United States probably had at this time not over $20,000,000 invested in China. (As late as 1914, American investment totaled only $42,000,000, excluding $10,000,-

ooo by that time invested in mission property.) On the other hand, Russia, Britain and Japan each had investments of well over $200,000,000, Germany had only slightly less and France had almost $100,000,000. In 1914, American exports to China were less than 1% of the total of United States exports.

During the Boxer Rebellion, Russia had occupied Manchuria and thereafter refused to evacuate. Hay protested on several occasions in 1902 and 1903. The Chinese-American Treaty of October 8, 1903, translated the Open Door policy into formal agreement and, for the time, forced Russia to keep Manchuria open to foreign trade. By this time, Britain had liquidated the Boer War and was in the process of settling her differences with France in Egypt and Morocco. British attention was now focused upon stopping Germany on the seas and halting Russia in the Far East. The Russian advance in Manchuria (which looked toward Korea) threatened Japan's penetration of Korea (which aimed at Manchuria); Japan was now strong enough to risk a trial of force. Before embarking upon this venture, however, the Japanese wished to make sure of an ally, in case any other power should intervene on Russia's side. This had led to the Anglo-Japanese alliance of January 30, 1902. The stated purpose of the alliance was to maintain the status quo in the Far East and to guarantee the continued integrity and independence of China and Korea.

At the outbreak of war between Russia and Japan, in 1904, the United States appealed to both belligerents to preserve Chinese neutrality and territorial integrity. In January, 1905, while both belligerents were busily engaged in trying to seize Chinese territory, Hay once more reaffirmed the interest of the United States in protecting China's integrity. At about this time, Britain, with its hands freed in South Africa and Morocco, secretly agreed to give Japan an implied free hand in Korea while Britain obtained a similar implicit right to invade Chinese sovereignty in Tibet.

After the great Japanese victory at Mukden (on March 10, 1905) France offered mediation of the Russo-Japanese conflict but Japan, distrusting the French, preferred the mediation of President Roosevelt. Roosevelt was only too eager. The Kaiser supported the suggestion, fearing a democratic revolution in Russia, if the conflict should drag on longer.

Peace negotiations began in early August and resulted in the Peace of Portsmouth, signed on September 5. While the envoys were on their way to the United States, Roosevelt sent Secretary of War Taft to Tokyo to confirm a previously implied promise to agree to Japan's free hand in Korea, provided that Japan would renounce any aggressive designs against the Philippines. The bargain was confirmed in the secret Taft-Katsura memorandum of July 29, 1905. This was the first ransom payment for the Philippine hostage. The irresponsible annexation of the Philippines had now led not only to the even more irresponsible Open Door guarantee of Chinese integrity but to the cynical selling out of the independent kingdom of Korea.

Under the Treaty of Portsmouth, Japan, in effect, obtained control of both Korea and southern Manchuria. In addition, Russia ceded to Japan the southern half of Sakhalin Island. Roosevelt was "dee-lighted" with the treaty and received the Nobel Peace Prize. Actually there was little reason to be pleased. Russia had been halted, it is true, but Russia had also been given a grievance which she would nourish through the years and for which she would in time exact a heavy price. Japan, which had every reason to be pleased, resented the fact that she had not been awarded all of Sakhalin Island and blamed the United States. Japanese resentment increased as the Open Door policy continued to frustrate Japanese designs for further conquest.

During the last years of his administration, Roosevelt realized that the sell-out of Korea had only increased both the appetite of Japan and the vulnerability of the Philippines. After a period of tension over Japanese immigration into California, he obtained an invitation for the fleet to visit Japan on a cruise around the world. After this demonstration of naval power he consummated another Executive agreement—the Root-Takahira Agreement of November 30, 1908. Once more, both powers declared their peaceful intentions, their respect for each other's position, and their desire to preserve the independence and integrity of China. Actually, the agreement seems to have expressed the intention on Roosevelt's part to take out another insurance policy for the Philippines by giving Japan a free hand in Manchuria, much as the Taft-Katsura Agreement had given the Nipponese the green light for the absorption of Korea. If this was, indeed, the intention, it was not carried out by Roosevelt's successor.

Viewed in retrospect, the Far Eastern diplomacy of Roosevelt and Hay appears as the piling of one error in judgment on top of another. Annexation of the Philippines led to the guarantee of Chinese territorial integrity, in which the United States had no vital interest and which it had no intention of defending by armed force. The vulnerability of the Philippines and of the Open Door guarantee led to the attempted appeasement of Japan by betraying Korea into its hands. Anglo-American support of Japan against Russia in Manchuria did not serve the intended purpose of preserving the status quo and the balance of power; it actually destroyed the balance and made Japan the dominant power in the Far East. Moreover, the Russian defeat at the hands of Japan disturbed the precarious balance of power in Europe, touching off revolutions first in Russia and then in the Ottoman empire of Abdul Hamid II.

The elements of American public opinion which supported this unwise Far Eastern policy were many and varied. Perhaps the strongest factor was the general, muscle-flexing mood resulting from a victorious war, but there were also specific group pressures which could be identified. While American commerce with China was so small as to be almost negligible, the traders formed a well-organized pressure-group which exercised disproportionate influence. Secretary Hay was peculiarly susceptible to British pressures, and these were exercised with considerable skill. The American Jewish community was hostile to Russia because of the persecution of the Jews by the Tsarist regime. (A Jewish banking house floated the loan which Japan obtained in the United States.) The Protestant churches had a strong interest in expanding their missions in China and in protecting mission property. All these and other wholly disparate elements operated in one way or another to support Hay's Far Eastern policy. In view of the subsequent development of American sentiment, it is of interest to note the almost total absence of any anti-Japanese feeling at this time, except on the part of West Coast labor.*

Europe and Africa

The inefficiency and corruption of the Tsarist regime, brought to light by the fiasco of the war against Japan, precipitated the revolution of 1905 which compelled the Tsar to acquiesce in the creation of a parliament as a check upon his despotic authority. The intended constitutional reform was largely frustrated when Nicholas II obtained a sufficient sum in foreign loans ($450,000,000) to enable him to circumvent the Duma's control over expenditures. Strangely enough, the largest part of these loans (about $230,000,000) was extended to the Tsarist regime by republican France. This anomaly resulted from the frantic balance-of-power maneuvering which had begun with Bismarck's great blunder of 1871.

The German annexation of Alsace-Lorraine created a vengeful irredentism in France, weakening the liberal forces within the republic and putting the conservative nationalists in control of French policy. While Bismarck remained in power, he pursued a non-aggressive policy, seeking to nail down the gains of 1871 and to preserve the status quo. Realizing that he had made France into an implacable enemy, the Iron Chancellor forged the League of the Three Emperors of Germany, Russia and Austria-Hungary, jealously maintaining this alliance in spite of the incompatible interests of Germany's two allies. After Bismarck's fall, his successors—Holstein and Prince von Bülow—abetted the Kaiser in a more aggressive policy, pursued with Bismarckian ruthlessness but without Bismarck's self-confident skill. As a result, Russia broke away and entered into an alliance with France, while Germany became more and more dependent upon the crumbling but aggressive Hapsburg monarchy. Thus, in 1905, France had an unnatural interest in preserving the absolutist power of the Tsar.

* References: Tyler Dennet, *Roosevelt and The Russo-Japanese War* (Doubleday, 1925); William Langer, *Diplomacy of Imperialism* (Knopf, 1935); M. J. Bau, *The Open Door in China* (Macmillan, 1923); Allen Nevins, *Henry White* (Harper, 1930).

During the first decade of the century, European diplomacy was engaged in a continual making and breaking of alliances and counter-alliances—most of them secret—representing, on the one hand, the death-struggle of the balance-of-power system and, on the other, Germany's aggressive thrust toward its "place in the sun." After the Young Turk revolt and the break-up of the Sultan's European empire, both Russia and Austria-Hungary pushed into the Balkan vacuum. Germany, fearful of both Russia and France and seeking to shoulder its way forward, was tied to the rickety but explosive remnants of Hapsburg power. France, fearful of Germany and jealous of England, was tied to the crumbling power of the Romanovs. England, half afraid of Germany and half anxious to come to terms with it—half sympathetic and half hostile towards France—wavered uncertainly on the outskirts.

Within France, a counter-revolutionary trend had been stimulated by fear of Germany and a desire for revenge. Within Germany, a revolutionary trend was set in motion by popular resentment against the swashbuckling military and the arbitrary whims of the Kaiser. Within the United Kingdom, social revolution was taking form and Irish home rule was becoming an explosive issue.

If ever there was a time to remain aloof from the tangled affairs of the European continent and from their ramifications abroad, it was this decade of mounting crisis.*

Not content, however, with involvement in the Asian backyard of European politics, Theodore Roosevelt also meddled directly in European affairs. The European scramble for African colonies and spheres of influence had resulted, in 1902, in a French-Italian agreement which left Tripoli under Italian influence. In 1904, France and England signed the *Entente Cordiale,* under which France gave Britain a free hand in Egypt

---

* The following works throw useful light upon this period:
Henry W. Nevinson, *The Dawn in Russia* (Harper, 1906).
Alexander Kerensky, *The Crucifixion of Liberty* (Day, 1934).
Joseph W. Swain, *The Beginning of the 20th Century* (Norton, 1933).
William S. Davis, *Europe Since Waterloo* (Century, 1927).
Carlton Hayes, *A Political and Cultural History of Modern Europe* (Macmillan, 1936).
Thorsten Veblen, *Imperial Germany* (Macmillan, 1915).
J. H. Edwards, *David Lloyd George* (Sears, 1929).

in exchange for a free hand in Morocco. In 1905, Germany set out to break up this understanding and to make of Morocco a test of Germany's power position. All this had little or nothing to do with the United States. However, because the Roosevelt administration had recently acted with great firmness in obtaining the release of an alleged American citizen * kidnaped and held for ransom by the Moroccan bandit Raisuli, the Kaiser conceived the idea that it might be both possible and profitable to involve the United States in the Moroccan affair.

On March 31, 1905, William II landed from his yacht at Tangier, called upon the Sultan of Morocco and dramatically declared:

> The object of my visit to Tangier is to make known that I am determined to do all in my power to safeguard efficaciously the interests of Germany in Morocco, for I look upon the Sultan as an absolutely independent sovereign.

Ostensibly, this was a demand for an "open door" in Morocco, challenging the Anglo-French agreement. The Sultan, egged on by the Germans, called for an international conference. This was rejected by the French foreign minister, Théophile Delcassé, with the support of the British government. The French cabinet, however, feared war with Germany and repudiated the stand of its foreign minister, forcing his resignation and inflicting exactly that humiliation upon France which the Kaiser had desired.

The German Emperor now asked Roosevelt to urge the French to accept the proposal for a conference, promising to agree in advance to whatever solution Roosevelt might consider fair. The temptation to play the peacemaker was irresistible. Roosevelt urged France to accept a conference, at the same time hinting broadly that he would support French claims in Morocco. The French agreed and the Algeciras Conference was scheduled for January 16, 1906. German diplomacy had achieved the first step in its program.

The conference might well have resulted in another and more dangerous success for the Germans, had not the second step in their program—the breaking up of the Russo-French al-

* John Perdicaris, whose American citizenship was not established.

liance—in the meantime miscarried. At a secret shipboard meeting in the Baltic on July 25, 1905, the Tsar agreed with the Kaiser to withdraw from his French alliance, but subsequently decided not to carry out his pledge. This left Germany without the power position she had expected to exploit at Algeciras.

The Act of Algeciras, signed on April 7, 1906, effected a compromise acceptable to all concerned and, in fact, favorable to France. Once more, the President took great pride in his accomplishment. Actually, he had engaged in a very risky enterprise. The affair was one in which the United States had no interest, except the general interest of preserving peace. The danger of war had actually passed with the repudiation of Delcassé and the Tsar's backdown had already assured a compromise solution. At the cost of involving the United States in European affairs, Roosevelt had merely helped to bring about an already assured postponement of the inevitable showdown between France and Germany. Had not the Senate, in ratifying the Act of Algeciras, asserted very clear reservations as to the responsibility undertaken by the United States in "the settlement of political questions which are entirely European in scope," and disclaimed any purpose "to depart from traditional American foreign policy which forbids participation by the United States" in the settlement of such questions, this country would have found itself in a dangerous and embarrassing position at the time of the Agadir crisis, five years later.

Fortunately, President Taft did not suffer from the same sort of restless energy which impelled his predecessor to rash intervention.

Two credit items must be added to Roosevelt's foreign policy ledger: the building up of the United States Navy into a powerful fighting force; and the negotiation of some twenty-five arbitration treaties with other countries, designed to assure the peaceful settlement of disputes. These undertakings expressed rather aptly the two sides of Roosevelt's nature. The Navy was the "big stick" needed to back up "the cause of righteousness." The arbitration treaties provided the means for "speaking softly" with the big stick conveniently standing in the corner.

CHAPTER SIXTEEN

The Last Years of the Long Peace

(1909–1913)

1. The Taft Administration.

IT HAS BECOME customary to regard the administration of President William Howard Taft as a period of reaction from Theodore Roosevelt's reforms, followed by a resumption of forward-looking legislation under President Woodrow Wilson. In the light of the facts, this is less than fair to Taft and overlooks altogether the impact of Robert La Follette upon Theodore Roosevelt—an impact which made the latter-day Roosevelt assume far more radical positions than he had taken as President. Actually, Taft's domestic policy was, on the whole, a continuation of that of his predecessor. Taft was nominated, against the opposition of both extremes in the Republican Party, by Roosevelt's influence and stood pledged to carry out the Square Deal. That he tried to do precisely this is evidenced by the legislative acts undertaken during his administration.

The 16th Amendment, authorizing the laying of a graduated income tax, was passed by Congress and submitted to the states for ratification. (Because the amendment came into effect on February 25, 1913, it is usually credited to President Wilson.) A Federal tax was levied upon the net incomes of corporations. A Monetary Commission was appointed and did much of the preliminary work which led up to the Federal Reserve Act of 1914. The Mann-Elkins Act extended the authority of the Interstate Commerce Commission to cover express and sleeping-car companies as well as communications. The Drug Label Act strengthened previous legislation. An eight-hour day was enacted for workers on the Federal payroll.

Also, during Taft's incumbency—though not on his initiative

—Congress passed the 17th Amendment providing for the direct popular election of Senators.

Many of these reform measures were imperfect. Most of them originated from popular demand at least as much as from administration leadership. But the same thing might have been said of Theodore Roosevelt's Square Deal reforms. The truth of the matter was that Taft was only a little more conservative than his predecessor, but not nearly as shrewd a politician. Where Roosevelt would sense a popular issue and place himself at the head of the political parade, Taft failed to make the reforms his own. This left him without credit with the radical wing of his party, while his acceptance of the reform measures made him almost equally unpopular with the stand-pat conservatives. The latter were particularly enraged over the change in the House rules which deprived their stalwart, Speaker Joe Cannon, of the arbitrary power he had so long wielded over the House. At the same time—and this was even more important— the entrenched conservative leadership in the Senate was all but overthrown by the Mid-Western Progressives led by Wisconsin's "Fighting Bob La Follette."

Returning from a hunting trip in Africa, Roosevelt sensed the situation and proceeded to appropriate most of the ideas of the La Follette progressives in a program which he called "The New Nationalism." This program went very much further than Roosevelt had gone as President or than he had expected Taft to go when he chose him as a successor. By snatching from La Follette the leadership of the Left wing of the Republican Party, Roosevelt made Taft into the leader of the standpatters, though he actually had little in common with them. Up to that point, the only serious blemish on Taft's domestic record had been his betrayal of his campaign promise to revise the tariff. As promised, he promptly called a special session to consider this matter but the resulting Payne-Aldrich Act raised rather than lowered the rates. It is doubtful whether Roosevelt would have done much better with the Congress elected in 1908; Roosevelt, however, would have had the political sense not to justify the unsatisfactory legislation as "the best tariff bill the Republican Party has ever passed." *

* Taft at Winona, on September 17, 1909.

It was not so much Taft's failure, as alleged by Roosevelt, to carry on the Square Deal program as Roosevelt's own rapid shift to the Left in 1910 in order to capture the Progressive movement which ended the friendship between the two men and split the Republican Party. Taft's easy-going, kindly nature did not equip him particularly well to deal with the resulting situation. He began by inheriting Roosevelt's enemies and ended by losing most of Roosevelt's friends. The ultra-conservatives stuck by him because they had no other place to go.

In his conduct of foreign policy, Taft showed no particular brilliance, nor did his Secretary of State, Philander C. Knox.

In the Far East, Taft and Knox believed that the Open Door in China was threatened by the railway concessions obtained by Russia and Japan. A memorandum, dated December 14, 1909, to China, Japan, France, Russia and Germany, proposed a joint loan to China to enable her to buy up all railroads then owned or controlled by foreign powers. This, of course, applied to the railroads in Manchuria over which Japan and Russia had gone to war. Secretary Knox naively asserted that this would be "perhaps the most effective way to preserve the undisturbed enjoyment by China of all political rights in Manchuria and to promote the development of those provinces under a practical application of the Open Door . . ." Russia had never accepted the Open Door principle. Japan considered it merely an irritating obstacle already tacitly removed by the Root-Takahira Agreement. The proposal had just the opposite effect of what it had been intended to achieve, arousing the resentment of both Russia and Japan and causing them to agree with each other as to their spheres of influence (in the treaties of July 4, 1910 and June 25, 1912). Thereafter both Russia and Japan proceeded to build additional railroads and feeder lines. Japan, particularly, connected the south Manchurian coal fields with a line running south through Korea to Pusan.

After the failure of this attempt, Taft and Knox turned their attention to obtaining for American firms a share in financing China's development. This resulted in the formation of the so-called Chinese Consortium, which loaned China about $135,-000,000; of which American firms supplied about $7,300,000.

In Latin America, Taft followed in Roosevelt's footsteps.

Knox negotiated with Nicaragua and Honduras treaties designed to straighten out the tangled affairs of these two small countries under an American protectorate. Both efforts proved abortive and resulted in the two countries making their own arrangements with their foreign creditors.

A year later, in 1912, a new President of Nicaragua, Adolfo Diaz, requested American intervention to restore order. Taft sent a detachment of Marines, some of whom remained until 1925 while the United States endeavored to restore tranquility.

In the same year, rumored negotiations of Japan with Mexico for a base in Lower California led to a Senate resolution, sponsored by Senator Lodge, which declared—in amplification of the Monroe Doctrine—that:

> . . . when any harbor or other place in the American continents is so situated that the occupation thereof for military or naval purposes might threaten the communications or the safety of the United States, the Government of the United States could not see without grave concern the possession of such harbor or other place by any corporation or association which has such a relation to another Government, not American, as to give that Government practical power of control for national purposes.*

Taft's only other serious problem in Latin America arose over the bursting into flame of the long-smoldering Mexican revolution. In 1910, the Diaz dictatorship was overthrown by Francisco Madero. Taft promptly recognized the new regime and, with Congressional approval, embargoed shipments of arms to Madero's opponents. The Madero government, however, displayed alarming signs of weakness and Knox soon felt compelled to demand more effective protection of American interests. Henry Lane Wilson, Taft's envoy in Mexico City, counseled drastic action, without which he thought that Latin American countries would lose "the awe and respect with which they have been taught to regard us." Taft mobilized 100,000 troops in Texas and threatened, if Madero failed to protect American interests, to permit shipments of arms to the anti-

---

* The rumored acquisition was not by the Japanese government but by a Japanese fishing company.

Madero insurrectionists. On February 9, 1913, just before Taft left the White House, Huerta successfully carried out a *coup d'etat* and Madero was brutally executed. Wilson urged prompt recognition of the counter-revolutionary government, but Taft declined to do so.

A second Moroccan crisis—the Agadir affair—occurred in 1911. Once more, the German Emperor rattled his sword. Thanks to the Senate reservations with respect to the Act of Algeciras, Taft was able to keep the United States aloof from the rapidly deteriorating situation in Europe.

Taft's endeavor to keep the Payne-Aldrich tariff from disrupting American trade with Canada by means of a reciprocal trade agreement was frustrated by one of those irresponsible outbursts by individual members of Congress which have so often plagued American diplomacy. Champ Clark, a Democrat from Missouri soon to be Speaker of the House, stated as his reason for supporting the agreement that he hoped to "see the day when the American flag will float over every square foot of British North American possessions clear to the North Pole." As a result of this tactless and wholly unnecessary utterance Canada rejected the agreement.

If President Taft achieved little of diplomatic gain during his four years in the White House, at least his administration was marked by greater restraint and consideration than that of his predecessor.

At the Republican Convention of 1912 Taft had the solid backing of the stand-pat Old Guard. Roosevelt might well have stampeded the convention and won the nomination had not the Old Guard controlled the credentials committee and settled almost all the disputes between rival delegations in Taft's favor. The Progressives thereupon bolted the party and, at a separate convention, nominated a third ticket, with California's Hiram Johnson named as Roosevelt's running-mate. Bryan guided the Democratic Convention's choice to Woodrow Wilson, the reform governor of New Jersey.

The real fight in the election was between Roosevelt and Wilson, the question being whether the new "Bull Moose" Progressive Party could attract a sufficient number of Democratic votes to offset the conservative Republicans who might be expected to stay with Taft. This might have been possible, if the Democrats had nominated a more conservative candidate. Wilson, however, appealed to the reform wing of the Democratic Party and succeeded in keeping most of it in line. The result was a popular vote of 6,286,214 for Wilson, 4,126,020 for Roosevelt and 3,483,922 for Taft. In the Electoral College, Wilson had 435 votes, Roosevelt 88 and Taft 8. The country was overwhelmingly in favor of progressive reform.

2. *The First Wilson Administration.*

The first Wilson administration will be considered here, rather than in the next chapter, because Wilson's "New Freedom" belonged, like Theodore Roosevelt's "Square Deal," to the end of an era in which the United States went through the growing pains of adolescence, pursued the self-centered course of a nation not yet fully mature and finally became conscious of at least some of its responsibilities. So also, the foreign policy of Wilson's first term marked a continuation of the past; the break came when the United States entered World War I in April, 1917.

Bryan picked Woodrow Wilson as a Democrat who could meet the Progressives on their own ground. As a consequence, Wilson made Bryan his first Secretary of State—a choice which turned out to be none too felicitous. Wilson's most important adviser in foreign affairs was a man who held no public office but who exercised a greater influence than the whole cabinet combined; this was the President's old and trusted friend, Colonel E. M. House, of Texas.

During his first year in office, Wilson put through two major reforms. The Underwood Tariff Act brought about a downward revision of the Payne-Aldrich rates, increased the free list, and created a Tariff Commission to study the differences between labor costs here and abroad. The measure also included a graduated income tax, which had been made possible by the ratification of the 16th Amendment.

The second great reform was the enactment of the Owen-Glass Bill, creating the Federal Reserve System. The Act divided the country into twelve regions, each with a Federal

Reserve Bank authorized to act as a central re-discount and note-issuing institution for the national and state-chartered banks in its region. This system provided, for the first time in the history of the United States, a paper currency with a strong metallic reserve and a re-discount facility through which the member banks could at any time borrow on their eligible commercial paper.*

Also in 1913, a law was enacted authorizing the Interstate Commerce Commission to make a thorough study of the value of railroad properties, with a view to establishing the basis for a fair rate of return.

After the Supreme Court had upheld the validity of state anti-trust laws (in the case against the International Harvester Company), President Wilson successfully urged a radical strengthening of the Federal Sherman Anti-Trust Law. The resulting amendment outlawed discriminating freight agreements, interlocking directorates and certain types of holding companies. The Federal Trade Commission was established on September 26, 1914, to regulate concerns other than banks and carriers engaged in interstate commerce and to establish rules of fair practice.

These were the major legislative enactments of the "New Freedom." In addition there were other manifestations of the growth of a social conscience. There was a tremendous increase in vocational schools and colleges. The demand for more and better public education led to the enactment of the Smith-Hughes Bill, in 1917, authorizing substantial Federal aid to states willing to match Federal grants for the improvement of the public schools.

The organization of labor progressed considerably during this period. As the unions grew in strength, many of them demanded the closed shop and this led to frequent disputes, some of them resulting in sympathetic strikes and boycotts. The American Federation of Labor quietly concentrated its efforts upon obtaining an eight-hour day and a minimum wage. The more radical Industrial Workers of the World (I.W.W.)

* Paul M. Warburg; *The Federal Reserve System;* Macmillan, 1930; also W. P. G. Harding; *The Formative Period of the Federal Reserve System;* Houghton Mifflin, 1925.

brought on a number of tumultuous disturbances. A threatened strike of railroad workers led President Wilson to demand
that Congress enact a law granting them an eight-hour day with
pro rata pay for overtime (the Adamson Act of September 3,
1916).

These highlights will perhaps suffice to indicate the temper
of the times and to illustrate the manner in which all three
branches of the Federal government were now moving toward
curbing the excessive power of wealth and toward the creation
of economic democracy. Unhappily, developments in the field
of foreign affairs were soon to bring this period of progress to
a halt.

It is an interesting fact that Wilson's first Inaugural Address
contained no reference to foreign policy problems. During the
first years of the Wilson administration, foreign policy was, in
fact, conducted almost solely in hemisphere terms and in almost total disregard of the growing crisis in Europe. This was
in part due to Wilson's preoccupation with domestic reform
and in part to the fact that both Wilson and Bryan were moral
pacifists. Neither seemed aware that a major conflict was brewing in Europe or that such a conflict might involve the vital
interests of the United States.

In the Far East, President Wilson's major interest centered
upon liberalizing the government of the Philippines. He persuaded Congress to enact the Jones Bill (1916), giving the Filipinos more opportunity for self-government and a promise of
independence as soon as they might demonstrate that they were
ready for it. This was an important step toward the redemption
of McKinley's great blunder. The President was successful in
fending off a Japanese Exclusion Act for which there was considerable demand in Congress. Wilson's other act of major importance in Far Eastern policy was to reverse Taft's program
with respect to the Chinese Consortium; he did not repudiate
the Open Door Policy in general.

Wilson's Latin American policy was substantially a continuation of that of his predecessors, except that the same course of
action was now clothed in moral precepts. The protectorates
over Cuba and the Dominican Republic were maintained and
a similar policy was extended to cover Haiti and Nicaragua.

The purchase of the Virgin Islands was finally consummated. The inhabitants of Puerto Rico were given self-government and American citizenship. Bryan's attempt to appease Colombian resentment over Theodore Roosevelt's Panamanian policy resulted in the already mentioned treaty which Roosevelt denounced as "blackmail" and which the Senate failed to ratify until 1921.

The moral missionary aspect of Wilson's attitude was most clearly expressed with regard to Mexico. Continuing Taft's refusal to recognize the Huerta regime, Wilson explained his action by a new moral doctrine. The United States, he declared, would support governments which rested "upon the consent of the governed," but "would have no sympathy for those who seek to seize the power of government to advance their own personal interests or ambitions." This was an early example of Wilson's habit of stating foreign policy in terms of subjective moral absolutes—a habit which led to moral crusading, irreconcilable with power politics and with another Wilsonian thesis—the right of every people to "self-determination."

Wilson replaced Taft's interventionist envoy to Mexico with former Governor Lind of Minnesota whom he instructed to tell Huerta that, if he would allow free elections in Mexico and the creation of a constitutional government, the United States would approve a Mexican loan by American bankers. Here was power politics—the very "dollar diplomacy" which Wilson condemned —employed to achieve a moral purpose. When Huerta rejected this proposal, Wilson proceeded by every means short of open intervention to seek Huerta's overthrow. Britain advised acceptance of the American proposal for constitutional reform. Once more, the Mexican President refused. Wilson then lifted the embargo on arms shipments to Huerta's opponents and sent warships to Vera Cruz in order to prevent similar supplies from reaching the regime. An incident involving the arrest of American sailors at Tampico, for which Huerta refused to apologize, led to the seizure of Vera Cruz. With the two countries on the verge of war, Argentina, Brazil and Chile offered mediation. Wilson promptly accepted. The Huerta regime collapsed and Huerta fled the country. This, however, did not restore peace; the new Carranza government was immediately threatened by two insurrectionary movements: one led by Emiliano Zapata in the South and the other by Francisco Villa in the North. Nevertheless, after consultation with six Latin American governments, Wilson recognized the Carranza regime.*

Carranza proved incapable of controlling the warring factions but rejected American aid as interference. Fifteen American engineers, invited by Carranza to help in reopening the mines, were intercepted and murdered by Villa. Not content with this outrage, Villa conducted a raid across the New Mexican border. With the quickly granted consent of Congress, Wilson sent General John J. Pershing with 15,000 men in a futile pursuit of Villa's bandits. One hundred fifty thousand National Guardsmen were mobilized on the Texas border.

The carrying out of this mobilization showed the total unpreparedness of the United States and emboldened both Villa and Carranza. When the bandit leader undertook two more raids into United States territory, the Carranzista forces in northern Mexico refused to cooperate with an American column sent in pursuit. The American troops actually clashed with Carranzistas at Carrizal.

The ineffectiveness of American policy aroused considerable criticism and a number of newspapers followed Theodore Roosevelt in demanding full-scale intervention. Wilson, by this time thoroughly alarmed over the war in Europe, clung to his policy of "watchful waiting" in the hope that the undeclared war with Mexico might be terminated by negotiation. In the end, there were no such negotiations; the American troops were withdrawn without Carranza's having given any of the assurances demanded. In March, 1917, with the United States on the brink of entering the war against Germany, Wilson sent Henry P. Fletcher as ambassador to Mexico to renew the severed diplomatic relations. The American envoy was received with catcalls and hisses, while the German ambassador was greeted everywhere with cheers.

We must now turn back to the outbreak of war in Europe in August, 1914.

* This procedure was in accordance with Colonel House's advice to "Pan-Americanize the Monroe Doctrine."

PART FIVE

The First World War and Its Aftermath

CHAPTER SEVENTEEN

Neutrality and Belligerence
(1914−1917)

WORLD WAR I broke out in Europe in August, 1914, in a manner which from the outset gave the Allies (Great Britain, France, Belgium and Russia) a moral advantage over the Central Powers (Germany, Austria-Hungary, Bulgaria and Turkey). The uncompromising Austrian ultimatum to Serbia and the ruthless German violation of Belgian neutrality put the Central Powers in the wrong from the start, at least so far as American public opinion was concerned. Most historians agree that by no means all of the responsibility for the first World War belongs to Germany and Austria. The Tsar's mobilization, French irredentism and Britain's failure to take a firm position all contributed to the final disaster, though it seems clear that Germany provided the basic cause of the conflict by its ambitious thrusting toward world power. Whatever the ultimate judgment of history,* American public opinion was quick to adopt the Anglo-French view that the Kaiser was almost solely responsible. This was not a unanimous view; there were dissenting groups, chiefly among Americans of German or Irish birth or descent and among Jewish and other East European groups hostile to the Tsarist regime.

Preponderant sympathy for the Allies did not, however, signify any inclination to go to war at their side. When President Wilson proclaimed strict neutrality, he expressed the sentiments of the vast majority. Yet he displayed an astonishing ignorance

---

* Charles Seymour, *The Diplomatic Background of the War* (Yale, 1916); Sidney B. Fay, *The Origins of the War* (Macmillan, 1928); E. M. Carroll, *Germany and the Great Powers, 1866-1914* (Prentice-Hall, 1938) ; and C. C. Tansill, *America Goes to War* (Little, Brown, 1938).

of human nature—and particularly of the American character—when he asked the American people to be "neutral in thought and feeling" as well as in action. It was one thing to express the popular desire to keep out of the conflict; it was a wholly different matter to expect the American people not to choose a side and to root for its victory.

As the Mexican imbroglio demonstrated, the nation was in any case wholly unprepared for war. The Army of 87,000 men possessed but four heavy field-guns, not a single trench-bomb or mortar, not a single plane suitable for combat duty and no stocks of munitions other than a supply of 800,000 excellent rifles. Thanks to Theodore Roosevelt the Navy had a strong fleet of modern battleships, but practically no submarines and few light cruisers, destroyers or escort vessels. Secretary of State Bryan showed how little he and many others in the administration understood the nature of the unfolding conflict when he declared that the United States needed to undertake no measures of preparedness because it could "raise a million men between sunrise and sunset."

Unready for war and disinclined to prepare for it, the nation was equally unprepared for the difficult diplomatic task of defining its neutral rights and defending them. The Secretary of State was temperamentally unsuited to carry out the particular kind of neutrality policy which the President chose to follow. Most of the American diplomats abroad had little experience or background knowledge of European history. Some of them—notably Walter Hines Page at the Court of St. James—were quite incapable of preserving that neutrality "in thought and feeling" which Wilson wished the American people to maintain. Wilson himself did not understand at first that this conflict differed from those of the past and that it had a vital bearing upon the future of the United States.

In 1914 and 1915, the United States government acted much as it had in the days of the Napoleonic Wars, seeing its sole problem in preserving freedom of the seas and the neutral rights of its citizens. The American people were just as little aware of their vital interest as their government. They were not "neutral in thought and feeling"; they wanted the Allied side to win, much as they wanted a favorite team to win a crucial game; but it occurred to very few Americans that their own future was at stake in the bloody battles being fought in Flanders and Picardy.

While the government and the people remained neutral in action, if not in sentiment, business did not remain neutral. Once the Germans were stopped at the Marne, the war became a war of attrition. In such a struggle, it soon became clear that the Allies could win only if they could blockade Germany and force it to consume its own substance while they themselves drew on the United States for supplies and the money with which to pay for them. Recognizing this, Britain and France bent every effort to influence American opinion in their favor, to stimulate American production of their needs and to get American bankers to grant them loans. In these efforts they were extremely successful. With great wisdom, Britain refrained from putting blockade measures into effect which might alienate American opinion until after the American economy had become readjusted to Allied needs and thoroughly dependent upon Allied purchases to maintain the war boom. The speed with which this boom developed can be seen from the following figures. In 1913, the United States had a favorable trade balance of $690,000,000. In 1915, it was $1,770,-000,000. In 1916, the figure rose to $3,000,000,000. Shipments of gold, sales of American securities by Anglo-French holders and war loans floated by J. P. Morgan & Company paid for the Allied purchases. Farm prices skyrocketed. Munitions plants paid unheard-of wages and drew people into the hastily improvised boom towns. The labor shortage was increased by a huge back-flow of immigration.[*]

It was not until after this boom was well under way that the British tightened up their blockade in such a way as to interfere seriously with American shipping. This led to the German declaration of a submarine counter-blockade of the British Isles. The blockade and the counter-blockade raised the familiar problems of neutral rights, with Britain in a position to cite the Civil War precedents to back its "paper blockade" of the Central Powers. The traditional American counter-measure had

* The net increase from immigration fell from 1,200,000 in 1914 to a mere 300,000 in 1916.

been the embargo. Speaker Champ Clark and the Democratic Majority Leader, Claude Kitchin, urged the use of this weapon, but Wilson would have none of it. An embargo might well have forced Britain to forego the illegal methods which made the blockade effective; this, in turn, might have prevented Germany from using unrestricted submarine warfare and—as some have argued—might have kept the United States out of the war. But by this time, an embargo would have collapsed the American war boom and would very likely have ruined Wilson's chances of re-election.

With American business booming and American bankers * marketing Allied war bonds, economic interest soon made American neutrality a matter of form only. To be sure, the United States government issued an almost continuous stream of formal protests against Allied and German invasion of neutral rights; but these notes were almost complacent in tone, as if intended to build up future claims for damages rather than to compel compliance. When Germany, for example, declared a "zone of danger" around the British Isles, Wilson declared that he would hold the Germans "strictly accountable" for any loss of American lives or property, but he gave no indication of what "accountability" would mean.

Wilson faced a choice. He could, as Bryan urged, warn Americans to stay off belligerent ships and order American vessels to stay out of the danger zone. Or, he could insist upon full neutral rights and freedom of the seas, which would logically mean resorting, if necessary, to armed neutrality or to actual war. His choice of the latter course brought about Bryan's resignation and the appointment of Robert Lansing as Secretary of State. On the other hand, Wilson showed extreme reluctance to enforce the kind of neutrality he had chosen. A few days after the sinking of the *Lusitania* (May 7, 1915), he declared to the Sen-

* To state these facts is not to endorse the theory that the munition makers and Wall Street were responsible for getting the United States into World War I. Given the kind of neutrality policy Wilson elected to pursue, the results were inevitable. It is, however, a fact that J. P. Morgan & Company, in addition to heading the syndicates which marketed Allied war bonds, also acted as purchasing agent and earned about $30,000,000 in commissions on purchases of about $3,000,000,000. See Report of the Nye (Senate) Investigating Committee, G.P.O., 1931.

ate: "There is such a thing as a man being too proud to fight. There is such a thing as a nation being so right that it does not need to convince others by force that it is right." Yet his note to Germany was firm, demanding assurance that unarmed merchant ships would not be attacked without warning.

The Kaiser hesitated. As yet, Germany had only about 40 sea-going submarines—not enough to make further antagonizing of the United States worth while. When the unarmed liner *Arabic* was sunk without warning in August, the German government disclaimed responsibility, claiming that the ship must have struck a mine. A second sinking, this time in the Mediterranean, was attributed to an Austrian submarine, and a third to Turkish action. On each occasion, Wilson protested the loss of American lives but took no other action.

During the latter part of 1915, a large part of the American public became restive. "Preparedness" groups were formed. Colleges began raising regiments. Theodore Roosevelt, the leading pro-Allied spokesman, poured contempt upon Wilson's cautious neutrality. Acts of sabotage, instigated by the German and Austrian embassies, aroused indignation and public sentiment was inflamed by none too scrupulous Allied propaganda.*

Realizing that the country was drifting into war, Wilson accepted Colonel House's advice and sought to mediate peace. House was authorized to tell Sir Edward Grey that Wilson expected to approach both sides; that, if the Allies accepted and the Central Powers refused mediation, the United States would *probably* enter the war on the Allied side; and that if both sides accepted and the conference should then fail because of German intransigence, the United States would also *probably* join the Allies. Grey turned down this chance to involve the United States, partly because the Allies were unwilling to state their terms and partly in the belief that the United States would be drawn into the war in any case.†

* For a brilliant, if somewhat one-sided, account of Allied propaganda, see Walter Millis, *The Road to War* (Houghton Mifflin, 1935); also C. H. Grattan, *Why We Fought* (Vanguard, 1929).

† This effort remained secret. See E. M. House, *Intimate Papers*, edited by Charles Seymour (Houghton Mifflin, 1951), Vol. II, pages 166-204.

On March 24, 1916, just a month after the British had rejected the House proposal, the English transport *Sussex* was sunk without warning in the English Channel, causing injury to a number of American passengers.* This brought forth the sharpest note Wilson had yet sent to Berlin. Under threat of breaking off diplomatic relations, Wilson demanded that the Imperial German Government abandon "its present methods of waging submarine warfare." The German reply amounted to a capitulation, although it insisted that the President demand the termination of the Allies' "illegal blockade." The determining factor, as we now know, was that the Germans still had only 52 U-boats—not enough to take the great gamble.

The German reply and the subsequent cessation of sinkings cooled off interventionist sentiment in the United States. Discouraged by the British refusal of mediation, Wilson now fell back upon strict neutrality. He had gone about as far as he could go in attempting to secure a just peace favorable to the Allies and had gained the impression that both sides were now so committed to the struggle that neither would settle on reasonable terms.

During the summer of 1916, the German offensive at Verdun and the Allied counter-offensive on the Somme with their fearful casualties showed that the war had entered into a stalemate on the Western front. With the Germans occupying highly favorable positions in Russia and the Balkans, it was difficult to see how even American intervention could bring about an Allied victory. In these circumstances, Wilson's neutrality policy had the support of the majority of the American people, despite attacks leveled against it by Roosevelt and other interventionists. The Democrats renominated Wilson for a second term and the Republicans nominated Chief Justice Charles E. Hughes— a man of cautious restraint—rather than the fire-eating Roosevelt. Participation in the war was not an issue between the two parties, but the most effective slogan used by the Democrats

---

* The unarmed *Sussex* was proceeding without escort through a danger zone littered with the wreckage of torpedoed ships. Some writers have voiced the suspicion that both the *Lusitania* and the *Sussex* were deliberately exposed to attack in order to bring about an American break with Germany. See S. F. Bemis; *op. cit.,* page 616.

was: "He kept us out of war." The popular vote was close, with California giving Wilson the decisive votes in the Electoral College.

After his re-election, Wilson resumed his efforts to make peace, asking both sides to state their terms. Prime Minister Lloyd George stated Britain's answer in the House of Commons on December 19, 1916: "Complete restitution, full reparation and effectual guarantees." Germany replied that she was prepared to attend a peace conference but would not state her terms of peace in advance. Privately, these terms were indicated to be such that Wilson knew the Allies could not be expected to accept them.*

In a speech to the Senate, on January 22, 1917, Wilson deplored the intransigence of both sides and declared that it should be clear to all that there could be no "peace with victory." In despair of bringing about a peace without victory, the President turned to the idea of arming American merchant vessels. His proposal was blocked in the Senate by the famous filibuster of the eleven "willful men," led by Robert La Follette.

While the Armed Neutrality Bill was under discussion, the die had already been cast at Berlin. The Kaiser decided, on January 9, 1917, that Germany's only hope of a victorious peace lay in the resumption of unrestricted submarine warfare. By this time Admiral von Tirpitz could muster over 100 submarines and was able to persuade the Kaiser that he could bring Britain to its knees within a matter of months. Asked about the effect of probable American intervention, the Admiral is said to have remarked that "an elephant cannot swim," and to have assured the Emperor that not a single American soldier would ever set foot on European soil.

A few days after Wilson's speech to the Senate, Ambassador von Bernstorff delivered a note announcing that Germany would resume unrestricted submarine warfare on February 1. Wilson promptly broke off diplomatic relations. The country

* These terms were later disclosed when Germany resumed unrestricted submarine warfare. They provided for German annexation of certain French territory and retention of control, though not ownership, of Belgium. Bulgaria was to have a free hand in Rumania. Germany was to receive colonies and indemnities from all the Allies.

was now feverishly preparing for war, but the President still hesitated to take the final step. At this point Britain gave matters a decisive push.

On January 19, the British had intercepted a message to Count von Bernstorff giving the substance of the notorious "Zimmermann Note" instructing the German ambassador in Mexico to approach the Mexican government with the suggestion that, if the United States should enter the war on the side of the Allies, Mexico should join the Central Powers and use the opportunity to recapture her "lost territory." The British, having obtained and deciphered this message by illegal interference with the United States diplomatic correspondence, did not publish it or turn it over to Washington at once. However, when the resumption of undersea war failed to bring about more than a rupture of diplomatic relations, the intercepted note was handed to President Wilson. This was on February 24. After hesitating for a week, Wilson gave the note to the press, knowing that the result would be an almost unanimous sentiment for a declaration of war.

Even this, however, was not the decisive event. It remained for the Russian revolution of March 12, 1917, to provide Woodrow Wilson with the moral basis for declaring war which he had hitherto lacked. The sudden overthrow of the Tsar made it possible to regard the conflict as a struggle between democracy and autocracy. It was no longer merely a contest between two equally intransigent belligerent groups, each striving for domination over the other. On April 2, 1917, Wilson went before Congress and asked for a declaration of war on the grounds that "the world must be made safe for democracy." War was declared four days later.

The crucial importance of the March revolution was appraised by Winston Churchill in these words: *

If the Russian revolution had occurred in January instead of March, or if, alternatively, the Germans had waited to declare unlimited U-boat war until the summer, there would have been no unlimited U-boat war and consequently

* Winston Churchill, *The World Crisis* (Houghton Mifflin, 1929), Vol. III, pages 212-215.

no intervention of the United States. If the Allies had been left to face the collapse of Russia without being sustained by the intervention of the United States, it seems certain that France could not have survived the year, and the war would have ended in a peace by negotiation or, in other words, a German victory.

Churchill may or may not have been right in assuming that, if there had been no U-boat war, neither Wilson nor the American people would have realized, before it was too late, what a German victory would mean to the United States. Be that as it may, the indisputable fact is that the decision to intervene was not reached by any clear analysis of the vital interests of the United States. It was reached because Wilson had come to the end of the road in the particular course of neutrality which he had chosen, and because the overthrow of Tsardom gave him the moral absolute without which he was unwilling to go to war.

The factors which *should* have been determining were:

1. That the acquisition of a Pacific empire had made the United States dependent upon a British alliance, unless and until the United States possessed sufficient sea power to match both Germany in the Atlantic and Japan in the Far East.

2. That the survival of Britain as a great sea power had become dependent upon the survival of France as a land power blocking German domination of the Atlantic coast of Europe.

3. That the survival of France had become dependent upon American intervention.

4. That the ability of the American economy to sustain the Allied war effort had become dependent, in a sort of vicious circle, upon the continuance of that war effort.

In asking for a declaration of war against Germany, President Wilson cited none of these reasons of vital national interest. He cited merely the German invasion of American neutral rights, the brutal inhumanity of the U-boat war and the crusading cause with which the accident of the Russian revolution had presented him. Instead of saying that technological progress and the advent of the air age had made peace indivisible—that the United States could, in future, hope for peace only if it helped to maintain world peace—Wilson merely told the American people that "the world must be made safe for democracy." To most Americans this meant simply that autocracy must be overthrown and that, once this had been accomplished, world peace—or at least peace for the United States—would be assured.

Thus the American people went to war with wholehearted enthusiasm and a crusading spirit, but without the slightest idea of what they were really fighting for. This led to a whole series of costly consequences affecting not only the Peace of Versailles but the subsequent course of events throughout the first half of the twentieth century.

Woodrow Wilson personified the basic ambivalence of the American people with regard to international relations—the conflict between a moral pacifism which rejected both war and *Machtpolitik* as evils to be abolished, and a nationalism which accepted the need for "living in the world as it is" and the use of whatever means—including war and power politics—might be necessary to defend and promote the national interest. This ambivalence dated back to the earliest days of the republic and had found expression in the policies pursued by most of the American Presidents. Jackson, Tyler, Polk, Pierce and Buchanan had been outright believers in and practitioners of power politics. Theodore Roosevelt was the outstanding believer in *Machtpolitik*—"The Big Stick"—in the post-Civil War era. All the other American Presidents, including even William McKinley, had in varying degrees felt and expressed a sense of moral guilt when confronted with the question of using force or the threat of force as an instrument of foreign policy. Wilson, once he was driven into power politics and war, became the first American President to translate moral pacifism into a course of positive action, attempting—no matter how unsuccessfully—to create a world in which war and power politics would no longer be essential to national survival and prosperity. ity.

CHAPTER EIGHTEEN

Wilson's Wartime Diplomacy and Peace Aims

(1917–1919)

ALTHOUGH he failed utterly to make the American people aware of their own stake in the outcome of the war, Woodrow Wilson perceived sooner than any other statesman of the time that only a just peace could be expected to be enduring and that the making and preserving of a just peace required more than the mere re-establishment of a balance of power. Strangely enough, Wilson did not use the entry of the United States into the war to persuade the Allies to define their peace aims in a manner consistent with his concept of a just and durable settlement. Clearly, this was the one moment when he had the bargaining power to compel a consideration of what he considered proper war aims. Yet, once the decision had been reached to declare war, Wilson made no effort whatever to make American participation contingent upon any sort of agreement as to the peace settlement.

The opportunity to bargain did not, moreover, vanish at the moment when Congress voted for a declaration of war; it existed for some time thereafter, until the United States was committed to an all-out military effort on the Continent. That the British and the French expected some such discussion of war and peace aims was clearly evident at the time of the visit of the Balfour mission in the spring of 1917, followed by the French, Belgian and Italian representatives. The British foreign minister brought with him a map, showing the effect of five secret treaties to which the Allies had committed themselves during the course of the war. Presumably he brought with him also the actual texts of the treaties. It is known that Balfour had long talks with Wilson and House about these commitments but, so far as is known, there was no discussion with the other Allied delegations and no American demands for change were expressed to the British. This was apparently due to the urgent advice of House against holding any discussion of peace aims at that time.* "If the Allies begin to discuss terms among themselves," House wrote to the President, "they will soon hate one another worse than they do Germany . . . It seems to me that the only thing to be considered at present is how to beat Germany in the quickest way."

The five secret treaties were:

1. *The Anglo-French Treaty with Russia of March, 1915.* This gave Russia the right to annex Constantinople and the Asiatic shore of the Bosporus and Dardanelles and provided for the break-up and partition of the Turkish empire. The Anglo-French (and, later, the Italian) spheres of influence were defined in the Sykes-Picot Agreement of May, 1916, and the April, 1917, modification thereof in favor of Italy. This disposed of Turkey's future.

2. *The Treaty of London between the Allies and Italy, April, 1915.* This was an agreement to give Italy a part of the Austrian Tyrol, possession of the head of the Adriatic, a part of Albania, the Dodecanese Islands and a share in the partition of the Turkish empire. At the price of these concessions, Italy switched over to the Allies.

3. *The Treaty of Bucharest, August, 1916.* This brought Rumania to the Allied side at the price of being promised the Hungarian province of Transylvania and the Serbian Banat region. (The Germans had offered Rumania the Russian province of Bessarabia.)

4. At the beginning of the war Britain and Japan had agreed to divide up the German islands in the Pacific—those north of the equator to go to Japan, those south of the equator to go to Britain. This was confirmed by an *Anglo-French-Italian-Russian agreement in March, 1917,* which also

* E. M. House; *op. cit.;* Vol. III, pages 29-63.

gave Japan the right to take over all German rights to the Chinese province of Shantung.

5. In *the Russo-French agreement of March, 1917,* each signatory gave the other a free hand in fixing its frontier with Germany. This meant promising Germany's Polish provinces to Russia and *at least* a return of Alsace-Lorraine to France.

These secret arrangements for the disposal of German, Austrian, Hungarian, Turkish and South Slavic territory were wholly inconsistent with the idea of a "peace without victory" and with the right of "self-determination" for all nations, considered by Wilson as indispensable to an enduring settlement. Arthur Balfour must have been agreeably surprised that Wilson made no effort to reopen these questions as the price for all-out American participation.

In April, Congress appropriated $7,000,000,000 of which $3,000,000,000 was to be loaned to the Allies. In May, Congress enacted national conscription and the President promised the Allies 1,500,000 American troops on the Western front by the end of 1918. The chance to bargain was past. Instead of having to haggle with a new ally as they had with each other, the Entente powers found that they had acquired an "Associate"— Wilson carefully maintained the distinction—who promised full cooperation without asking anything in return. The productive power of American factories and farms, the wealth of the American people and the flower of American youth were thrown into the scales unhesitatingly, without a question being asked as to the objectives for which these resources were to be spent. Never had so desperate a cause received so much for so little.

The advice which House gave President Wilson turned out to be fatally bad advice. When it came to the peace conference, Wilson found it far more difficult to deal with the victorious Allies than he had anticipated—far more difficult than it would have been in the spring of 1917. This not only prevented the making of a just and durable peace but established a disastrous principle which was to govern this nation's conduct in a later world conflict—the principle of military expediency, of winning a war first and talking about the peace only after the war had been won.

While the United States was preparing to throw its decisive weight into the balance but was as yet unable to offer much immediate military assistance, Allied fortunes sank to a low ebb. Italy all but collapsed after the defeat of Caporetto in the autumn of 1917. The Bolshevik revolution of November, 1917, sealed the fate of Russia as a useful ally and opened the way to a separate peace between Russia and Germany. Bolshevik disclosure of the secret treaties undermined Allied morale. Mutiny was brewing in France and the German General Staff was preparing to stake all on a last great spring offensive. Only at sea, where the convoy system was beginning to bring the submarine menace under control, were there any hopeful signs for the future. It was in these gloomy circumstances that Wilson endeavored to lift Allied morale and to undermine the German will to resistance by putting forward his famous Fourteen Points. This program for peace was stated to the Congress on January 8, 1918. Its chief points were:

1. Open covenants of peace, openly arrived at with no private international understandings, and diplomacy to proceed always frankly and in the public view.

2. Absolute freedom of navigation upon the seas, outside territorial waters, alike in peace and in war, except as the seas may be closed in whole or in part by international action for the enforcement of international covenants.

3. The removal, so far as possible, of all economic barriers and the establishment of an equality of trade conditions among all the nations consenting to the peace and associating themselves for its maintenance.

4. Adequate guarantees given and taken that national armaments will be reduced to the lowest point consistent with domestic safety.

5. . . . impartial adjustment of all colonial claims, based upon strict observance of the principle that . . . the interests of the populations concerned must have equal weight with the equitable claims of the government whose title is to be determined.

6. The evacuation of all Russian territory and such a settlement of all questions affecting Russia as will secure the best and freest cooperation of the other nations of the world in obtaining for her an unhampered and unembarrassed opportunity for the independent determination of her own political development and national policy and assure her of a sincere welcome into the society of free nations under institutions of her own choosing; and, more than a welcome, assistance also of every kind that she may need and may herself desire. The treatment accorded to Russia by her sister nations in the months to come will be the acid test of their good will, of their comprehension of her needs as distinguished from their own interests, and of their intelligent and unselfish sympathy. [This paragraph, written in the hope of keeping Bolshevik Russia in the war, was later to make strange reading.]

7. Evacuation of Belgium and full restoration of its sovereignty.

8. The freeing and restoration of invaded French territory and the restoration to France of Alsace-Lorraine.

9. A readjustment of Italian frontiers along clearly recognizable lines of nationality.

10. Freest opportunity of autonomous development for the peoples of Austria-Hungary.

11. Rumania, Serbia and Montenegro to be evacuated and restored; Serbia to have access to the sea; relations between the Balkan states to be determined along lines of allegiance and nationality and their independence guaranteed.

12. The Turkish portions of the Ottoman empire to remain Turkish but other nationalities assured of autonomous development; the Dardanelles to be open to all nations.

13. An independent Poland to be created, including the territories inhabited by indisputably Polish populations. This new state to have free and secure access to the sea.

14. A general association of nations to be formed under specific covenants for the purpose of affording mutual guarantees of political independence and territorial integrity to great and small nations alike.

The wording of points 9-13 was such that their meaning, especially in relation to the secret treaties, remained largely a matter of interpretation. If victorious, the Allies—except Russia—would be able to interpret these points in such a way as to get pretty much what they wanted. Although the proposal could scarcely be called a definitive program for peace, it served its purpose as an extremely effective instrument of propaganda, especially points 1, 3, 4, 5 and 14, which gave expression to Wilson's idealism and his conception of a just peace. Points 9 to 13 provided for the break-up of the Austrian and Turkish empires and a seizure of German territory on conditions which might or might not—according to later interpretation—be consistent with a peace of justice.

The Germans' contention that they were misled and betrayed by the final interpretation of the Fourteen Points might have been well founded, had it not been for the fact that the Germans themselves had stultified their case by showing—in the disgraceful treaty of Brest-Litovsk, signed in March, 1918—what kind of a peace they would have imposed if victorious. Two wrongs did not make a right, but, certainly, the ruthless behavior of the Germans as conquerors undermined their case against the peace imposed by the Allies a year later.*

The final German offensive in the West failed in July, 1918. American troops were beginning to arrive in great numbers to bolster the exhausted Allied armies. During this period, Wilson made a number of public addresses in which he amplified the principles of the Fourteen Points.†

The collapse of the Central Powers came suddenly. In mid-September, Austria proposed a discussion of peace on Wilson's

---

* For an admirable study of the events leading up to the Bolshevik revolution and the separate peace with Germany, see John Wheeler-Bennett; *The Forgotten Peace;* Morrow, 1939.

† To Congress, February 11, 1918; at Mt. Vernon, July 4, 1918; and in opening the Fourth Liberty Loan Campaign on September 27, 1918. In these addresses Wilson elaborated and emphasized the meaning of "impartial justice," the need for each part of a settlement to be just in itself; the principle that "peoples and provinces are not to be bartered about from sovereignty to sovereignty as if they were mere chattels . . . in the game of power politics"; and the need for making all settlements "upon the basis of the free acceptance . . . by the people immediately concerned, and not upon the basis of the material interest or advantage of any other nation . . ."

principles. Two weeks later, Bulgaria surrendered unconditionally. With the Allies now rapidly advancing in the West, the German High Command panicked and urged the Kaiser to seek peace. On October 6-7, the German and Austrian governments appealed to Wilson for an armistice. Wilson replied to Berlin that before transmitting this request to the Allies, he must know whether he was dealing with a German government that had the support of the people. To Austria he said that the Czechs and Jugoslavs would have to decide upon their own future destiny. Meanwhile the Allied advance continued. On October 31, Turkey withdrew from the war and accepted an armistice. The end was near. On November 3, the rapidly crumbling Austro-Hungarian empire capitulated without making the Wilsonian terms a condition of surrender. The proclamation of a socialist republic in Germany finally induced Wilson to submit the German request for an armistice to the Allies. The Kaiser fled ignominiously to Holland. General Pershing favored continuing the Allied advance into Germany. Marshal Foch, however, overruled him, saying: "One makes war only to get results." It was Foch, rather than Wilson, who dictated the military terms of the armistice. These terms ultimately contained two major reservations as to the Fourteen Points: the British, in effect, struck out Point 2 guaranteeing freedom of the seas; the French introduced the demand that Germany must pay reparations for all damages done by Germany to the Allies. With these two major modifications, Wilson's pronouncements became the basis for the armistice signed on November 11, 1918.

From here on, the tragic story of Wilson's failure becomes very largely a story of mishandled domestic politics. Wilson's first great mistake was to appeal to the American people for the election of a Democratic Congress. (The Congressional elections were held during the armistice negotiations.) Partisan politics had been almost entirely submerged, but, during the months preceding the elections, both Taft and Roosevelt had appealed to the electorate to insure a peace of unconditional surrender by electing a Republican Congress. Roosevelt had explicitly denounced the Fourteen Points as "soft." Wilson's counterappeal for a Democratic majority was doubtless based upon the fear that a Republican Congress might repudiate the "just peace" for which he was striving. Had he appealed to the country on a non-partisan basis, he might well have obtained a friendly though not necessarily Democratic Congress. It must be borne in mind that the country, in 1918, was still normally Republican. The result of the partisan appeal was an overwhelming defeat for the President. Theodore Roosevelt declared to the world: "Our Allies and our enemies, and Mr. Wilson himself, should all understand that Mr. Wilson has no authority whatever to speak for the American people at this time. His leadership has just been emphatically repudiated by them . . ." It is difficult to understand just what patriotic purpose Roosevelt thought he was serving by such a statement; and it was, of course, wholly untrue to say that Mr. Wilson had "no authority whatever to speak for the American people." He was still, and would be for two more years, the duly elected Chief Executive.

A man with greater political sagacity would, in Wilson's place, have realized that he could not, with cavalier disregard of the Congressional elections, proceed to act for the American people in negotiating the peace without close consultation with the leaders of a hostile Congress. It was Wilson's second great mistake that he assumed full and almost sole responsibility for the negotiations, taking with him to the Peace Conference not a single Congressional leader and not even a delegation appointed with the advice and consent of the Senate.* The men whom Wilson took with him were: Secretary Lansing, Colonel E. M. House, General Tasker H. Bliss and the veteran diplomatist, Henry White, plus a large group of "experts" mostly recruited by Colonel House.

Turning now to Wilson's negotiations with other powers, we recall that the United States had missed its first and most promising opportunity to clear away the commitments of the five secret treaties. On November 29, 1918, a second such opportunity was presented. The French government suggested that the United States, Britain, France, Italy and Japan hold a preliminary meeting, throw out all the secret treaties and agree

* Henry M. Wriston, *Executive Agents in American Foreign Relations* (Johns Hopkins, 1929).

among each other upon the principal terms of peace; that a five-power proposal then be submitted to the other interested powers; and that, thereafter, all the nations meet to work out the permanent structure of the League. Although both House and Lansing were inclined to favor such a procedure, Wilson did not even reply to the French proposal. He was determined to get the League first and to make the peace treaties dependent upon its creation. He was convinced that the unassailable moral principles to be embodied in the covenant would overcome both Republican resistance at home and the selfish nationalistic ambitions of the European powers. Realizing that he stood more or less alone among the world's statesmen in his reliance upon moral right, Wilson never hesitated over the decision to go to Paris himself as the chief proponent and negotiator. In so deciding, he sacrificed the great reserve power which he might have wielded, had he remained at home and issued instructions to plenipotentiaries at Paris after consultation with Congressional leaders.*

However much Wilson's leadership had been repudiated at home, his prestige, when he arrived at Paris in January, 1919, was far greater than that of any other statesman. For one thing, he came as the Chief of State of the nation which had rescued the Allies from disaster. Even more important—he came as the friend of mankind, as the champion of impartial justice, and as the exponent of carrying into the hitherto cynical realm of international affairs the principles and ideals of Christianity.

Wilson insisted that the Covenant be drafted and agreed to as the first integral part of the peace treaty. To accomplish this, he was compelled to make a number of sacrifices of principle in the various peace settlements.

Great Britain and the Dominions were unwilling to apply the principle of "impartial adjustment" (Point Five of the Fourteen Points) to the former German possessions. General Jan Smuts of South Africa, one of the leading proponents of the League, put forward a system of League mandates for the new

* Wilson's own Secretary of State felt that it was a mistake for the President to descend from his dominant position to negotiate on the level of the Paris Conference. See Robert Lansing, *The Peace Negotiations, A Personal Narrative* (Houghton Mifflin, 1921).

countries to be formed out of the non-Turkish parts of the former Ottoman empire, but neither Britain nor the Dominions were willing to apply this principle to the former German colonies. Wilson finally accepted a system of "graded mandates" for all conquered territories, which theoretically avoided outright annexation. In practice, however, it developed that in almost every instance the mandate was given either to the nation which had conquered a former German possession or to the nation to which that territory had been promised in one of the secret treaties.

In shaping the new states of central and eastern Europe, the principle of "recognizable nationality" was fairly well carried out as to Finland, Latvia, Estonia and Lithuania—all formerly parts of the Tsarist empire. In the formation of the remnant and succession states created out of the former Austro-Hungarian empire, Wilson agreed to several dangerous departures from the principles of the Fourteen Points. Czechoslovakia was awarded the ethnically German Sudetenland for strategic reasons; a considerable Hungarian minority was left in Slovakia and a White Russian-Ukrainian minority in the strategic tip of Ruthenia. Austria was reduced to a rump with insufficient hinterland for the great city of Vienna and without access to the sea. A part of the Tyrol, inhabited by 250,000 Austrians, was given to Italy, along with considerably more territory at the head of the Adriatic than could be justified on ethnical grounds, leaving Slavic peoples under Italian rule in the Trieste area, and Italians under Jugoslav rule in Fiume. All these concessions contained the seeds of future trouble. Worst of all, however, were the compromises made in the creation of Poland and in the effort to satisfy French demands for security guarantees and reparations.

In attempting to restore independence to the long-suffering and often-partitioned Polish nation, it was necessary to amputate parts of three former empires. The so-called Curzon Line, as the new frontier between Russia and Poland, was probably as fair, on ethnical grounds, as any feasible line of demarcation, yet it failed to satisfy the Poles and resulted in Polish aggression in 1920. The amputation from Germany and Austria of the predominantly Polish provinces was also, on the whole, a fair solution,* but the attempt to give Poland access to the sea through the Danzig Corridor left German East Prussia as a German island in a Slavic sea, creating insecurity and resentment on both sides.

It was inevitable that the attempt to remake the map of Europe in such a way as to give its peoples national sovereignty in accordance with the Wilsonian principles would create certain difficulties. Moreover, one may doubt whether it was wise to break up the Hapsburg empire without creating in its place some sort of Danubian federation to prevent the Balkanization of central Europe. In any case, Wilson's purposes could have been more successfully achieved if—as France proposed—the table had first been swept clean of the secret treaty commitments.

The most disastrous compromises of all were made in the attempt to meet the French demands for reparations and for adequate guarantees against renewed German aggression. France, as the chief sufferer, had a reasonable case in both respects, but Clemenceau's rancor led him to make excessive demands. In addition to paying for all war damage, he insisted that Germany should also pay France a sum sufficient to defray French separation allowances to soldiers' families, and pensions to relatives and survivors of the dead. This ran the already astronomical reparation account into fantastic figures. To assure French security, Clemenceau demanded that all of Germany west of the Rhine should be set up as a permanently demilitarized buffer state, ostensibly independent, but subject to French control. Alsace-Lorraine was, of course, to be returned to France and, in addition, Clemenceau wished to annex the ethnically German Saar.

After long negotiations, Clemenceau agreed—against the advice of Foch—to modify these terms, provided that the United States and Britain would sign a treaty guaranteeing French security. When Wilson and Lloyd George agreed to this, the French dropped their claims for repayment of separation allowances and pensions and accepted the following security arrangement: (1) France to take back Alsace-Lorraine; (2) the

---

* The Silesian border was settled by plebiscite after a German protest against the original proposal.

prewar frontiers to remain otherwise unchanged, except that France was to take over the Saar under a League mandate until 1935, when its final disposition would be settled by plebiscite; (3) Germany to agree to the permanent demilitarization of the Rhineland and of a zone fifty kilometers in depth east of the Rhine; (4) France to occupy the left bank of the Rhine and its bridgeheads for a limited period, withdrawal to be made in five-year stages.

Wilson signed the Anglo-French-American treaty but made no very great effort to obtain its ratification. When the Senate rejected it—as Wilson probably expected it would—Clemenceau finally agreed to let the territorial arrangements stand, on condition that the French claim for repayment of pensions and allowances be reinstated. Wilson agreed to this unhappy compromise, probably in the hope that the League would ultimately satisfy French security requirements and that common sense would eventually bring about a more realistic calculation of Germany's capacity to pay.

Had Wilson possessed the political acumen to match his statesmanship and thus been able to carry his own country with him, many of the defects of the peace settlements might have been remedied. American withdrawal from all responsibility left the French without adequate guarantees and destroyed the influence of those French leaders who would have wished to pursue a moderate policy. France became vengeful and intransigent, evoking a fatal resurgence of German nationalism, and the provisions for modification contained in the Treaty of Versailles were never used. This, in turn, led to the creation of the German myth that Germany had been "betrayed" into acceptance of a dictated peace.

There can be no doubt that the Treaty of Versailles was harsh and that it was imposed, rather than negotiated. It stripped Germany of all colonies, reduced its armed forces to 100,000 and imposed a state of demilitarization "in order to render possible the initiation of a general limitation of the armaments of all nations." It forced the Germans to accept the responsibility "for causing all the loss and damage to which the Allied and Associated Governments and their nationals have been subjected as a consequence of the war imposed upon them by the aggression of Germany and her allies" (Article 231). It imposed upon Germany an impossible burden of reparations; by doing so it confused the calculations of the whole Western world and led to a period of disastrous economic nationalism.*

Yet, with all its faults, two things should be remembered about the Treaty of Versailles:† it did not dismember or destroy Germany; and its provisions were such as to make subsequent modifications possible. Much of the harm done by the concessions which Wilson made to the power politics of Clemenceau, Lloyd George and Orlando would have been—or, at least, might have been undone, if the League had come into being, as Wilson hoped, with the United States as a participant.

Wilson gambled everything upon the assumption that, once the nations of the world would have united in the League Covenant, their common interest in the preservation of peace would bring them to accept justice as the only basis for lasting peace; and that whatever injustice might be committed in the settlements of 1919-1920 would in due course be remedied. In view of the nature of the Covenant, which assumed that the great powers would be willing to apply sanctions to maintain peace when their own vital interests were not directly at stake, it is doubtful whether Wilson's hope was justified. The mere

* The decision to permit Germany to have an army of 100,000 professionals, enlisted at long term, instead of an army of 200,000 conscripts serving only a year, was taken against the advice of Marshal Foch. Foch foresaw the danger of permitting the creation of professional cadres which might readily be expanded.

The decision to make Germany acknowledge moral responsibility for the entire cost of the war while accepting actual liability only for the civilian damage has been attributed to Mr. John Foster Dulles. See Paul Birdsall, *Versailles Twenty Years After* (Reynal & Hitchcock, 1941), pages 241-243. This was the basis of the much-discussed Article 231—the war-guilt article—which provided Hitler with the psychological basis of resentment upon which to base a repudiation of the Versailles Treaty.

The classical work on the reparations clauses of the Treaty is John Maynard Keynes' *The Economic Consequences of the Peace* (Harcourt, Brace, 1919). A rebuttal of Keynes was published in 1946 by a French writer, Etienne Mantoux, in a book entitled *The Economic Consequences of Mr. Keynes.*

† The peace settlements consisted of five treaties: (1) the Treaty of Versailles, June 28, 1919, which fills a full printed volume; (2) the Treaty of St. Germain with Austria, signed September 10, 1919; (3) the Treaty of the Trianon with Hungary, signed June 4, 1920; (4) the Treaty of Neuilly with Bulgaria, signed November 27, 1919; and (5) the Treaty of Sèvres with Turkey, signed August 10, 1920.

entry of the United States into an inherently defective organization would not have brought about the far-reaching change in international morality and behavior upon which Wilson had set his heart. Yet it may be argued with some force that, if the United States had ratified the Covenant and the treaties, and if the American people had elected a new President empowered to pursue Wilson's high ideals, both the structure of the League and the peace settlements might, in due course, have been modified.

The fateful decision to win the war first and to leave the discussion of peace aims until the Germans had been defeated undermined Wilson's ability to deal with Lloyd George's greed for colonies, with Orlando's expansionist ambitions and with Clemenceau's vengeful desire to humiliate and destroy the German nation. The miracle of the Paris negotiations was not that Wilson failed to achieve a just peace but that he came so close to succeeding. The tragedy of his failure was that he relied too much upon human decency, understood too little Europe's deep-rooted addiction to cynical power politics, and, finally, that he lacked those comparatively minor qualifications of political leadership which would have enabled him to secure the approval of his own countrymen for the work which he had accomplished.

Before considering the disaster which befell Wilson at home after his return from Paris, it is necessary to take account of certain developments in Europe which not only affected the decision of the American people but which perhaps did more to undermine the future peace of the world than did the defects of the League and the injustices of the peace settlements.

CHAPTER NINETEEN

Revolution, Reaction and Repudiation

(1919 – 1920)

THE AMERICAN PEOPLE had gone into the war to make the world safe for democracy. The one, single factor which, more than any other, made the peace merely a twenty-one-year armistice was that the victorious Allies used their victory—not to promote the cause of democracy—but to restore or maintain in power much the same anti-democratic political and economic groups which had ruled the various countries of Europe before 1914.

The primary cause of this regressive behavior was fear inspired by the Russian revolution. It is important to recall some of the facts which were little noted at the time and have since been almost entirely forgotten by most Americans.

When the Tsarist regime was overthrown, in March, 1917, the new, constitutional government headed by Prince Lvov in many ways resembled the regime which overturned the Bourbons in the first stage of the French revolution. Later in the summer, Alexander Kerensky became head of the new government. These events were welcomed by President Wilson and by most Americans with much the same sentiments as those evoked by early Jacobinism. The British and French governments, however, took quite a different view. For various reasons, they considered their vital interests threatened by the overthrow of the Tsar and almost immediately began to intrigue with reactionary Russian restorationists. Although the Lvov-Kerensky government reaffirmed and remained faithful to the Entente alliance, British and French support was secretly given to both General Korniloff and Admiral Kolchak, the two outstanding Tsarist leaders who were trying to overthrow it. At the time, little was known of these maneuvers outside of official government circles. This was true not only in the United States but also in Britain and France; but it remains a fact of historical importance that the new, democratic Russian government was undermined from the start—not merely by the Germans, who smuggled Lenin back into Russia to overthrow Kerensky and take Russia out of the war—but by the British and French governments.

The explanation is not easy to discover. It is true that the Tsar had been an ally, but the new government from the outset declared its faithfulness to the alliance. It is true that Britain had a dynastic interest in preserving monarchy and that the Tsar was related to the British Royal family, but this did not apply to France and, for that matter, the German Kaiser too was related to the British King. The only logical explanation is that the democratic revolution in Russia frightened both the British and French governments and, therefore, incurred their hostility. Had this fear been merely one of losing a sorely needed ally, Anglo-French diplomacy would have exerted itself to the utmost to strengthen a regime which had pledged continuance of the war and which might win greater popular support for the war effort than its predecessor. The conclusion seems inescapable that the democratic revolution in Russia frightened the British and French governments precisely because it was a democratic revolution—because it meant a change in the social structure which threatened the European status quo and which might awaken the underprivileged masses in other countries, including their own. This would explain why the people of Britain and the people of France did not share the fear of their governments and were as little alarmed by the March revolution as the people of the United States.

The Bolshevik revolution of October-November, 1917, was a wholly different matter. It was only logical that this second phase should frighten and alienate Western sentiment, much as the second phase of the French revolution had reacted upon Western opinion and sympathy. The March revolution had been about as non-violent as a revolution could be which would successfully overthrow the heavily intrenched ancient regime. The Bolshevik revolution horrified the Western world by its bloody violence. The March revolution had been wholly indigenous. The October-November revolution was to a large extent engineered by the Germans, for the express purpose—realized within four months—of getting Russia out of the war.[*]

The Allies made practically no attempt to win Lenin to a policy of continuing the war. Quite deliberately, they decided that the Bolshevik government must be overthrown and continued their assistance to Kolchak in Siberia and to Korniloff (later, to Denikin) in the south. Once the Germans surrendered, the United States joined in this policy. British-American expeditionary forces were sent to Archangel and Murmansk under the command of the British general Ironside. Another Allied force of Japanese and American troops landed in Siberia.[†] Anglo-French forces strengthened Denikin's army in the south. In spite of all this, the attempt to overthrow the Bolshevik regime ended in failure. After a little over a year, the Allied expeditionary forces were withdrawn, but not before American troops had staged the first serious mutiny in American history.

The unsuccessful attempt to overthrow the Soviet government did more than prejudice the future relations between Russia and the West. It exercised a profound influence upon the future foreign policy of the Western nations and immediately affected Allied treatment of the defeated Central Powers.

When the Kaiser fled and the German High Command confessed defeat, revolution broke out in Germany. War weariness and President Wilson's reply to German peace overtures, stating

[*] The Bolsheviks actually took over the government on November 7, 1917. The Treaty of Brest-Litovsk was signed on March 3, 1918.

[†] The landings at Vladivostok were undertaken in part to cover the rear of the Czechoslovak Legion's march across Siberia. This extraordinary feat was accomplished by the Czechoslovak soldiers who, as prisoners taken by Russia from the Austro-Hungarian army, had been held in Siberian camps. The Japanese at one time had as many as 72,000 troops in Russian territory. The American contingent of approximately 7,000 men was sent primarily to prevent the expedition from becoming a purely Japanese affair leading to possible Japanese annexation of territory. Japanese troops remained in Siberia until 1922 and in Northern Sakhalin Island until 1925. During the war, the United States made various efforts to restrain Japanese expansionism on the mainland. For an account of Japan's notorious "21 Demands" on China and the secret Lansing-Ishii agreement of 1917, see S. F. Bemis, op. cit., Chapter XXXV. See also H. B. Morse and H. F. MacNair, Far Eastern International Relations (Houghton Mifflin, 1931).

that the Allies would talk peace to an Imperial regime only on the basis of unconditional surrender, had created the necessity for the Kaiser's abdication. Sailors in the fleet had already mutinied and various other incidents had occurred before the armistice was signed. The most popular slogan was *"Nie wieder Krieg"* (Never again war) and the German people overwhelmingly desired a republican form of government. In the confusion of the collapse of Imperial Germany, only the Social Democrats were capable of assuming the responsibilities of government. Their party comprised the majority of German workers and had the support of many of the soldiers in the defeated army. Unused to responsibility, the Socialists knew what they wanted but were caught unprepared to carry their program into effect. They wished to break up the Junker estates into small farms, to socialize the heavy industries controlled by the industrial barons and to create a people's defense force to protect the new republic which would be free from the domination of the hitherto all-powerful officer-caste.

The Socialist leaders were, however, confronted with a highly articulate minority of "Spartakists" and "Independent Socialists"—the former more or less outspoken followers of Lenin, the latter early prototypes of the fellow travelers. To control this radical minority, the Socialists needed the help of the army, but the army leadership could not be won to any program which would destroy the officer-caste's position. Friedrich Ebert, the first President of the Weimar Republic, managed to achieve an alliance with General Wilhelm Groener, the only high-ranking officer at General Headquarters who had preserved a cool head in the disaster of defeat. Groener, in effect, undertook to bring the army home in good order and to help establish lawful government on condition that the honor of the army would be upheld. This agreement, while undermining the democratic revolution and ultimately making the army once more the arbiter of German affairs, need not have had quite such disastrous consequences, had it not been for the policy pursued by the Allied armies of occupation.

Immediately prior to the armistice, Soldiers' and Sailors' Councils had sprung up all over Germany and a number of "peoples' governments" had been established in various cities and towns. These revolutionary organizations were by no means dominated by the extremists and could have been weeded out so as to become nuclei of spontaneous democratic government. However, on November 10, 1918—the day before the signing of the armistice—the Supreme Allied Command decreed, in effect, that it would deal with none but the local authorities of the ex-Kaiser's Imperial government.* The Allied military government then proceeded to insist upon the re-instatement of these officials in place of the revolutionary groups.

The Allies, in other words, welcomed a German "revolution" insofar as it meant the substitution of a formal republic for the Kaiser's empire, but they feared and vigorously objected to any change in the basic social-economic structure of Germany, refusing to permit the displacement of the bureaucracy which had been subservient to the ruling cliques of Imperial Germany. The Allied High Command—over Wilson's protest—even went so far as to enforce this counter-revolutionary edict by a food blockade until April, 1919.

Thus Allied policy unwittingly combined with Ebert's need of army support to abort a democratic revolution. Formal political democracy was established with the adoption of the Weimar constitution, but social and economic democracy were strangled at birth by Allied governments so frightened of Bolshevism that they had become hostile to any basic change.

These events took place long before the Treaty of Versailles was written. They probably did more to warp the future of Germany than all the mistakes embodied in the peace settlements. One may legitimately question whether, even without Allied intervention, the German people would have carried through a real democratic revolution—whether the traditions of a long, authoritarian past would not, in any case, have reasserted themselves and subverted the Weimar Republic. The fact remains that the Bolshevik revolution and the fears which it inspired among the ruling groups in Western society changed the Allied aim of making the world safe for democracy—if, indeed that had ever been the Allied objective—into the aim of

---

* The official report to the United States War Department of Colonel I. L. Hunt states that paragraph V of the Armistice Agreement "was so interpreted that 'local authorities' meant officials of the old regime."

making the world safe from any revolutionary change. The fact that the Bolsheviks openly avowed the intention of bringing about a world revolution in accordance with their own pattern exaggerated the impact. Fear of a world-wide challenge to the moral and intellectual foundations of Western society as well as to its economic structure engendered a hostility to all change, because any change might lead to the horrible extremes then being demonstrated in Russia. It was too soon to recognize that what was happening in Russia was in many respects more counter-revolutionary than revolutionary, that a democratic revolution had been distorted rather than carried too far and too fast. The result of the status quo reorientation of Allied policy—as the succeeding years were soon to demonstrate—was actually not to make the world safe from change but to make the world safe for counter-revolution and anti-democratic reaction.

The alteration in the climate of Western opinion between March, 1917, when a war to overthrow autocracy had an almost universal appeal, and Wilson's return from Paris in the summer of 1919 perhaps had as much to do with his repudiation as had Lodge's partisan hostility, Wilson's own political ineptitude and the defects in the proposals which he submitted to the American people.

Although Woodrow Wilson was the founder of the League of Nations, he neither originated the idea nor was he its sole protagonist. On both sides of the Atlantic, the idea of a world peace organization had long been discussed and considered.* Republican leaders, such as Taft, Root, and even Roosevelt and Lodge, had expressed themselves in favor of a world peace organization and a non-partisan *League to Enforce Peace* had functioned since 1915 as a propaganda agency in favor of a League. Dissension in the United States began when Wilson rejected Taft's advice to take with him to Paris at least some of the Republican leaders in order to insure bipartisan support.

* David Hunter Miller, *The Drafting of the League of Nations* (Putnam, 1928). Felix Morley, *The Society of Nations, Origin and Development* (Brookings, 1932). Ruhl J. Bartlet, *The League to Enforce Peace* (Chapel Hill, 1944). D. F. Fleming, *The U. S. and the League of Nations* (Putnam, 1932).

The merging of the League and the peace treaty into a single proposal increased the cleavage in American opinion, with some leaders unwilling to support the treaty because they opposed the League and others unwilling to support the League because they opposed the treaty.

When Wilson returned to the United States for a short visit, in February 1919, in order to attend to his Constitutional duties, he made the additional mistake of discussing the Covenant in public addresses, rather than with the Senate or with the Senate leaders. One result of this procedure was that 39 Senators or Senators-elect went on record in a statement demanding that the treaty and the Covenant be separated.

Among the supporters of the League there developed a strong desire for amendments to the Covenant, of which the most important were: that the Covenant should recognize the Monroe Doctrine; that the United States should stipulate that it would not be obligated to cooperate in imposing sanctions under Article X without a vote of Congress; that in all matters of League action affecting domestic affairs (the chief concern here was about tariffs and immigration laws) there must be a unanimous vote of the Council (this amounted to a demand for a veto); and that member nations should have the explicit right of withdrawal.

Wilson at first opposed any amendments whatever, particularly those affecting Article X and the sanctions against aggressors, which he considered "the heart of the Covenant." After his return to Paris in March, Wilson yielded to Taft's repeated urgings to the extent of demanding an amendment recognizing the Monroe Doctrine. Taft begged Wilson to consider as well an amendment explicitly providing for unanimous consent to actions involving domestic affairs, although he believed that "the Monroe amendment alone would probably carry the Treaty."

Upon Wilson's return, Lodge rejected the amended Covenant and, under his leadership, there were submitted 45 amendments and 4 reservations. The Foreign Relations Committee adopted delaying tactics and made public its extensive hearings. Wilson decided to appeal to the people and embarked upon a nation-wide speaking tour in the midst of which he collapsed (September 26). The Senate then adopted the 14 so-called Lodge reservations.*

Viewed in retrospect, the Lodge reservations do not seem as destructive as they appeared to Wilson and his supporters at the time. In fact, there is good reason to believe that the Allies might have accepted the revised treaty rather than to forego American participation. Colonel House advised letting the Senate take full responsibility and discussing the matter with Sir Edward Grey, then newly appointed ambassador to Washington. Wilson, perhaps because he was already a very sick man and perhaps because the open hostility of Lodge evoked in him an irrational stubbornness, rejected the amendments, refused to see Grey, had a near-break with House, and declared that he would take the whole matter to the people.

The elections of 1920 were in no sense the plebiscite which Wilson intended them to be. Governor James M. Cox of Ohio, the Democratic nominee, was a strong Wilson supporter, but the Democratic platform adopted a plank favoring the Covenant *with such amendments as would not destroy the effectiveness of the League.* The Republicans—in the famous "smoke filled room" caucus—selected Senator Warren Gamaliel Harding of Ohio, an extreme conservative who declared himself in favor of "an association of nations." This ambiguous declaration was interpreted in a statement signed by some thirty Republican leaders—including Elihu Root, Herbert Hoover, A. Lawrence Lowell and Nicholas M. Butler—as meaning that Harding favored the League. Thus, the issue was not drawn between the uncompromising positions of Wilson and Lodge; it was not even clearly drawn as between support of the League or opposition to it. Considerations of domestic policy and a general feeling of wanting to be done with the war and with foreign involvement entered strongly into the picture. The favorite Republican slogan in the campaign was "Let's be done with wiggle and wobble." Harding won in a landslide.

* For a full account of this whole matter see T. A. Bailey, *Woodrow Wilson and the Great Betrayal* (Macmillan, 1945). For a brief statement of the 14 Senate reservations, see S. F. Bemis, *op, cit.,* page 653.

Although the election had not been fought on a clearly defined League issue, its result was interpreted as a repudiation of Wilson and all his works, including the League and the treaty. The truth of the matter was that Harding had been elected by a nation weary of war and disillusioned with the peace—a nation which had gone to war without knowing that it was fighting for its own vital interests, and which had now disavowed the idealistic aims for which it had believed itself to be embattled. The United States had become the most powerful nation in the world, but realized neither its power nor its responsibility. The people seemed more inclined to trust business leaders than politicians, and the business leaders wanted a return to *laissez-faire* government, even if it meant veterans selling apples on the streets.

President Harding's favorite campaign phrase had been "return to normalcy." This meant, in effect: "The war is over. Let's go back to where we were before we got mixed up with those foreigners. We don't want any more of their wars; and we certainly don't want any of their radical ideas. We want to be left alone. Let's have America for Americans, free enterprise, a little old-fashioned horse sense, and no government meddling with business." President Harding did not create these sentiments. He merely coined the ungrammatical phrase which articulated them. He was the logical product of the times, accurately representing the two prevalent misconceptions: first, that the war had been merely an interlude; and, second, that the nation's former isolationist irresponsibility had constituted "normalcy."

The war had, however, changed many things. It had transformed the United States into a world power, enormously stimulating its economic growth, while weakening the economies of the European powers. It had shifted the center of gravity of the Western world from London and Paris to New York and Washington. Most important of all, the war had transformed the United States from a debtor to a creditor nation so radically altering its international balance of payments that its high protective tariff had become a menace both to world trade and to the expanded American economy. Neither

Harding nor his advisers nor the Congress elected in 1920 were aware of what these changes implied in terms of shaping the nation's policy.

CHAPTER TWENTY

"Normalcy," Irresponsibility and Disaster

(1921 – 1932)

ONCE IN OFFICE, President Harding declared that his administration had "definitely put aside all thoughts of entering the League of Nations." It had, he said, no intention "to enter by the side-door, the back-door, or the cellar-door." There was little dissent. Disillusionment with our recent Allies and guilt over the severity of the peace imposed upon Germany were beginning to reverse previous sympathies. The public mind was confused and resentful. Fear of Bolshevism set off a witch-hunt for "Reds," in which little distinction was drawn between Socialists and Communists, or between alien ideologies and native radicalism. The Ku Klux Klan reappeared. Refusal to obey the Volstead Act gave rise to bootlegging, gangsterism and a general disrespect for law.

Because the war seemed to have been futile, people began to create various myths to account for American involvement. The munitions-makers were held responsible or the bankers, or British propaganda. Under Harding, the nation returned to Wilson's pacifist isolationism, but without Wilson's high ideals or universal moral concepts. It was the great era of "debunking," in which more bunk was produced than ever before.

During the war, the United States had loaned over $10,500,-000,000 to the Allies—about $4,000,000,000 to Britain, slightly less to France, $2,000,000,000 to Italy and the rest scattered. (Britain had loaned to the other Allies more than she had borrowed from the United States; France alone owed her $3,500,000,000.) Because President Wilson had never grasped the vital American interest in British and French survival, he had regarded and caused the country to regard these debts as ordinary loans to be repaid at the end of the war; whereas they could more properly be considered as a partial offset to British and French sacrifices made before the United States became a belligerent. Because Wilson had not recognized this even at the war's end, he had been powerless to combat the demand that the whole cost of the war should be extracted from Germany, to set a total limit to German reparations, or to limit the period during which Germany would be compelled to continue payments.

The British were quick to realize the danger created by the dual fiction of German reparations and war debts. Just before Wilson left office, they suggested that the Allies and the United States cooperate in the reconstruction of Germany in order to avoid the creation of a dangerously explosive situation in that country. Wilson replied:

> You have suggested that we all address ourselves to the problem of helping to put Germany on her feet. But how can your experts and ours be expected to work out a *new* plan to furnish working capital to Germany, when we deliberately start by taking away all Germany's *present* capital? How can anyone expect America to turn over to Germany . . . new capital to take the place of that which the European nations have determined to take from her?

After Harding took office, British and French liberals urged a general maintenance of wartime economic controls in order that there might be an orderly economic reconstruction of Europe. But the business interests here and abroad would have none of this. They insisted that the governments abolish their controls, "get out of business" and leave reconstruction to private initiative and enterprise. The business interests won and, with their victory, accepted the responsibility for carrying out the impossible assignment which the politicians had created—

namely, to bleed Germany white and, at the same time, to reconstruct her economy. The business interests, in effect, undertook to make the fiction of reparations and war debts come true.

During the Harding administration conditions in Europe grew steadily worse. In 1920, Poland invaded Russia and captured Kiev. A Russian counter-offensive carried to the gates of Warsaw, where it was stopped by Marshal Pilsudski with the help of the French general, Weygand. (This was when Poland acquired the territory east of the Curzon Line, reclaimed by Russia at the end of World War II.) The Silesian plebiscite settled the Polish-German frontier and the demarcation of the Danzig Corridor. Russia and Germany were developing a common interest in suppressing the new independent Poland. In 1921, the German foreign minister, Walter Rathenau, startled the West by his Treaty of Rapallo with the Soviet Union. A substantial credit was granted by Germany to Russia, ostensibly for the promotion of business between the two countries, but actually as a cloak for secret cooperation in building airplane and tank factories in Russia and training the cadres of an illegally enlarged German *Reichswehr*.*

Toward the West, Germany pursued a "policy of fulfillment" while, at the same time, frantically seeking a revision of the reparations clause. France, denied an Anglo-American guarantee of her security, adopted an uncompromisingly harsh policy refusing to consider any modifications of the Versailles Treaty. British sentiment, consistent with Britain's traditional balance-of-power policy, began to veer from pro-French to pro-German.

In Italy, mass unemployment and severe suffering created a revolutionary atmosphere. Fearing Bolshevism and unwilling to undertake the needed reforms of an outmoded social-economic structure, the ruling clique of industrialists, large landowners and courtiers connived, together with the King, at the establishment of Mussolini's Fascist dictatorship. The "March on Rome" set the pattern soon to be followed in Germany, Austria and Spain—the pattern of unconstitutional seizure of

* For the history of German rearmament in 1920-1926, see J. W. Wheeler-Bennett, *The Nemesis of Power* (St. Martin's Press, 1954), Chapters I and II.

power by an illegally armed minority.* In the United States there was no awareness of the new threat to democracy posed by counter-revolution from the Right. People commented with satisfaction upon the fact that, at last, Italian trains ran on time and that Italy appeared to have established an "orderly government."

In 1922, the British government offered to cancel all debts owed to it by the other Allies, if the United States would cancel its war loans. (As already stated, Britain was owed considerably more than it had borrowed.) Harding and his Secretary of the Treasury, the multi-millionaire Andrew Mellon, bluntly refused this suggestion; they were far too busy reducing taxes and retiring the public debt on the pleasant assumption that the war debts were "good assets." In the same year, France agreed to the first reduction of German reparations, but this concession proved insufficient to halt the flight of German capital and the rapid depreciation of German currency.

By the end of 1923, the German mark had become practically worthless and the savings of the German workers and of the middle class had been wiped out. (Actually, German savings had in large measure been destroyed by the huge war expenditures, but this became apparent only when the currency panic was precipitated.) The German government now declared that it could no longer meet its schedule of "payments in kind," consisting for the most part of deliveries of coal. Thereupon, France and Belgium sent troops to occupy the Ruhr. This occupation lasted until 1925. Its results were disastrous. The French discovered, in the face of passive resistance, that "coal cannot be mined with bayonets"; and a sullen spirit of resentment was kindled in Germany.

While leaving the question of European reconstruction to take care of itself—except for the food relief organized under Herbert Hoover—the Harding administration undertook a series of moves which had a fatal effect upon the future of the Far East. Imbued with a wholly honorable spirit of pacifism, Secretary of State Charles E. Hughes summoned the former

* G. A. Borghese, *Goliath, the March of Fascism* (Viking, 1938); G. Salvemini, *Under the Axe of Fascism* (Viking, 1936); F. S. Nitti, *Bolshevism, Fascism and Democracy* (Macmillan, 1927).

Allies to a Disarmament Conference. No attempt was made to deal with land armies. First of all, the United States insisted that Great Britain abrogate its alliance with Japan. This demand was based upon the strange theory that the United States could agree to limit its naval construction only if there were no alliance between British and Japanese sea-power. During the war, the American people had failed to understand that the acquisition of a Pacific empire had made the United States dependent upon British control of the Atlantic—that, ever since the annexation of the Philippines, the United States had entered into what amounted to a tacit alliance with Britain. This was bad enough. But the Harding administration now proceeded to act upon the assumption that Britain was actually a potential enemy. The proper conclusion from that assumption would have been to build a two-ocean navy to provide against possible attack by Britain and Japan. Instead, the Harding administration coupled its demand for the termination of the Anglo-Japanese alliance with a proposal to limit the construction of British, Japanese and American sea power. In order to limit the strength of a potential enemy (Japan), it proposed to limit its own strength and that of its only potential ally.

British acceptance arose from a disillusioned pacifism similar to that which predominated in the United States. Moreover, a limitation of naval armaments offered relief to the sorely tried British taxpayer.

The Japanese also accepted, and why not? Once their alliance with Britain was severed, the proposed treaty might actually work in their favor, particularly if they could some day find a new partner who would keep Britain preoccupied in Europe. The Japanese understood our tacit alliance with Britain far better than we understood it ourselves. They knew also that a pacifist Britain and a pacifist United States would strictly abide by the limitations of naval construction, while they themselves intended to do so only so long as it might suit their purposes. Above all, they knew that, without such a treaty, the United States could easily outbuild them, even if it should decide to construct a two-ocean navy.

The Washington Treaty of 1922 dealt only with capital ships of over 10,000 tons. It established, as between the United States,

Britain and Japan, a ratio of 5-5-3. (France and Italy, the other two participating powers, accepted a ratio of 5-5-3-1.7-1.7.) Under this agreement, the United States not only halted new construction but sank 25% of its World War I fleet.

Unfortunately, this was not all. The Harding-Hughes diplomacy also attempted to settle the political affairs of the Far East in such a manner as to contain any future Japanese expansion. This it attempted to accomplish by an agreement not to fortify Guam and the Philippines, in exchange for Japanese agreement not to fortify the former German islands in the Marshall, Marianas and Caroline groups. Here again, the Japanese could be reasonably certain that the pacifist and economy-minded United States would leave its vulnerable outposts in a state of utter defenselessness, while they—at the proper moment—would do as they pleased. (The Japanese mandated islands were in due course secretly fortified and served as valuable bases by the time Japan decided upon open aggression.)

In order to prevent future Japanese aggression against China, the United States took the lead in internationalizing the Open Door Policy in the Nine-Power Treaty of February 6, 1922. (Japan's signature did not prevent the invasion of Manchuria in 1931.)

To cap the climax, Congress insisted upon passing the Japanese Exclusion Act of 1924, thus adding a mortal insult to the diplomatic maneuvers which sought to frustrate Japanese ambitions while, at the same time, emasculating American and British sea power.

The sudden death of President Harding, on August 2, 1923, was followed by unexpected revelations of malfeasance and corruption in his cabinet. The notorious Teapot Dome scandal, involving Harding's Secretary of the Interior, Albert B. Fall, and the charges brought against Attorney General Harry Daugherty—both involving sales to private interests of government-owned oil reserves—shocked the nation.

During the unexpired part of Harding's term, Calvin Coolidge, a taciturn, economy-minded New Englander, so well satisfied his party that he was nominated at the 1924 convention without opposition. That he satisfied the country as well was demonstrated by his overwhelming victory over John W. Davis, the Democratic nominee chosen after a protracted deadlock between William G. MacAdoo and Governor Alfred E. Smith of New York. The campaign was unusually quiet, its most significant feature being the large protest vote polled by the Progressive Party. This arose chiefly from dissatisfaction in the farm belt over tumbling commodity prices and a rising cost of living. (Coolidge received 15,075,016 votes, Davis polled 8,386,-503 and La Follette 4,822,856.)

With Andrew Mellon continuing as Secretary of the Treasury, the national debt was rapidly reduced from its wartime peak of over $26,500,000,000. Taxes were cut and expenditures pared down. The funding of the British war debts, carried out under Harding, was followed by funding agreements with other former Allies. The terms of these agreements provided a generous scaling down of accumulated interest, but maintained the fiction that the debts would be repaid out of German reparations.

As to the latter, General Charles G. Dawes was entrusted by Coolidge, in 1924, with the mission of working out a method of payment. Under the Dawes Plan, Germany was given a large loan secured by a lien on German railways and factories and reparation payments were reduced to a series of annual instalments. This lightened the immediate burden upon the German economy, but fixed no time limit and left the Germans without knowledge of what their ultimate liability would be. The chief benefit of the Plan was that it made possible the reorganization and stabilization of the German currency. On the other hand, its very harmful effect was to create an apparent German prosperity which not only served to maintain the fiction of the ultimate collectibility of reparations and war debts, but also opened the way to a disastrous flood of foreign loans to German industries, states and municipalities.

President Coolidge's own view of the war debt problem was expressed in one simple sentence: "They hired the money, didn't they?" To help the Allies repay, Coolidge did his best, by sending the Dawes mission, to straighten out the immediate German tangle. Then he sat back and waited for American bankers to make loans which would help rebuild German productive power.

This scheme of things was helped along by the vastly improved atmosphere created in Europe by the Treaties of Locarno (1925) in which Germany voluntarily agreed to a permanent settlement of her relations with her Western neighbors, even though she refused to recognize as permanent the settlement of her Eastern frontier. A relatively small cloud—so it appeared at the time—appeared upon the horizon when Foreign Minister Gustav Stresemann next signed a friendship pact (The Berlin Treaty) with Russia. The West did not suspect that the Rapallo Treaty of 1921 had already laid the foundations for the secret training of German cadres in Russia and that Stresemann's treaty foreshadowed Russo-German cooperation against Poland. One of Stresemann's intimate friends and advisers was Konrad Adenauer, then President of the Prussian State Council and later to become the first Chancellor of the Federal Republic of West Germany.

It was at about this time—when American bankers were embarking upon an orgy of investment in Germany—that the preconditions for the National Socialist counter-revolution were being created. Inflation had destroyed the stable lower middle class in German society and a new group of inflation profiteers had come into being. Most of the big industrialists and bankers had managed to preserve and even to augment their wealth and power, but the little people had been utterly incapable of protecting themselves against the complete destruction of their savings. This produced two ingredients of Fascist counter-revolution: a strong anti-capitalist sentiment among the masses; and a fear of socialist revolution among the privileged few. For the time being, the strictly unpolitical *Reichswehr* under General von Seeckt's leadership guaranteed order, but von Seeckt's days were numbered and, under the leadership of the crafty Kurt von Schleicher, a favorite of the venerable von Hindenburg, the *Reichswehr* was soon to descend into politics with disastrous results. The harsh Versailles Treaty and the occupation of the Ruhr united all kinds of Germans in a common resentment of outraged nationalism and played into the hands of the militarists and nationalist leaders who were already thinking about the next war. Thus, both the socialist and nationalist ingredients of what was soon to become National Socialism were latent in the Germany which Americans were so anxious to rebuild, in order that the war debts might remain a sound asset on Mr. Mellon's books.

Here at home the reduction of taxes and the plentiful supply of money set off a business boom in which bankers were only too eager to find employment for their funds. Soon there was a scramble to see who could offer the most attractive terms to the German steel manufacturers and other industrialists. In this respect Mr. Coolidge's scheme began to work nicely. But, if Germany was to keep up her reparation payments, she needed not only to obtain loans to increase her production but also to find outlets for that production. She needed not only capital but access to markets in which she could earn the foreign exchange with which to make reparation payments. American business was, however, not at all prepared to expose itself to German competition. Under the Harding administration, the relatively liberal Underwood Tariff Act of 1913 had been repealed and the much more restrictive Fordney-McCumber Tariff of 1922 enacted. This was only a foretaste of what was yet to come during the administration of President Hoover. In the Harding-Coolidge-Hoover era the idea was to keep all of the domestic market, to capture the world markets from the British to the greatest extent possible, and to frown upon any German intrusion into Anglo-American rivalry. Thus, while American and British loans were helping to build up German productive capacity, Anglo-American trade policies were making it impossible for Germany to sell its goods for foreign exchange.

It did not take the Germans long to realize that eager American bankers might supply them with the foreign exchange which American manufacturers were unwilling to let them earn by exporting their products. Accordingly, the German government encouraged not only the industries but every conceivable government agency, provincial government and municipality to contract long-term loans in dollars or sterling.

Had the American government not left the whole problem to business—had it been aware of the interests of the American people—it would have taken measures to prevent the orgy of foreign lending which began in 1925 and ended only with the collapse of 1929-1930. Under the Coolidge-Big Business policies, other countries fell more and more hopelessly into debt to the United States.

The domestic manifestation of this false prosperity was a wild inflation of security prices and a speculative mania which seized almost the entire population. Under a complacent, do-nothing government, Big Business reverted to the standards of the McKinley era. The great monopolies found ways to circumvent the anti-trust laws. The regulatory bodies established in the reform era fell into impotence. Irresponsible bankers exploited the holding company device, pyramided inflated securities and sold the public new holding company "equities" which were nothing more than thin speculative margin accounts. The public bought whatever it was offered, causing security prices to rise still further and making the originally thin margins into substantial paper equities. The most foolhardy investments turned out to be the most profitable—until the crash.

In this atmosphere of irresponsible financial anarchy, the opportunity to float German and other foreign loans represented to many bankers nothing more than a way to make profits by selling more securities to an insatiable public. As a matter of fact, the German loans were, for the most part, better secured than many of the domestic issues sold to the public at the same time. Few ever defaulted because the individual German borrower was unable to meet his payments, but all the German loans eventually defaulted together when the German government was unable to convert the borrower's interest and sinking-fund payments into foreign exchange. This did not happen until several years later, by which time the unhappy Mr. Hoover occupied the White House.

Before concluding this highly compressed summary of the events which led up to the great disaster of 1929-1932, two actions in the field of foreign affairs undertaken by the Coolidge administration should be noted.

The Immigration Act of 1924 introduced the so-called quota system of immigration control. This was a major departure from the traditional, non-discriminatory American policy, deliberately designed to exclude or limit immigration from Eastern Europe, the Near East and Asia and to favor immigration from those West European countries which had in the past supplied most of the American population. Henceforth, insofar as their opportunity to become American citizens was concerned, all men were *not* to be considered equal. A sign was now hung upon the American door, reading: "Nordics, Anglo-Saxons and other West Europeans preferred."

The Paris Pact of August 27, 1928, originally suggested by the great French statesman, Aristide Briand, was negotiated by Secretary of State Frank B. Kellogg, who had succeeded Hughes in 1925. This three-paragraph document, condemning recourse to war as a method of settling international disputes and renouncing war as an instrument of national policy, was signed within a year by 15 nations. Had it not been for the irresponsible economic policies of the time, the Kellogg-Briand Pact might have marked the first important step in a new approach to the problem of preserving world peace.

Both Presidents Harding and Coolidge unsuccessfully urged American participation in the Permanent Court of International Justice, established at The Hague under League auspices in 1920. Ironically enough, President Coolidge's effort failed to win Congressional approval because the League had adopted an American proposal * for strengthening the Court's jurisdiction.

Coolidge tried to arrange another Disarmament Conference, at which he hoped to extend the existing limitations to cruisers and aircraft carriers. When Britain and France rejected this proposal, Coolidge recommended a large naval construction program, which Congress approved only in part, considering an increase of the fleet inconsistent with the Kellogg-Briand Pact.

Distress in the farm belt and in the coal industry remained the outstanding blemishes upon the record of "Coolidge prosperity." The President was unable to put through any satisfactory farm relief legislation and a major coal miners' strike during his administration underlined the unhealthy condition of that important industry.

With Coolidge renouncing re-election ("I do not choose to

* By Dr. James T. Shotwell of the Carnegie Endowment for Peace.

run") and Hughes unavailable, Secretary of Commerce Hoover was nominated without serious opposition as the Republican candidate. Governor Alfred E. Smith of New York became the Democratic nominee. The Democrats denounced Republican corruption and the failure to supply farm relief or unemployment cures. Smith personally espoused a repeal of the 18th (Prohibition) Amendment. Hoover made only a few noncommittal speeches but won 40 out of the 48 states, for the first time making a dent in the solid Democratic South. The fact that Smith was a Roman Catholic undoubtedly contributed to his defeat.

When President Hoover took office, the process of financial anarchy already described was in full swing, but firm action might still have arrested the boom and put a stop to the excessive foreign lending. Far from taking any such action, the new administration continued the complacent course of its predecessor. In April, 1929, the Dawes Plan was supplanted by the Young Plan,* which again revised German reparations payments downward and provided another large international loan to the German government. This created even greater confidence in German recovery and loans to German borrowers flowed faster than ever.

At least one banker warned, in the spring of 1929, that a collapse of the inflated security markets was imminent.† Nothing was done to restrict speculation and further over-expansion. In October, the stock market finally collapsed of its own weight, wiping out margin accounts and bringing ruin to a large part of the investing public. Even then, the Hoover administration did not seem to realize what was happening. Hoover himself issued a series of reassuring statements and insisted that there was no cause for alarm. "Prosperity," he said, was "just around the corner,"

So little did the Congress and the administration understand the fundamental fallacies upon which the false boom had been created that they proceeded to enact the incredible Smoot-

* Named after Owen D. Young, who headed the new mission.
† "Paul Warburg, a great financial authority and a great man who had given years of his life to the original building up of the Federal Reserve System, issued early in 1929 public warning that speculation had gone wild and that the country would have to pay for it." Franklin D. Roosevelt; *Looking Forward;* John Day, 1933, page 219.

Hawley Tariff, raising import restrictions to the highest level in our history. It was world-wide disaster—not prosperity—that now waited around the corner.

Here at home the depression spread slowly at first because of various palliative measures which, in the end, only made matters worse. But it spread nevertheless—from the stock markets into the banking structure, and from the banks into industry and the already depressed farm area. People began to lose homes and farms under foreclosure. Factories began to close down or reduce their output. Mass unemployment set in.

No one now wanted to lend or invest money. Everyone wanted to borrow. Banks began to call in their short-term loans and credits to German banks and commercial borrowers. British, Dutch, French, Swiss and Swedish bankers followed suit. By the middle of 1930, the depression had spread over most of Europe, being felt most keenly in those countries which had become dependent for their foreign exchange upon new loans, instead of upon their ability to sell their goods in foreign markets. In Germany and Austria the whole machinery of business threatened to come to a standstill. President Hoover declared a moratorium and the bankers of the various lending countries agreed to stop further withdrawals. And yet the crisis deepened. Banks began to crash in Austria and Germany as well as in the United States. In 1931, Britain was forced to abandon the gold standard; she could no longer settle her accounts by shipping gold. All the gold in the world was being sucked into the United States. Since the tariff prevented other countries from selling their goods in the American market, and since Americans were selling more abroad than they bought, there was no way for foreign countries to settle their balances of payment with the United States except by shipping gold. This could be done only so long as the supply of gold lasted. When a country's gold reserve neared exhaustion, its currency depreciated and a flight of capital would set in. Soon economic anarchy gripped the whole Western world, with each nation frantically taking measures to cut down its imports and to force up its exports in order to protect itself. Economic nationalism—the pattern which the United States had set in its selfish irresponsibility—became by sheer necessity the guiding principle for all nations. World trade dried up. Some countries approached starvation while others were smothered in surplus foodstuffs for which no market could be found.

In Germany, the dangerous state of mind of 1923-1924 was re-created. Five years of false prosperity had put off the evil day but had not averted the disaster. With the collapse of the foreign borrowing racket, business came to a standstill and mass unemployment set in. Once more the German people were desperate and disillusioned. The weak, democratic government of the senile President von Hindenburg and his irresolute Chancellor, Heinrich Bruening, became more and more of a dictatorship—a flabby, indecisive dictatorship which discredited democratic theory but failed to solve the economic problem. Indeed, there seemed to be no solution for the economic problem without a wholesale repudiation of debts and reparations. A sense of almost universal helplessness and frustration set the stage for the emergence of Hitler. In October, 1930, the National Socialists gained their first big block of seats in the Reichstag. In the Presidential elections which followed, von Hindenburg barely managed to defeat the Nazi *Fuehrer* because the dominant, reactionary nationalists were not yet quite ready to embrace the Austrian upstart. Thereafter, the crisis deepened. In 1932, the intrigues of General von Schleicher and Franz von Papen forced Chancellor Heinrich Bruening's resignation. The ambitious general and the bumbling Junker diplomat, between them, then proceeded to write the last pages of the tragic history of the Weimar Republic. When von Papen induced Hitler to accept the Vice Chancellorship, the nationalist clique thought it had captured the Nazi movement, but the rude awakening was soon to come. Within a short time, the nationalists were to find that Hitler had captured them and, along with them, the army and the entire power of the German state. From that moment, it became certain that Europe would either have to accept German hegemony or fight to preserve its independence.*

* Konrad Heiden, *History of National Socialism* (Knopf, 1936). Frederick Schuman, *The Nazi Dictatorship* (Knopf, 1936). *Nazi Conspiracy and Aggression* (United States Government Printing Office, 1946). Hermann Rauschning, *The Revolution of Nihilism* (Longmans, Green, 1939).

In the Far East, too, the war clouds were gathering. On April 22, 1930, the United States, Britain and Japan signed the Treaty of London, under which the naval disarmament begun in Harding's day was carried further, with limitations now imposed upon cruisers as well as battleships. This merely continued the process of disarmament so favorable to Japan and so fatal to the United States and Britain. By 1931, with a resurgent Nazi Germany looming over the European horizon, Japan's military leaders could already envisage a possible alliance with a partner who would keep Britain occupied in Europe. Nor was it necessary to wait for that hope to be fulfilled before taking the first aggressive step toward the creation of a Japanese empire on the mainland. With the Western world gripped by depression and near-panic, the Japanese leaders felt safe in launching an invasion of the long-coveted Chinese province of Manchuria.

The background to this action arose out of the complicated developments which had taken place in China between 1923 and 1929. During the first part of this period, the Nationalist revolutionary movement led by Dr. Sun Yat-sen had worked closely with Moscow, but in 1927 the Kuomintang had broken with the Communists. Under the leadership of Chiang Kai-shek, the new Nationalist government rapidly gained control over most of China south of the Great Wall and aggressively asserted Chinese independence. A strong, independent China constituted a threat to Japanese expansion on the mainland but, under the leadership of Baron Shidehara, the Japanese pursued a moderate policy, keeping a loose control over the northern provinces by an understanding with the war-lord, Chang Tso-lin. When the latter showed signs of becoming friendly with the Nationalist government and the Nationalists advanced their hold on the northern provinces, the militarist faction, led by Baron Tanaka, gained ascendancy, asserting that only a strong, "positive" policy would preserve Japan's rightful interests. On two occasions, once in 1927 and again in 1929, Japanese troops were landed in Manchuria to protect Japanese concessions, but in each case they were subsequently withdrawn. In December, 1931, the militarists decided that the time had come to drop all pretense and to seize permanent control.

President Hoover's far-seeing and courageous Secretary of State, Henry L. Stimson, issued a forceful protest, but his action received little support at home or abroad.* The League of Nations appointed an investigatory commission under the chairmanship of Lord Lytton. The League itself possessed no military or naval power; without strong British support, it was impotent to halt Japanese aggression, but Britain was no more ready than the United States to go to war for the integrity of China. Whitehall rebuffed Stimson's protest and President Hoover—much to Stimson's chagrin—decided to take no further action. Thus the first overt challenge to the League, the Paris Pact and the Nine Power Treaty, went unanswered, except for the appointment of a League commission to investigate a matter which scarcely required investigation. The precedent for aggression was set. The curtain was rising on World War II.

Here at home a Senate committee, headed by Gerald P. Nye, of North Dakota, was preempting the headlines with its investigation of how the United States had become involved in World War I.

The society of Western nations had demonstrated its bankruptcy. Its most powerful member, the United States, had led the way into an economic disaster which produced political paralysis in the face of aggression in Europe and in Asia. The senseless quarrels of Europe and the irresponsibility of the United States had combined to make the world safe for aggressors. Blind adherence to the fiction of reparations and war debts had been the first step toward economic disaster. Do-nothing government and runaway capitalism had done the rest.

In November, 1932, the American people voted overwhelmingly to discontinue the Republican administrations which, for twelve years, had left the welfare of the country in the hands of Big Business. President Hoover was defeated by a Democrat who had served as Assistant Secretary of the Navy under Wilson, had run with James M. Cox on the Democratic ticket of 1920, served as governor of his native state of New York and had gallantly conquered a crippling disease which would have ended the careers of most other men. Franklin D. Roosevelt's

* For Stimson's own account of the Far Eastern crisis of 1931-1932, see his *On Active Service* (Harper, 1948), Chapter IX, pages 220-263.

great popular plurality was not a mandate for social revolution, nor did Roosevelt's campaign speeches indicate that he interpreted it as such. The vote was primarily a vote against the depression, against do-nothing government and against Big Business leadership.

The social revolution of the New Deal was shaped to a greater extent by what happened after the November elections than by what had gone before. In the winter of 1932-1933, conditions changed so radically for the worse that, by the time Roosevelt took office, the popular demand was not merely for relief and measures to bring about recovery but for basic reform. Before President Hoover left the White House, the depression reached the acute stage of a nation-wide panic, with banks closed, money unavailable, business at a standstill and unemployment reaching the neighborhood of 15,000,000. Naked fear went stalking through the land. Had it not been for the fact that a change of leadership was at hand, almost anything might have happened.

PART SIX

The Diplomacy of Franklin D. Roosevelt

CHAPTER TWENTY-ONE

The New Deal Submerges Foreign Policy
(1933 – 1937)

THE OUTSTANDING FEATURES of Franklin D. Roosevelt's first term were: (1) the acceptance by the Federal government of the responsibilities of leadership in bringing order out of chaos in domestic affairs; and (2) the conscious decision to subordinate foreign policy to the demands of domestic recovery.

The recognition of the Soviet Union in 1933 and the granting of independence to the Philippines in 1934 were the two notable exceptions to a period in which the United States turned its back upon world affairs, concentrating all its energies and resources upon lifting itself out of the worst depression in its history. From March 3, 1933 until October 5, 1937—the date of President Roosevelt's famous "quarantine the aggressors" pronouncement—the United States was, to all intents and purposes, an absentee member of the community of nations. Even the shift—actually begun by Stimson—from "Dollar Diplomacy" to the "Good Neighbor Policy" in Latin America constituted a withdrawal rather than a positive action.

During this five-year period, the shadow of Fascist aggression was to fall across Europe and gradually across the world. Italy was to rape the helpless little kingdom of Abyssinia. Hitler was to unleash a fury of brutality against the remnants of German culture, religion and human decency; and, having conquered his own people, to denounce the Versailles Treaty, to rearm, to remilitarize the Rhineland and to seize Austria. Spain was to become the first battleground where democracy would stand and fight the rising tide of totalitarian tyranny. Japan was to proceed with its conquest of China. Men throughout the world were to lose their faith in collective security and proud nations were to embark upon the despicable effort to appease aggressors by betraying the weak and defenseless into their hands.

Throughout this fateful period, the American people were to keep their eyes averted from the world beyond their own borders.

From the point of view of domestic affairs, it was a happy accident that a new administration came into office at precisely the moment of greatest danger and that a calm, fresh voice, telling the people that they had "nothing to fear but fear itself" should, almost overnight, restore confidence and hope. The new President and the new Congress set to work with a will to organize relief, to stimulate recovery and to enact measures of reform designed to prevent a recurrence of the catastrophe while the catastrophe itself was still fresh in people's minds. Many of these reform measures aroused opposition from the vested business interests but they conformed, on the whole, to what the majority of the people wanted. The people had lost confidence in business leadership; they wanted their government to step in to protect their savings, their homes, their farms and—most of all their jobs. Roosevelt, his advisers and Congress endeavored to carry out what the people wanted. Inevitably, they made some mistakes. The National Recovery Act, designed to put industry back on its feet, tended in some respects to foster monopoly. The Agricultural Adjustment Act, with its plowing under of "surplus" crops and slaughtering of little pigs, over-emphasized raising prices at the expense of getting full production under way. The same was true of the inflationary monetary measures. But none of these mistakes were as important as they seemed at the time to those who were still clinging to *laissez-faire* doctrines and belief in the magic powers of unregulated free enterprise.

The devaluation of the dollar aroused a particularly stormy controversy. The action was denounced by economists and bankers to whom the orthodox gold standard had become a sacred cow. The more radical theorists and the cheap money advocates traditionally spawned by any depression were inclined to blame the orthodox gold standard for the breakdown of international trade, for the collapse of the banking system and for the heavy burden of the debt structure. The truth of the matter was that the gold standard had broken down because international trade had been destroyed by the economic nationalism—most of all by the tariff and foreign trade policies of the United States—and that the collapse of the banks and the top-heavy debt structure had been caused by an uncontrolled boom, irresponsible lending and wild speculation on borrowed money. There had been no real scarcity of gold, as there had been after the Civil War. The trouble was that the world's gold supply had been drained off into the United States Treasury and, from there, into the private hoards of panicky citizens. The international gold standard had been a device for settling temporary disequilibria in the balance of trade between nations. It broke down when disequilibrium became permanent and when gold shipments were used to offset the one-way flow of goods and foreign investment.*

After Britain was forced off gold in 1931, many of the countries of Europe joined the British Dominions in attaching their currencies to the pound sterling which dropped from its gold parity of $4.8665 and fluctuated rather wildly between $3 and $4. This depreciation gave the "Sterling Bloc" countries an advantage in competing for exports so that the "Sterling Bloc" began to recover from the depression before the "Gold Countries." It was this phenomenon which, more than anything else, caused Roosevelt's decision to cut the dollar loose from gold and, later, to devalue it permanently, reducing its gold content by 41%. Whatever the merits of this move as a stimulant to domestic recovery, the devaluation of the dollar to 59 cents in effect raised our tariff by 66% against imports from all nations whose currencies were not correspondingly devalued. Thus the move contributed to a further strangulation of international trade.†

The consequences of Roosevelt's monetary policy were greatly magnified by its effect upon the World Economic Conference, scheduled to open at London on June 12, 1933. At

---

* For a fuller discussion of the gold standard and its relation to the great depression, see Chapters I-XIV, pages 1-77, of the author's *Money Muddle* (Knopf, 1934).

† For a detailed discussion of the monetary policies of 1933 and the fiasco of the World Economic Conference at London, see *ibid.*, pages 71-272.

President Roosevelt's invitation, most of the nations intending to participate sent delegations to Washington for preliminary discussions. Prime Minister MacDonald of Great Britain, Premier Herriot of France, Finance Minister Jung of Italy, and Hitler's notorious Dr. Schacht headed their respective delegations, followed by many others from Europe and Latin America. At these preliminary talks a tentative program was worked out, comprising various measures to free international trade from the various artificial restrictions which had brought it to a standstill. It was agreed that a stabilization of the world's widely fluctuating currencies would have to be the first step in this direction.

During the preliminary Washington conversations, Roosevelt suddenly decided to abandon the gold standard and to permit the dollar to depreciate. By June, a certain amount of recovery had taken place in the American economy. Attributing this in large measure to the abandonment of the gold standard, Roosevelt decided, while the London Conference was in session, that a stabilization of the dollar in terms of the other currencies would not be in the interest of further domestic recovery. He so advised the American Delegation, thereby nullifying its carefully worked out instructions. The result of the American decision was the complete failure of the Conference and an acceleration of the world-wide trend toward *sauve-qui-peut* economic nationalism.

Whatever the wisdom of Roosevelt's decision from the domestic point of view—and about this, opinions differ—the sudden reversal of American policy in July, 1933, stands out as the symbol of a period in which domestic considerations were aggressively placed ahead of cooperation in straightening out the tangled affairs of a world rapidly drifting toward catastrophe.

While American foreign policy as such, during the first Roosevelt term, was based upon narrow nationalistic considerations, the domestic New Deal reforms had an effect reaching far beyond the borders of the United States. The New Deal served notice that American democracy had once more become dynamic, that the American people had regained their momentum as leaders in the march toward greater human dignity and freedom, and that—in America at least—the "forgotten man" had once more been remembered. The New Deal did more than save the American people from the worst consequences of their own folly. It showed the world that Western society's apparent dilemma between Fascism and Bolshevism was actually a false dilemma and that industrial capitalism could be reconciled with political democracy. Neither the New Deal's imperfections nor its contradictions, nor the intense opposition which it aroused, could alter the dynamic fact that it demonstrated the determination of the American people to discover the means whereby freedom and opportunity might be made compatible with social justice and security.

The major reforms enacted under the New Deal dealt with the abolition of certain existing abuses, the recognition of hitherto unrecognized rights and the provision of certain new public services. The separation of commercial banking from the investment business and the regulation of the issuance of new securities were designed to protect the people's savings. The restrictions placed upon holding companies and the pyramiding of equities limited the power of concentrated wealth. The outlawing of child labor, the recognition of labor's right to bargain collectively, and the establishment of old age and unemployment insurance were steps in the direction of greater social justice and security. New agencies were established through which the Federal government might lend assistance to farmers, home-owners and small business. Rural electrification was promoted by government subsidy. The Tennessee Valley Authority demonstrated what might be done for the people in flood control, river valley development and power production and provided a yardstick against which to measure the services performed by privately owned utilities. Through the assumption of vast new responsibilities and powers, the Federal government transferred the nation's emphasis from property values to human values.

These manifold activities brought into being a huge Federal bureaucracy and a tremendous increase in the Federal budget; they also raised the question whether the powers assumed by the Federal government exceeded those given to it under the Constitution. The latter issue led President Roosevelt into an ugly fight with the ultra-conservative Supreme Court, consistently hostile to the New Deal. While Roosevelt's attempt to "pack" the Court was unsuccessful and unpopular, the New Deal itself enjoyed the support of the vast majority of the American people. In many ways, the Roosevelt revolution resembled the Jacksonian revolution. Much the same outcries were raised against it and much the same popular enthusiasms were engendered. Most of the reforms proved lasting, though many of them were later modified. In time, the Supreme Court once more got into step with the creation of the new instruments of public power, proceeding—as Mr. Dooley had put it—to "follow the illiction returns." In the seesaw battle between people and property which had been going on since the foundation of the republic, the New Deal took its place beside Jefferson's victory over Hamilton, the Jacksonian revolution and the reform period begun by Theodore Roosevelt and carried on by Taft and Wilson.

How far the New Deal would have carried, or to what extent it would have been reversed by the traditional pendulum swings of American politics, will never be known, because the long-ignored and rapidly deteriorating world situation overshadowed and distorted the succeeding years.

On January 30, 1933, Adolf Hitler came to power in Germany. On March 17, 1933, Japan served notice of withdrawal from the League of Nations; this was the Japanese reply to a League resolution condemning the invasion of Manchuria, belatedly adopted on February 24 in accordance with the recommendations of the Lytton Commission. On October 14, 1933, Germany withdrew from the League and from the Disarmament Conference which had been dragging along at Geneva, thereby indicating its intention to rearm in defiance of the Versailles Treaty.

Russia was more acutely aware than the Western nations of the rising threats of aggression. Soviet policy, directed by Stalin and Maxim Litvinov, aimed at organizing resistance, its immediate objectives being to obtain American recognition and admission to the League of Nations. The first aim was realized in November, 1933; the second in September, 1934.

Roosevelt's recognition of the Soviet government was induced primarily by the pressure of business groups desiring access to the Russian market. Prior to Roosevelt's inauguration, Senator William E. Borah, of Idaho, and Raymond Robins, the long-time friend of the Soviet Union, had led a campaign for recognition. William C. Bullitt, soon to become the first American ambassador to Moscow, strongly urged the President to establish diplomatic relations and had preliminary conversations with Litvinov during the London Economic Conference. The chief opposition came from certain patriotic societies and from the holders of defaulted Tsarist bonds. The agreement reached between Roosevelt and Litvinov ostensibly took care of the two chief objections: Litvinov promised that the Soviet Union would refrain from supporting subversive activities in the United States; and provision was made for taking care of the defaulted securities. Failure to carry out the somewhat ambiguous agreements resulted in mutual recriminations.*

During the second year of the New Deal, Japan enthroned Pu Yi as Emperor of the puppet state of Manchukuo (Manchuria). In the "Night of the Long Knives" (June 30, 1934), Hitler purged the Nazi party and caused the murder of Ernst Roehm, leader of his Brownshirt Storm Troopers, and of General Kurt von Schleicher. A month later, Chancellor Dollfuss was assassinated in the course of the first Nazi attempt to annex Austria, but the coup was balked by Mussolini's prompt mobilization at the Brenner Pass. On October 9, 1934, King Alexander of Jugoslavia and French Foreign Minister Barthou were murdered at Marseilles; this was a serious blow to the French system of alliances. In December, Mussolini moved against Ethiopia; Emperor Hailie Selassie asked for League arbitration and Mussolini refused.

In 1935 the pace quickened. In January, the Saar plebiscite returned the Saar to Germany in accordance with an overwhelming vote of the population. In March, Hitler suddenly announced that Germany had built an air force. The re-tooling of German industry had been so well concealed that the world was confronted with the accomplished fact of the repudiation

---

* See *Memoirs of Cordell Hull* (Macmillan, 1948); Edward H. Carr, *The Soviet Impact on the Western World* (Macmillan, 1947); and William Appleman Williams, *American Russian Relations* (Rinehart, 1952).

of the Versailles Treaty. This shocking announcement was followed by Hitler's declaration that a new German army would at once be raised by conscription. Two British ministers, Sir John Simon and Anthony Eden, flew to Berlin and were flatly rebuffed. At the Stresa Conference, Britain, France and Italy agreed to cooperate in preserving peace and a special session of the League Council condemned Hitler's action. Shortly thereafter, France and the Soviet Union signed a mutual assistance treaty.

The illusion that the European powers would unite to check Hitler's plans was, however, short-lived. In June, 1935, the British government took the first step in what was soon to become known as the "policy of appeasement." A naval treaty with Germany tacitly sanctioned German land rearmament, provided that Hitler would refrain from challenging British supremacy at sea.

Noting the weakness of Anglo-French policy, Mussolini now launched a full-scale invasion of Ethiopia; this brought about the notorious agreement between Premier Joseph Laval and Sir Samuel Hoare to permit the partitioning of Ethiopia. Repudiation of the Hoare-Laval agreement by the House of Commons very nearly caused the overthrow of the Baldwin cabinet. The British people were more inclined than the French to appease Germany. Laval, on the other hand, admired Mussolini and sought to win him as an ally against Hitler, while British sentiment opposed any concessions to the Italian dictator. Under British and Soviet leadership, the League voted to invoke economic sanctions against Italy.

Britain was slowly realizing the futility of pacifist ideals and attempted disarmament. Yet, paradoxically, the existence of a powerful German air force acted as a deterrent rather than as a spur to British rearmament. Only Winston Churchill and Duff Cooper (later Lord Norwich) raised their voices against the government's indecisive vacillation. Duff Cooper, demanding rapid rearmament, was denounced in the House of Lords as "a deliberate, disgraceful and dangerous scare-monger."

American reaction to the rising threat of war in Europe was merely to seek more complete isolation. The Neutrality Acts of 1935 and 1936 enacted into law some of the misconceptions which had gained wide credence. They provided that, in the event of war between other nations, the President would forbid the shipment of arms, ammunition and implements of war directly or indirectly to any belligerent. (This prohibition derived from the belief that the United States had been drawn into World War I by the munitions makers.) The new laws prohibited the granting of private loans or credits to belligerents. (This clause rested upon the belief that the bankers had involved the United States in the last conflict.) Finally, American ships were prohibited from carrying implements of war—a provision later expanded to forbid the arming of merchant vessels and their entry into zones of combat. (This precaution originated from the conviction that insistence upon neutral rights and freedom of the seas had unnecessarily caused the United States to become a belligerent.)

Among the people there was resentment against Italy for its unprovoked attack upon a helpless, small nation and disgust at the Hoare-Laval agreement, but the latter sentiment served only to fortify the prevailing desire to have nothing more to do with European affairs. There was widespread hostility toward the Nazi regime because of its brutal persecution of Jews and other minorities but, on the whole, the American attitude toward German rearmament was not unsympathetic. In part, this was due to a feeling that the Versailles Treaty had been unduly harsh and, in part, to the belief that a rearmed Germany might prove a useful bulwark against Russia. Having failed to understand that their own security had been threatened by the Kaiser's Germany, Americans were almost wholly unaware that it was once more endangered by a rearmed Third *Reich*. What they wanted was to insure against renewed involvement, if necessary by putting foreign policy into a strait-jacket and abandoning the rights of neutral trade. The fact that 1936 was an election year increased preoccupation with domestic affairs to the point where almost no attention was paid to the fatefully rapid march of events abroad.

On March 7, 1936, Hitler's new *Wehrmacht* marched into the Rhineland, without previous notice and in direct violation of both the Versailles and the Locarno Treaties. French public opinion favored strong counter-action and, had such action been taken, Hitler would have been driven to ignominious retreat. It is now definitely known that the German military leaders tried to dissuade the *Fuehrer* from what they considered an extremely rash adventure. Hitler, however, was certain that France would not act without British support and that British support would not be forthcoming. His intuition proved correct. The Baldwin government deprecated Germany's unilateral action but "after all, the Rhineland is a part of Germany; why shouldn't the Germans be allowed to occupy it?" Britain accepted the *fait accompli*. France might well have acted alone. Her army was still vastly superior to the new *Wehrmacht* and no one knew this better than the German generals; but powerful French interests feared Russia more than Germany. The old Franco-German steel cartel was once more in operation. Unemployment and widespread suffering during the depression had stimulated the workers' demand for social reform and had frightened conservatives and business interests into forming such reactionary organizations as the *Cagoulards* and the *Croix de Feu;* these gained considerable support among the officers in the French army.*

The French government's failure to stop Hitler's march into the Rhineland caused its overthrow in the general elections of May, 1936. Leon Blum's Popular Front took office amid sit-down strikes and disorder. Frightened by these developments in France, King Leopold of Belgium abrogated the Franco-Belgian alliance—a fateful decision which later contributed to the collapse of the Allied defenses.

Meanwhile, Mussolini had completed the conquest of Ethiopia and King Victor Emmanuel had assumed the title of Emperor. In July, General Francisco Franco launched a rebellion against the government of Spain with the concealed support of Hitler and Mussolini. In August, the Moscow purge trials took place; and in September, the Nazis proclaimed a world-wide crusade against Communism.

During this fateful year, the United States, Britain and

* Charles Micaud, *The French Right and Nazi Germany* (Duke University Press, 1943), gives a clear picture of how France was rendered impotent at this decisive moment.

France were, strangely enough, still discussing the limitation of naval armaments.

In the electoral campaign here at home, the Republican candidate, Governor Alf M. Landon, of Kansas, singled out for attack the one New Deal policy which ran counter to the prevailing nationalistic trend; namely, the program of reciprocal trade treaties to effect tariff reductions, inaugurated by Secretary of State Cordell Hull. Thus the Republican Party stultified its position by plumping for two mutually exclusive objectives: it launched its major attack upon the excessive centralization of power in the Federal government, while at the same time advocating a foreign economic policy of national self-sufficiency and narrow nationalism which could be carried out only with an even greater control by government over the economic life of the country.

In spite of the fact that more than two-thirds of the press supported Landon and that a number of conservative Democrats came out in opposition to the New Deal, Roosevelt won an overwhelming victory. Landon carried only two rock-ribbed Republican states—Maine and Vermont.*

Armed with the impressive authority of his victory, President Roosevelt visited South America, delivering the opening address at the Inter-American Conference held at Buenos Aires. The purpose of this trip was to cement the bonds already forged by the Good Neighbor Policy which Roosevelt had adopted in place of the "Dollar Diplomacy" of previous Presidents. The collective security, non-intervention and neutrality protocols adopted by the Conference went far toward establishing hemispheric solidarity but, in effect, they merely extended the isolationist pacifism of the United States over the southern continent. They constituted no recognition that the vital interests of both the Americas were threatened by the aggressive expansionism of the Fascist dictators in Europe and the rising power of Japan in the Far East.

The year 1937 marked the unrecognized beginning of World War II.

A military revolt in the Chinese province of Shensi presented

* Note the striking similarity between this election and Jackson's re-election in 1832.

the Japanese with an opportunity to intervene under the pretext of "pacifying China." A trumped-up incident resulted in the full-scale overrunning of the northern provinces and the capture of Peiping. Next, the Japanese blockaded the China coast, captured Shanghai and moved inland up the Yangtze valley. The Chinese forces, led by Chiang Kai-shek resisted fiercely but, step by step, the Chinese government was forced to withdraw, first to Nanking, then to Hankow and finally to Chungking. The barbaric behavior of the Japanese invaders surpassed any savagery known in modern times. Mild diplomatic incidents were caused by the allegedly accidental bombing of the American gunboat *Panay* and by Japanese violation of European concessions, but neither the United States nor any European power took action to halt the aggression. Large sums of money were privately raised in the United States for Chinese relief. The newspapers fulminated against the invaders; but that was as far as it went.

In Europe, the year began with a "gentleman's agreement" between the British government and Mussolini. By this time Italian "volunteers" were fighting side by side with Franco's rebels at the gates of Madrid and Hitler was testing his latest planes and weapons allegedly by sending "only a few technical groups" to Franco's assistance. The Spanish government had asked for and obtained help, mostly in the form of planes and pilots, from the Soviet Union. It had obtained as well the help of an International Brigade composed of true volunteers—young men from the United States, France and Britain (and even a few anti-Nazi Germans), who recognized what Fascism was and wanted to fight it, even if they fought side by side with Communists.

These young men and the liberals who supported the Loyalist cause did not represent majority opinion in their home countries. In both Britain and France, conservative opinion favored Franco. Powerful church elements supported the Fascist rebellion in Europe and in the United States. The governments of Britain and France entered into a farcical "neutrality agreement" with other nations, *including the Soviet Union, Germany and Italy who were openly participating in the civil war.* German and Italian warships joined British and French vessels in patrolling the Spanish coast "to enforce non-intervention," while German and Italian troops fought under the banner of the rebellion. The effect of this "non-intervention" was to shut off outside aid to the government forces and to permit such aid to the rebels to continue.

The conduct of the United States in this affair was scarcely better than that of Britain and France. It was both dishonest and stupid—dishonest, because the United States government used the pretext of neutrality to aid the rebellion; and stupid, because, in company with Britain and France, the United States failed utterly to understand that the Spanish affair was actually the beginning of a joint bid for European, and eventually world supremacy on the part of Hitler and Mussolini.

On May 1, 1937, a new Neutrality Resolution, passed by Congress, was proclaimed by the President as an amendment to the previous legislation. This provided that the prohibitions applying to belligerent nations should apply equally to countries engaged in civil war, if, in the judgment of the President, such application should be in the nation's interest. The prohibition against American vessels carrying implements of war to belligerents was extended to cover certain other articles as well, and made applicable to countries in which civil war might exist. Finally, the "cash and carry" provision stipulated that any sales of goods to belligerents *or to nations engaged in civil strife* be completed in the United States and that title must have passed to the purchaser prior to exportation from the United States.

The Resolution of 1937 was clearly framed so as to justify withholding assistance to the legitimate Spanish government. By exercising the option given to him and applying the Resolution's provisions to Spain, President Roosevelt, in effect, caused the government of the United States to aid the Fascist rebellion and, in so doing, to further the designs of Hitler and Mussolini. The President was doubtless persuaded to take this action because the American people were still deeply committed to pacifist isolationism; because most Americans were more afraid of Communism than of Fascism; and because the legitimate Spanish government had become identified, in the public mind, by Fascist propaganda, spread through certain church and business groups, as a "Communist government." Actually, the government against which the rebellion was launched did not contain a single Communist or even Left-wing socialist.* Whatever the motivations behind the President's action, it is difficult to justify it on either moral or pragmatic grounds.

The first repercussions of "non-intervention" were felt in France. Blum's government had made the mistake of yielding to conservative pressure not only as to Spain but also against devaluing the franc so as to bring it into line with the devalued pound and dollar. This prevented his social reforms from bringing about recovery and disappointed the working class while at the same time the reforms antagonized the conservatives. Many of the "best people" expressed the opinion: "Better Hitler than Blum." When the French Senate refused to ratify his financial proposals, Blum was forced to resign. The so-called French New Deal failed and the Popular Front government was supplanted by a conservative administration, headed by Camille Chautemps, in whom British appeasers were to find a willing collaborator.

With Neville Chamberlain succeeding Stanley Baldwin as Prime Minister, the appeasement policy was now clearly formulated; it consisted of rather leisurely rearmament and an endeavor to "remove the causes of war" by making every possible concession to the aggressive dictators. It was based not only upon the illusion that the dictators could be appeased by concessions but also upon the realization that Britain's tardy preparations would not take effect for another two years. It was a policy of gaining time, but the price paid for the time turned out to be far greater than the time was worth. Churchill, still a voice crying in the wilderness, was beginning to gain a following.

Toward the end of 1937, President Roosevelt, too, became aware of the mounting danger. In his famous "Quarantine Speech" of October, he said:

> The present reign of terror and international lawlessness began a few years ago. It began through unjustified interference in the internal affairs of other nations or the invasion of alien territories in violation of treaties, and has

* See U.S. Ambassador Claude Bowers' *My Mission to Spain* (Simon and Schuster, 1954), pages 190-194.

now reached a stage where the very foundations of civilization are seriously threatened . . .

Nations are fomenting and taking sides in civil warfare in nations that have never done them any harm . . . If we are to have a world in which we can breathe freely and live in amity without fear, the peace-loving nations must make a concerted effort to uphold the laws and principles on which alone peace can rest secure. The peace-loving nations must make a concerted effort in opposition to those violations of treaties and those ignorings of human instinct which today are creating a state of international anarchy and instability *from which there is no escape through mere isolation or neutrality* . . . (Italics added)

It seems to be unfortunately true that the epidemic of world lawlessness is spreading. When an epidemic of physical disease starts to spread, the community approves and joins in a quarantine of the patients in order to protect the health of the community against the spread of the disease.

The speech evoked widespread criticism and disapproval, partly because it ran counter to prevailing isolationist sentiment and partly because it was utterly inconsistent with the President's own recent conduct of foreign affairs. Mr. Roosevelt did not pursue the discussion. He seemed to realize that any efforts to gain support for the firm interventionist policy which he now knew to be necessary would prove futile, so long as Britain and France continued their appeasement. He saw that it would be almost impossible to arouse the American people to a danger which neither the more exposed British nor the much more exposed French people seemed to recognize. And so the President retreated from his forthright position to bide his time for a more favorable opportunity—an opportunity which did not come until it was almost too late. Nevertheless, the "Quarantine Speech" marked the end of the period of New Deal nationalism and heralded the beginning of a period of transition which was to last until the fall of France in the fateful summer of 1940.

CHAPTER TWENTY-TWO

The Betrayal of Central Europe
(1938–1939)

EARLY IN 1938, Hitler summoned Chancellor Kurt Schuschnigg to Berchtesgaden and demanded that the Austrian government cease suppression of the Nazi party. With Mussolini's Blackshirts present in Spain in greater numbers than ever before, Chamberlain told the House of Commons that he intended to seek another "gentleman's agreement" in which he hoped that the Italian dictator would "give some evidence of sincerity" by "withdrawing a substantial number of volunteers from Spain." This produced the first showdown over the appeasement policy. Foreign Secretary Anthony Eden vigorously opposed any further negotiations and resigned when Chamberlain insisted that confidence be placed in "the perfect good faith" of the Italian government and its "sincere desire to reach agreement."

Eden's stand aroused a considerable amount of public sympathy in the United States, but the government remained silent. A month earlier, however, the President had sent a significant message to Congress on the subject of national defense. Proposing a substantial increase in naval construction and a re-tooling of the aircraft and munitions industries, Mr. Roosevelt said:

Adequate defense means that for the protection not only of our coasts but also of our communications far removed from the coast, we must keep any potential enemy many hundreds of miles away from our continental limits. We cannot assume that our defense would be limited to one ocean and one coast and that the other coast would with certainty be safe. We cannot assume that the connecting link

—the Panama Canal—would be safe. Adequate defense affects, therefore, the simultaneous defense of every part of the United States of America.

It was clear from this message that the President was convinced of the likelihood of war—more so, perhaps, than most European statesmen. It was also clear that he entertained no doubt that such a war would endanger the security of the United States and that an attack might come across either ocean. While a reluctant Congress was debating whether or not to follow the President's recommendations, the next move toward war was already in the making.

On March 11, 1938, Hitler proclaimed the annexation of Austria and German troops marched unopposed into Vienna. This time, Hitler had reached a prior agreement with Mussolini.

Britain and France addressed sharp notes of protest to a defiant and triumphant *Fuehrer*. The French ambassador called at the British Foreign Office and announced that France would honor its alliance and fight in the event that Hitler should next invade Czechoslovakia, demanding to know what Britain would do in that eventuality. Chamberlain did not know what Britain would do; he felt sure that "Herr Hitler" would now be reasonable and that Mussolini would see that Germany must not be allowed to acquire domination over Europe. French public opinion was outraged, but not Chautemps, who agreed with Chamberlain and was shortly forced to resign. A second Blum administration lasted only a few weeks and was replaced, after another financial crisis, by a cabinet headed by Edouard Daladier, with the subtle and wholly unreliable Georges Bonnet as foreign minister.

Neither the British nor the French government was convinced that war was inevitable. Britain relied upon the power of a naval blockade and France upon the assumed impregnability of the Maginot Line. Both hoped that Hitler would follow the formula laid down in his book, *Mein Kampf,* and attack Russia. As for the attitude of the Soviet government, Maxim Litvinov made this unequivocally clear in a proposal for joint action sent to London, Washington and Paris. Outlining the recent history of Fascist aggression, the Russian note concluded with these significant paragraphs:

> Thus far, the menace has been directed against the . . . small nations; but the inevitable enslavement of these countries will create a basis for pressure and even for attacks against large countries as well.
>
> In the first place, there arises a menace to Czechoslovakia, but, owing to the contagious character of aggression, the danger threatens to grow into new international conflicts and already manifests itself in the alarming situation which has arisen on the Polish-Lithuanian frontier.
>
> The present international situation places before all peace-loving nations, and the great powers in particular, the question of their responsibility for the destinies of the peoples of Europe, and not only of Europe. The Soviet government, being cognizant of its share in this responsibility and being cognizant also of its obligations under the League Covenant, the Kellogg-Briand Pact and the treaties of mutual assistance concluded with France and Czechoslovakia, I can state on its behalf that, on its part, it is ready as before to participate in collective actions that would be decided upon jointly with it and that would aim at checking the further development of aggression and at eliminating an aggravated danger of a new world massacre. It is prepared immediately to take up in the League of Nations, or outside it, deliberation with other powers on practical measures that circumstances demand.
>
> Tomorrow may be too late, but today the time for it is not yet gone, if all states, and the great powers in particular, take a firm and unambiguous stand on the problem of the collective salvation of peace.

There was no reply from Britain, France or the United States. In part this was due to the prevailing fear of Communism; in part to an underestimation of Russia's military capability. The West had not comprehended the true significance of the Russian purge and the elimination of the Trotskyite opposition. The trials had seemed merely a hollow mockery, designed by Stalin to get rid of personal enemies. It was widely believed that Stalin had "killed off the best of his generals" and that Russia would not be of much use in a war. This attitude, fostered by Charles Lindbergh's deprecatory comments on the Red air force and his glowing description of Goering's *Luftwaffe,* had much to do with the subsequent behavior of the Western powers. (Indeed, the underestimate of Russian strength persisted until well into 1941; at the time of Hitler's attack on Russia, the estimate of most Western military authorities, including our own, was that Hitler's armies would "cut through Russian resistance like a knife through cheese.")

No sooner had Hitler annexed Austria, than the campaign for the "liberation" of the Sudeten Germans in Czechoslovakia went into high gear. On May 20, a border incident appeared likely to precipitate an invasion. The Czech army mobilized and the prompt issuance of French mobilization orders caused Hitler temporarily to back off. But the German army announced maneuvers in September and it became known that hundreds of thousands of workmen were employed in constructing a "Siegfried Line" along Germany's western frontier. In a state of panic, Chamberlain sent Walter Runciman to Prague to attempt "mediation." Chamberlain was still most anxious to "talk to Mussolini," but Franco's rejection of a British appeal to oust all foreign troops from Spain held up negotiations.

In the first week of September tension became acute. Hitler demanded an immediate plebiscite in the Sudetenland and announced, at the Nuremberg rally, that Germany would, if necessary, fight to "free" the Sudeten Germans. On September 15, Chamberlain flew to Berchtesgaden to talk to "Herr Hitler." Having ascertained that Hitler would not recede from his demand—"the last territorial demand he would ever make"—Chamberlain returned and met with Daladier. The British government wished to tell President Beneš that he must submit to the plebiscite. The French cabinet was divided.

On September 19, Mussolini declared that, if war were to come, Italy had chosen her side. A day later the British and French governments told Beneš that he must accept the plebiscite. Litvinov, speaking before the League Assembly, declared Russia's willingness to fight, if France would live up to her obligations to support Czechoslovakia. Again, no reply.

Under the unremitting pressure of the French and British governments, Beneš finally agreed to the plebiscite, knowing that this would mean the loss of the Sudetenland and the breaching of Czechoslovakia's strategic defenses. Chamberlain flew back to Germany to report his "success" to Hitler at Bad Godesberg, only to be met with far stiffer demands, including immediate German occupation of the Sudeten territory. Reporting on his unhappy journey, Chamberlain said: "I was taken completely by surprise when I got back to Germany and found that Herr Hitler insisted that the territory should be handed over to him immediately, and immediately be occupied by German troops, without previous arrangements for safeguarding the people within the territory who were not Germans or who did not want to join the German *Reich*." Then, with a pained expression, he added: "I must say that I find that attitude unreasonable."

Chamberlain was not alone in clinging to the belief that a peaceful settlement could be made with Hitler. On the same day—September 26, 1938—President Roosevelt cabled to both Hitler and Beneš urging that peaceful negotiations be continued. Hitler replied with a long denunciation of Wilson, the Versailles Treaty, the Czech government and the Western democracies, declaring that a postponement of the issue was no longer possible, and that it rested with the Czech government alone "to decide whether it wants peace or war." To this uncompromising and rude reply, Roosevelt added another plea urging the avoidance of armed conflict. In addition, the President cabled to Mussolini urging him to mediate.

Mussolini acted promptly. On September 28, Hitler postponed the invasion of Czechoslovakia and announced that, at Mussolini's suggestion, he would agree to a four-power parley of Britain, France, Germany and Italy to be held at Munich. The parley, held two days later, was short. Chamberlain and Daladier signed Hitler's "peace terms," including an agreement that the German army was to march at once into the Sudetenland. Czechoslovakia was not represented, except by the men who betrayed her. Russia was not consulted. Having signed a mutual peace pledge with "Herr Hitler," Chamberlain returned home triumphantly with what he described as "peace with honor" and "peace for our time." For a brief moment it looked as if the betrayed Czechs might fight alone, but that moment passed and, with it, vanished the possibility that France might still honor her solemn alliance. Had such been the case, had World War II begun in October, 1938, instead of a year later, Germany's defeat would almost certainly have been accomplished at less cost and in a far shorter time.

The surrender involved more than the Sudetenland. It involved the strategic control of Central Europe, handing over to Hitler the Moravian Gateway into the Danubian plain. It enabled the Nazi *Fuehrer* to coerce and bribe Hungary into becoming a satellite and to seduce the corrupt Polish government to its own destruction. The "Peace of Munich" destroyed at one stroke the whole French system of continental alliances, alienating not only Poland but Rumania and Jugoslavia as well. With Anglo-French prestige at an all-time low, all the small nations of Eastern and Central Europe now found themselves in the position of having to make whatever terms they could with Hitler. Worse yet, the betrayal of Czechoslovakia alienated the Soviet Union and destroyed the Soviet-French alliance, giving Hitler the one thing he needed most; namely, the assurance that he would not have to fight a two-front war. Without this assurance, one may doubt whether even so reckless a man as the *Fuehrer* would have risked starting a major conflict.

Within Germany, Munich killed the last serious opposition to Hitler's policy of aggressive expansion. Once more—as in the previous case of the Rhineland—the German generals had opposed risking a major war over the Sudeten issue; they knew that the *Wehrmacht* was not ready. Once more, Hitler had said: "Wait. There will be no war." And, once more, Hitler had been right. The German people were as frightened of war in 1938 as the people of France and Britain. Had Hitler's intuition proved wrong, there might have been serious disturbances among the workers and disaffection in the High Command. After Munich, Hitler stood before the German people as the genius who had led them from triumph to triumph without getting them into war. Henceforward they would follow him blindly.

The consequences of the "Peace of Munich" reached far beyond the war and into the post-World-War-II era. It was at

Munich that Eastern Europe was cut loose from its traditional moorings to the West, leaving it a prey to Hitler and—after Hitler's defeat—a prey to the Soviet Union. It was at Munich that the European community was partitioned and the fixtures erected from which the Iron Curtain was later to descend.

All that Chamberlain and Daladier gained from the betrayal was a brief reprieve from the dreaded horrors of aerial bombardment. That short respite enabled Britain to train and equip an army of about 300,000 men, considerably less than the thirty-five well-trained and well-equipped Czechoslovak divisions which, together with Czechoslovakia's formidable strategic position, had been abandoned. As for France, the period from Munich to the outbreak of war a year later was put to better use by the Nazi fifth column than by the French government.

When Daladier returned from Munich, he expected to be stoned. Instead, he was mobbed by a grateful populace which realized only that it had been released from the terrible threat of war. The French Right rejoiced over the "Peace of Munich," because it "locked Russia out of Europe." The Left accepted the surrender with mixed feelings of relief and dismay. The majority of French citizens had become resigned to German hegemony in Eastern Europe, believing that the French army could successfully fight a defensive war behind the Maginot Line, but that it was incapable of waging an offensive war. For the most part, French opinion accepted the slogan, coined for it by the Nazi fifth column: "Why die for Czechoslovakia?" *

In Britain, a large part of the population welcomed Chamberlain as their deliverer, but there was also strong criticism. Major Clement Attlee, leader of the Labour opposition, denounced the betrayal. Sir Samuel Hoare and Viscount Halifax defended it. Eden and the Liberal leader, Sir Archibald Sinclair, were sharply critical; Duff Cooper resigned from the Admiralty in protest; but it remained for Winston Churchill

---

* Micaud, *op. cit.*, and Edmond Taylor in his *Strategy of Terror* (Houghton Mifflin, 1940), give an excellent picture of how Nazi propaganda penetrated and undermined the French nation. See also Heinz Pol, *The Suicide of a Democracy* (Reynal & Hitchcock, 1940); and André Maurois, *Tragedy in France* (Harpers, 1940).

to cut through to the heart of the matter. In a flaming speech of denunciation, Churchill said:

> Do not suppose that this is the end. It is only the beginning. It is only the first foretaste of the bitter cup which will be proffered to you year after year, unless, by a supreme recovery of moral health and martial vigor, we rise again to take our stand for freedom as in olden times.

When the government's critics demanded to know why Russia had been left out of the Munich conference, Sir John Simon offered the explanation that to have invited Russia would have "offended Hitler and Mussolini."

In the United States, too, there was mingled relief, dismay and disgust. The Undersecretary of State, Sumner Welles, officially hailed the Munich Pact, characterizing the President's intervention as "an historical service to humanity." The President himself asked to be "excused from an opinion." He, who a year before had recommended quarantining the aggressors, now found himself in the unhappy position of having helped to bring about an abject and disgraceful surrender to aggression.

On the other side of the globe, Japan was making rapid progress in the conquest of China. The fall of Canton cut China off from outside contact, except over the caravan routes to Siberia and the precarious back door of French Indo-China. The Chinese government was in desperate straits. But the Far Eastern policy of the great powers was very similar to their policy in Europe; namely, to let the aggressors satisfy their lust, so long as it did not encroach directly upon their own interests. If Japan could gratify its ambitions in China, and if Germany could be induced to turn East and attack Russia, all might yet be well. The trouble with this cynically immoral policy was that it rested upon a complete failure to comprehend the cumulative nature of aggression.

Neither the events in Europe nor those in Asia were as interesting to the American people in an election year as the fact that domestic recovery had been arrested. The President's fight with the Supreme Court, his attempted purge of the Democratic Party and a serious slump in business aroused the strongest opposition yet encountered by the New Deal. The Congressional elections weakened the Democratic control of both Houses, creating a serious obstacle to the President's leadership in preparing against a war which, he well knew, might break out at any time.

The country as a whole was still very far from recognizing its own vital interests or the dangers which threatened them. The events of 1938 merely confused the American mind. Common interests with Britain and France were obscured by the lack of respect which the Munich betrayal had inspired. Disgust at Anglo-French appeasement rationalized American connivance and made it possible to bury any feelings of guilt under a pretext of righteous indignation. The "Peace of Munich" caused a resurgence of American isolationism and presented the aggressors with three years in which to exploit American indecision.

CHAPTER TWENTY-THREE

War and Short-of-War Assistance

(1939–1941)

ON JANUARY 4, 1939, President Roosevelt told Congress in blunt words that the state of the world demanded that the nation arm itself for self-defense. "There comes a time in the affairs of men," Mr. Roosevelt said, "when they must prepare to defend not their homes alone but the tenets of faith and humanity on which their churches, their governments and their very civilization are founded. The defense of religion, democracy and good faith among nations is all the same fight. To save one, we must now make up our minds to save all." In a frank commentary on the recent past, the President said: "A war which threatened to envelop the world in flames has been averted, but it has become increasingly clear that peace has not been assured." Declaring that the law-abiding democracies "cannot safely be indifferent to lawlessness anywhere," Mr. Roosevelt proceeded to promulgate a new policy for the United States—the policy of short-of-war resistance to aggression.

> The peaceful democracies cannot forever let pass without effective protest acts of aggression against sister nations—acts which automatically undermine all of us. Obviously, they must proceed along peaceful lines. But the mere fact that we rightly decline to intervene with arms . . . does not mean that we must act as if there were no aggression at all. Words may be futile, but war is not the only means of commanding a decent respect for the opinions of mankind. There are many methods short of war, but stronger and more effective than mere words, of bringing home to the aggressor governments the sentiments of our own people.

The weakness in this policy was obvious. Against wholly unscrupulous and lawless aggressors, methods short of war would be effective to prevent war only if backed by superior force and the determination to use it, should all else fail. To proclaim that "we rightly decline to intervene with arms" (a phrase reminiscent of Wilson's "too proud to fight") was to imply that we would not resort to arms if methods short of war should fail to stop aggression. To imply this was actually to notify aggressors that they would encounter only moral disapproval and economic sanctions.

The President was doubtless aware of this, but he also knew that, if he went further, it was doubtful whether Congress would enact even the most vitally necessary measures of defense —measures which the nation's safety demanded, no matter what policy it pursued. He had now to deal with a preponderantly isolationist and refractory Congress, and a direct appeal to the people so soon after a Congressional election held forth little promise. In his anxious dilemma between what he knew the international situation demanded and what he thought Congress and the people would accept, the President embarked upon a course of action which thereafter held him prisoner until the Japanese attack upon Pearl Harbor untied his hands.

The isolationist opposition was quick to mobilize. Mr. Hoover told the country that the President's policy would mean taking the country into war through meddling in affairs which were none of its business. Minimizing the danger of conflict, he said: "There are more realistic pressures for peace in Europe today than there are for war."

One had to use a strange pair of lenses to discern these "pressures for peace." Hitler had just made a speech demanding the return of the former German colonies and endorsing Mussolini's territorial ambitions. He had just unblushingly revealed that as early as May 28, 1938 he had ordered preparations for the invasion of Czechoslovakia *on October 2*. Mussolini had not fulfilled his Munich promise to withdraw Italian troops from Spain; instead, he was making threatening gestures toward France's Mediterranean possessions. Barcelona had fallen and, on February 11, the *New York Herald Tribune* reported that Franco's forces had captured Minorca, "ably assisted by the intervention of the British cruiser *Devonshire*." (To keep the Balearic Islands out of Mussolini's clutching hands, the British were now aiding Franco!)

Such were the "pressures for peace." The vision of Mr. Hoover's Secretary of State was clearer than that of his former chief; on March 6, 1939, Mr. Stimson announced his support of President Roosevelt's policy.

There were a few Americans at this time who not only disagreed with Mr. Hoover but felt that the only hope of averting a second World War lay in a much stronger policy than that proposed by President Roosevelt. At a meeting of the Economic Club of New York on March 22, the author advocated an immediate American declaration of solidarity with Britain and France, making it unequivocally clear that an attack upon either of them would involve war with the United States. This proposal—in essence the same as the Atlantic Treaty to be signed ten years later—drew sharp disagreement from two other speakers: Senator Burton K. Wheeler, of Montana, and Mr. John Foster Dulles, later to become Secretary of State.*

* For the full text of this debate, interesting chiefly because of the light which it throws upon Mr. Dulles' thinking of the time, see the author's *Our War and Our Peace* (Farrar & Rhinehart, 1941).

What illusions remained as to Mr. Chamberlain's "peace for our time" were shattered on March 13, when Hitler suddenly ordered Slovakia to break away from the Prague government and pledged his support to the puppet premier Tiso. On the following day, German troops occupied Prague and set up a Nazi regime under the guise of a "Protectorate." Simultaneously, Hungary seized the Carpatho-Ukraine at the eastern tip of Czechoslovakia, thereby establishing a common frontier with Poland. All this was in direct violation of the Munich Pact, contradicting not only "the last territorial demand" but the pretense that Hitler wanted only Germans in his Third *Reich*.

Berlin truculently rejected Allied protests. In the House of Commons, Neville Chamberlain asked and left unanswered a question which indicated that even he had come to the end of his faith in the promises of "Herr Hitler." "Is this," he asked, "a step in the direction of an attempt to dominate the world by force?" As if by way of reply, Hitler seized the port of Memel from Lithuania and announced a trade agreement with Rumania. Roosevelt's reaction was prompt: he imposed a super-tariff upon all German goods, amounting to an embargo, and decided to seek modification of the Neutrality Laws.

With Hitler ranting about the "impossible Danzig Corridor" and massing troops on the Polish frontier, Britain and France held anxious consultations. Should they accept the Soviet Union's renewed offer of a triple alliance or proceed, alone, to guarantee the integrity of Poland and Rumania? They decided in favor of the latter and invited the Polish foreign minister, Josef Beck, to London. Beck was not overenthusiastic about accepting a guarantee from the powers which had betrayed Czechoslovakia, but did accept it when he obtained the promise of a loan as well. He flatly refused to have Russia join as a guarantor of Polish integrity. Hitler's immediate reply to the announcement of the Anglo-French guarantee, which had not mentioned Danzig, was a speech declaring that Danzig was none of Britain's business.

Meanwhile, Madrid had fallen. On March 30, Hitler welcomed home the first 7,000 men of the Condor Legion. A few days later, he revealed that he had ordered intervention at the very beginning of the Franco rebellion and that German planes

and troops had been in Spain since July, 1936. Not to be out-
done in claiming credit for the Fascist victory, Mussolini
boasted that the Italian navy had carried "at least 100,000
Italian troops" (no longer referred to as "volunteers") to fight
for Franco. Thus ended the Spanish republic and thus ended
a shameful chapter in Western diplomacy. Relatively few Americans realized then or later the extent to which they had been
tricked and misled by pro-Fascist propaganda.

The facts were that the Fascist rebellion against the legitimate, republican government had been stimulated and aided
from the start by both Hitler and Mussolini; that the government was not a "Red" government but a democratic Left-of-
center coalition; and that this government, faced with German
and Italian intervention on behalf of Franco, had sought, received and paid for Soviet aid. By misrepresenting the nature
of the legitimate government, magnifying Soviet assistance and
denying and concealing their own much more formidable intervention on behalf of Franco, Hitler and Mussolini, aided by
pro-Fascist propagandists here and abroad, made the Spanish
civil war appear as a fight against Communism, whereas, in fact,
it was a fight against Fascism seeking to usurp power and to
destroy democracy. So effective was this Fascist propaganda that
any American who volunteered to fight in Spain or who contributed to medical aid for the loyalists forces has continued to
this day to be suspected of pro-Communist leanings and disloyalty to the United States.

It was true that the appeasement policy of the democracies
made many Communist sympathizers both in Europe and in
the United States. The extent to which the Soviet Union had
become a repressive police-state was not generally understood.
The Soviet Union and its Communist fifth columns seemed—
and, to a large extent, they actually then were—the only strong
forces operating against the continued encroachment of Fascist
aggression. Some disillusioned democrats did join the Communist party at that time. Many more, who never lost their democratic faith but were disgusted with appeasement, became, for
the time being, "Communist sympathizers," in the sense that
they sympathized with Communist resistance to Fascism. This
could be said of most West European workers and intellectuals,

but few Europeans drew the broad inference that a man who had fought for democracy in Spain had renounced his loyalty to his own country. The deeper penetration of Fascist propaganda in the United States was evidenced by the fact that only here was a stigma permanently attached to an individual who had aided the Spanish loyalists—only here was that action equated with a strong presumption of disloyalty—only here was coined that curious term of opprobrium: "Oh, he was a premature anti-Fascist." (As if only a Communist could have had the brains to recognize the Fascist threat at that time!)

A week after Fascism's triumph in Spain, Mussolini's Blackshirts invaded Albania and made it part of the new Roman empire. Britain announced a guarantee of Greek integrity. President Roosevelt asked Hitler and Mussolini for assurances that they had no further designs for conquest and suggested a conference to discuss international disarmament and the freeing of international trade. The Italian dictator coldly brushed off this appeal in a speech to an Italian audience. Hitler ignored it altogether. Before the month ended, Britain adopted conscription and Hitler repudiated the Anglo-German naval agreement with which the appeasement policy had begun.

On May 3, 1939, the Soviet government served notice that it had reached the end of its patience by announcing the replacement of Maxim Litvinov by Viacheslav Molotov. French diplomatists, quick to understand the significance of this announcement, urged Britain to enter an Anglo-French-Russian alliance. Chamberlain resisted, still hoping to seduce Mussolini from his allegiance to Hitler. Daladier was insistent that Britain's course would dangerously alienate the Soviet Union, and not only the Labour leadership but Britain's World War I leader, Lloyd George, urgently demanded a Russian alliance. Yielding to public pressure, Chamberlain sent a mission of second-rank representatives to Moscow.

Molotov insisted that not only Poland and Rumania but Latvia, Estonia and Lithuania be jointly guaranteed by Britain, France and Russia, but the Baltic states, fearful of provoking Hitler, declined a guarantee and thereby sealed their own doom. The negotiations stalled and ominous hints appeared of a Russo-German trade agreement. On June 29, Lord Halifax declared that Britain would tolerate no further expansion by force or threat of force, but within a month Britain appeased Japan by withdrawing financial support from Chiang Kai-shek, and opened negotiations with Dr. Wohltat for the extension of large British credits to Germany. When news of the latter negotiation leaked out, Mr. Robert Hudson was declared by Chamberlain to have acted without the authority of the cabinet.

This sort of thing played directly into the hands of the American isolationists. Ignoring the fact that the Chamberlain government was being sharply criticized at home, they asked: "If this is how Britain deals with the aggressors, why should the United States take any action to stop them?" The President and Secretary Hull pleaded in vain with Congress to amend the Neutrality Laws. Senator William E. Borah, of Idaho, leading a "Peace Bloc" opposition, declared that he had "better sources of information than the State Department" and that he was quite certain that there would be no war in Europe. Congress adjourned without taking action.

During the eventful summer of 1939, Japan extended its control over most of China, but Japanese troops clashed in Mongolia with Russian forces. The unexpected strength of the Russian army displayed in this short, undeclared and little-publicized war had an important bearing upon the subsequent Japanese decision to attack the United States rather than the Soviet Union. On July 26, the United States served six months' notice of its intention to abrogate the Japanese-American Trade Treaty of 1911. This amounted to declaring that an embargo would go into effect in January, 1940. The action, initiated by Republican Senator Vandenberg, of Michigan, received widespread bipartisan approbation. The American people were far more ready to take drastic action against Japan than against Germany. Japan seemed a natural enemy, but the menace of Nazi Germany was obscured by Anglo-French appeasement. The notice of abrogation brought about a cabinet crisis in Japan.

In Europe, events moved inexorably toward the final crisis. Hitler demanded the cession of Danzig and the whole Polish Corridor. Count Ciano, Italy's foreign minister, dissociated his country from this demand. Border incidents broke out and were played up by Nazi propaganda. Count Czaky, the Hungarian foreign minister, was summoned to Berlin. On August 18, Hitler formally took over Slovakia and simultaneously announced that Polish silence constituted a refusal of Germany's "legitimate" demands, shouting: "The time for words is past!" And so it was.

Two days later came the announcement of a Russo-German trade treaty. While the stunned Western world was still trying to persaude itself that this had no great significance, von Ribbentrop announced that he was leaving for Moscow to sign a non-aggression pact.

Britain, aghast and angry, reaffirmed that she would fight if Poland were attacked. Simultaneously Chamberlain permitted Germany to buy large quantities of British copper and other essential war materials.

France called half a million reserves to the colors. Rome maintained an ominous silence. The King of Belgium, the Pope and the President of the United States all issued peace appeals; Roosevelt's message was addressed to the Italian King.

At Moscow, the Anglo-French mission packed its bags, but then decided to delay its departure. Russia was still willing to talk, but demanded that Poland and Rumania join an alliance against Germany. Poland and Rumania—allied with each other against Russia but not against Germany—stubbornly refused. That settled it. Molotov waited until August 31 to see whether, under the increasing threats from Berlin, Beck would change his mind at the last minute and permit Russian troops to come to Poland's assistance. The Poles stuck to their refusal; the die was cast. Without a backward glance, Russia embarked upon a cynically realistic course of self-preservation. For the time being, Communism and Fascism, each considering the other its implacable enemy, entered into alliance.

In the last week of August, Hitler wrote Daladier, declaring that he had nothing but the friendliest feelings for France and would never want Germany to fight France again. (In *Mein Kampf* he had said: "France is and remains the inexorable enemy of the German people.") To Chamberlain, Hitler gave assurance that he would accept British mediation of the Polish dispute and even laid down somewhat milder terms—which the

Polish government never received until after the invasion had been ordered.

On September 1, 1939, the German tanks rolled into Poland. Two days later Britain and France declared war; the Dominions followed suit.

In a radio address, President Roosevelt condemned the use or threat of force and declared that the war which had broken out endangered peace everywhere. Announcing that a neutrality proclamation was being prepared, he asked for adjournment of partisanship. Where, in similar circumstances, Wilson had asked the people to be "neutral in thought and feeling," Roosevelt said:

> This nation will remain a neutral nation, but I cannot ask that every American citizen remain neutral in thought as well. Even a neutral has a right to take account of facts. Even a neutral cannot be asked to close his mind or conscience.

In effect, the President said to the American people:

> It is up to you to think about this war, to watch its course, and to let your minds and consciences tell you whether it is right for us to remain neutral or whether, at some point, our vital interest will demand that we enter the conflict. I shall preserve American neutrality by every means at my command, so long as the American people wish me to preserve it.

In the minds of those who knew him well, the President left little doubt as to his own feelings. He himself was not and made no attempt to be "neutral in thought and feeling." He wanted the Allies to win and he wanted to help them win, without involving the United States in war. Whether he believed that this was possible is a matter of conjecture; it seems probable that he did, at least until the fall of France. What appears certain is that Roosevelt knew that, if ever the time should come when only American intervention could save Europe from Nazi conquest, it would be a long, hard job to persuade Congress and the people that the United States should become a belligerent.

By the middle of September, Polish resistance was broken, Warsaw lay under siege and the Polish government was in flight.* On the 16th, Soviet troops crossed Poland's eastern frontier and advanced as far as the old Curzon Line. Here they met the advancing German armies and Polish resistance ceased. The Soviet government then declared that Russia would remain neutral in the Anglo-French war against Germany.

The Russian action against Poland created a furor of excitement in the United States. The move was denounced as treachery and it was generally assumed that Russia had now become Germany's ally. In Britain, a calmer attitude prevailed. Russia's declaration of neutrality was taken seriously. Churchill, now First Lord of the Admiralty and certainly no friend of the Soviet Union, stressed Russia's common interest with the Allies in keeping Germany out of the Balkans. Lloyd George wrote to the Polish ambassador:

> It is essential to draw a distinction between the action of the Soviet Union and that of the Nazis. The latter seek to annex territory essentially Polish. . . On the other hand, the Russian armies marched into territories which were not Polish and which were forcibly annexed by Poland after the Great War despite fierce protests and armed resistance by the inhabitants . . . It would be an act of criminal folly to place the Russian advance in the same category as that of the Germans, although it would suit Herr Hitler's designs to do so.

Had the Soviet Union been content with recapturing the Polish Ukraine, anti-Russian sentiment in the United States might have subsided and the whole future course of American-Soviet relations might have developed along happier lines. The Russians, however, were far more concerned with protecting themselves against a future German attack than about Western opinion. Anxious to create the largest possible buffer between the Germans and their own vital centers, they used coercive threats to obtain military concessions from the three Baltic

---

* The Polish government fled first to Rumania, then to France and eventually to Britain where it remained with the other governments-in-exile.

states and Finland. The Baltic states complied under duress. Finland, however, refused the Russian demand to grant the Soviet Union a naval base at Hangö and to move back its frontier on the Karelian Isthmus, where it came within 20 kilometers of Leningrad.* Thereupon Russia declared war and invaded Finnish territory. This was too much for the American people.

Molotov's curt rebuff of President Roosevelt's proffer of mediation raised American sentiment against Russia to a higher pitch than the feeling against Germany. All through the winter, the American press and the public were far more concerned with Finland's heroic resistance than with the minor skirmishes of the "phony war" between Germany and the Western powers. Private citizens contributed generously to Finnish war relief and a public loan of $10,000,000 was extended to the Finnish government. After giving a magnificent account of themselves, the Finns were overpowered and forced to surrender on March 12, 1940.

No one knew, or could know then, that the brutal Russian actions in the North were eventually to save Leningrad and to play a vital part in enabling the Soviet Union to halt the Nazi steam roller. Nor did this outcome provide any moral justification for the Soviet action. Having failed to enlist the Western democracies in a joint effort to halt Nazi aggression, Russia embarked upon a policy of ruthless, unilateral defense of its own security. In so doing, it saved itself—and perhaps the Allied cause—from defeat; but, in so doing, it placed itself—in American eyes at least—on a moral level with the Fascist aggressors.

After a violent nation-wide debate over repealing the

* Churchill recounts how Stalin, reminiscing at Yalta, gave this version of how the Finnish war had begun. "The Finnish frontier was some twenty kilometers from Petersburg. The Russians asked the Finns to move it back thirty kilometers, in exchange for territorial concessions in the north. The Finns refused. Then some Russian frontier guards were shot at by the Finns and killed. The frontier guards detachment complained to Red Army troops, who opened fire on the Finns. Moscow was then asked for instructions. These contained the order to return the fire. One thing led to another and the war was on. The Russians did not want a war against Finland." *History of the Second World War* (Houghton Mifflin, 1953), Vol. VI, page 364.

Neutrality Laws, in which former Secretary of State Stimson led the fight for repeal while Senator Borah and Charles Lindbergh led the opposition, the President concluded that the most he could hope for would be a repeal of the Arms Embargo. Addressing the Congress, he characterized the Embargo as dangerous to peace, recalling how a similar law had involved the United States in the War of 1812. Calling the whole Neutrality Act of 1935 a mistake, he declared: "I regret that the Congress passed that act. I regret equally that I signed that act."

After a month of acrid debate, the Arms Embargo was repealed. During the discussion there emerged the five major isolationist arguments which were to be heard over and over again until debate was ended by Japanese bombs on Pearl Harbor. These were:

1. *"Our help is not needed."* This was first proclaimed by former President Hoover, who assured the country that British sea power and the French Maginot Line defenses made Allied victory certain.

2. *"War means abandoning democracy."* This was also propounded by Mr. Hoover, warning against the "emotionalism" which, he said, had drawn us into the last war and which, if permitted to involve us again, would change the republic into a dictatorship.

3. *"It is already too late. We shall have to do business with Hitler."* This was Lindbergh's favorite line, contradicting Mr. Hoover's "Our help is not needed." Since the Fascists were going to win anyway, Lindbergh counseled doing nothing which might offend them.

4. *"We are secure behind our oceans."* In propounding this thesis, later to become the main theme of the America First Committee, Lindbergh attacked Canada for "bringing the war to this hemisphere," eventually advancing the idea that the United States ought, in self-defense, to take over Canada.

5. *"This is just another imperialist war of power politics."* Senator Borah firmly believed that Hitler and Mussolini would become reasonable if they were given colonies, access to raw materials and export markets and that Allied refusal to make

these concessions was in large measure responsible for the conflict. This argument appealed to a certain group of intellectuals and was, until Hitler's attack on Russia, the favorite line of the American Communist Party.

These five arguments were used in varying combinations by a strangely assorted opposition to Roosevelt's short-of-war aid policy. Apart from the Nazi *Bund,* the "Christian Front" and various other native or foreign-inspired Fascist groups—and, for a time, the Communists—the isolationist movement was composed mostly of American citizens who sincerely believed that our own interests were not at stake in the war and that the President's policies were taking us into a wholly unnecssary and disastrous involvement. There were, to be sure, some whose business interests inclined them toward "doing business with Hitler." There were the Franco partisans, conditioned to believe that the Nazis were the only bulwark against Communism. There was the curious case of Charles Lindbergh, who had accepted Nazi decorations and become intimate with at least one French Fascist leader. There were Americans who unwittingly became dupes and tools of Fascist, Nazi and Communist professionals. But the vast majority of the isolationists were wholly loyal Americans unable to see that our national safety was in danger, that our whole civilization was threatened and that the United States could not hope to remain a happy island of freedom in a world enslaved by Fascist tyranny.

The President's task of arousing the country to its peril was rendered difficult not only by strictly partisan opposition but even more by the inherent contradiction in his own policy: if American vital interests were at stake—and this was the only justification for short-of-war aid to the Allies—then, logically, they would have to be defended by the full military power of the United States, if nothing less would suffice to defend them.

Those Americans who were prepared to fight, if necessary— and there were many such—found themselves more and more hampered by this contradiction in the President's policy. They could not disagree with the President without jeopardizing the limited program of preparedness and aid which he advocated. Thus, for a long time, they had to restrict themselves to the advocacy of "defending America by aiding the Allies" * in order not to jeopardize defending America at all.

For over two years the nation-wide argument was largely irrelevant. Instead of debating the basic question of whether or not American vital interests—and not just American sympathies—were really at stake in Anglo-French survival, the discussion proceeded on the assumption that the one vital national interest was to stay out of war. Moreover, the issues were confused by the peculiar nature of the war in its early stages, with an apparently permanent Nazi-Communist alliance in the East and a "phony war" in the West.

When the *Sitzkrieg* ended with the sudden Nazi descent upon Denmark and Norway, in April, 1940, the American public finally began to take a greater interest and hostility began to shift from Russia to Germany. On the other hand, the fiasco of Anglo-French intervention in Norway reinforced the Lindbergh thesis that it was already too late to prevent a Hitler victory.

In May, the world witnessed the incredible spectacle of the collapse of the entire Allied front in the West. Winston Churchill became Britain's prime minister and offered his people the forever unforgettable "blood, toil, tears and sweat." The battered British army escaped through the heroic rescue at Dunkerque. Norway surrendered. The Nazi tanks crunched on toward Paris. Mussolini, now sure of Hitler's triumph, declared war on a tottering France and President Roosevelt denounced his action as a "stab in the back." Paris fell to the Germans. The French government fled to Tours and, finally, to Bordeaux. Franco seized the International Settlement of Tangier, across the straits from Gibraltar. Stalin occupied the Baltic states and forced Rumania to yield Besserabia and a part of Bukowina.

In the hope that the French government would flee to Algiers with its fleet and continue the fight, Churchill made a spectac-

* A nation-wide citizens' organization to support the President's policies and to combat the propaganda of the America First Committee was organized under the title of "The Committee to Defend America by Aiding the Allies." A more forthright interventionist group split off from this organization to operate as the Fight for Freedom Committee. (The writer was one of the founders of the latter organization.)

ular offer of Anglo-French union which, had it been accepted, might have altered the whole postwar picture. The French parliament, however, voted itself out of existence. The cabinet resigned; Marshal Pétain became the ruler of a defeated French nation, long enough, at least, to ask for an armistice and to accept the German terms of surrender. When Britain seized the French warships in British-controlled ports and attacked a French squadron at Oran which refused to surrender, Pétain broke off diplomatic relations. He and a clique of Fascist-minded collaborationists, among whom the most prominent were Joseph Laval and Admiral of the Fleet Darlan, now became caretakers for the Germans of that part of southern France which Hitler agreed to leave unoccupied, so long as the French fleet remained at its base of Toulon. A relatively unknown French general, Charles de Gaulle, fled to England and became the symbol of the continued resistance of a betrayed people.

The victorious German armies now stood poised opposite the chalk cliffs of Dover. Hitler was master of Western Europe. Britain, practically unarmed after the evacuation of Dunkerque, stood alone across 21 miles of blue water. The British people had their fleet, their small but highly efficient air force, the strength of their distant empire and a fearless, indomitable leader. Above all, they had their own unconquerable spirit and the hope, as Churchill expressed it, that "in God's good time, the New World might come to the rescue of the Old."

President Roosevelt promptly ordered the shipment to Britain of large quantities of rifles, machine-guns, ammunition and artillery from the stocks remaining after World War I. These supplies played a vital part in making it possible for the British people to prepare against apparently imminent invasion, while British workers toiled to replace the equipment lost in France. Yet the greatest danger to British survival soon became that of German submarine warfare against British shipping. It was here that a fortunate turn of the wheel in domestic American politics made possible an action which saved the British Isles from probable starvation.

Immediately after the fall of France, President Roosevelt asked for over $1,000,000,000 in additional defense appropriations, appointed a Defense Council to coordinate production, and called for a mechanized army and 50,000 airplanes. In a somewhat daring move—considering that 1940 was an election year—Mr. Roosevelt appointed two outstanding Republican leaders to his cabinet: Henry L. Stimson as Secretary of War and Frank Knox (Vice-presidential candidate in 1936) as Secretary of the Navy.

Mr. Hoover's argument that our help was not needed had been knocked into a cocked hat, but the Lindbergh argument for isolation—that it was too late to prevent a Nazi victory—had gained wide acceptance. Governor Thomas E. Dewey of New York, an eager aspirant for the Republican nomination, ridiculed as fantastic the President's call for production of 50,000 planes;* in other respects his views on foreign policy were enigmatic. The other leading Republican contender, Senator Robert A. Taft, of Ohio, son of the former President, was an outright isolationist. When the Republican convention met, it unexpectedly nominated Wendell Willkie, a public utility lawyer with no political experience, whose forthright speeches in support of aid to the Allies, combined with slashing attacks upon some of the domestic reforms of the New Deal, made him a promising candidate against Mr. Roosevelt without risking a nationwide debate over foreign policy.†

When, in spite of the no-third-term tradition, the Democrats renominated Mr. Roosevelt, the foreign policy issue was removed from the campaign. Each candidate asserted that American interests were deeply involved in British survival, that the United States should render all possible aid short of war, and that—if elected—he would keep the country out of armed conflict. Each was careful to avoid throwing the isolationist-pacifist vote to the other. The contest thus became largely a question of whether the Republican reaction of 1938 would carry further, especially in view of sentiment against a third term, or whether support for the New Deal and reluctance to change leadership at a critical moment would be decisive. After a cam-

* American aircraft production had risen, due to Allied orders, from 6,000 planes in 1939 to 12,000 in 1940. By 1943 it reached 100,000.

† For the best account of Wendell Willkie's rise to political prominence and of the Presidential campaign of 1940, see Joseph Barnes, *Wendell Willkie* (Simon and Schuster, 1952).

paign conducted on an unusually high level of patriotism and dignity, Roosevelt was overwhelmingly re-elected.

During the interval between the nominations and the election, the President was enabled by his adversary's support to override isolationist opposition to an action which crucially affected Britain's chance of survival. The famous "Destroyers for Bases Deal" transferred 50 American World War I destroyers to Britain in exchange for 99-year leases on certain British bases in the Western hemisphere. Thus two things were accomplished: the British anti-submarine defense received desperately needed reinforcement; and the United States strengthened its position in the event that it might have to rely upon hemisphere defense. Also with Willkie's support, the President succeeded in obtaining enactment of the first peacetime conscription in American history, over the bitter resistance of the majority of the Republicans in Congress. Thus the unpredictable course of domestic politics vitally affected both British survival in 1940 and American preparedness for the events of 1941.

In September, 1940. the Luftwaffe began its attack upon England magnificently overcome by the heroic RAF and an almost unbelievably steadfast civilian population.

In October, Mussolini invaded Greece and met unexpected repulse. German troops marched into Rumania unopposed, halting at the newly established Russo-Rumanian border. Much to the dismay and disgust of Churchill and Roosevelt, Pétain carried out his craven policies in Asia as well as in Europe, conceding Japan the right to erect airbases and to maintain troops in French Indo-China, thus throwing open the back door to Singapore and enabling Japan to prepare for the conquest of Malaya and the East Indies. Up to this time, Japan had refused all German overtures for a military alliance. A week after the Vichy government's concessions, Japan signed up in the Tripartite Axis Pact.

The quickening pace of Japanese aggression was due in part to Russia's plight and in part to the vacillations of American policy. Since January, 1940, American trade with Japan had been on a day-to-day basis. The United States had signed no new treaty to take the place of the one it had abrogated as a warning against further Japanese aggression. At the same time, however, the American government continued to license shipment to Japan of scrap steel, oil and gasoline, thereby nullifying the effect of its own policy.

Toward the end of 1940, British forces succeeded in driving the Italians back from an attempted invasion of Egypt and in crippling the Italian fleet by a torpedo-plane attack at Taranto, but the strain of home defense, of fighting in Africa and of keeping open the vital lines of communication had all but stripped the British Treasury. Without dollars with which to buy food and war material in the United States, the British Isles were doomed. President Roosevelt was acutely aware of the mistakes committed in World War I and flatly refused to consider the creation of new "War Debts." In what was perhaps the most inspired action of American diplomacy up to that time, Mr. Roosevelt and his advisers worked out the Lend-Lease formula of reciprocal aid. Harry L. Hopkins, the President's most trusted adviser, was sent to England to become in effect the link between Roosevelt and Churchill.*

On January 6, 1941, the President sent a special message to Congress urging all-out aid to Britain, China and Greece and defining the "Four Freedoms" as the basis for eventual peace. (Freedom from want, freedom from fear, freedom of worship and freedom of speech.)

> We are committed to the proposition that the principles of morality and considerations for our own security will never permit us to acquiesce in a peace dictated by aggressors and sponsored by appeasers. We know that enduring peace cannot be fought at the expense of other peoples' freedom.
>
> The world order which we seek is the cooperation of free countries working together in a friendly civilized society.

* The two works which are indispensable to an understanding of Anglo-American relations during World War II are Robert E. Sherwood's *Roosevelt and Hopkins* (Harper, 1948) and Sir Winston Churchill's monumental six-volume *History of the Second World War* (Houghton Mifflin, 1948-1953). See Sherwood, *op. cit.* Chapters XI and XII for Hopkins' first visit to London and the development of Anglo-American cooperation.

This nation has placed its destiny in the hands, heads and hearts of its millions of free men and women and its faith in freedom under the guidance of God. Freedom means the supremacy of human rights everywhere. Our support goes to those who struggle to gain those rights and to keep them. Our strength is our unity of purpose.

To that high concept there can be no end save victory.

This message, reaffirming the Jeffersonian championship of freedom for all men everywhere, echoed around the world, proclaiming both the American will to further democratic progress at home and the American determination to help establish freedom throughout the world.

Unlike President Wilson, however, Mr. Roosevelt was not content with a statement of lofty ideals. His message was followed by the largest military budget in the history of the nation (over $10,000,000,000), by the setting up of three separate fleets (Atlantic, Pacific and Asiatic), and by the introduction of the Lend-Lease Bill. The debate now reached its climax. The whole nation lined up on one side or the other. The isolationist opposition included a strange mixture of disparate elements. The ultra-nationalistic conservative Hearst-McCormick-Patterson newspapers found themselves working in alliance with the Communist *Daily Worker*. Loyal and unsuspecting American citizens parroted arguments and phrases coined in Berlin or Moscow. On March 11, after two months of angry debate, the Lend-Lease Bill was enacted into law.

Meanwhile, the Nazis had marched into Sofia, Bulgaria had joined the Axis and a Jugoslav government which had signed the Axis Pact was overthrown; the new Belgrade government defied Hitler and offered heroic resistance to Nazi invasion. Having subdued Jugoslavia, the Germans crossed the Greek frontier, conquering that country too, in spite of a gallant British attempt at rescue, which cost England the fruits of a hard-won victory in the desert and compelled the British army to retreat once more into Egypt. A Nazi-inspired revolt in Iraq was quelled by British troops, but Crete was lost to the first great paratroop operation.

Hitler now held sway over the European continent, with

only Switzerland remaining as an island of neutral freedom, while on the periphery Sweden, Turkey, Spain and Portugal lived in uneasy fear. Britain's ports and cities were taking an unmerciful pounding from the air. Submarine sinkings were rising at an alarming rate. . . .

On June 14, the President ordered the "freezing" of Axis funds in the United States, except those of Japan. Two days later he ordered the closing of all German consulates. The sinking of an American ship, the *Robin Moor,* was branded by the President as the act of "an international outlaw," and in a special message to Congress delivered on June 20, he said: "We are not yielding and we do not propose to yield." Anti-German feeling reached a new peak. The Fight for Freedom Committee called for the full use of the American Navy to keep the sea lanes open, even if this should involve a "shooting war." It seemed as if any day might see the United States enter the conflict.

And then the totally unexpected happened. At dawn, on June 22, 1941, the Nazis launched a furious, unheralded attack upon the Soviet Union. Overnight, the whole picture changed.

Winston Churchill wasted no time in making his country's position clear. Revealing that he himself had warned Stalin of the impending attack, he pledged Britain's aid to Russia against "this bloodthirsty guttersnipe" and defined British policy in a sentence: "Any man or state who fights against Nazism will have our aid." President Roosevelt, too, declared that Russia would receive short-of-war aid from the United States, subject to the prior needs of Britain, and sent Harry Hopkins to Moscow.* But the Nazi attack on Russia gave the isolationist opposition a new lease on life.

Mr. Hoover opined that the turn of events furnished "half a dozen reasons for the United States to stay out of the European conflict." Senator Wheeler, leading spokesman for America First, declared: "I don't think the American people will stand for us to tie up with the Communists." John T. Flynn, another vocal America Firster, asked: "Are we going to fight

* For a full account of Hopkins' mission and the extraordinarily frank disclosures of the Russian position made by Stalin to Hopkins, see R. E. Sherwood, *op. cit.,* Chapter XIV.

to make Europe safe for Communism?" and added the strange opinion that British intervention had "caused the destruction of the Low Countries and France." A sentence attributed to Senator Harry S. Truman, of Missouri, expressed a widespread sentiment: "Let the Nazis and Communists kill each other off."

The interventionist Fight for Freedom Committee hailed the attack as providing a supreme opportunity for the nations resisting Fascist aggression, but the most strident of all the voices clamoring for American belligerence now became that of the Communist *Daily Worker*. Turning an overnight somersault, the Communists suddenly discovered that what had been a "capitalist-imperialist war" on June 21, had become a holy crusade for democracy on June 22. The embarrassment of Communist support was now transferred from the isolationists to the supporters of all-out intervention.

It is appropriate to consider here the origin and effects of President Roosevelt's so-called Vichy Policy. When France fell, there were three groups of Frenchmen with whom it was necessary to reckon: the Free French—mostly outside of France— who stood with de Gaulle for continuation of the fight against Hitler; the outright collaborationists who, under the leadership of Laval, stood openly for joining the Germans in their conquest of Europe and hoped to displace Mussolini as Hitler's number-one partner; and the clerical, Fascist-minded defeatists who, under the leadership of Pétain, wished to re-create a pre-republican, authoritarian France which would cooperate with the hated invaders to the extent made necessary by what the old Marshal called "the rope around my neck." The majority of the French people rallied, for want of other leadership, around the mystic, remote and cheerless figure of the venerable military leader who had been as ready to accept defeat in 1918 as he was in 1940.

After Pétain had broken off Anglo-French relations, Britain recognized de Gaulle as the leader of the Free French. The United States, on the other hand, maintained diplomatic relations with Vichy, officially ignoring de Gaulle. This was in part due to the fact that the United States was still neutral and maintained relations with Berlin and Rome; in part it was due to the desire to keep open at least one French window to the

West in the hope of helping Pétain to resist the outright collaborationists. In making this deliberate decision, approved
by Churchill, Mr. Roosevelt and Secretary Hull were probably
influenced by an underestimate of the French spirit of resistance and by a too rosy appraisal of the old Marshal. Pétain had
not only been a defeatist in World War I; he was an outspoken
foe of democracy, connected with the reactionary, semi-Fascist
Cagoulard clique in the army, and an intimate friend of his
erstwhile pupil, Francisco Franco.*

British approval of the divergent American policy was based
upon anxiety lest the French fleet and the African colonies fall
into Axis hands. Both Britain and the United States were no
doubt conditioned to deal tolerantly with the Vichy government by their previous indirect support of Francisco Franco.
Whether or not the Vichy policy was wise is still a matter of
lively debate. Some historians justify it on the ground that it
made possible the North African invasion. Others minimize its
contribution to that campaign and hold that it stultified the
moral position of the United States. It is an indisputable fact
that the American dealings with Pétain and the prolonged
American refusal to recognize de Gaulle alienated the Free
French leader and imbued him with a permanent hostility to
the United States. (This would have been a matter of more serious regret, if de Gaulle had turned out to be a great democratic
leader as well as a military man of courage and pertinacity,
instead of an authoritarian whose political inclinations were
almost as anti-democratic as those of Pétain.) Whatever the
value of the Vichy Policy in terms of military expediency, there
could be no doubt that it was at variance with the idealistic
principles enunciated by President Roosevelt.

These principles, stated in broad terms in the January 6,
1941, message to Congress, were re-affirmed in more precise

* At the postwar trial, which convicted Pétain of treason, it was shown that
his complacent attitude toward French defeat derived largely from his hatred
of the republic and his wish to see it destroyed. For a good account of the
Anglo-American negotiations with the French government before and after the
surrender, see Forrest Davis and Ernest Lindley; *How War Came;* Simon &
Schuster, 1942; for a history of the whole Vichy Policy see William Langer, *Our
Vichy Gamble* (Knopf, 1947); also Admiral William Leahy's memoirs, *I Was
There* (McGraw-Hill, 1950).

terms in the Atlantic Charter Declaration, signed by Roosevelt and Churchill on August 14, 1941, at their first wartime meeting—the famous shipboard conference off Argentia. Here was forged the first great propaganda instrument of the anti-Axis powers, giving to the peoples of the world the first clear alternative to Hitler's "New Order" of peace enforced by conquest and slavery. In making this joint declaration, the President asserted the intention of the United States to take a hand in the shaping of the peace, even though it might or might not become a belligerent in the war. Recognizing the futility of a unilateral declaration, such as Wilson's promulgation of his Fourteen Points, Mr. Roosevelt entered into a joint commitment with Great Britain which was soon to become a commitment of the entire anti-Axis coalition.

After a preamble stating that the two statesmen had considered "the dangers to world civilization arising from the policies of military domination" upon which the Axis leaders had embarked, the aims of the signers were set forth in eight points:

First, their countries seek no aggrandizement, territorial or other;

Second, they desire to see no territorial changes that do not accord with the freely expressed wishes of the peoples concerned;

Third, they respect the right of all peoples to choose the form of government under which they will live; and they wish to see sovereign rights and self-government restored to those who have been forcibly deprived of them;

Fourth, they will endeavor, with due respect for their existing obligations, to further the enjoyment by all States, great or small, victor or vanquished, of access, on equal terms, to the trade and to the raw materials of the world which are needed for their economic prosperity;

Fifth, they desire to bring about the fullest collaboration between all nations in the economic field with the object of securing, for all, improved labor standards, economic adjustment and social security;

Sixth, after the final destruction of the Nazi tyranny, they hope to see established a peace which will afford to all nations the means of dwelling in safety within their own boundaries, and which will afford assurance that all the men in all the lands may live out their lives in freedom from fear and want;

Seventh, such a peace should enable all men to traverse the high seas and oceans without hindrance;

Eighth, they believe that all of the nations of the world, for realistic as well as spiritual reasons, must come to the abandonment of the use of force. Since no future peace can be maintained if land, sea or air armaments continue to be employed by nations which threaten, or may threaten, aggression outside of their frontiers, they believe, pending the establishment of a wider and permanent system of general security, that the disarmament of such nations is essential. They will likewise aid and encourage all other practicable measures which will lighten for peace-loving peoples the crushing burden of armaments.

The first, second and fourth articles were self-denying declarations which added up to a renunciation of the traditional spoils of victory, pledging the signatories to take no territory from the vanquished and to countenance only such changes of sovereignty as might be desired by the majority of the inhabitants of a given region. (This might, for example, apply to the Austrian Tyrolese who had been placed under Italian rule and to the Sudeten Germans in Czechoslovakia.) In addition, the signatories renounced seeking commercial advantage for the victors, going further to promise equal access to markets and sources of raw material for all nations, subject to the reservation (introduced by Churchill) that this concession would be made "with due respect for their existing obligations." (Without this reservation, the fourth article would have committed Britain to the abandonment of preferential tariffs within the Commonwealth and Empire and might have been construed to commit the United States to the abandonment of its protective tariff.)

The third article was clearly designed to restore free and independent government to such countries as Poland, Czechoslovakia, Holland, Belgium and Norway which had been conquered and occupied by the enemy. It was not clear whether the signers considered that the people of Spain—or, for that matter, the people of Italy and Germany—had been "forcibly deprived" of self-government. It was even less clear whether it was intended that "the right of all peoples to choose the form of government under which they will live" applied to the dependent or semi-dependent peoples of Asia and Africa.

Article seven promised freedom of the seas, but only in times of peace.

The sixth and eighth articles looked toward some sort of world organization to enforce peace, to promote economic cooperation and the abolition of national armaments.

The most precise and most significant paragraphs were clearly those which renounced a victor's peace and promised justice to victor and vanquished alike.

Wilson's effort to achieve a just peace had foundered upon his failure to establish a firm agreement as to peace aims before the United States became a belligerent. Roosevelt did not repeat this mistake, but Roosevelt and Churchill later deliberately sacrificed to military expediency the just peace to which they pledged themselves in August, 1941.

In the following month Averell Harriman was sent to Moscow by the President together with Lord Beaverbrook, in order to ascertain what supplies were most urgently needed to maintain Soviet resistance. In October, Hitler boasted that the power of Russia had been broken, that the Soviet air force had been destroyed and that the final "battle of annihilation" was now beginning. Leningrad was besieged. The Nazi tanks stood within sixty miles of Moscow. The diplomatic corps was evacuated to Kuibyshev on the Volga. Odessa fell, the Russians retreated across the Dnieper, blowing up the great Dnieper dam, and were forced to evacuate the great industrial city of Kharkov. The coal, iron and manganese of the Ukraine were in Nazi hands. The oil of the Caucasus was threatened.

Meanwhile, President Roosevelt had sent American troops to occupy Iceland to protect the Atlantic convoy routes and to Dutch Guiana to protect the bauxite deposits in the Dutch colony. An American destroyer was attacked by a submarine and the President issued orders to the Navy to "shoot at sight." A drastic amendment of the Neutrality Act lifted the ban on

American shipping and permitted the arming of merchant vessels. A bill extending selective service passed Congress—by the narrow margin of one vote. Pacifist-isolationist sentiment was still strong, but the country was unmistakably moving toward war with Germany. The Great Debate was going into its final phase.

And then, before the American people had made up their minds to go to war in defense of their own vital interests and the survival of Western civilization, the decision was taken out of their hands—not by Germany, but by Japan.

The events leading up to Pearl Harbor have been related in detail in the memoirs of Secretary of War Henry L. Stimson, and Secretary of State Cordell Hull. In addition, they have been somewhat more critically analyzed by Mr. Joseph Grew, a veteran diplomat and former Undersecretary of State, serving at the time as United States ambassador to Japan.[*]

In July and August, 1941, Britain and the United States took advantage of Hitler's preoccupation with Russia to turn at least some of their attention to the Far East. Japan, with the full consent of the Pétain regime, was then proceeding toward a complete military occupation of French Indo-China. Washington and London first "froze" all Japanese assets in the United States and Britain and then jointly issued a formal warning to the Japanese government to keep its hands off Thailand. (Malaya seemed to be Japan's next probable objective and the obvious invasion route lay through the Thai peninsula.) The President's actions were approved by the vast majority of Americans. Public sentiment was far more ready to support a belligerent attitude toward Japan than to intervene against the Axis in Europe.

Once again, Mr. Roosevelt's Far Eastern policy was undermined by inconsistency. In spite of the warnings issued to Japan, Japanese purchases of strategic materials—except aviation gasoline—continued to be licensed. The effect of this strange mixture of firmness and appeasement, which Mr. Roosevelt described as "babying Japan along," was to provoke anger without commanding respect or fear of reprisal. The "mod-

---

[*] Cordell Hull, *Memoirs* (Macmillan, 1948). H. L. Stimson, *On Active Duty* (Harper, 1948). Joseph Grew, *The Turbulent Era* (Houghton Mifflin, 1952).

erate" Konoye government was overthrown by the Japanese war party and Admiral Hideki Tojo, avowed friend of Nazi Germany, became prime minister. On November 5, a special envoy, Saburu Kurusu, started for the United States bearing the new government's "last proposals."

Churchill declared that if the United States were to become involved in war with Japan, Britain would join "within the hour." On November 29, Tojo demanded the "purging of British and American influence from the Orient." The President asked for a definition of Japanese aims in Indo-China and the ill-fated British battleships *Prince of Wales* and *Repulse* steamed into Singapore as a belated warning. The Japanese war plan had already been determined. On December 6, with the Hull-Kurusu negotiations at an impasse, the President cabled an appeal for a peaceful settlement to Emperor Hirohito. At this moment, Japanese carriers were within a day's steaming of Pearl Harbor.

In the midst of a quiet Sunday, the American people suddenly heard the radio announcement of the Japanese attack. Later, the news trickled in of attacks upon the Philippines, Malaya and Hong Kong. On December 8, an angry Congress declared war upon Japan. In a radio address, President Roosevelt minimized the damage to the fleet and warned the people against giving credence to wild rumors. Relating the sneak attack to the long and black record of Nazi perfidy and aggression, Mr. Roosevelt declared that the Axis powers must now be defeated "on one, gigantic battlefield." The next day, Germany and Italy declared war against the United States, thus clearly revealing that there was indeed a coordinated Axis plan to preoccupy the United States in the Pacific and thus to frustrate the effectiveness of its intervention in Europe.

Pearl Harbor destroyed overnight the illusion that we were "safe behind our oceans." It ended all doubt that the nation was now fully engaged in a struggle for survival. It taught the American people the lesson which they had failed to learn from World War I—that the United States had a direct and vital interest in the survival of Britain and of British control of the sea lanes; and that British survival was inseparable from the survival of Western Europe.

But Pearl Harbor did not resolve—it merely suspended—the debate as to whether the United States had a vital interest in the defeat of all totalitarian dictatorships and in the establishment of world peace enforced by world law. The isolationists were no longer pacifists after Pearl Harbor; most of them became embattled patriots overnight; but many of them remained unconvinced that the nation was now at war for any other reason than that the Axis powers had unbelievably dared to attack it. Not a few of them thought that "only our own meddling in other peoples' business" had provoked an attack which might otherwise not have occurred.*

* A not inconsiderable number of historians have in recent years developed what they call a "revisionist" interpretation of the United States' entry into World War II. These writers have sought to build up a case to show that Roosevelt "lied the country into war"; that he vainly sought to provoke Hitler into attacking the United States, and that, being frustrated in this design, he then deliberately provoked a Japanese attack in order to get the United States into the war by "the back door." The student who is interested to sample this "revisionist" literature will find a useful symposium in *Perpetual War for Perpetual Peace*, edited by Harry Elmer Barnes, with contributions by William Henry Chamberlain, Percy L. Greaves, Jr., George A. Lundberg, George Morgenstern, William L. Neumann, Frederic R. Sanborn and Charles Callan Tansill. (Caxton Press, 1953.) It should be pointed out that the "revisionists"—irrespective of the strength or weakness of the case which they seek to build against Roosevelt and irrespective of whatever their motivation—uniformly imply that the Axis powers never constituted a threat to the vital interests of the United States. They resent being called "isolationists" or "nationalists" yet their main thesis seems to be that peace is still divisible and that the foreign policy of George Washington is still applicable to the world of 1950.

The author, while sharply critical of certain aspects of President Roosevelt's foreign policy, and even more critical of that of his successor, emphatically rejects the "revisionist" aspersions cast upon Roosevelt's integrity. He rejects as well the thesis that the nation's vital interests were not threatened by the Axis dictators.

CHAPTER TWENTY-FOUR

Win-the-War Expediency
(1942 – 1943)

ONCE AT WAR, the people of the United States lost no time in getting down to the business of winning it. The President called for a vast two-year program of building planes, ships, tanks and guns. By the end of 1942, Congress had appropriated over $100,000,000,000.

In the winter of 1941-1942, however, the picture was grim. Just before Christmas, Churchill arrived in Washington for the first of many wartime conferences. It would be many months before the damage to the Pacific fleet could be repaired and before the American training and production programs could be expected to deliver men and supplies at the battle-fronts. It was agreed that the first major effort must be made in Europe, while Russia was still able to preempt most of Hitler's energies and resources.

The Europe-first decision did not please those former isolationists whom Pearl Harbor had converted into fire-eating patriots; to them it seemed that the first objective should be to punish Japan. Many of the "America-Firsters" became and remained throughout the war "Japan-Firsters" who bitterly resented the priority given to the European theater.

On January 2, 1942, the United States, Britain, Russia, China and 22 other nations at war with one or more of the Axis powers signed the *United Nations Declaration*. (This was the first use of the term "United Nations," not in its later sense as the title of a world organization, but as the official designation of the anti-Axis coalition.) The Declaration was carefully phrased so as to avoid committing the Soviet Union to war with Japan, but all the signatories—including the Soviet Union—agreed not to make a separate peace and subscribed to the eight principles of the Atlantic Charter. Thus the entire coalition pledged itself to a just peace, without spoils for the victors.

The road to victory and peace was to be long and arduous.

In the first three months of 1942, the Japanese conquered the whole of Southeast Asia, pushing their "Co-prosperity Sphere" to the gates of India and the northern shores of the Australian continent and seizing more than 1,000,000 square miles of territory inhabited by over 100,000,000 people. In just 100 days, they seized the world's most important sources of rubber, tin, hemp and quinine as well as plentiful supplies of oil, foodstuffs and mineral deposits for which Japan had hitherto depended upon imports from other nations. When Corregidor surrendered after a siege lasting until May 6, 1942, the last organized resistance within this vast new empire came to an end. Japan had now secured every resource required for fighting a long war.

The white man's prestige in Asia reached an all-time low. Except in the Philippines, where the native population had briefly known independence, the Japanese were received by the natives more as liberators than as invaders or conquerors. The slogan of "Asia for the Asians" had a powerful appeal. The sight of white men in flight before an Asian liberator was a welcome spectacle.

On the other side of the world, the coalition's position was a little, though not yet much, better. The Germans had been flung back at the gates of Moscow. Leningrad still held out. The Nazi steam roller had for the first time been halted. But in the Mediterranean area, the picture was grim. Malta held out against continuous attack, but the British Mediterranean fleet was so badly battered that most of the convoys to Egypt and the Near East were taking the long route around the Cape of Good Hope. Here, too, they were constantly harassed by submarine attacks.

The U-boat menace was, in fact, at its height. Not only was deadly damage inflicted on the Atlantic convoys but Nazi submarines were preying almost at will upon American coastal shipping, sinking freighters and tankers within sight of the Florida coast.

In the United States a tremendous job of preparation was going forward. The armed forces expanded from 2,000,000 to 4,000,000 during the year. By April, the gigantic task of converting American industry to war production had practically been completed. During 1942, 10,000,000 new workers went into war industries; 8,000,000 tons of new shipping were constructed, in addition to hundreds of new naval vessels of all kinds and sizes; 49,000 planes and 32,000 tanks and self-propelled guns rolled off the American assembly lines.

In the last days of January, 1942, the first American troops landed in Northern Ireland and, across the world, in Australia. In April, American troops occupied the French islands of New Caledonia and American fliers carried out their first raid on Tokyo. In the first week of May, American naval task forces defeated two Japanese invasion fleets in the Coral Sea, between New Guinea and the Solomon Islands. A month later, the crucial three-day battle of Midway resulted in a decisive victory over a Japanese invasion armada heading for Midway Island. These actions crippled the Japanese carrier strength and saved the American supply line to Australia.

Even as the tide turned slightly in the war against Japan, the situation in Europe deteriorated. In the latter part of May, the Germans launched a two-pronged assault against the Near East. One arm of the Nazi pincer reached for the Caucasus; the other aimed at Egypt and the Suez Canal. American supplies were slow to reach the British Eighth Army in Africa and even slower to arrive in Russia. Moscow urgently demanded a Second Front. Foreign Minister Molotov went to London and signed a 20-year mutual assistance pact with Britain. Then he visited Washington and conferred with the President. Britain and the United States successfully resisted Molotov's determined effort to obtain agreement as to Russia's European frontiers and spheres of influence.*

On June 18, 1942, Churchill arrived in Washington for another conference. While there, he received the shocking news that the British Eighth Army was in retreat toward Alexandria

* See Sherwood, *op. cit.*, pages 556-579.

and that the fortress of Tobruk, with its garrison of 25,000 men, had surrendered. The Russians, too, were faring badly, being driven out of the Crimea and back to the valley of the Don. The great question was how and where to take the offensive in order to relieve the pressure of the twofold Nazi thrust against the Near East. The Anglo-American forces being built up in the British Isles were not yet sufficient to undertake a perilous cross-Channel invasion of France. Should the available troops and equipment be hoarded in order to assure the eventual success of that operation, or should they be used as quickly as possible in some diversionary attack which might draw Axis forces away from their objectives? And, if the latter, where and when should such an attack be launched? Unless the Allies did something more than bomb Germany from the air, there was great risk that Russia would be hopelesly beaten or make a separate peace.

The American leaders were convinced that the invasion of France offered the best chances of bringing Germany to her knees, but the British were not over-enthusiastic about an operation likely to entail huge casualties; the memories of World War I still haunted them. Churchill in particular had a predilection for Mediterranean strategy, not only because it would assure the safety of the Empire life line but because he believed that the Axis was most vulnerable in what he called its "soft underbelly." Finally, the Vichy Policy, though not undertaken for that reason, now provided the hope that Pétain might cooperate in some manner with an American force suddenly appearing in French North Africa. This idea intrigued the President.

The decision was to concentrate upon preparing the cross-Channel invasion of France, with the idea of undertaking a full-scale operation as early as posible in 1943, or, if the Russian situation should become desperate, of launching a smaller operation in 1942, designed merely to create and hold a limited bridgehead. British hesitation and doubts over this plan—and a certain amount of doubt on the part of the President—led Mr. Roosevelt to send General Marshall and his most trusted adviser, Harry Hopkins, to England in July to re-survey the situation. Much to the disappointment of Secretary Stimson,* this meeting resulted in the decision to keep the cross-Channel invasion as the major project but to put it off until 1943, meanwhile undertaking an invasion of French North Africa at the earliest posible date. This meant the abandonment of any possible emergency operation in France during the summer of 1942.

The decision to descend upon the North African coast involved several important political consequences. It required intensified wooing of Pétain, in spite of the old marshal's increasingly overt collaborationist policy. It meant side-tracking de Gaulle and keeping the Free French out of the proposed operation altogether.† Finally, since passage through the Straits of Gibraltar would be vital, it meant that Franco would have to be cultivated assiduously by continued shipments of oil and other scarce supplies, in spite of the fact that his Blue Legion was fighting for the Nazis on the Russian front. From a political point of view, the plan was the lineal descendant of "non-intervention" in Spain and of the Vichy Policy.

Neither Roosevelt nor Churchill entertained any illusions as to how their decision would "sit with" Stalin. Its effectiveness as a Second Front was clearly limited and its political implications dubious. It fell to Churchill's lot to carry the unwelcome tidings to Moscow. He has fully described Stalin's original lack of enthusiasm and his eventual concurrence.‡

Stalin had every reason for anxiety. During the late summer, the German drive toward the Caucasus assumed ominous proportions. September and October marked the high tide of Nazi penetration. The German armies reached the Volga, captured the oil fields at Maikop and began an assault upon the passes leading through the Caucasus mountains to the major oil fields at Baku. A fierce battle raged in the ruins of the great industrial city of Stalingrad.

In Egypt, things were going somewhat better. Rommel's

---

* Stimson, *op. cit.*, pages 420-428; and Sherwood, *op. cit.*, pages 580-614.

† Apart from the natural antagonism between the Free French and Vichy, de Gaulle's abortive attempt to capture Dakar had destroyed Anglo-American confidence in his military usefulness.

‡ Churchill; *op. cit.*; Volume IV, pages 477-493.

drive for Alexandria was halted at El Alamein, about 100 miles short of its goal. Newly arrived American Sherman tanks played a vital part in General Auchinlek's successful stand.

The large-scale night raids which had for some time been carried out by the Royal Air Force on German cities and industrial centers were augmented during the summer by the daylight raids of the Britain-based American Eighth Air Force. This not only increased the effectiveness of the air bombardment but placed a heavy strain upon the *Luftwaffe's* fighter command.

In August, the successful landings of United States Marines on Tulagi and Guadalcanal in the Solomons marked the passing of the offensive from the Japanese aggressors into the hands of the United Nations. Grim fighting on land and sea still lay ahead, but the Japanese march of conquest was ended.

Toward the end of the year, naval construction began to fill the gaps torn in the United States Navy during the early months of the war, particularly in aircraft carriers; and new merchant-ship building began to catch up with submarine sinkings.

The American public, however, was unaware, as the Congressional elections approached, that the turn of tide was imminent. The North African plan was a closely guarded secret. The losses incurred in the Solomons were known, but not the full significance of the costly action. Rommel still stood at the gates of Alexandria, and the Russian armies seemed in dire straits. People were dissatisfied with the conduct of the war, disgruntled over inflation controls and grumbling about the rationing of gasoline. On November 3, the Republicans gained 43 seats in the House and 9 in the Senate, leaving Congress in the control of a tacit coalition of Republicans and reactionary Southern Democrats. Had the elections occurred a week later, the results might have been very different.

On October 28, General Montgomery, the new commander of the British Desert Army, had launched a furious attack upon Rommel's position at El Alamein. By November 2, the *Afrika Korps* was in full flight out of Egypt, abandoning its Italian divisions to their fate. Montgomery launched a swift pursuit across northern Egypt and the battle-scarred Libyan Desert.

On November 8, a great American Expeditionary Force appeared off the coast of Morocco, having crossed the Atlantic unobserved and without losing a single ship. These troops landed at various points on the Moroccan coast, encountering stiff resistance from the Vichy French forces at Casablanca. Simultaneously, two other British-American convoys sailed from Britain through the Straits of Gibraltar and landed at Algiers and Oran. The whole operation was under the command of General Dwight D. Eisenhower. After 76 hours of sporadic fighting, all resistance ceased. Allied forces raced into western Tunisia while German and Italian troops landed at its northern tip to contest the Allied thrust. The surprise offensive had caught the German High Command completely off guard. Within a few days, the French North African possessions had passed into Allied hands and French West Africa—the arrow pointed at Brazil—was neutralized and cut off. The Germans swiftly took over the unoccupied zone in southern France, including the harbor of Toulon, where most of the remaining French fleet lay at anchor.

In spite of Washington's coddling of Pétain, the French forces under General Nogues had, on Pétain's orders, offered fierce resistance, which might have been protracted for some time, delayed the Allied advance into Tunisia and altered the whole complexion of the subsequent campaign, had it not been for an accident of political as well as military consequence. The Allies had planned to place in supreme authority over French North Africa General Honoré Giraud, recently escaped from a German prison camp. Quite unexpectedly, they found Pétain's deputy, Admiral François Darlan, in North Africa. (He had come to Algiers to visit a sick son.) General Nogues in Morocco was reported willing to cease resistance only if ordered to do so by Pétain or by Admiral Darlan as the representative of the Vichy government. Acting upon the advice of Robert Murphy of the Department of State and in consultation with British representatives, General Eisenhower made the famous "Darlan Deal," under which the French admiral ordered a cessation of all resistance by the Vichy forces on condition that he be appointed as the supreme authority over the French African possessions. Thus, for cogent reasons of military expediency, the liberation of French Africa was accomplished without the cooperation of the only French forces which had remained true to the Allied cause, and the liberated territory was turned over to a leading French collaborationist.*

A strong protest over the Darlan appointment arose in Britain and the United States. President Roosevelt endeavored to calm the storm by a statement declaring that General Eisenhower's decision had been dictated solely by military expediency, that it had saved unnecessary loss of life, and that the French people would in due course be given the opportunity to choose whatever government they might desire. On November 27, the "Darlan Deal" paid a final dividend when the French fleet at Toulon scuttled itself to prevent falling into German hands. When, less than a month later, Darlan was assassinated by a young French patriot, it looked as if the cause of democracy might yet be redeemed through a general housecleaning of collaborationist officials. Such, however, was not to be the case.

Meanwhile, on November 19, the Russian army had launched its great counter-offensive at Stalingrad and Rhzev, soon to result in the worst disaster ever to befall a German army.

On January 14, with the Russian offensive in full swing and the Anglo-American forces driving forward in Tunisia, the President, Churchill and the Anglo-American high command met dramatically at Casablanca. The conference resulted in the fateful declaration of the Anglo-American aim to achieve the "unconditional surrender" of the Axis powers. The phrase was Roosevelt's borrowed from Grant's terms to Lee at Appomattox. What it meant was that the United States and Britain committed themselves to the total destruction of German, Italian and Japanese power. To all intents and purposes, this declaration foreclosed the possibility that Hitler and Tojo might be overthrown and that peace might be made with such democratic regimes as might accomplish their overthrow. This was the opposite of Wilson's policy with regard to the Kaiser. Its effect

* Sherwood, *op. cit.*, Chapter 26. For General Eisenhower's own account, see his *Crusade in Europe* (Doubleday, 1948). Also Harry Butcher, *My Three Years with Eisenhower* (Simon and Schuster, 1946).

was to insure a last-ditch stand by both Germany and Japan and to magnify Russia's postwar position. (The effect upon Italy was different due to the development of an Anglo-American policy toward that country which bore no relation to the policy pursued with respect to the two major Axis powers.)

Both Giraud and de Gaulle were induced with some difficulty to attend the Casablanca Conference and to be photographed shaking hands. For the moment, all seemed to be well. But, as time wore on, the Vichy officials remained in power and the American State Department even went so far as to import from the Argentine, as governor of Algiers, the notorious collaborationist, Marcel Peyrouton. (Peyrouton enjoyed the distinction of having caused the arrest of Laval—not because he disagreed with him, but because the two men were rivals—but he had also been instrumental in establishing Nazi concentration camps in unoccupied France.) The Vichy Policy had by now taken the bit into its teeth.*

Similarly, although American shipping and petroleum resources were strained to the utmost, the United States continued to permit American tankers to carry oil and gasoline to Spain, at a time when Franco was providing war materials to Germany and conducting pro-Axis propaganda in Latin America. The reason was, of course, anxiety for the safety of the lines of communication past Gibraltar and Spanish Morocco.

Thus the North African campaign committed the United States anew to the policy of appeasing Fascism, wherever such a course might hasten the attainment of military objectives. While it was true that the Anglo-American Allies did not at first have sufficient military strength to undertake the North African adventure on any other basis, it was also true that—as their strength grew—it became more and more difficult to break away from this policy. Each step tended more and more to commit them to the next, and the rationalization of each action taken made it appear more and more that they believed in what they were doing rather than merely following the dictates of military necessity.

From an immediate military point of view, the policy was

* Sherwood, *op. cit.,* Chapter 27.

effective. French resistance was shortened. The French fleet did not fall into German hands. Franco did not make a hostile move. The Germans did not come down through Spain—but this was due less to Allied policy than to the fact that Hitler had his hands full in Russia and Tunisia.

On February 2, 1943, General von Paulus surrendered what was left of the 22 German divisions which had been encircled in front of Stalingrad. The Germans were driven from the Caucasus and across the Don. The British Eighth Army chased Rommel across Tripoli into Tunisia—a retreat of over 1,300 miles. The *Afrika Korps* managed to join up with the German and Italian forces landed in northern Tunisia, only to be pinned against the sea and finally forced to surrender. With the fall of Tunis and Bizerte, more than 175,000 prisoners fell into Allied hands. By the middle of May the Axis powers had been driven out of the African continent and Mussolini's empire had ceased to exist.

During the last stages of the Tunisian campaign, Churchill again visited Washington in order to discuss the next steps in Allied strategy. Having driven the Germans back to a line running just east of Orel, Belgorod and Kharkov, the Russians were now preparing to meet a renewed German offensive and insistently demanded a Second Front in the West. On May 22, Moscow announced the dissolution of the Comintern; this appeared to be the official burial of the Bolshevik doctrine of world revolution and was widely acclaimed as such. Pro-Russian sentiment in the United States reached its high-water mark, even though a slight rift had appeared in the honeymoon atmosphere when Moscow broke off relations with the Polish government-in-exile over the latter's demand for an investigation of the "Katyn murders"—a wholesale slaughter of Polish officers charged against Russia by the Nazis.

In spite of the Russian demand for a major Second Front, echoed by considerable popular sentiment in Britain and the United States, the Anglo-American leaders decided to put off the cross-Channel invasion of France until 1944. The Tunisian campaign had taken longer than expected. It had shown that the American troops needed seasoning and, above all, there were as yet insufficient landing-craft available for the major operation. In these circumstances, Roosevelt and Churchill determined upon an invasion of Sicily as the next step. If successful, this might lead to knocking Italy out of the war. It would also go far toward clearing the Mediterranean.

Between the Washington Conference and the launching of the Sicilian invasion on July 10, a number of significant events occurred. Representatives of 44 nations met at Hot Springs, Virginia, and reached a tentative agreement for the handling of postwar food relief. The openly pro-Nazi Castillo government of the Argentine was overthrown. De Gaulle had finally been permitted to enter North Africa and had brought together the anti-Vichy factions in a Committee of National Liberation. Peyrouton, Nogues and other Vichy officials were ejected and the Nazi-inspired "Vichy laws" were abrogated. Admiral Robert, the Vichy commander at Guadaloupe and Martinique, was induced to surrender to American occupation. Giraud decided upon a sudden trip to Washington, hoping to obtain stronger backing for his position as against the rising power of de Gaulle. Finally, a week before General Eisenhower's forces landed on the Sicilian beaches, the long-awaited German summer offensive was launched in the Kursk salient; a week later, the Red army, having taken everything the Germans had to offer, went over to the offensive. The initiative had passed permanently into the hands of the Soviet forces.

On July 25, with Anglo-American troops overrunning Sicily, Mussolini was suddenly overthrown by a "palace revolution" within the ruling Fascist clique. The King, who had hitherto supported all of Mussolini's adventures, ordered Marshal Badoglio, conqueror of Ethiopia, to head a new government. His first act was to issue a proclamation declaring: "The war continues. Italy, grievously stricken in her invaded provinces and in her ruined towns, maintains her faith in her given word."

There now followed a series of gyrations in Allied policy which must have been utterly confusing to the Italian people, since they confused even some of the Anglo-American officials. Until now, Allied propaganda had consistently urged the Italian people to throw off the yoke of their Fascist oppressors; it had taken the line that the Allied armies would come as liberators, not as conquerors. Now, suddenly, Allied propaganda

created the impression that the British and American governments considered the Badoglio regime with some favor, even
though it had pledged itself to continue the war and was clearly
no less Fascist than its predecessor. President Roosevelt publicly reproved the "Voice of America" for quoting a commen-
tator who had referred to King Victor Emmanuel as "the mo-
ronic little king"; yet, a day later he declared in an address
that the United States would "have no truck with Fascism." *
General Eisenhower added to the confusion by issuing a proclamation denouncing Badoglio as a traitor to the Italian people.

In August the conquest of Sicily was completed. During a
mysterious lull, surrender negotiations went on at Lisbon. The
apparent truce ended when British troops landed at the toe
of the Italian boot and moved north through Calabria. On
September 8, it was announced that the Badoglio government
had "unconditionally surrendered." General Maxwell Taylor
secretly visited Rome to arrange for an airborne descent on the
Rome airfields and General Clark's new Fifth Army landed at
Salerno, hoping to capture Naples and move quickly to Rome.
The Germans, however, got wind of the surrender and moved
swiftly, sending troops from the north to seize the Rome airfields and to pin down the invading forces on their narrow
beach head. Here they remained in a precarious position until
relieved by Montgomery coming up through Calabria. On October 1, Naples was captured, but by this time the Germans
had established a strong line below Rome before which the
Allied advance was brought to a halt. The Badoglio government escaped to Brindisi and, on October 13, re-entered the
war on the side of the Allies.

The Italian fleet sailed into Malta and surrendered. The
Italian army in the Balkans disintegrated, parts of it joining
the Greek and Jugoslav resisters. Foggia became an important
base for air operations. Corsica and Sardinia fell to the Allies
and the entire Western Mediterranean was cleared. A British

* President Roosevelt's attitude was clearly expressed in his cable of July 30,
1943, quoted by Churchill in *op. cit.*, Vol. V, page 64. It read in part: "There
are some contentious people here who are getting ready to make a row if we
seem to recognize the House of Savoy or Badoglio. They are the same element
which made such a fuss over North Africa."

attempt to seize Rhodes and the Aegean Islands, thus clearing the Eastern Mediterranean, ended in failure because, much to Churchill's chagrin, insufficient forces were allotted to the effort.

The Italian campaign bore somewhat dubious political fruit: a Fascist ally in the crusade for freedom, designated for the time being as a "co-belligerent."

While the Italian campaign was under way, the French Committee of National Liberation was reorganized: de Gaulle became the civilian head of a provisional French government while Giraud remained as commander-in-chief of the armed forces. After almost a month of deliberation, the British and American governments issued simultaneous announcements, recognizing the National Committee of Liberation as the supreme French authority outside of France for the duration of the war, but not as the provisional government of France itself. The Soviet Union extended full, unqualified recognition. The result of this Anglo-American decision was to build de Gaulle into a formidable political figure nursing a strong grievance, while, at the same time, alienating the resistance movement within France and giving it a strong impetus toward friendship with Russia. Much of the later prestige of the French Communists, as leaders of the French resistance, derived from this divergence between Anglo-American and Russian policy. The rationalization for the Anglo-American action was the American contention that the people of France must, when liberated, have the unprejudiced right to choose the form and personnel of their government. This point of view would have been more persuasive, had not the British and American governments extended full, unqualified recognition to Polish, Greek and Jugoslav governments-in-exile which could not, by any stretch of the imagination, be considered to represent the free choice of the peoples concerned.

The restorationist attitude of the British government was clearly avowed in Churchill's declaration of August 31, 1943:

> I take this opportunity to send a message of encouragement to the Kings of Greece and Jugoslavia . . . whom we hope to see restored to their thrones by the free choice of their liberated peoples.

The traditional British predilection for monarchy, combined with the momentum of the American policy of military expediency, had taken the two countries, at the moment of their first military triumphs, into a political position far removed from that crusade for freedom which Mr. Roosevelt had proclaimed. The extent to which the United States and Britain had become the prisoners of a policy which placed quick victory ahead of all political considerations was best illustrated by the attitude of the two governments toward Spain. With the Germans on the run in Russia, with Italy knocked out, with the Western Mediterranean firmly in Allied hands and a great reserve of power built up in North Africa, the American ambassador to Madrid went out of his way to assure General Franco that his regime would have nothing to fear from an Allied victory.

By the end of 1943, it was clear that Germany was headed for defeat. Exceeding the most optimistic expectations, the Russian armies had driven across the Dnieper, recaptured Kiev and Smolensk, and were approaching the Latvian and Polish borders. In the war against Japan, the road ahead was still long, but the United States Navy already held control of the Southwest Pacific and General MacArthur's land forces were steadily moving northwestward along the coast of New Guinea. The Axis powers were not going to conquer the world. But the great question now before the United States and Britain was what to do next.

At the first Quebec Conference, in August, the plan for the cross-Channel invasion had been confirmed and the date tentatively set for May 1, 1944. This meant that a part of the Anglo-American troops in the Mediterranean and most of their landing-craft would have to be transferred to the British Isles during the intervening months. What were the remaining forces to do during the winter and spring in order to take some of the pressure off the Red Army? Should another attempt be made to capture the Aegean Islands and to bring Turkey into the war on the Allied side, thus opening up a supply line to Russia through the Black Sea? Should more substantial assistance be given to the Greek and Jugoslav partisans, who were keeping more German divisions occupied in the Balkans than the Allied armies held engaged in Italy? Should the Allied armies, once they had captured Rome, hold a line across the narrow neck of Italy and move in force up the Adriatic to seize Istria and pose a threat to Vienna through the Ljubljana Gap?

The American Chiefs of Staff favored concentrating the entire Allied effort on "Overlord"—the cross-Channel invasion—using such forces as might be freed in Italy for "Anvil," the code name for a secondary invasion of France from the Mediterranean coast and up the Rhone valley. Churchill, while equally committed to the success of "Overlord" and to its priority over all other plans, urgently desired to clear the Eastern Mediterranean, to bring Turkey into the war, to clear the Adriatic and seize Istria. Admittedly, this Mediterranean strategy might cause a slight delay in the launching of the cross-Channel invasion. Churchill was willing to face this possibility. The American Chiefs of Staff were not. Clearly, the question was one in which Russian wishes should be considered.

But what were the Russian desires, beyond a definite assurance that the cross-Channel invasion of France would be undertaken in the spring? It was urgently necessary for Roosevelt, Churchill and Stalin to met.

CHAPTER TWENTY-FIVE

The Great Wartime Decisions
(1943–1945)

IN THE AUTUMN OF 1943, the major problem of the postwar future was already discernible, even though it was not clearly envisaged by the makers of Anglo-American policy. The problem could be stated in a single word: Russia.

It was evident that the Soviet Union would emerge from the

war as a far more powerful factor in world affairs than Russia had ever been, even in Napoleonic times. Germany and Japan, the traditional barriers to Russian expansion in Eastern Europe and Asia, would presumably be eliminated as power factors. Britain, which had traditionally contained Russian expansion southward, was clearly going to emerge from the war in a much weakened position. The only military power capable of restraining the Soviet Union from enlarging its sphere of influence, if not its actual empire, would be the United States. Hence, one of two assumptions would have to be made: (1) that the Soviet Union could be induced by diplomacy and fair treatment to abandon all expansionist aims and to cooperate in making and maintaining a just peace; or (2) that the war must be fought in such a way as to bring about not only the elimination of the German-Japanese threat to the freedom and independence of other nations but also the threat of Soviet imperialism. The first hypothesis would assume a loyal maintenance of the anti-Axis coalition not only throughout the war but after it. The second might well contemplate the possibility that it might suit Anglo-American policy to stop short of the utter destruction of the military power of Germany and Japan, provided that democratic revolutions could be induced to occur in these two countries.

Without consciously adopting anything like the second hypothesis, Britain and the United States had already pursued a policy in Italy which suggested that it might not be altogether impossible for the remaining Axis powers to obtain a peace short of "unconditional surrender" and, perhaps, to switch sides. Such an inference must have occurred to Stalin. On the other hand, past Soviet dealings with Nazi Germany made the Western Allies suspicious of Soviet loyalty to the coalition and fearful lest, having cleared the Nazis from Russian soil, the Soviet leadership might make a separate peace permitting Hitler to throw his full energies once more against the West. It was, in fact, this fear which made both Roosevelt and Churchill —but especially Roosevelt—anxious to ascertain, in the fall of 1943, what Stalin would most like the Western powers to do next.

On October 18, 1943, Secretary of State Hull, Foreign Secretary Eden and Foreign Minister Molotov, each with their advisers, met at Moscow to lay the groundwork for a meeting of Roosevelt, Churchill and Stalin. The communiqué, which prefaced three separate declarations, stated that military decisions had been taken and that "second only to the importance of hastening the end of the war was the recognition by the three governments that it was essential in their own national interests and in the interest of all peace-loving nations to continue the present close collaboration and close cooperation in the conduct of the war and in the period following the end of hostilities."

The military discussion revealed that Stalin was interested in little else than a Second Front in France. He wished formal assurances that this operation would be undertaken in the spring of 1944. The assurance was given, though no definite date was promised. The Soviet leader expressed interest in seeing Sweden and Turkey enter the war. Eden, after consulting Churchill, expressed cautions and conditional agreement.* These discussions remained secret.

The conferees announced the decision to establish in London a European Advisory Commission for "the examination of European questions as the war develops . . . and to make joint recommendations to the three governments." The creation of an Advisory Council for Italy was likewise announced, consisting of the three powers plus the French Committee of National Liberation, with provisions for the later addition of Greece and Jugoslavia. The restoration of the independence of Austria was declared to be the common purpose of the three powers and "consideration was given to questions concerning the treatment of Hitlerite Germany and its satellites."

The three separate declarations issued were:

1. A declaration by Roosevelt, Churchill and Stalin warning that at the time of granting any armistice to the German government, German war criminals would be "taken back to the countries in which their abominable crimes were committed to be charged and punished according to the laws of those countries." (This was Churchill's proposal.)

* Churchill, *op. cit.,* Vol. V, Chapter XVI.

2. A four-power declaration, with China as the fourth signatory, pledging united action until the unconditional surrender of the nations with which the signatories were at war and the earliest possible establishment of a "general international organization based on the principle of the sovereign equality of all peace-loving states and open to membership by all such states, large and small, for the maintenance of international peace and security." The declaration further pledged that "after the termination of hostilities" the signatories "will not employ their military forces within the territories of other states except for the purposes envisaged by this declaration and after joint consultation." Finally, the four signatories agreed to "confer and cooperate" to regulate armaments in the postwar period. (This was Hull's major achievement.)

3. A three-power declaration on Italy asserting that "Allied policy toward Italy must be based upon the fundamental principle that Fascism . . . shall be completely destroyed and that the Italian people shall be given every opportunity to establish governmental and other institutions based upon democratic principles."

The decisions of the Moscow Conference would, if adhered to, mean a momentous change in the traditional policy of each of the three participants. For the Soviet Union, they meant the abandonment of its implacable hostility to capitalist countries and of its aim to foment a world "socialist" revolution. For Britain, they meant the abandonment of the traditional balance of power policy, under which Britain had almost invariably sided with the second-strongest power on the Continent against the strongest; by this agreement Britain now aligned itself with the strongest power. For the United States the decisions reached at Moscow meant the abandonment of its traditional habit of moving in and out of international cooperation, according to its changing conceptions of its own interest; they meant the acceptance of responsibility commensurate with its power.

When Secretary Hull reported to Congress on the results of the Moscow Conference, he received a great ovation. Both Houses had for some time been debating resolutions asserting American determination to "cooperate with our comrades-in-arms to secure a just and lasting peace." The Fulbright Resolution in the House and the Connally Resolution in the Senate were now altered so as to confirm expressly the four-nation declaration drawn at Moscow.

Whatever the ultimate value of the agreements reached, their immediate effect was to sound the death-knell to Nazi hopes of a separate peace with either Russia or the West.

The next step toward postwar cooperation followed almost immediately. On November 9, 44 nations, assembled at the United Nations Relief and Rehabilitation Conference in Atlantic City, agreed as to the machinery and methods by which each nation would contribute in accordance with its ability.

Secret negotiations now proceeded for a meeting of the Big Three. Churchill urgently desired a prior meeting of the Anglo-American groups; Roosevelt declined to hold such a meeting for fear of offending Stalin. Roosevelt wanted Chiang Kai-shek to attend the meeting; Stalin rejected this idea, because Russia was not at war with Japan. Stalin also declined to hold the meeting at any place outside of the Soviet Union other than Teheran. Ultimately, two conferences were held: the first at Cairo, on November 22-25, attended by Roosevelt, Churchill and Chiang Kai-shek; the second at Teheran on November 28-December 1, 1943.*

The Cairo communiqué announced that Japan was to be "stripped of all the islands in the Pacific which she had seized or occupied since the beginning of the first World War in 1914, and that all the territories Japan has stolen from the Chinese, such as Manchuria, Formosa and the Pescadores, shall be restored to the Chinese Republic." It was further affirmed that "Japan will also be expelled from all other territories which she has taken by violence and greed" and that Korea should "in due course become free and independent."

Apart from the announced decisions, Roosevelt and Churchill disclosed to the Chinese leader their plans for regaining control of the Bay of Bengal and for the reconquest of Burma, as well as the American program of driving the Japanese back toward their home islands. There was not much immediate solace in this for the Generalissimo.

* *Ibid.*, Vol. V, pages 300 to 407.

Churchill's complete lack of interest in China is characteristically expressed in his account of the Cairo Conference. Of the 16 pages devoted to this meeting—as against 75 pages describing the subsequent meeting at Teheran—only 2 relate to Chinese affairs.

"What we had apprehended from Chiang Kai-shek's presence," he writes, deploring the fact that the Cairo meeting was not a purely Anglo-American affair, "now in fact occurred. The talks of the British and American staffs were sadly distracted by the Chinese story, which was lengthy, complicated and minor . . . the President, who took an exaggerated view of the Chinese-Indian sphere, was soon closeted in long conferences with the Generalissimo. All hope of persuading Chiang and his wife to go and see the Pyramids . . . fell to the ground, with the result that Chinese business occupied first instead of last place at Cairo." Churchill then relates how the President promised Chiang "a considerable amphibious operation across the Bay of Bengal within the next few months. This would have cramped 'Overlord' for landing and tank-landing craft . . . far more than any of my Turkey and Aegean projects."

There was more than petulance behind this Churchillian attitude. What troubled Churchill was the thought that, if the Allies made no other move than "Overlord" and no move at all until May, 1944, Russia might well end up in control of the Balkans and the Eastern Mediterranean, as well as being in control of Poland, Hungary and perhaps Austria. What he had hoped to accomplish in an Anglo-American meeting prior to Teheran was to win Roosevelt and the American Chiefs of Staff to some move or moves in the Eastern Mediterranean, even if this should cause a month's delay of "Overlord" and the abandonment of the subsidiary landings in the south of France. The one argument which might have convinced Roosevelt was an argument which Churchill did not make—namely, the desirability of fighting the war in such a way as to limit Russia's postwar influence in Europe. The argument which he did make—that the forces in the Mediterranean should be utilized during the winter months and that his Mediterranean projects would draw off more German strength from northern France than "Anvil" —were not sufficiently convincing. Roosevelt's mind was preoccupied with keeping Russia in the war against Germany, with getting Russia to participate in the war against Japan after Germany had been defeated and with making sure of Russian cooperation in the postwar period. The question which Churchill instinctively wanted to raise was actually one which went to the root of the agreements just reached at Moscow. The troubled state of mind expressed throughout most of his account of the winter of 1943-1944 probably arose from a deep ambivalence as to the wisdom of gambling the whole future upon the assumption that Russia, if fairly treated, would adhere to her agreement not to use her infinitely enlarged power for selfish imperialist expansion. Had Churchill been fully conscious of this motivation, he would doubtless have expressed his misgivings to Roosevelt. Whether or not this would have changed the President's attitude is a matter of conjecture; there is no evidence to suggest that Roosevelt himself had any such misgivings until the last weeks of his life, after the Yalta Conference had made the gamble irrevocable.

At Teheran, the question of how the Allied forces in the Mediterranean should be employed after the capture of Rome was laid before Stalin. After being assured that, no matter what else might be undertaken, the cross-Channel invasion would take place in May or—at the latest—in June, Stalin expressed the feeling that the landings in southern France would do more to assist the main operation than either an attempt to force the Alpine passes (which no one had suggested) or a move up the Adriatic and, through Istria, toward Vienna. To clear the Eastern Mediterranean and bring Turkey into the war seemed to him desirable, provided this could be done without affecting "Overlord."

To Churchill, this was satisfaction enough. There would be plenty of time to discuss again at a later date whether "Anvil" was actually the most effective method of helping "Overlord." Meanwhile, his project in the Eastern Mediterranean could be carried through. The fact that it had been Roosevelt who had raised the question of Istria and the Ljubljana Gap approach to Vienna and that Stalin had raised no violent objection, expressing merely a preference for southern France, left this matter sufficiently open. Churchill could not foresee that all his hopes were doomed to disappointment by a delay of many months in capturing Rome.

Apart from the crucial questions of major strategy and the obtainment of Stalin's firm assurance that Russia would enter the war against Japan at an appropriate time after the German surrender, the Teheran Conference dealt chiefly with the questions of Poland, Finland and Germany.

The Polish question involved two matters—frontiers and the nature of the Polish government. As to frontiers, Stalin demanded the 1939 border, which corresponded roughly to the old Curzon Line, except that it left the city of Lvov to Russia, but hinted that, if he could have the German port of Koenigsberg, he would not argue about Lvov. To Roosevelt's question whether this change could be brought about by a voluntary exchange of Russo-Polish populations, Stalin replied that he thought it could. This seemed to settle the question without doing violence to the Atlantic Charter pledges, since Russia was demanding only the return of territory which all agreed had never rightfully belonged to Poland. The claim to Koenigsberg, however, was a wholly different matter. In agreeing tentatively to this suggestion, Roosevelt and Churchill allowed the camel to get its head into the tent; this was "territorial aggrandizement" pure and simple, against which the entire anti-Axis coalition had solemnly pledged itself. The point seems not to have occurred to either Roosevelt or Churchill. Both men were more concerned over the question of the Polish government, but here no satisfactory understanding was reached. Stalin flatly refused to discuss anything with the London exiles whom he accused of collaborating with the Germans against the partisans.

As to Finland, Stalin was more reasonable. He would insist upon keeping the Finnish frontier away from Leningrad, but he was prepared to give back Hangoe and take Petsamo instead. Nevertheless, here too, the proposed solution was inconsistent with the basic principles of the Atlantic Charter.

When it came to Germany, all three of the great statesmen seemed to have forgotten the Atlantic Charter altogether. Roosevelt proposed a dismemberment of Germany into five states, with the Ruhr and the Saar under international control. Stalin said that he, too, favored dismemberment. Churchill thought that Prussia should be isolated and south Germany perhaps incorporated in a Danubian federation. Stalin disliked that idea. He thought the Prussians were beasts but not much worse than all Germans: it would be far better to break up and scatter the German tribes. Churchill pointed out the danger that, if this were done, the Germans would inevitably try to reunite. Roosevelt, according to Churchill, nevertheless remained in agreement with Stalin. If Churchill's recollections of this discussion are accurate, he himself was the only one of the Big Three who showed any sense of history and of justice. Stalin's vengefulness was understandable in view of what Russia had suffered at German hands; Roosevelt's attitude, if correctly pictured, is difficult to explain. By common agreement, the matter was left as having been only "a very preliminary discussion." *

The Big Three then agreed that Poland should be compensated for yielding the territory east of the Curzon Line by advancing its frontier into Germany to the line of the Oder and Neisse rivers. (A dispute arose later, at Potsdam, as to whether this had meant the Western or Eastern branch of the Neisse River.) This arrangement was impossible to reconcile with any principles of justice or with the specific pledges solemnly laid down in the Atlantic Charter and confirmed in the United Nations Declaration. If Poland was to cede the lands east of the Curzon Line because they had been seized by force in 1920-1921 and had never rightfully belonged to Poland, then why should Poland be compensated for giving back what it had never rightfully possessed? And, if compensation were considered in order, why should it come from Germany rather than from Russia? The Polish annexation of German territory would clearly violate the pledge against "territorial aggrandizement." Equally, the contemplated annexation could not possibly be accomplished by any "voluntary exchange of populations" or "in accordance with the freely expressed wishes of the peoples concerned." It could be accomplished only by the forcible expulsion of the German population.

The fact that the Teheran agreement, confirmed at Yalta and

* *Ibid.,* Vol. V, pages 400-403 and 406-407.

executed at Potsdam, was a direct violation of pledges solemnly signed by Poland as well as by the United States, Great Britain and Russia, seems never to have played any part in the deliberations of the statesmen who shaped the nature of the postwar world. (Even eight years later, when Churchill wrote the history of 1943, he saw no reason to regret the decision, except insofar as it had not clearly stated that the line should be at the Eastern rather than the Western Neisse.) This was not a good beginning toward making a peace based upon mutual respect for the sanctity of contracts.

In his account of the Teheran Conference, Churchill records the skillful manner in which Stalin drove the entering wedge toward Russian territorial aggrandizement in the Far East.

> Stalin asked what could be done for Russia in the Far East.* [This was after Stalin had declared his intention of entering the war against Japan.] I replied that Russia had Vladivostok, but he replied that the port was ice-bound, and also depended on the Straits of Tsushima. I answered that I wished to meet the Russian grievance, because the government of the world must be entrusted to satisfied nations, who wished nothing more for themselves than they had. If the world-government were in the hands of hungry nations, there would always be danger. But none of us had any reason to seek for anything more . . . We were like rich men dwelling at peace within their habitations.

Even at this early date, the "world-government" contemplated by Churchill—and by Stalin—was, in effect, a government of the world by the Big Three. Roosevelt's conception was apparently not essentially different, except that he steadily insisted upon including China. Churchill's statement that world-government "must be entrusted to satisfied nations" must have appeared as an attractive invitation to Stalin to state, in due course, just what it would take to make the Soviet Union a "satisfied nation."

Thus Churchill's attitude toward Russia—once he had decided to take the great gamble of foregoing Britain's traditional

* *Ibid.,* Vol. V. pages 381-382.

balance of power policy—and Roosevelt's determination to pay whatever price might be necessary to get Russian help against Japan combined in such a way as to undermine the peace which both men were earnestly striving to attain. Instead of showing, in their first dealings with their Russian partner, the clarity of purpose and firmness of principle which Stalin might have understood and perhaps even respected, the Anglo-American leaders displayed an over-eagerness to please which a man like Stalin was certain to exploit to the utmost. The danger-signals were all there at Teheran, but Roosevelt's supreme confidence that he could handle Stalin, and Churchill's ambivalence, not only toward Russia but toward the nature of the new world then taking shape, prevented both men from seeing the abyss which lay ahead.

The Teheran Conference fixed the timetable of the major Anglo-American effort against Germany and of a Russian spring offensive timed to assist that effort. It left open what the Anglo-American forces in the Mediterranean should do in the intervening six months. Stalin had expressed no great interest in the capture of Rome, but, for Churchill, this became a prestige objective of utmost importance, to be accomplished before large numbers of troops and landing craft would have to be withdrawn from the Mediterranean. The persistent pleading of the British leader obtained somewhat reluctant American agreement to the undertaking of a surprise landing at Cape Anzio, behind the strongly held German front. This entailed a considerable risk that the return of landing craft to Britain might be delayed, as well as the possibility that, if the break-out failed, so many troops and vehicles might be committed as to endanger the timetable of the subsidiary invasion of southern France.

The result turned out as the American high command had feared. The landing was brought off with complete surprise, but the two divisions placed ashore failed to advance quickly enough to exploit the advantage. Instead of being forced back from their outflanked main front, the Germans brought up reinforcements, held on grimly and launched a furious counter-attack against the beach head. Many more troops than were originally intended had to be thrown into Anzio and a stalemate ensued, which lasted throughout the rest of the winter and early spring, with repeated Allied failure to break through the German defenses and the Germans unable to eliminate the beach head in their rear.

The result of this costly operation was that Churchill's projects in the Eastern Mediterranean had to be abandoned.

Between Teheran and June 6, 1944, when the cross-Channel invasion of France was launched, the highly successful anti-submarine campaign, the gallant convoys to Murmansk and the stepped-up air war against Germany were the sole Anglo-American contributions to the defeat of Hitler. During the same period, the Russian armies drove forward to a line running south from the Baltic Sea, swinging westward in a wide bulge along the Polish, Czechoslovakian and Rumanian frontiers and back to the mouth of the Dniester River.

As the Russian armies approached their own frontiers, Moscow made a number of political moves. The Russians stated their rather moderate terms of peace to Finland, which were endorsed as fair by the British government. They signed a mutual assistance treaty with Czechoslovakia, leaving the door open for Poland and Rumania to sign similar agreements. Upon crossing the Rumanian frontier in April, they announced that "the invasion is dictated exclusively by military necessity" and declared that they had no desire to acquire more territory or to "change the social structure" of Rumania.

Meanwhile, the Anglo-American Allies were having plenty of political trouble. Roosevelt, yielding at last to the pressure of American public opinion, urged the formation of an anti-Fascist, democratic Italian government. Churchill stubbornly resisted, on the grounds that any such move should be deferred until after Rome was in Allied hands. Stalin confused the issue by suddenly extending recognition to the Badoglio government, a move the significance of which is much clearer today than it was then. (Reactionary or Fascist regimes provide a far more favorable opportunity for a Communist revolution than democratic governments.) Shortly thereafter—with Rome clearly not destined to fall until the spring—Churchill yielded to the extent of agreeing to the formation of a new Italian government with the participation of the anti-Fascist parties, but still under the King and Badoglio. The King announced that, after the capture of Rome, he would resign in favor of his son, Prince Umberto. (The latter, like his father, had been a sycophant of the Mussolini regime.)

In Jugoslavia, where the partisan leader, Josip Broz (Tito), rather than General Mikhailovitch, emerged as the real hero of the resistance, Churchill struggled to effect a reconciliation between Tito and the exiled government which would permit the return of King Peter to his throne. A similar effort to restore King Paul of Greece involved the forcible repression of a mutiny among Greek troops.*

Negotiations with Turkey failed to produce more than a stoppage of chrome shipments to Germany. A suspension of oil shipments to Spain and a demand that Franco pursue a more neutral policy produced a few nominal concessions, but the Blue Legion remained at the Russian front and Falangist propaganda urged Britain and the United States to make common cause with Hitler against Russia.

De Gaulle remained a problem-child. The French National Assembly at Algiers gave him a unanimous vote of confidence when he demanded assurance that no Allied military government would be established in France. (Such assurances had been given to Belgium, Holland and Norway.) On April 5, 1944, de Gaulle deposed General Giraud as commander of the French forces. Churchill's attempts to mollify the arrogant and vain French leader were haughtily rebuffed. It was an unhappy fact that Anglo-American dislike and distrust of de Gaulle—largely created and justified by his own behavior—tended only to build up his importance in French eyes and to alienate French sentiment.

In the United States, criticism of all sorts was vocal. From the more liberal friends of the Roosevelt administration came protests against what appeared to be a reactionary Anglo-American policy. From the opposition came cries of alarm about the concessions made to Churchill on the one hand and to Stalin on the other. The stalemate in Italy and impatient uncertainty as to the invasion of France created dissatisfaction with the conduct of the war; this was only partially offset by the good news

* *Ibid.*, Vol. V, Chapters IX and XIII.

of Admiral Nimitz' successful island-hopping in the Pacific and the steady advance of MacArthur in New Guinea and New Britain.

On April 9, Secretary Hull made a significant broadcast aimed at clarifying the aims of American policy and drawing attention to three important developments:

1. We and those nations who are now our Allies have moved from relative weakness to strength.
2. We in this country have moved from a deep-seated tendency toward separate action to the knowledge and conviction that only through unity of action can there be achieved in this world the results which are essential for the continuance of free people.
3. We have moved from a careless tolerance of evil institutions to the conviction that free governments and Nazi and Fascist governments cannot exist together in this world.

The Secretary declared that we could "no longer acquiesce in" neutral nations drawing upon our resources and at the same time aiding the enemy. He asserted that while chaos must be avoided after the fall of Hitler, "stability and order do not and cannot mean reaction," and that it was to our interest "to encourage the establishment in Europe of strong and progressive popular governments."

Speaking of the formulation of our policy toward enemy countries, Mr. Hull again emphasized: "There can be no compromise with Fascism or Nazism. It must go everywhere."

Unhappily, it had not been merely a lack of power which had led from "non-intervention" in Spain through Pétain, Darlan and Peyrouton to Badoglio. Military expediency, Tory restorationism and fear of Communism had caused us to support the status quo, not realizing that, in so doing, we were handing over the leadership of revolution to the Communists.

On May 23, 1944, Mr. Churchill addressed the House of Commons to render a report upon a somewhat unsatisfactory period. He revealed that the Allies had hoped to bring Turkey into the war and that these hopes had been disappointed, largely because of two factors: the fiasco of the Aegean adventure and Turkish underestimation of Russian power. Acknowledging Turkey's friendly attitude and her halting of chrome shipments to Germany, Churchill nevertheless expressed the opinion that, as a consequence of their decision to remain neutral, the Turks would not have "the strong position at the peace table which would attend their joining the Allies."

Reviewing the campaign in Italy, Churchill admitted that Allied action after the fall of Mussolini "might have been more swift and audacious" and that perhaps some mistakes had been made. Yet he defended Allied support of the King and Badoglio, adding that the Italian people would in due course have "free and fair opportunity of deciding whatever form of democratic government, whether monarchical or republican," they might desire. "We shall not," he added, "allow any form of Fascism to be restored or set up in any country with which we have been at war."

Then came the reverse twist. "From Italy one turns naturally to Spain, once the most famous empire in this world and down to this day a strong community in a wide land with marked personality and distinguished culture among the nations of Europe. Some people think that our foreign policy toward Spain is best expressed by drawing comical or even rude caricatures of General Franco, but I think there is more than that." Recalling that Franco had not attacked Gibraltar nor interfered with the North African invasion, Mr. Churchill said: "I have no sympathy with those who think it clever or even funny to insult or abuse the government of Spain . . . I am here today to speak kindly words about Spain. Let me add this hope that she will be a strong influence for the peace of the Mediterranean after the war. The internal political arrangements in Spain are a matter for the Spaniards themselves. It is not for us to meddle in these affairs . . ."

Thus, Mr. Churchill declared that the friendly Turks would have little to say at the peace table because they had remained neutral, but that Franco should exercise strong influence because—though he had not even pretended to be neutral—he had not actually attacked Britain. Answering criticism of his statement, Mr. Churchill denied that it was in conflict with what he had said about Italy. "There is a clear line of distinction," he said, "between nations who go to war with you and nations who leave you alone." The distinction, strangely reminiscent of Neville Chamberlain, was wholly at variance with Secretary Hull's pronouncement that "free governments and Nazi and Fascist governments cannot exist together in this world."

Mr. Churchill's words were a strange sort of inspiration to the youth of Britain and America, waiting for the great adventure in the peaceful loveliness of an English spring. "The war," he had said, "is losing its ideological character." Where Mr. Hull had defended past appeasement of Fascism on the grounds of lack of power, Mr. Churchill justified it as a policy of strength and proposed to continue it into the future.

Beyond saying that he thought Spain's actions as a "neutral" somewhat less than satisfactory, President Roosevelt refrained from comment. Mrs. Roosevelt went somewhat further. She thought the speech "very characteristic of Mr. Churchill" and remarked: "Mr. Churchill has thought a certain way for sixty years and doesn't want to change."

The day after Mr. Churchill's speech, the Allied armies in Italy finally breached the German defenses and linked up with the Anzio beach head. On June 4, Rome fell and Marshal Kesselring began a general retreat. Two days later, the long-awaited landings in France took place on the beaches of Normandy. The great concentric drive against *Festung Europa* had begun.

To the uninformed, it seemed as if the attack on Rome had been magnificently planned to distract the Germans and draw off strength from France. Actually, the long delay in Italy had frustrated the Allied plan for a simultaneous landing on the French Riviera, but the delayed Italian offensive served the same purpose. For the following two months, while the "Overlord" operation developed successfully and while the promised Russian offensive roared forward to the gates of Warsaw, Churchill exhausted every resource at his command to have the landings in Southern France called off altogether. He pleaded in vain that their purpose had been fulfilled by the Italian campaign, that a move up the Adriatic and through Trieste toward Vienna would be more profitable and—finally —that a landing in the Bordeaux region would serve "Overlord" better than opening up the long supply route up the

Rhone valley. Roosevelt was adamant against a move up the Adriatic, which he quite unjustly characterized as a move "into the Balkans." (Churchill never wanted to invade the Balkans; he wanted to establish a third front threatening Hitler and, if possible, to reach Vienna before the Russians liberated it. Roosevelt considered this a breach of faith with Stalin.) The idea of landing in the Bay of Biscay, instead of on the Riviera, and opening up additional Atlantic ports to receive the rapidly flowing American reinforcements appealed to Eisenhower's Chief of Staff, but not to Eisenhower. When "Anvil" was finally launched, it was mid-September before the forces that landed on the Riviera could effect a junction with General Eisenhower, but the Teheran promises had been fulfilled.

Anglo-American diplomacy failed to keep pace with the magnificent military successes achieved. After the fall of Rome, the King appointed Prince Umberto as his lieutenant governor, but the anti-Fascist parties were now sufficiently strong to refuse to have anything to do with the monarchy or the Badoglio regime. On June 9, without royal consent, they formed a cabinet under the veteran liberal Ivanoe Bonomi. After ten days of vain effort to have Badoglio included in the new government, the United States and Britain recognized the Bonomi government. As for France, de Gaulle was kept in total ignorance of the invasion plans until the last minute and no French contingents were permitted to participate in the Normandy landings. (This, sadly enough, was made necessary by legitimate doubts as to de Gaulle's security.) Once firmly ashore, Churchill urged that the French National Committee be recognized and brought into the picture but at this point Washington remained obdurate. It was not until the Riviera landing that French troops were permitted to participate in the liberation of their country, and not until late October that the United States finally agreed to recognize the National Committee as the provisional government of France. By this time it was abundantly clear that the vast majority of all Frenchmen had given their allegiance to the de Gaulle organization. The generally known fact that both Russia and Britain had so long postponed recognition only in deference to Washington's objections did not provide a happy beginning for postwar relations between the United States and France. The chief beneficiary of de Gaulle's lasting hostility to the United States was the Soviet Union.

At about the time when the Western world was rejoicing over the liberation of Paris, the liberation of Warsaw also seemed imminent; but here a dreadful and ominous tragedy occurred. When the Russians crossed the Vistula in late July and news came to Warsaw of the July 20 plot against Hitler,* General Bor Komorowski, commander of the Polish resistance forces organized under the government-in-exile, decided that the moment had come to assist the Russian advance by a general uprising. The insurrection began in the first days of August and lasted through the first week of September. Instead of continuing their advance upon the city, the Russians halted and not only failed to render any assistance to the insurrection which they themselves had encouraged, but even refused to allow Allied planes to parachute supplies and refuel on Soviet-held territory. British opinion was outraged at what appeared to be a cold-blooded betrayal, designed to kill off a Polish resistance movement which might not be friendly to Russia. Churchill's protests to Stalin received no very enthusiastic backing from President Roosevelt.†

Here in the United States, the tragedy of Warsaw aroused relatively little public interest. The liberation of France, the storming of Saipan and MacArthur's return to the Philippines engaged American attention to the extent that it was not wholly

* For an account of the plot against Hitler, see J. W. Wheeler-Bennett, *Nemesis of Power*, Chapter 6 (St. Martin's Press, 1954); also Hans B. Gisevius, *Bis zum Bitteren Ende* (Zurich, 1946).

† The full facts concerning this tragic episode and the subsequent cleavage within the coalition are still not available. The Russians were convinced that the Polish exile government in London was not only reactionary but anti-Soviet and that some of its supporters in Poland had actually collaborated with the Germans against Polish Communist partisans. This would explain Stalin's intransigent hostility to the London government which had been recognized and supported by Britain and the United States, though it would in no sense condone the treacherous betrayal of the Warsaw uprising. It is a known fact that the British made constant efforts to bring about a liberalization of the exile group. In one short passage of his narrative (*op. cit.*, Vol. VI, pages 425-426) Churchill himself indicates that the extreme Right wing of the Polish underground, "the so-called N.S.Z.," may have given the Russians just cause for suspicion.

preempted by domestic politics. Thomas E. Dewey finally achieved the Republican nomination. Roosevelt reluctantly declared his willingness to accept a fourth term and was renominated without opposition, but an interesting struggle developed over the Vice-Presidential nomination. Roosevelt let it be known that he lacked confidence in the incumbent, Henry A. Wallace; the White House suggested War Mobilizer James F. Byrnes, an influential conservative from South Carolina. When the pro-Roosevelt labor leaders rejected Byrnes, the choice fell upon a relatively unknown Senator from Missouri, Harry S. Truman. In the ensuing campaign, Roosevelt remained almost wholly inactive, leaving the field to his Republican rival while he himself undertook a trip to the Pacific theater of action. It was not until October, when a whispering campaign about his health aroused his fighting spirit, that the President went into action.

Meanwhile, Roosevelt, Churchill and their advisers met at a second Quebec Conference. The chief subjects slated for discussion concerned military strategy but another matter much on the mind of the British leader was the question of British financing after the tapering off of Lend-Lease aid which would follow German surrender. It was this last consideration which no doubt influenced Mr. Churchill's attitude toward a plan for the post-surrender treatment of Germany unexpectedly produced by Secretary of the Treasury Henry Morgenthau.

This strange proposal provided for the drastic "de-industrialization" of Germany, including the permanent closing and flooding of the Ruhr coal mines. Its purpose was to destroy forever the German military potential and to prevent Germany from again becoming a competitor in world markets. (If carried out, it would also have prevented any reasonable degree of recovery in all of Europe.) Churchill records: * "At first I violently opposed this idea. But the President—with Mr. Morgenthau from whom we had much to ask—were so insistent that in the end we agreed to consider it." Whether or not the President really was insistent, or merely acquiescent toward this

---

* *Ibid.*, pages 156-157. For a full discussion of the Morgenthau Plan see the author's *Germany—Bridge or Battleground* (Harcourt, Brace, 1947); and his *Germany—Key to Peace* (Harvard University Press, 1953).

ill-considered plan, both he and Mr. Churchill approved and initialed it, with disastrous consequences.

At Quebec, Churchill pleaded again for "a right-handed thrust from Italy into the armpit" through Trieste to Vienna. This time the proposal received approval, but, once again, the slow progress of the denuded Allied forces in Italy was destined to frustrate the cherished project. Other developments were to preempt Churchill's attention.

In October 1944, with Roosevelt busy with the election campaign, Churchill revisited Stalin, primarily in order to reach some sort of understanding as to the future of Poland and the Balkans. The result as to Poland was an inconclusive meeting of the London and Lublin leaders which seemed more promising than it later turned out to be. The visit, however, produced an agreement as to Rumania, Jugoslavia and Greece which was not at all pleasing to President Roosevelt and even less so to Secretary Hull. Stalin agreed to give Churchill a free hand in Greece in exchange for a free hand in Rumania, with the understanding that Britain and Russia would respect each other's equal influence in Jugoslavia. Hull objected strenuously to this reversion to old-fashioned, spheres-of-influence power politics. Roosevelt finally consented to the arrangement, but only for three months. During those three months, Churchill undertook an armed intervention against the threatened domination of Greece by the communist-led E.L.A.S. resistance movement which opposed the return of King Paul and his exiled government.

During October, the President threw himself into the campaign with his old-time vigor, winning easily in the November elections and gaining a stronger control over Congress. This was of great importance to the approaching peace negotiations and to the assurance of American participation in the United Nations.

Mr. Churchill's speech of May 23, 1944, already referred to, had contained a somewhat vague passage concerning the new world organization, in which the British leader envisaged a "Great Power Executive Council" as the essential agency for maintaining peace, with an "assembly of nations" whose functions he had declared himself unable to define. This had brought forth a protest from the Dutch foreign minister, Van Kleffens, declaring such an arrangement to be unsatisfactory and suggesting at least rotating representation on the directorate for the smaller nations. Secretary Hull, on June 1, had reassured the smaller nations that the world organization would be all-inclusive and that the lesser nations would be kept "in a position of equality."

On June 15, just after the successful Normandy landings, President Roosevelt had disclosed in somewhat more specific terms the nature of the contemplated structure.* "We are not thinking," he said, "of a super-state with its own police forces and other paraphernalia of coercive power." (Thus it was made clear for the benefit of those concerned over the maintenance of full national sovereignty that the new organization would be another league of sovereign nations and not a league of sovereign peoples.) "The maintenance of peace and security," Mr. Roosevelt continued, "must be the joint task of all peace-loving nations. Accordingly, it is our thought that the organization would be a fully representative body with broad responsibilities for promoting and facilitating international cooperation . . ." and "that the organization would provide for a council, elected annually by the fully representative body of all nations, which would include the four major nations and a suitable number of other nations. The council would concern itself with the peaceful settlement of international disputes and with the prevention of threats to the peace or breaches of the peace." (Thus the formula emerged by which the "idealistic" concept of a universal organization was to be merged with the "realistic" design of a peace enforced by the power of the Big Four.)

* In the complicated political maneuvering for the Democratic nomination at the Chicago convention of 1932, Franklin D. Roosevelt is generally believed to have made some sort of agreement to drop his advocacy of the League of Nations. During the subsequent campaign he did belittle the League and foreswear American membership in it. The shaping of the United Nations was doubtless greatly influenced by Roosevelt's determination not to let the old questions of sovereignty once more wreck American participation in a world organization. The result was a structure acceptable to the moderate nationalists and, therefore, reasonably sure of ratification. This, however, involved the creation of a new world organization endowed at the outset with insufficient powers to enforce peace.

Finally, Mr. Roosevelt had said: "We are seeking effective agreements and arrangements through which the nations would maintain, according to their capacities, adequate forces to meet the needs of preventing war and of making impossible the deliberate preparation for war, and to have such forces available for joint action when necessary." (This made it clear that collective force would be applied against an aggressor only when the Big Four were in agreement and that no effort would be made to create machinery strong enough to deal with possible disputes among the Big Four themselves.)

The dangers inherent in the plan thus foreshadowed were apparent to anyone who had studied the period beginning with the Japanese aggression in Manchuria in 1931 and ending with World War II, during which aggression could have been halted by concerted action of the great powers at any one of several stages, but remained unchecked because of their failure to act in concert. On the other hand, the plan had the virtue of acceptability; indeed, it had been devised and carefully discussed with Congressional leaders in order to insure against a repetition of the disaster which had befallen Woodrow Wilson. But, if this was to be the plan for peace, everything would depend upon reaching a firm and lasting understanding between the United States, Great Britain, China and the Soviet Union.

During August and September, representatives of these four countries met at Dumbarton Oaks and gave form and substance to the United Nations plan, adumbrated by President Roosevelt. Agreement was reached on all major matters, save one— the question of voting rights in the all-important Security Council. Neither the Soviet Union nor the United States was ready to submit itself to majority rule on that body; an acceptable formula remained to be devised.

Domestic politics, trouble in Greece and the German breakout in the Ardennes preempted American attention in the succeeding months. For many reasons, it was urgently necessary that the Big Three should have another meeting, but the President's Constitutional duties prevented his leaving the country prior to his re-inauguration and Stalin was as unwilling to leave Russia as he had been in 1943. Plans were laid for a secret meeting to be held in the Crimea, during the first week of February.

On this last of his journeys, President Roosevelt was accompanied by his usual advisers, plus the new Secretary of State, Edward R. Stettinius, who had replaced the aging and infirm veteran, Cordell Hull. Another new addition to the American team was Mr. James F. Byrnes, President Roosevelt's Defense Mobilizer whom he had sought to have elected Vice President.

The Yalta Conference has been described in detail by some of the American participants as well as by Winston Churchill.* Its published decisions were at the time almost universally praised. Since then, the "Yalta Deal" has been both widely attacked and sturdily defended. Actually, the Yalta Conference did little more than carry out the agreements reached and the tendencies established at Teheran.

In a secret agreement, which followed Stalin's definite promise to enter the war against Japan within three months after German surrender, Stalin was promised in the Far East just about what he might have been expected to demand after the encouragement given to him at Teheran. This consisted of: (1) the restoration of Russian rights lost after the Russo-Japanese War; (2) the preservation of the rather obscure status quo in Outer Mongolia; and (3) the acquisition of the Kurile Islands. The first item included recovery of the Southern half of Sakhalin; the internationalization of Dairen under predominant Russian interest; the restoration of the lease of Port Arthur as a Russian naval base; and the joint operation with China of the Chinese Eastern and South Manchuria Railway, with the understanding that predominant Russian interest would be safeguarded and that China should retain full sovereignty over Manchuria. The agreement signed by the Big Three was made subject to Chiang Kai-shek's consent, which Roosevelt undertook to obtain. It contained also an expression of Russian readiness, later fulfilled, to enter into a treaty of alliance with the Chinese government.

This Far Eastern agreement was later to be attacked as a betrayal of China. It is difficult to see how it can be so construed,

* James F. Byrnes in *Speaking Frankly* (Harper, 1947); W. A. Harriman in testimony before the Senate; Harry Hopkins in Sherwood's collection of his private papers; Admiral Leahy in *I Was There* (McGraw-Hill, 1948); and E. R. Stettinius in *Roosevelt and the Russians* (Doubleday, 1947).

since Chiang accepted it without demurral and welcomed the treaty of alliance. On the other hand, it is now evident that Roosevelt's eagerness for Russian help against Japan led him to pay a price for an action which Russia would in any case have taken in its own self-interest. Stalin was only too eager to be in at the death and to collect his share of the spoils. In fact, it seems doubtful whether he could have been prevented from so doing. Moreover, as it turned out, Roosevelt was badly misinformed by his military advisers as to the Japanese capacity to resist. Even without the then as yet unproven atom bomb, victory was much nearer than was indicated by the intelligence estimates upon which Roosevelt based his policy.*

As regards Europe, the Yalta Agreements were, with one extion, merely the logical extension of Teheran. The exception was in the procedure adopted for the treatment of Germany. The Roosevelt-Stalin idea of dismemberment was dropped and a plan adopted instead which produced, contrary to intention or expectation, a much worse form of dismemberment than would have resulted from the orderly, planned creation of several German states. This can be more appropriately discussed in relation to the subsequent Potsdam Agreement. The Teheran decision to fix the frontiers of Poland at the Curzon and Oder-Neisse lines was reaffirmed, again leaving unclear which Neisse River was intended to be the boundary with Germany. Reparations, too, were left in the same cloudy state as at Teheran, with Stalin restating the Russian demand for $10,000,-000,000 and the Anglo-American leaders replying that the matter would have to be studied.

Once again, only more emphatically than at Teheran, Roosevelt and Churchill sought assurance as to the future of Poland and the Balkan countries. What they got was a verbal agreement to establish "freely chosen democratic governments"

* These estimates indicated that it would take eighteen months after the surrender of Germany to bring Japan to its knees and that it would be necessary to invade the Japanese home islands. The invasion of Honshu alone would, it was estimated, cost 500,000 casualties. A much more accurate dissenting estimate by Admiral Zacharias is said never to have reached the President. Admiral Leahy, in *op. cit.*, states that he also held the view that Russian help was neither necessary nor desirable.

which meant one thing to Stalin and quite another to Roosevelt and Churchill.

Churchill has fully recorded the protracted discussions which took place at Yalta over the creation of a Polish government satisfactory to both sides. In the interval between Churchill's visit to Moscow in the preceding October and the Yalta meeting, Prime Minister Mikolajczyk and one of his cabinet had gone to Warsaw and reached a tentative understanding with the "Lublin government," only to have the London government repudiate the agreement and force Mikolajczyk's resignation. The Russians had then recognized the Lublin or, as they called it, the "Warsaw government" and relations between the two groups were worse than ever. All access to Poland had been denied to the Western powers, so that there was no agreed basis of fact upon which to conduct negotiations. The "solution" reached at Yalta was an agreement by Stalin to foster the establishment of "a fully representative Provisional Polish Government, based upon all the democratic and anti-Fascist forces in Poland, and including democratic leaders from Poles abroad." Molotov, W. A. Harriman and Sir Archibald Clark Kerr were entrusted with the task of approaching such leaders and submitting proposals to the consideration of the three governments. It was further agreed that the government thus established should as soon as possible hold "free and unfettered elections" in which "all democratic parties would have the right to participate and to promote candidatures . . ."

The Russo-Polish failure to carry out this agreement, together with the imposition by Russia of a Communist-dominated regime in Rumania, opened up the breach between Russia and the Western powers which was soon to develop into a chasm.

Before discussing these post-Yalta developments, it is necessary to note one other important achievement of the Crimean meeting. The vexing question of voting rights on the Security Council of the United Nations was solved by the acceptance of an American proposal that each member should have one vote, but that all decisions of major importance should require the unanimous consent of the permanent members of the Council. Thus the later much-discussed "Veto" was born. Stalin asked and was granted the right for two Soviet republics—the Ukraine and White Russia—to become members of the United Nations in their own right and to have one vote each in the Assembly. It was agreed that the United Nations should be convened at San Francisco on April 25, and that all those nations should be invited to become members which had declared war on the common enemy by March 1, or had already signed the United Nations Declaration.

When President Roosevelt reported to Congress, he received a great ovation. He did not, for obvious reasons, report on the Far Eastern agreement as to the price paid for Russia's secretly promised help against Japan, nor did he mention the concession of separate membership for the Ukraine and White Russia.*

The last two months of Mr. Roosevelt's life were not happy ones. Not only was his health rapidly failing but the turn of events must have made him question seriously and perhaps for the first time whether the basic premises of his policy had been valid. With the German front in the East collapsing, Rumania had switched sides. On February 27, Vyshinsky suddenly appeared in Bucharest and demanded that King Michael dismiss his coalition government. Soviet tanks rolled into the city and, on March 2, the King was forced to submit to the installation of a Soviet-designated government. Churchill was deeply troubled but in no position to protest, since Stalin had raised no objection to British armed intervention in Greece. The Polish question, too, dragged on without a solution; here, Churchill tried to spur Roosevelt into action but found the President reluctant to risk a break with Stalin.

Toward the end of March, the Allied armies crossed the Rhine and began a rapid encirclement of the Ruhr. Simultaneously, the German High Command in Italy put out peace feelers to the representatives of the United States Office of Strategic Services (O.S.S.) in Berne, Switzerland. These exploratory conversations, possibly leading to a surrender of the German forces in Italy, were reported to Stalin on March 21. This occasioned a rude and angry outburst from Molotov and an ex-

* The belated disclosure of this agreement raised public apprehension as to what other secret concessions might have been made to Russia.

tremely bitter exchange of cables between the President and Stalin, in which the Russian leader made an entirely unwarranted charge of bad faith indignantly repudiated by the President. The incident closed with Stalin's disavowal of any intention to impugn the personal integrity of either Roosevelt or Churchill, the alleged fault being that of subordinates. There the matter was allowed to drop.*

On April 12, 1945, the President cabled to Churchill:

> I would minimize the general Soviet problem as much as possible because these problems, in one form or another, seem to arise every day and most of them straighten out, as in the case of the Berne incident.

A day later, Roosevelt was dead. . . .

In domestic affairs, Franklin D. Roosevelt's leadership had reached its peak during the first, dynamic hundred days of the New Deal. In foreign affairs, his statesmanship reached its apogee in the period between the fall of France and Pearl Harbor. Prior to the fall of France, Roosevelt had first turned his back upon world affairs and then, from 1937 to 1940, wavered unhappily between his sound intuition and the false hope that appeasement might somehow bring peace. From the fall of France to Pearl Harbor he had shown brilliant leadership in preparing a reluctant nation for war and in providing essential aid to the forces holding the line against the aggressors. The culminating achievements of this period had been the Lend-Lease Act, which laid the foundations for eventual victory, and the Atlantic Charter, which laid the foundations for peace.

After Pearl Harbor, Franklin D. Roosevelt had become more Commander-in-Chief than President. As such, he became a military leader probably superior to any American President since George Washington. But, just because he became more Commander-in-Chief than President, his diplomacy dropped from the high level of the preceding period. With military expediency as the paramount consideration, Roosevelt achieved a brilliant pursuit of victory but, in the process, lost his clear vision of the path to just and lasting peace. The military aspects of the war obscured the revolutionary forces which criss-crossed

* Churchill, *op. cit.*, Vol. VI, pages 440-454.

the national struggle for survival. The great crusade for human freedom degenerated into an effort to restore as much as possible of the prewar world.

Roosevelt understood much more clearly than had Wilson the vital interests of the United States. He avoided Wilson's great error of not stating American war aims at the outset of the conflict. Through the ingenious invention of the mutual aid formula of the Lend-Lease Act, he escaped from the disastrous war-debt entanglement in which Wilson became enmeshed. And finally, by not demanding too much in the way of surrendering national sovereignty to a world organization, Roosevelt achieved acceptance of his plan for peace, where Wilson had suffered defeat and repudiation. But, where Wilson's idealistic aims had been frustrated by failure to understand the realities of power politics, Roosevelt's preoccupation with power politics diluted his idealistic vision. Where Wilson's moral absolutes had made him incompetent to deal with the art of the possible, Roosevelt's natural aptitude and liking for the art of the possible made him lose sight of the moral absolutes.

When Roosevelt died, he had to all intents and purposes achieved victory, but he had not achieved peace. He was, in fact, further from achieving peace than he had been in August, 1941, when he had laid down the principles of peace in the Atlantic Charter.

Wilson's hope of peace resided in his confidence in the power of an idea; Roosevelt's hope of peace rested in his confidence in his own extraordinary ability to improvise solutions to successive crises. Had he lived beyond final victory, had his great energy and superb courage once more been directed toward the creative, affirmative tasks of peace, he might well have succeeded in holding together the great coalition which he had led to victory in war.

If Wilson had died in the autumn of 1918, he would have left a plan for peace which others might have been able to execute, perhaps with greater success than Wilson himself. When Roosevelt died, he left an unfinished series of negotiations the successful outcome of which depended upon his own peculiar talents which, unhappily, were extinguished by his death.

PART SEVEN

Disenchantment and Cold War

CHAPTER TWENTY-SIX

The Disintegration of the Coalition
(1945)

THE LAST, unfinished paper of Franklin D. Roosevelt was a draft of the speech which he intended to deliver at the opening of the San Francisco Conference, at which the United Nations was to be brought into being. President Truman fell heir to this assignment with less than two weeks in which to familiarize himself with the complicated background of negotiations and agreements, many of which were wholly unfamiliar to him.

In addition, Mr. Truman took over the conduct of foreign policy at the moment when, with victory over Germany in sight, the first serious cracks had appeared in the anti-Axis coalition. Although Mr. Truman fully intended to carry out the Roosevelt policies and at first retained most of Mr. Roosevelt's advisers, it was inevitable that the smooth continuity of Anglo-American relations would be interrupted and that something of a hiatus should develop in Anglo-American policy toward the Soviet Union. This could not have happened at a worse moment.

It was too late to postpone the San Francisco Conference for which all arrangements were already made; on the other hand, the whole United Nations project rested upon the assumption of continuing friendly cooperation with the Soviet Union, an assumption now subject to grave doubts and misgivings. President Roosevelt's last cable to Mr. Churchill had contained the advice to "minimize the Soviet problem" and had expressed the belief that it would straighten itself out, but the events which followed immediately upon Mr. Roosevelt's death would undoubtedly have caused him to reconsider that optimistic opinion and, perhaps, to take even so drastic a step as to postpone the San Francisco Conference until a better understanding had been reached with the Kremlin. For the new President to take such a step, before he had had time to familiarize himself with the complex causes of misunderstanding, was clearly out of the question. Moreover, military events were now moving so rapidly toward a climax that a political crisis had at all costs to be avoided.

On April 9, the Russian armies had entered Vienna. By April 22, they were massing at the Oder before the gates of Berlin. On the 25th, the day when President Truman opened the San Francisco Conference, Russian and American troops met at Torgau on the Elbe. On the 29th, the German armies in Italy surrendered. On May 1, Hitler committed suicide; and, a day later, Berlin fell to the Red Army. On May 8, 1945, the unconditional surrender of Hitler's Third *Reich* was consummated.

During this eventful month, Winston Churchill became increasingly apprehensive over Soviet intentions. From him flowed a stream of cables, messages and minutes, all directed toward the single purpose of limiting the penetration of the Russian armies into Europe. General Eisenhower's decision to strike southeastward to forestall a last stand in southern Germany, leaving the capture of Berlin to the Soviet forces, filled Churchill with dismay. Vainly he endeavored to persuade President Truman to override the decision. Field Marshal Montgomery's British forces, proceeding across the northern German plain, were urged at all costs to get to Lübeck before the Russians and thus to insure Denmark's liberation by British rather than Russian forces. After the surrender of the Germans in Italy, Field Marshal Alexander was instructed—with President Truman's concurrence—to seize Trieste in order to forestall seizure by Tito's partisans. Both Montgomery and Alexander succeeded by narrow margins of time in accomplishing these assignments.

With the collapse of the German front in the West, refugees began streaming from the East, seeking haven from the advancing Russians in territory likely to be taken by the Western forces. Himmler tried, through a Swedish intermediary, to arrange for a separate surrender to the Western powers but was unhesitatingly told by the British and American governments that only complete unconditional surrender of all German forces to the united coalition would be accepted. Stalin expressed his appreciation to Churchill, but could scarcely have been unaware that the British leader, while loyally adhering to tripartite agreements, was doing everything in his power to limit the encroachment of Soviet forces. (No one, in fact, would understand this better than Stalin, since it was precisely what he would have done in Churchill's place.)

The real difficulties arose after the surrender of May 8. At this time the American forces had penetrated far beyond the line established months earlier by the European Advisory Council, as the boundary between the Anglo-American and Soviet zones of occupation. Eisenhower's troops held all of Thuringia and a part of Saxony and were at some points well over 100 miles beyond the zonal frontier. On the other hand, Eisenhower had halted his advance at the Czechoslovak frontier—much to Churchill's dismay—acceding to a Soviet request to leave the liberation of Prague to the Red Army. Vienna had, of course, already fallen to the Russians.

It had been agreed that Vienna, as well as the rest of Austria, should be divided into four zones of occupation. Once in control, however, the Russians refused the Allied request to fly in their missions, saying that this move must await the formation of a provisional Austrian government. This, together with the Russian delay in carrying out the Polish agreement, augured ill for the execution of all past agreements.

Churchill argued that the Anglo-American forces should on no account be withdrawn to the predetermined zonal boundaries until a satisfactory understanding had been reached with the Kremlin as to Poland, Vienna and the joint occupation of Berlin. He urged President Truman to come to London, proceeding from there to a joint meeting with Stalin. Through Eden, attending the San Francisco Conference, as well as by direct messages, the prime minister sought to impress upon the new American President the view to which he had now come. This was expressed so clearly in his cable of May 12 to the President, that anything less than a full quotation would do violence to history, especially since Mr. Churchill has stated in the last volume of his history, that he "would rather be judged by this" than any other document written at this time.

PRIME MINISTER TO PRESIDENT TRUMAN   12 May 45

I am profoundly concerned about the European situation. I learn that half the American Air Force in Europe has already begun to move to the Pacific theatre. The newspapers are full of the great movements of the American armies out of Europe. Our armies also are, under previous arrangements, likely to undergo a marked reduction. The Canadian army will certainly leave. The French are weak and difficult to deal with. Anyone can see that in a very short space of time our armed power on the Continent will have vanished, except for moderate forces to hold down Germany.

2. Meanwhile what is to happen about Russia? I have always worked for friendship with Russia, but, like you, I feel deep anxiety because of their misinterpretation of the Yalta decisions, their attitude towards Poland, their overwhelming influence in the Balkans, excepting Greece, the difficulties they make about Vienna, the combination of Russian power and the territories under their control or occupied, coupled with the Communist technique in so many other countries, and above all their power to maintain very large armies in the field for a long time. What will be the position in a year or two, when the British and American armies have melted and the French has not yet been formed on any major scale, when we may have a handful of divisions, mostly French, and when Russia may choose to keep two or three hundred on active service?

3. An iron curtain is drawn down upon their front. We do not know what is going on behind. There seems little doubt that the whole of the regions east of the line Lübeck-Trieste-Corfu will soon be completely in their hands. To this must be added the further enormous area conquered by the American armies between Eisenach and the Elbe, which will, I suppose, in a few weeks be occupied, when the Americans retreat, by the Russian power. All kinds of arrangements will have to be made by General Eisenhower to

prevent another immense flight of the German population westward as this enormous Muscovite advance into the centre of Europe takes place. And then the curtain will descend again to a very large extent, if not entirely. Thus a broad band of many hundreds of miles of Russian-occupied territory will isolate us from Poland.

4. Meanwhile the attention of our peoples will be occupied in inflicting severities upon Germany, which is ruined and prostrate, and it would be open to the Russians in a very short time to advance if they chose to the waters of the North Sea and the Atlantic.

5. Surely it is vital now to come to an understanding with Russia, or see where we are with her, before we weaken our armies mortally or retire to the zones of occupation. This can only be done by a personal meeting. I should be most grateful for your opinion and advice. Of course we may take the view that Russia will behave impeccably, and no doubt that offers the most convenient solution. To sum up, this issue of a settlement with Russia before our strength has gone seems to me to dwarf all others.

On this side of the Atlantic, other difficulties were simultaneously coming to the surface. Mr. Molotov insisted that the veto in the Security Council should apply not only to decisions for action but also to determination of what matters the Council should discuss. This occasioned acrimonious debate. The Russian delegation became incensed—not without justification—over the railroading of Argentina into the United Nations by the United States and the Latin American bloc. (Argentina, having been pro-Axis during most of the war, was certainly not eligible for membership under the spirit of the agreement reached at Yalta; the United States felt itself bound to support the Latin Bloc's sponsorship by the conflicting obligations assumed under the recent Act of Chapultepec, providing for hemisphere solidarity.) The Soviets countered with a demand for the inclusion of the provisional (Lublin) government of Poland. This brought the Polish hornet's nest into the forum of the United Nations and matters reached a point so serious that it was decided to persuade Harry Hopkins to leave a sick bed to undertake a trip to Moscow.

The story of Hopkins' last mission is eloquently told in Sherwood's biography.* Hopkins' efforts resulted in a sufficient relaxation of tension to enable the San Francisco Conference to adopt the United Nations Charter and so to reach a successful conclusion. The full text of Hopkins' reports supplies valuable insight into Stalin's thinking at this time, showing that, in Stalin's mind, the counterpart to Churchill's distrust of Russia was already formed; "Churchill," he said to Hopkins, "wants to establish a *cordon sanitaire* against Russia."

Churchill was extremely anxious for Hopkins to stop in London on his return, but Hopkins—much as he loved Churchill— wanted to fly home and Truman urged him not to delay his return. Churchill continued to urge a tripartite meeting, preferably in London, preceded by Anglo-American talks. At this point, Truman made two decisions, one of which deeply offended the British leader while the other filled him with a sense of frustration and despair.

Through Joseph E. Davies, former American ambassador to Moscow, Mr. Truman tried to persuade Churchill that—instead of what he called "ganging up" on Stalin by prior Anglo-American consultation—he, Truman, should try to see Stalin alone before the tripartite meeting. With great dignity, but with unconcealed indignation, Churchill rejected this proposal. (The suggestion was without doubt tactless, in view of Truman's recent entrance upon the scene, but one cannot help wondering what might have occurred if Truman and Stalin had met privately at this time and established a personal contact.)

Truman's second decision, about which historians will very likely judge him to have been wrong, was to insist that the Anglo-American forces be withdrawn to the zonal boundaries before any understanding had been reached with Russia. (The writer doubts whether Roosevelt would have done this. Churchill was not proposing that the zonal arrangements should be repudiated; he was merely suggesting that the Anglo-Americans delay the fulfillment of their undertaking until Stalin had either

* Sherwood; *op. cit.;* pages 883-916.

fulfilled his engagements or given clear evidence that he had no intention of doing so. Truman took the position, apparently concurred in by Eisenhower, that it was his duty to carry out Roosevelt's commitments and that the misunderstandings with Russia could best be straightened out if the United States and Britain came to the tripartite meeting with completely clean hands.) Churchill, at this time beset with the necessity for calling new elections and thus ending his wartime coalition government, accepted Truman's decision with good grace, but with a heavy heart. The tripartite meeting was set for mid-July in Berlin. The Anglo-American forces retired to their zonal boundaries in the first week of July; at the same time, the three Western powers took over their sectors in Berlin, without even securing a firm agreement as to their right to maintain free communications between these sectors and their respective zones of occupation.* At about the same time, the zones in Austria were established. Thus, before the United States and Britain had really faced the decision whether to continue their past policy, or to modify it to conform to what appeared to be a changed Soviet attitude, Russia was permitted to move into the heart of central Europe and within one hundred miles of the Rhine.

Two fateful cleavages had opened within the great coalition: Churchill had almost completely receded from the spirit of Teheran and Yalta; his suspicions had turned into overt distrust and apprehension; Truman as yet adhered to Roosevelt's faith in Russian cooperation and thus was temporarily split from Churchill, though not so deeply or permanently as Churchill and Stalin were now divided. A strange fate lay in store for Winston Churchill: dismissed from high office in his own country, he was soon to become the guiding spirit of American policy.

Never before had there been greater need for Western unity and less evidence that it existed. In the weeks before the Potsdam meeting, the only cheerful news came from the far side of the world. With the fall of Okinawa on June 21, the last chapter in the war against Japan had opened. From a base within easy

* See the author's *Germany—Key to Peace* (Harvard, 1953), pages 17-18; see also Lucius D. Clay, *Decision in Germany* (Doubleday, 1950), pages 26-27.

reach of the new B-29 bombers, the flimsily built cities of the Japanese home islands now lay exposed to devastating fire-raids. To Churchill, this was perhaps less important than the reconquest of Burma which saved India and opened the hope of regaining Singapore; but to Harry Truman, as he set sail for his first encounter with Stalin, it was of supreme significance. For the first time, it began to look as if Russian help in the war against Japan might not be needed.

With Truman and his other advisers went his newly appointed Secretary of State, James F. Byrnes, whom he had placed in office as soon as Mr. Stettinius had finished his labors at San Francisco.

During the week in which Churchill participated at Potsdam, before the results of the British elections removed him from office, he and President Truman acquired a considerable respect and liking for each other. Churchill found "the new potentate," whom he had been so anxious to meet, impressive because of his "gay, precise, sparkling manner and his obvious power of decision." The extent to which Churchill impressed Truman was to become evident before many months had passed. Stalin and the new President also seemed to get along well, each rather liking the blunt manner of the other. From the point of view of personal relationships, the conference got off to as good a start as could be expected. Unhappily, this was far from sufficient to insure a satisfactory result.

On July 17, the day when the conferees arrived in Berlin, Secretary of War Stimson received a cable telling him that "the babies were born." This meant that on the preceding day the first atomic bomb had been successfully exploded at Alamagordo in the New Mexican desert. Churchill was elated over the news, which meant to him that the Western Allies had "suddenly become possessed of a merciful abridgement to the slaughter in the East and of a far happier prospect in Europe." There was not the slightest doubt in Churchill's mind that the bomb should be used against the Japanese; British consent had, as a matter of fact, already been given on July 4. When President Truman informed Churchill of his intention to apprise Stalin of the momentous development, the British leader urged that only the barest statement be made concerning the new weapon.

During the succeeding days, while the Big Three were discussing Polish, German and European affairs, Truman and Churchill held several meetings with their staffs to discuss the next moves with regard to Japan. Stalin had informed Churchill privately that, just before he had left Moscow, "an unaddressed message had been delivered to him by the Japanese ambassador" stating that the Japanese could not accept "unconditional surrender" but "might be prepared to compromise on other terms." Stalin had replied that the message contained no definite proposals upon which the Soviet government could take action. In informing Churchill, Stalin explained that he had not mentioned the matter to Truman directly "lest he might think the Russians were trying to influence him toward peace." * Churchill, of course, informed Truman and, on July 26, an ultimatum was dispatched to the Japanese government over the signatures of Truman, Churchill and Chiang Kai-shek.

The essential text of the ultimatum, published on July 26, 1945, was as follows:

> The time has come for Japan to decide whether she will continue to be controlled by those self-willed militaristic advisers, whose unintelligent calculations have brought the Empire of Japan to the threshold of annihilation, or whether she will follow the path of reason.
>
> The following are our terms. We shall not deviate from them. There are no alternatives. We shall brook no delay.
>
> There must be eliminated for all time the authority and influence of those who have deceived and misled the people of Japan into embarking on world conquest, for we insist that a new order of peace, security, and justice will be impossible until irresponsible militarism is driven from the world.
>
> Until such a new order is established and until there is convincing proof that Japan's war-making power is destroyed points in Japanese territory designated by the Allies will be occupied to secure the achievement of the basic objectives we are here setting forth.

* The quotations are from Churchill's account on pages 641-644 of Vol. VI, op. cit.

The terms of the Cairo declaration shall be carried out, and Japanese sovereignty shall be limited to the islands of Honshu, Hokkaido, Kyushu, Shikoku, and such minor islands as we determine.

The Japanese military forces after being completely disarmed shall be permitted to return to their homes, with the opportunity of leading peaceful and productive lives.

We do not intend that the Japanese shall be enslaved as a race nor destroyed as a nation, but stern justice will be meted out to all war criminals, including those who have visited cruelties upon our prisoners. The Japanese Government shall remove all obstacles to the revival and strengthening of democratic tendencies among the Japanese people. Freedom of speech, of religion, and of thought, as well as respect for fundamental human rights, shall be established.

Japan shall be permitted to maintain such industries as will sustain her economy and allow of the exaction of just reparations in kind, but not those industries which would enable her to re-arm for war.

To this end access to, as distinguished from control of, raw materials shall be permitted. Eventual Japanese participation in world trade relations shall be permitted.

The occupying forces of the Allies shall be withdrawn from Japan as soon as these objectives have been accomplished, and there has been established, in accordance with the freely expressed will of the Japanese people, a peacefully inclined and responsible Government.

We call upon the Government of Japan to proclaim now the unconditional surrender of all the Japanese armed forces, and to provide proper and adequate assurances of their good faith in such action. The alternative for Japan is complete and utter destruction.

By far the greatest part of the plenary sessions at Potsdam was devoted to the question of the German-Polish frontier. Here Truman and Churchill found themselves presented with the accomplished fact of an established Polish administration in the German lands east of the Oder and the Western Neisse. In effect, Stalin had created a fifth zone of occupation, giving as the "unavoidable" reason for this action the need for preserving order in the rear of the Russian armies and the allegation that the Russian forces themselves were not trained or equipped to establish a military government. Churchill relates in full the strong argument which he put up against this action.* He pointed out sharply what it would mean to deprive Germany of an area which had in the past produced 25% of the foodstuffs for the whole German people, while at the same time expelling millions of Germans from their homes and crowding them into the already overcrowded rump of Germany in the West. Stalin's reply was that there would be no overcrowding because millions of Germans had been killed and millions more would probably die. As for expulsion, he said that every German had already fled from the land between the Vistula and the Oder. In the future, he said, replying to the matter of food production, Germany could buy food from Poland. The same was true of coal, if the Germans should need more than they could produce in the Ruhr.

Truman's attitude throughout this discussion seems to have been that the matter should be left to the decision of the peace conference. Churchill strongly objected to this, correctly foreseeing that, unless the Poles were forced to retreat now, the situation would probably become frozen. Truman pointed out that the Big Three had agreed at Yalta to consult the Polish government and that this ought to be done; he thought the question was not so much one of substance as one of the manner in which the Poles had been given a fifth zone without consultation. Stalin promptly agreed to consult the Polish government and President Bierut was sent for. As might be expected, this discussion proved wholly unproductive. This was on July 24. The following day Churchill left for London to await the results of the elections. The next morning he resigned and Clement Attlee became prime minister.

Churchill maintains† that "the overrunning by the Russian armies of the territory up to and even beyond the Western Neisse was never and would never have been agreed to by any government of which I was the head." He makes a point of

* Churchill, *op. cit.*, Vol. VI, Chapter 20, pages 647-667.
† *Ibid.*, pages 672-674.

insisting that, had he remained in office, he would have had a showdown and even a public break, if necessary, "rather than to allow anything beyond the Oder and the Eastern Neisse to be ceded to Poland." This, he says, "was no point of principle only, but rather an enormous matter of fact affecting about three additional millions of displaced people." He places less blame upon "the ministers of the new government" (in the United Kingdom) than upon the American government—not for what Truman did or failed to do at Potsdam—but for the American failure to support his demand for a showdown "before the Americans, and to a lesser extent the British, made their vast retirement on a 400-mile front to a depth, in some places of 120 miles, thus giving the heart and a great mass of Germany over to the Russians."

In claiming that the time to have a showdown was before the retirement to the zonal boundaries, Churchill was undoubtedly right. On the other hand, Churchill's great indignation over the seizure of the strip between the two Neisse rivers and his assertion that he would have risked an open break, rather than acquiesce in it, is not impressive. So far as indignation over violated principle was concerned, the evil principle of permitting annexations and the eviction of populations had been accepted by the Big Three at Yalta, in direct violation of their solemn pledges to the contrary. The question of *which* Neisse River was to be the new frontier had never been clearly settled, either at Teheran or at Yalta. There was, therefore, no question of principle involved in the matter over which Churchill insists that he would have risked an open break, had he been present up to the end of the Potsdam Conference. As for the "enormous matter of fact affecting about three additional millions of displaced people," Churchill had been and still was willing to have some nine million Germans, living in East Prussia, eastern Pomerania, eastern Brandenburg, and Upper Silesia, evicted from their homes and crowded into the West German rump; and, so far as food production was concerned, the relatively small strip of Lower Silesian territory between the two branches of the Neisse River would not have made a vital difference.

The sin against moral principle and the errors of practical

judgment as to the future of Germany were committed at Teheran and Yalta. Churchill's reason for wanting a showdown before the retirement of the Anglo-American forces to the zonal boundaries had not been to rectify those errors but to make sure that Russia intended to adhere to and carry out the Teheran and Yalta agreements. This applied more to Poland, Austria and the Balkans than to the unclear question of which Neisse River had been intended as the boundary between Germany and Poland. Had there been such a showdown, it might well have been possible to clarify this relatively minor matter as well; but it was certainly not the main issue.

Apart from the moral considerations involved in the violation of the Atlantic Charter pledges, the basic error which both Roosevelt and Churchill committed at Teheran and Yalta was that they sought to undo by a rather vague political agreement both the consequences of pre-war appeasement and of wartime military action. Appeasement had handed central Europe and the Balkans to Hitler. The course of the war had delivered central Europe and the Balkans, except Greece, into the hands of Stalin. It was clear at Yalta—if not at Teheran—that Russia would make the major contribution to German defeat, and that Russia—not the Western Allies—would liberate Poland, Rumania, Bulgaria, the Baltic states and, very likely, Hungary, Austria and Czechoslovakia as well. (Actually, the Anglo-American armies came nearer to liberating Czechoslovakia and pushed further into Germany than any one could reasonably expect at the time of Teheran, or even at the time of Yalta.) What Roosevelt and Churchill tried to do, and believed they had accomplished, was to insure that the countries betrayed into Hitler's hands by appeasement, which were about to be "liberated" by Russia, would be restored *by Russia* to full sovereign independence and that their peoples would be given *by Russia* a degee of democratic freedom (in the Western meaning of the term) which most of them had never enjoyed in their pre-war history. To indulge in this hope seemed to this observer fantastic at the time and seems no less fantastic in retrospect. It would have seemed a dubious assumption, even if the Soviet Union had been a free democracy instead of a totalitarian dictatorship. It was one thing to believe that Russia's help in conquering Japan was essential and to make concessions—even immoral concessions—to obtain it. It was quite another thing to believe that Russian "liberation" of Eastern Europe would result in anything other than the establishment of Soviet-style "peoples' democracies," subservient to the dictates of the Kremlin.

The anxious state of ambivalence in which Churchill found himself after Teheran—as evidenced by his persistent eagerness to alter the Anglo-American strategy—showed that he only half-believed in the efficacy of any undertaking by Russia to grant real independence to countries over which she would exercise full military control. But, while Roosevelt lived, this fundamental reason for the "underbelly" strategy was never stated. The arguments Churchill put forward were not such as might appeal to Roosevelt or his military planners. The restoration of pre-war Mediterranean regimes and the maintenance of the British Empire "life-line" to India were motives for which Roosevelt could have a sympathetic understanding, but which he could not share. Nor did Churchill's dread of heavy casualties in a cross-Channel invasion awaken much of an echo in the determined minds of General Marshall and the American Chiefs of Staff. Against such sincere but not fundamental arguments for a different strategy, Roosevelt's anxiety to make friends with Russia and to obtain Russian aid against Japan remained paramount.

If the ultimate verdict of history should be that the Teheran-Yalta policy was a mistake, it will not be easy to assess the major responsibility for that mistake as between Roosevelt—who apparently had no misgivings whatever—and Churchill, whose European background and sharp instinct gave him a warning which he failed to understand and heed.

If, on the other hand, when the secrets of Soviet Russia are unlocked, it should appear that Roosevelt's trust in Stalin was merited and that the Russian ruler sincerely desired a peace without great Soviet expansion—that his later aggressive expansionism was the result of fear, inspired by the distrust which he sensed in Churchill—then the blame will rest not upon the Yalta agreement but upon the failure on both sides to maintain that mutual respect and trust which the agreement implied.

Whatever the hindsight verdict of history as to the basic wartime agreements, it is not necessary to await that verdict concerning the manner in which the Potsdam Conference endeavored to put those agreements into effect with respect to Germany. The prior commitment to Polish annexations of German territory provided no excuse for at least three major blunders of deadly consequence.

The first of these mistakes was to leave the question of Germany's western frontier unsettled, after deciding, to all intents and purposes, what was to be done in the East. The second and almost incredible blunder was to give France a zone of occupation and an equal voice on the Allied Control Council, without obtaining French signature to the four-power contract under which the Council was chartered to operate. These two matters were closely related.

The de Gaulle government wished to annex the Rhineland and the Saar or—at the very least—to have these areas separated from Germany. Once the Atlantic Charter pledges had gone overboard, this was not an unreasonable demand, if considered in the light of past French experience with Germany. On the other hand, a Germany deprived of Upper Silesian coal and industry and of its eastern breadbasket, could not live, much less become reasonably prosperous, if it were also to be deprived of its major industries and coal deposits in the West. Not only Britain and the United States but Russia, too, recognized this fact and, therefore, refused to accede to the French demands. The logical consequence would have been that France would either give up its demands or take no part in the occupation and management of Germany until a satisfactory solution had been found. Logic, however, played little part in the proceedings. France, still stubbornly clinging to its demands, was seated on the Allied Control Council and, since the decisions of that body were to be made only by unanimous consent, France was thus given a veto over all action *under an agreement to which it was not a signatory*. For the first crucial six months of the four-power experiment, France vetoed every act through which the Council sought to execute its mandate of governing Germany as a political and economic entity, forbidding even such purely symbolic actions as the issuance of uniform postage stamps for the four zones. This French intransigence brought about the wholly unplanned division of Germany into four, separate, hermetically sealed compartments, among which all trade, all travel and all political intercourse were inhibited. It was not at first Russian violation of the Potsdam agreement but French obstructionism that brought about the breakdown of the four-power plan. Soviet exploitation of the breakdown came later.

The third and perhaps the most fundamental error committed at Potsdam was to make the assumption that four victorious nations could impose what amounted to a social and economic revolution, without having first reached agreement among each other as to what kind of a new Germany they desired to create. This was as if four doctors were to undertake to treat a patient, without first reaching agreement as to the nature of his illness, the cure to be prescribed and the definition of what would constitute good health.

In addition to these basic blunders, the Potsdam agreement failed to resolve the conflicting interpretations of the Yalta agreement as to reparations; laid the foundations for the disastrous farce of "denazification;" and took over from a secret American directive a most unsatisfactory compromise between the Morgenthau Plan and the War and State Department view that Germany must be made self-supporting as quickly as possible.*

Apart from these specific actions with relation to Japan and Germany, the Potsdam conferees created a Council of Foreign Ministers to prepare the definitive peace treaties with the Axis

---

* This compromise directive, JCS 1067, was not published until some time after the conference. When submitted to the European Advisory Council prior to the Normandy landings, it had been rejected and was then issued to General Eisenhower as a directive applying only to the American troops under his command. The absence of any directive applicable to all the Allied armies when they began the occupation of Germany was responsible for the fact that each of the four zonal commanders proceeded along his own lines to remake his particular zone in the image of his own country. Three months of this divergent procedure established a number of mutually incompatible methods and principles even before a four-power agreement was finally reached at Potsdam. For a much fuller discussion of these problems and the documents pertaining thereto, see the author's *Germany—Bridge or Battleground* (Harcourt, Brace, 1947), and *Germany—Key to Peace* (Harvard University Press, 1953).

powers and their satellites. Originally, it was intended that the representatives of the United States, the Soviet Union, Great Britain, China and France should compose this organ. (Later, China was excluded from discussion of the European treaties; and the treaty with Japan was eventually negotiated by the United States without reference to the Council and without the participation of the Soviet Union.)

But for one remaining question, the Potsdam Conference completed the long list of wartime decisions which shaped the nature of the peace. The one matter, which had now become one for President Truman's sole decision, was whether and how the atomic weapon should be used against Japan.

From July 26, when the ultimatum was delivered, to August 5, the Japanese home islands were submitted to a concentrated air bombardment, designed to create popular support for the Emperor in ordering surrender. Leaflets warned the population to flee from cities listed for attack, but no mention was made of the impending use of a weapon which would make preceding attacks pale into insignificance. (There was no certainty that an atomic bomb dropped from the air would actually detonate.) With the Japanese government still refusing to accept the terms of surrender, the decision was reached to drop the first bomb upon Hiroshima and the second (there were only two) upon Nagasaki. Secretary Stimson and others concerned in the decision have described the basis upon which it was reached. The considerations were purely military—to save lives and hasten surrender by creating a face-saving situation in which the Emperor might reverse his previous position. The military effect was precisely that desired. Surrender talks began within four days of the dropping of the first bomb on August 6, 1945, and were completed by August 14. The formal surrender ceremony took place the next day on board the United States battleship *Missouri*.

World War II had ended; and so had that part of the world's history in which war could be considered an instrument of foreign policy.

Whether it was right or wrong—wise or unwise—to use the atomic weapon in the existing circumstances must be left to later judgment. It is not too soon, however, to recognize that, while military considerations dictated the decision, its political effects were far more important than the military result achieved. So far as one can evaluate the consequences today, these political effects were unfortunate rather than fortunate.

The fact that President Truman had casually told Stalin about the existence of a new superbomb could hardly prevent the Russian leaders from receiving a terrific shock when the wholly unprecedented destructive power of the new weapon was demonstrated. For them—as for the rest of the world—an entirely new situation was presented. The Russian leaders had been expecting to play a major part in bringing about the defeat of Japan. They were on the very verge of fulfilling their engagement to declare war within three months of the German surrender and did, actually, declare war on August 8. Moreover, the Russian leaders had been confident in their belief that, when the war ended, the Soviet Union would find itself in possession of power at least equivalent to that of the United States and Britain with the additional advantage of occupying a huge continuous land mass impregnable to attack by sea or air.

As of August 7, all this was changed. Russian help was not only unnecessary but unwelcome, and, in any case, too late. Air power had suddenly been lifted into a wholly new predominance over land power. So long as the United States might hold a monopoly of the new weapon, its power would be vastly greater than that of the Soviet Union—greater, in fact, than that of all the other nations of the world combined. Even a dictator, ruling over a long-suffering people firmly shackled under the terror of a police-state, would, in these circumstances, have to feel some apprehension concerning the impact of Hiroshima upon public sentiment—all the more so, because official propaganda had educated the Soviet people to believe that theirs was without doubt the most powerful of all the nations, that Russia had won the war almost single-handed *and* that Soviet science was far in advance of scientific development in the Western countries.

This revolution in the balance of power might have made a weaker man than Joseph Stalin more tractable. From Stalin it could only be expected to evoke the grim determination to acquire the atomic secret, to catch up to and surpass the United States in atomic power and, meanwhile, to push even further away from the Soviet Union the frontiers of its expanding empire.

Secretary Stimson has left an illuminating account of his own thoughts, doubts and misgivings in deciding to let loose upon the world the unpredictable consequences of the new weapon.* Deeply conscious of the responsibility which the monopoly of atomic power imposed and fully aware that the monopoly would soon be broken, Stimson pondered over how this new destructive power might be brought under control and how the fruitful benefits of atomic energy might be given to the world. His memoirs show at one and the same time how decent and sincere were this great American's motives and how little he or any of his associates in the great decision understood its consequences.

One cannot help wondering whether Roosevelt—had he lived and remained in full possession of his powers—might not have taken a different course. Doubtless, Roosevelt would have been no less eager and willing than Truman and Stimson to shorten the war and to minimize casualties, probably using the bomb on Japan, if that seemed necessary. One cannot help speculating, nevertheless, whether Roosevelt, with his extraordinary instinct and his much more intimate knowledge of Stalin's nature, might not have pursued a different course as to prior disclosure. Without revealing the secret of making the bomb, he might—for example—have coupled a full disclosure of its power of devastation with a proposal for the immediate postwar creation of a supranational authority, endowed with the power to prevent the manufacture of atomic weapons by any nation, including the United States. (The relatively minor risk of having the first two bombs fail to live up to expectations could have been eliminated by a further secret test.) Such a proposal could scarcely have failed to impress even Stalin and, at the time of Potsdam, not even Stalin could have interpreted this kind of generosity as weakness. A procedure of this sort might not have allayed all Stalin's suspicions, but it might

* Stimson, *op. cit.*, pages 634-655.

have gone far in that direction; and it would most certainly have prevented—even if rejected—the deeply disturbing shock of Hiroshima and the resentment which it engendered.

It is true that the United States made a proposal for the international control of atomic energy a year later. It is true that this was, in its basic conception, a generous proposition. But, in the meantime, the damage had been done and the cold war, though not yet recognized as such, had already started. By then, when the Russians rejected the proposal, most Americans were ready to accept the conclusion that the Russians were impossible people and that it was a waste of time to try to talk to them in any language other than that of force.

It may well be that, had such a proposal been made simultaneously with the disclosure of the bomb's existence, at Potsdam, Russian policy would have been no different. This remains a matter of conjecture. But there can be no doubt whatever as to the disastrous effect which the discovery and use of the bomb had upon subsequent American policy. Having vastly increased the danger of Russian hostility and reduced the hope of concluding the kind of peace to which it was committed, the American government now proceeded to act as if no danger existed, dismantling its vast military establishment, demobilizing its manpower, disposing of its war supplies and putting its great navy into mothballs. One may question seriously whether this folly would have been committed, even in the face of the strongest kind of popular pressure to "bring the boys back home," if the government of the United States had not felt so secure in its sole possession of the atomic weapon.

A further consequence of the great discovery which might have been foreseen, had wiser counsel prevailed, was that the sole possession of the atomic secret would inevitably attract spies as a magnet attracts steel filings. Given the manner in which the bomb had been used, it was, or should have been obvious that Russia would resort to any and all means of penetrating American security. This should have led to a most careful tightening up of internal security measures; but the same sort of complacency which led to the premature demobilization of the armed forces also produced a period of laxity in guarding against fifth-column penetration.

Thus, the last of the great wartime decisions—however wise it may have been from the point of view of military expediency —set in motion both here and abroad political and psychological forces which infinitely complicated the already complicated problems of the peace.

The postwar era began with mutual distrust already far advanced toward invalidating the basic assumption upon which the wartime leaders had based their plans and hopes of enduring peace. The postwar era began with each side feeling that it had already been to some extent betrayed by the other, with the experiment of great power cooperation on explicit trial in Germany, and with a new destructive force let loose in the world with which no one as yet knew how to deal. The United Nations had been brought into being to preserve peace, but, before the peace could be preserved, it had to be established. Whether it would be established depended primarily upon the two nations in whom power had become concentrated—the United States and the Soviet Union.

CHAPTER TWENTY-SEVEN

The Nature of the Crisis

(1945)

WORLD WAR II had been a national struggle for survival against threatened physical conquest; but it had also been in part a revolutionary civil conflict which crossed and recrossed national frontiers. The war of survival had created strange bedfellows, throwing democracies into alliance with dictatorships. The revolutionary struggle had not ended on VJ Day; it contained at least as many of the seeds of future trouble as the wartime decisions and actions of the anti-Axis coalition.

The two outstanding facts of the postwar world were:

1. That both the distribution and the nature of national power had radically changed, and changed in such a manner that it was no longer possible, after World War II, to make or maintain a traditional balance-of-power peace.

2. That the majority of the human race was in open revolt against the past and on the march toward a different future, without any very clear concept of what that better future was to be.

Neither of these two facts was fully grasped by the Western statesmen who endeavored to patch up the peace. Whether the Russian rulers understood them any better is not clear; all we can say is that they profited by Western failure to comprehend the changed nature of the world.

The change in the *distribution of power* was primarily due to a shift in the center of gravity of the Western world which had been going on almost imperceptibly throughout the first half of the century until accelerated by the impact of the two great wars. This transference of the seat of Western power from Western Europe to the United States left the European nations with the habit of exercising a power which they no longer possessed and the United States in possession of world power without either the experience or the inclination to exercise it. The result was the creation of a power vacuum in those parts of the world which had formerly been owned, controlled or dominated by Western Europe. The Soviet Union pushed aggressively into this vacuum. The United States was drawn into the empty space partly by the suction of the vacuum itself and partly because Soviet expansion demanded a counter-force. Neither the United States nor the Soviet Union created this condition. Its fundamental cause was the decline of Western Europe; and this, in turn, was brought about primarily by Western Europe's age-old inability to live at peace with itself.

The change in the *nature of power* was, quite simply, that the invention of atomic weapons of mass destruction had made victory in any future conflict so nearly indistinguishable from defeat as to invalidate the old axiom of General von Clausewitz that "war is the extension of policy by other means." General

H. H. Arnold, chief of the United States Army Air Corps in World War II, recognized the transformation when he said: "You can't win a war any more than you can win a fire."

What had happened was this: power had become concentrated in two great nations—the United States and the Soviet Union—neither of which fully understood that military power had become an instrument of suicide rather than of self-preservation. With power polarized in two superpowers, there could no longer be any maneuvering for equilibrium through the traditional process of shifting alignments among a number of more or less equally powerful nations. There could now be only peace through agreement or a struggle for preponderance of power between the two surviving giants—a struggle in which each of the two superpowers would quite sincerely believe that only its achievement of preponderance would guarantee peace. Peace by agreement could be achieved only if both sides renounced any ambition to dominate the world and if both sides recognized that the attempt to attain world domination would result in a war of mutual annihilation. This was one side of the postwar picture; the other concerned peoples rather than nations.

The world-wide revolution could clearly not be arrested. How might it be guided toward the achievement of justice and freedom by peaceful means? Here the outstanding fact was extremely difficult for Western statesmen to understand and accept. It was, quite simply, that the world had reached the end of a long period of its history in which a relatively small part of the human race, inhabiting first Europe and then the larger Atlantic community, had been able to exercise domination over the great mass of the world's peoples chiefly by reason of its superior skill in mastering man's physical environment. Western man had been rapidly losing the advantage which had made him supreme in the past. His own technology had eliminated time and distance, so that what was known one day in the capitals of the Atlantic community was known the day after in Tel Aviv and Tokyo and, the day after that, in New Delhi, Moscow and Peiping. No more revolutionary ideas had ever been hurled into the world than the messages of Western science, telling all men everywhere that there *could* be relief from hunger, pestilence and oppression—that it was not a cruel, immutable fate which doomed the majority of mankind to grinding poverty and ignoble servitude, but ignorance and man's inhumanity to man. The revolutionary realization of this fact by the suffering masses of mankind was not the product of Communist conspiracy or Marxist propaganda; it was the product of the material progress of Western civilization.

The existence of a Communist conspiracy serving the interest of a power-hungry Soviet dictatorship, and seeking to distort and capture the revolution of the oppressed, blinded Western leadership to the much more important fact that this revolution would have existed, had there been no Soviet Union and no Communist ideology. The unpalatable but inescapable truth was that the underprivileged two-thirds of humanity, composed mostly of the colored races, was no longer willing to remain submerged, and that Western man faced the choice of allying himself with the accelerating revolution or being submerged by it.

The defeat of European power by Japan, followed by the elimination of Japan as a power factor, left the peoples of Asia more on their own than they had been since the first European ships reached Asian ports. From the Far East the realization that the end of the white man's rule was at hand spread to the remnants of the European empires in the Middle East and in Africa. With the dawn of freedom on two vast continents came the inevitable problems of emergence into national independence and the strains and tensions created by the conflict between the old order and the new.

It was here that the United States had and missed its greatest opportunity for leadership. Its natural role would have been that of the Western friend and counsellor of the peoples emerging into freedom—the Occidental nation which had not been involved in the hated colonial past and which had freed its one colonial possession—the great and powerful people which had itself broken the trail of revolt against European colonialism. Had the United States been able to fulfill this role, it might have been in a position to exercise a guiding influence upon the Asian and Near Eastern revolutions. Washington, instead of Moscow, might have become the magnet of political attraction or, in any case, a much more powerful counter-force to the appeal of Communism.

Two factors unhappily stood in the way of this development. One was the American failure to solve the problems of race relations at home, bringing with it an almost unconscious assumption of white supremacy in dealings with other nations and peoples. (From the Asian point of view, using the atomic bomb only against Japan implied a contempt of the yellow race, even when it became known that the weapon had not been developed before the German surrender.)

The second limiting factor arose out of the nature of American postwar involvement in the affairs of Europe, which caused the United States to abandon its traditional anti-colonialism for the sake of strengthening European alliances contracted to contain the Soviet Union. In combination, these two factors made the United States appear to the emerging peoples as hostile to their aspirations and as the most powerful defender of the old order, rather than as the friendly guide to the new. The dissipation of what had been a great reservoir of good will toward the United States in the so-called underdeveloped areas of the world left the field open to Communist exploitation. This, more than any other single element, was responsible for the successes which Communism achieved in Asia.

(Ironically enough, it remained for the traditional leader of the European colonial powers to provide the greatest offset to American failure. The British action in freeing India, Burma and Ceylon, in 1948, went far toward establishing the much-needed new relationship between the colored peoples of Asia and the West. By then, it was too late to save China, but the Labour government's break with past centuries of empire-building and with Churchill's grim determination to hold on to every foot of empire soil probably saved the Indian sub-continent from a similar fate. At the very least, it prevented white prestige in Asia from falling to a point from which no recovery would have been possible.)

Before attempting to trace the origins of the European involvement which so largely stultified American policy in Asia, it is necessary to note certain wartime developments within

China which conditioned subsequent events. Differing with
Churchill's low appraisal of China's importance, Roosevelt had
firmly believed that China would and should become one of the
five most important nations in the postwar world. Roosevelt's
policy was directed not only toward helping China to expel the
Japanese but also toward healing the breach between the Nationalist government at Chungking and the Communist regime
at Yenan. Stalin gave every indication during the war that he
wished to see Chiang Kai-shek consolidate his power, expressing
on at least one occasion a rather contemptuous disdain of the
"so-called Chinese Communists." This may, of course, have been
guile, but it seems more likely that Stalin actually had little
interest in Mao Tse-tung until the latter had won his surprising
and spectacular victory. In any case, there is no evidence that
Russia in any way helped the Chinese Communists prior to
Japanese surrender.

American wartime policy in China had been more or less
neutral as between Chiang and Mao, seeking above all else to
bring about a reconciliation and a consequently stronger effort
against the Japanese. A sharp conflict over military strategy,
however, had political repercussions. One school of thought, led
by Major General Claire Chennault, held that the Japanese
could be driven from China by air power, provided that a
sufficient number of American planes, crews and supplies could
be flown in over "The Hump." The opposing school, led by
Lieutenant General Joseph P. Stilwell, asserted that the way to
defeat Japan in China was to insure land access from Burma
and to train and equip the maximum number of Chinese divisions. The Chennault school had little faith in Chinese troops.
The Stilwell school believed that, properly trained and
equipped, the Chinese would be equal to the Japanese. Moreover, the Stilwell people contended—and in this they were
proved correct—that the Chennault strategy would provoke
Japanese land offensives against the American air bases and thus
lead to a more extensive occupation of Chinese territory. The
compromise reached was "to try a little of both." This left each
commander feeling that his strategy would have succeeded if
supplies had not been diverted to the other. Secretary Stimson's
account of the controversy indicates that he thought Stilwell was

basically right. Chiang Kai-shek, however, could not tolerate Stilwell's crusty insistence upon reforms in the Chinese high command and eventually demanded his recall. Stimson expresses regret that President Roosevelt complied with this request, remarking somewhat ruefully that Stilwell "never quite made his number with the President." * The decision was important in its effect upon postwar developments.

Insofar as Stilwell's policy prevailed, it resulted in providing the Nationalist government with well-trained and well-equipped divisions which, had they been more numerous and more wisely employed after the Japanese surrender, might have succeeded in re-establishing Nationalist control over the northern provinces, or, at the very least, in preventing the total conquest of China by the Communist forces. As it turned out, the relatively few American-trained and American-equipped divisions gave an excellent account of themselves but were sacrificed by Chiang Kai-shek in an ill-advised move into Manchuria before he had consolidated his position south of the Great Wall. As early as November 20, 1945, Lieutenant General Albert C. Wedemeyer had warned Chiang against over-extending his position and reported to Washington: †

> I have recommended to the Generalissimo that he should concentrate his efforts upon establishing control in North China . . . logistical support for National Government forces and measures for their security in Manchuria have not been fully appreciated by him or his Chinese staff.

Subsequent disregard of this advice and the loss of the crack Nationalist divisions in Manchuria was the beginning of the military disaster which befell Chiang's armies.

With this background, we may now take up President Truman's conduct of postwar foreign policy.

* Stimson, *op. cit.*, pages 528-541.
† Department of State Publication 3573, page 131.

CHAPTER TWENTY-EIGHT

Truman, Byrnes and Marshall
(1945–1948)

WITH VICTORY ACHIEVED, President Truman faced two major tasks, one at home and the other abroad. The two problems were closely inter-related, although Mr. Truman did not appear to realize this for some time.

The domestic task was to reconvert an enormously expanded economy to the work of peace and reconstruction without letting it slip into a depression and another relapse into irresponsible "Normalcy." This presented less immediate difficulty than most economists had anticipated. It proved relatively easy to bring about reconversion without allowing the time-lag to bring on a serious slump. The backed-up demand for consumer goods, which had been scarce or unobtainable during the war, plus the accumulated savings of a fully employed population, created a ready market for just about everything that could be produced. The re-equipment of plants and a tremendous demand for new housing, new schools and new roads created a similarly insatiable market for the machinery of production. Instead of the expected deflation there was a strong inflationary trend marked by scarcity of goods and rising prices. In the face of this unexpected phenomenon, Big Business insistence upon the abolition of wartime controls and a return to "free enterprise," plus a lack of alertness on the part of the government, resulted in a premature jettisoning of rationing, price controls and allocation of scarce materials. This led to an unhealthily rapid rise of prices, profits and wages. Had it not been for unforeseen factors, arising outside of the framework of our domestic economy, the unhealthy boom would in all probability have collapsed in a major depression about two years after the war ended. It was not wise planning that prevented a serious depression but the suddenly realized need to create military strength in order to meet the catastrophic deterioration which had taken place in the relations between the West and the Soviet Union.

Before considering how this deterioration came about, it should be noted that the economic behavior of the United States in the early postwar period justly aroused doubts abroad as to American capacity for responsible leadership. With Great Britain and Western Europe struggling for bare subsistence and with food and consumer goods scarce in every part of the world, the picture of the world's wealthiest nation indulging itself in unrestrained luxury was not one to inspire confidence or respect. It looked, in fact, very much like another return to "Normalcy." This impression was heightened by President Truman's abrupt termination of Lend-Lease assistance without any apparent awareness of the problems of transition faced by our recent allies. When the Soviet Union requested a loan to assist its reconstruction of the devastated areas, the request was first "lost" for a period of several months in the files of the Foreign Economic Administration and then brusquely turned down. When Great Britain asked for similar assistance, the amount was cut in half and conditions attached which very nearly wrecked the British economy altogether. In the first winter of "peace," it became clear that the United States alone possessed the surplus resources to push the world economy off dead center and to start it toward recovery, but both the people and the government of the United States seemed almost wholly unaware of their responsibility.

This absence of American leadership and the apparent indifference of the American people toward what was going on in the rest of the world played directly into Soviet hands. The immediate postwar policy of the Soviet Union was one of nationalistic expansion combined with revolutionary penetration. Throughout the Continent of Europe and especially in those countries which had been occupied by the enemy, the Communist parties had gained enormously in prestige and influence. In part, this was due to the reflected glory of the Red Army; but, in large measure, it was because, throughout enemy-occupied Europe, the Communists had provided the disciplined spearhead of the resistance movement. In addition, the demoralization of European middle class leadership and the absence of a clear, pro-democratic Anglo-American policy during the war had permitted the Communists to pose as the standard-bearers of liberation. Thus the fifth-column tools of penetration were ready to Moscow's hand. In the winter of 1945-1946 they were used to the fullest possible extent.

In the one case where Moscow used the old-fashioned techniques of imperialist expansion, Western counter-action was effective; Soviet failure to evacuate northern Iran as per agreed schedule produced a prompt protest by the United Nations and forced a Soviet withdrawal. In other cases, where the Kremlin employed the more modern methods of fifth-column penetration, the Western powers found themselves frustrated in attempting to enforce—through the United Nations or outside of it—pledges which they thought they had obtained at Yalta. Western protests bogged down in endless wrangling over the meaning of "democracy" and "free elections." It became belatedly clear that these words had one meaning in London, Paris or Washington and quite another meaning in Moscow. The United Nations became more and more a forum for mutual recrimination.

During this unhappy period, the United States put forward its ill-fated proposal for the supra-national control of atomic energy. If adopted, this would have been a first step toward making the United Nations into an organization capable of administering and enforcing world law. Russia countered with an ambiguous proposal for international disarmament. Both proposals contained potential merit. Both were lost in the confusion of a debate which had little to do with the intrinsic matter.

With the dream-world of Yalta collapsing, with the United Nations rendered impotent, and with the laboratory test of great-power cooperation—the four-power experiment in Germany—clearly headed for disaster, one might have supposed that the United States would proceed cautiously in dismantling its military power. Granted that there was a great and understandable pressure to "bring the boys back home," two facts stand out clearly: no government which understood the situation it faced would have succumbed to that pressure; and the pressure itself would not have existed to such an extent if the American people had developed a political purpose in fighting the war—if they had been conscious of fighting not merely to defeat the enemy but to create conditions in which there could be reasonable hope of lasting peace. Instead, the American people were led, or led themselves to believe that peace would come semi-automatically with the cessation of war and that, thereafter, it would be semi-automatically preserved by the new machinery of the United Nations—provided only that they themselves did not repeat the mistake of refusing to join the world organization. President Roosevelt had made the fulfillment of that one condition easy by making the United Nations "acceptable." But acceptability had been purchased at the price of making the effectiveness of the world organization dependent upon the continuance of a coalition which was now rapidly disintegrating. If the American people had understood these facts—if these facts had been presented to them by their government—common sense might well have overruled emotion and the great power vacuum resulting from premature demobilization might never have been created.

The failure was not the failure of a man or a party in power. It was the result of a great delusion in which Republicans and Democrats alike had participated. By the time this was realized, the nation had stripped itself of power and the first phase of American postwar policy had ended.

The outstanding characteristic of the next phase of United States policy was disillusionment—disenchantment as to the good intentions of Russia, as to the effectiveness of the United Nations and as to the efficacy of diplomacy, with a corresponding shift to reliance upon physical force and a tendency toward unilateral action. Unfortunately, disillusionment did not mean facing reality. It meant escaping from reality into a second illusion, no less dangerous than the first. It meant swinging from naive over-optimism as to the nature and intentions of the Soviet regime to the conviction that an evil and implacable enemy was solely responsible for the failure to make and preserve a just peace—an enemy who did not want peace and with whom no agreement was possible.

Instead of trying to understand where and how we had gone wrong, we adopted the easy escape of finding a scapegoat. This change did not happen overnight. It began—if one can date such a phenomenon—with a speech at Fulton, Missouri, by Winston Churchill on March 5, 1946, with President Truman sitting by his side, beaming apparent approval. Shorn of its characteristic embellishments, the speech amounted to this:

> The world is now divided into capitalist and Communist blocs. To check the expansion of the Communist bloc, the English-speaking peoples—a sort of latter-day "master-race" —must sooner or later form a union. They should immediately contract a military alliance and coordinate their military establishments. They must lead "Christian" civilization in an anti-Communist crusade. They must hold on to the secret of the atom bomb. Only thus can a probable war be averted because the Soviet rulers respect strength and would probably come to terms with a powerful and determined Anglo-American alliance.

The speech was promptly repudiated by the British Labour government. In this country, the reaction was also generally unfavorable. One leading newspaper called it a "bombshell dropped into the peaceful streets" of the postwar world. Moreover, the suggestion that the United States should underwrite the British Empire was not considered very helpful in persuading a reluctant Congress to approve the then pending British loan. Yet, within a year, the essence of Churchill's proposal was to become the basis of a new American policy and, within two years, it was destined to become the policy of the British Labour government as well. The crux of Churchill's thesis was that the hopes entertained at Yalta were dead, that the Western camp must rearm and hold on to its atomic monopoly. Clearly implied was a renunciation of hope in the United Nations.

There was considerable speculation as to whether, by his apparent sponsorship, President Truman had meant to convey agreement or approval. This was denied, and it was undoubtedly true that Mr. Truman had not yet reached the somber conclusions at which Mr. Churchill had arrived.

During 1946, Secretary Byrnes traveled from one international conference to another, often failing to keep Washington informed as to the course of his negotiations. These concerned the working out of the Italian and Axis satellite peace treaties. Although the German settlement was clearly the central problem of the European peace, Mr. Byrnes proceeded, after a number of futile negotiations, to leave this matter aside, approaching it only from the periphery.*

Toward the end of 1946 a long-germinating precarious situation at the eastern end of the Mediterranean showed signs of coming to a head. Russia pressed Turkey for concessions in the control of the Dardanelles and—through Bulgaria and Jugoslavia—brought pressure upon Greece for frontier revisions. An American naval demonstration in the Eastern Mediterranean served notice that the United States might step in to take over British commitments in that area, if Britain's weakened condition should make such a move necessary. Nevertheless, Mr. Truman was still trying to think in terms of reconciliation. In his message on the State of the Union, delivered on January 7, 1947, he said:

> Whatever differences there may have been between us and the Soviet Union . . . should not be allowed to obscure the fact that the basic interests of both nations lie in the early making of a peace under which the peoples of all countries may return, as free men and women, to the essential tasks of production and reconstruction. . . Our policy toward the Soviet Union is guided by the same principles as will determine our policies toward all nations. We seek only to uphold the principles of international justice which have been embodied in the charter of the United Nations.

By this time Mr. Truman had accepted the resignation of Secretary Byrnes and asked General George C. Marshall to take his place. In part, this decision was probably due to the President's dissatisfaction with Mr. Byrnes' peripheral approach to the European peace and to his rather personal conduct of the Department's affairs. In part it may have been influenced by

---

* For a full account of the German negotiations and especially for a summary of the important speech delivered by Secretary Byrnes at Stuttgart on September 6, 1946, see *Germany—Bridge or Battleground, op. cit.*, Chapter 12, pages 99-118.

incompatibility of personality and outlook, especially in the matter of race relations. A more decisive factor, however, was that the Congressional elections of November, 1946, had given the Republicans control of both Houses; this made it essential for Mr. Truman to have a Secretary of State who stood above partisan politics and could command the respect of Republicans and Democrats alike. No one fulfilled these requirements as well as the wartime Chief of Staff.

In considering the development of the United States foreign policy during the two years of Secretary Marshall's tenure, it is important to bear in mind that throughout this period the President was operating with a hostile Congress. This handicap was to some extent overcome by the continuation of the "bipartisanship" which had originated during the war. Secretary Hull had long followed a policy of working closely with the Senate leadership. In 1944, by arrangement between President Roosevelt and Governor Dewey, Mr. John Foster Dulles had been taken into the inner circle of the State Department as Republican consultant. Mr. Byrnes had been accompanied on most of his travels by Senators Tom Connally, of Texas, and Arthur H. Vandenberg, of Michigan—the former Chairman of the Foreign Relations Committee, the latter its senior Republican member. From 1946 to 1948, this arrangement continued, except that the roles of Senators Vandenberg and Connally were now reversed.

When General Marshall took office he had just returned from a difficult mission in China. His assignment had been to mediate peace between the Nationalists and the Communists by getting both sides to agree to the formation of a non-Communist, left-of-center, progressive government. This had proved impossible, partly because of Communist intransigence and partly because the Nationalists were unwilling to undertake a long-overdue housecleaning and reform.

The fatal error of American policy in China had already been committed in the winter of 1945-1946 when the United States had straddled between washing its hands of the Chinese civil war or intervening with sufficient force to make its intervention decisive. The choice had been clearly put before the American government by its commander in the Chinese Theater, Lieutenant General Albert C. Wedemeyer. Defense Secretary Forrestal's record reveals that, on November 20, 1945, Wedemeyer's recommendation was either to withdraw all American troops at once or to announce continued military and economic support for Chiang. On the 23rd, he emphasized again that it would be impossible to support Chiang and at the same time stay clear of Chiang's war with the Communists, stating:

> "Such United States support to the National government will definitely involve American forces in fratricidal warfare. There can be no mistake about this. . . . If the unification of China and Manchuria under Chinese National forces is to be a United States policy, involvement in fratricidal warfare, and possibly in war with the Soviet Union, must be accepted and would definitely require United States forces far beyond those presently available in the theater to implement this policy." *

Faced with this dilemma, the Truman administration did the worst thing it could have done in the circumstances: it intervened on behalf of the Nationalists, thus incurring the lasting enmity of Mao Tse-tung, without intervening with sufficient force or determination to make its intervention effective. By granting large financial subsidies and supplying military equipment, without insisting upon reform of the Nationalist government, the United States burdened that already unpopular regime with the additional handicap of appearing in Chinese eyes as a foreign-sponsored puppet. Thereafter, it was clearly impossible for the United States to assume the role of impartial umpire and peacemaker. Yet this was essentially what President Truman had asked General Marshall to attempt.

President Truman's unwillingness to undertake a full-scale military intervention in order to insure Chiang's victory was based upon the correct assumption that the American people were in no mood to embark upon another war—least of all a war which might involve the Soviet Union. Furthermore, it seems doubtful in retrospect whether full-scale intervention could have saved the Chiang regime, even if Russia had stayed

* James V. Forrestal, *Forrestal Diaries* (Viking, 1951), page 111.

aloof. Only a self-reform so drastic as to capture the revolution from the Communists could probably have saved the regime, and such self-reform was no part of Chiang Kai-shek's program. On the other hand, President Truman's unwillingness to take the alternative of observing neutrality in the Chinese civil war stemmed directly from the traditional American proclivity to guarantee Chinese integrity. The result of the straddle was not that "we lost China to Communism," but that we lost all chance of establishing friendly relations with a Communist regime already destined to come to power, allying ourselves with a Nationalist regime already doomed by its own incompetence and corruption. Not even the wisest American policy could at this time have saved China from Communism, but a wiser American policy might not have driven Red China into the arms of Moscow; at the very least, it might have kept China neutral as between the emerging rival power orbits.

Having failed as a peacemaker, General Marshall wisely recommended withholding further aid to the Nationalist government, unless and until it might undertake the necessary reforms. This was a realistic view which recognized that the Chinese revolution could not be halted nor the Chinese people be forced back into the pattern of the past—that the only hope lay in recapturing the revolution from the Communists. For this, unhappily, it was too late.

Trouble was also brewing in French Indo-China, where France was seeking to re-establish colonial rule over the empire betrayed by Pétain. When the French decided to "teach the natives a lesson" by bombarding the defenseless port of Haiphong on November 27, 1946, they entered upon a war which was to drain France of strength and eventually to lead to a world crisis.

Returning from the Far East and appraising the situation with which he would have to deal in Europe, especially that brewing at the eastern end of the Mediterranean, Marshall at once invited John Foster Dulles to accompany him on his forthcoming trip to Moscow for the long-delayed conference on Germany. Next, he suggested to President Truman that, before the American delegation arrived at Moscow, it would be well for the United States to have assumed what he called "a military posture," indicating greater firmness of purpose than displayed in the past. The opportunity for the assumption of such a posture had for some time been knocking at the State Department's door.

The British had for weeks been urging that the United States take over their position in Greece and Turkey. Recently, they had announced that they would in any event be compelled to withdraw from Greece at the end of March, 1947. President Truman now laid before a group of Congressional leaders a proposal for assuming "a military posture" by taking over the guardianship of the Eastern Mediterranean. At this meeting, Senator Vandenberg is reported to have said: "Very well, Mr. President, if that is what you want, there is only one way you can get it. That is to make a personal appearance before Congress and scare the hell out of the country." The attribution and the quotation may be inaccurate, but it is reasonably certain that President Truman's famous message of March 12, 1947, delivered in a personal appearance before both Houses of Congress, was deliberately shaped to meet this requirement. With that message, the second phase of American postwar policy went into operation.

The President asked Congress for $400,000,000 to spend in Greece and Turkey "to maintain their national integrity," describing both countries as being in great danger unless they were helped to bolster their economies and their military establishments. In addition, Mr. Truman asked Congress to authorize "the detail of American civilian and military personnel" to provide for "the instruction and training of Greek and Turkish personnel." This was the concrete proposal. The President said that he was "fully aware of the broad implications involved" and proceeded to speak of them at length.*

Two excerpts give the main tenor of what was soon to be known as the Truman Doctrine, involving the United States in the preservation of "freedom" and "independence" in every part of the world.

* See author's *Put Yourself in Marshall's Place* (Simon & Schuster, 1948), pages 12-14 and 47-49.

One of the primary objectives of the foreign policy of the United States is the creation of conditions in which we and other nations will be able to work out a way of life free from coercion. . . . To insure the peaceful development of nations, free from coercion, the United States has taken a leading part in establishing the United Nations. The United Nations is designed to make possible lasting freedom and independence for all its members. We shall not realize our objectives, however, unless we are willing to help free people to maintain their free institutions and their national integrity against aggressive movements that seek to impose upon them totalitarian regimes. This is no more than a frank recognition that totalitarian regimes imposed on free peoples, by direct or indirect aggression, undermine the foundations of international peace and hence the security of the United States.

One should note here the implication that American objectives could not be realized through the United Nations but must be pursued by unilateral action. This was what Churchill had said a year earlier, except that he had pictured joint Anglo-American action.

The broad denunciation of all totalitarian regimes apparently harked back to Cordell Hull's speech of April, 1944, but it turned out to have a much narrower meaning. The President was not repeating Hull's assertion that totalitarian and democratic governments could not co-exist; he was not speaking of Franco's Spain, Salazar's Portugal or Peron's Argentina. Here, too, he was following Churchill's line as to "people who don't knock you down." He was not speaking of *all* totalitarian dictatorships but only of those imposed by Moscow. This became more explicit in the succeeding paragraphs:

The peoples of a number of countries of the world have recently had totalitarian regimes forced upon them against their will. The Government of the United States has made frequent protests against coercion and intimidation, in violation of the Yalta Agreement, in Poland, Rumania and Bulgaria. I must also state that in a number of other countries there have been similar developments.

At the present moment of world history, nearly every nation must choose between alternative ways of life. The choice is too often not a free one.

One way of life is based upon the will of the majority and is distinguished by free institutions, representative government, free elections, guaranties of individual liberty, freedom of speech and religion and freedom from political oppression. The second way of life is based upon the will of a minority forcibly imposed upon the majority. It relies upon terror and oppression, a controlled press and radio, fixed elections and the suppression of personal freedoms.

I believe that it must be the policy of the United States to support peoples who are resisting attempted subjugation by armed minorities or by outside pressure. . . .

The free peoples of the world look to us for support in maintaining their freedoms. If we falter in our leadership, we may endanger the peace of the world—and we shall surely endanger the welfare of our own nation.

The President was now for the first time endorsing Churchill's thesis that the world was divided between "good" and "evil"; that there were only two ways of life between which all peoples must choose. He was painting a world of blacks and whites, but his definition of white included such black regimes as that of Franco in Spain. It was not, in fact, a moral definition at all; it was power-political. What Mr. Truman really said was that the United States would help any nations threatened by Russian imperialism and Communist conspiracy—that the United States had appointed itself as global policeman and protector. To carry out this function would clearly require vast rearmament and the forging of military alliances. This was not mentioned. The President described his concrete proposal as requiring only $400,000,000, "less than one-tenth of 1%" of American investment in World War II.

In itself, the Greco-Turkish aid proposal was sound and courageous, necessitated not by moral considerations but by strategic needs. The over-all policy statement which accompanied the proposal was less a demonstration of "military posture" than of emotion-charged confusion. Its effect was to bewilder the American people, to frighten friends and potential allies abroad, and to serve notice upon the Kremlin that the United States had declared an undefined state of ideological and power-political war.

In the long and confused debate which followed, Senator Vandenberg managed to prevent an open affront to the United Nations by introducing an amendment, making American action subject to United Nations approval. While this debate was going on, Secretary Marshall was at Moscow, trying for the first time to come to grips with the situation which had arisen in Germany, but the Truman pronouncement had already wrecked what hope there might have been of coming to an understanding.

French obstruction to the working out of the four-power plan had brought about a peculiar and unforeseen situation. The Russians discovered that the unplanned partition of Germany actually worked out to their distinct advantage, because their zone produced more food than it consumed, while the deficit of the British and American zones required a subsidy from the occupying powers. Having discovered that they could milk the German cow at one end, while the Western powers were compelled to feed it hay at the other, the Russians were in no hurry to end this state of affairs. By the end of 1946, they rather than the French had become the chief obstructors to the working out of the Postdam Agreement.

During the first year of the occupation, the Russians took out of their zone about every moveable machine or piece of equipment. Having learned that this procedure did not greatly help their own reconstruction while destroying the productivity of their zone in Germany, the Russians then switched to a policy of taking reparations out of current East German production, rather than in capital assets. This was a clear violation of the Potsdam Agreement and produced one of the two major stumbling-blocks at the Moscow Conference of March-April 1947.

The other major issue upon which no agreement could be reached concerned the nature of the All-German state to be created and the structure of its government. The Russians wanted a strong central government through which they hoped to influence the course of future German development. The

French wanted extreme decentralization amounting to a loose confederation of German states. Britain and the United States stood in between, favoring a federal government of limited powers, with a considerable degree of home rule left to the component states. Disagreement among the Western powers placed them at a serious disadvantage in dealing with the Russians. An additional disadvantage resulted from Secretary Byrnes' ill-advised earlier agreement with France permitting the separation of the Saar from Germany and its incorporation in the French economy. This stultified the moral position of the Western powers in opposing the excessive annexations of German territory by Poland and the Soviet Union; it also gave Mr. Molotov the opportunity to cater to German sentiment by objecting to the Saar deal as unfair to Germany.

After weeks of fruitless negotiation, the Moscow Conference ended in complete failure. It served to clarify the issues but resulted in no progress toward their resolution. Secretary Marshall had done precisely what Secretary Byrnes should have done and had failed to do in 1946; that is, he had tried to grapple directly with the central problem of the European peace. Unfortunately, a settlement in Germany had now become dependent upon an over-all understanding between Russia and the United States. Whatever might have been the Kremlin's intentions on March 10, 1947, when the Conference opened, the Truman pronouncement of March 12 made Germany into merely one of many battle-fronts upon which the cold war would now have to be fought. The Russians were difficult after March 12 precisely because they wanted to be difficult and to delay a solution, hoping that, if a solution were postponed, the whole West European economy might collapse and alter the picture radically in their favor. Given the state of affairs in Britain and Western Europe in the spring of 1947, this was not an unreasonable expectation.

Western Europe was rapidly approaching the point at which actual starvation in the coming winter loomed as a serious probability. Its productive machine was almost at a standstill for lack of foreign exchange with which to buy raw materials. Without producing, it could not earn the dollars with which to buy much-needed food in the western hemisphere. An unusually harsh winter had made matters worse. The proceeds of the British loan were rapidly being exhausted—far more rapidly than had been anticipated, chiefly because of the uncontrolled, inflationary price rise in the United States which reduced the purchasing power of the borrowed dollars. The financial conditions attached to the loan were clearly going to bankrupt the British Treasury by mid-summer, unless the stipulated resumption of currency convertibility were to be waived or modified.

Without prompt and substantial American aid, it looked as if the Russian bet on economic chaos might well pay off in creating precisely the sort of political conditions best suited to Communist exploitation. European despair over American failure to understand the impending crisis had been increased not only by the belligerent and yet vague Truman Doctrine but by some remarks made by the President a week earlier in a speech at Baylor University. Speaking chiefly about foreign economic policy, Mr. Truman had declared:

> We are the giant of the economic world. Whether we like it or not, the future pattern of economic relations depends upon us. The world is waiting and watching to see what we shall do.

Having made this assertion, the President then proceeded to outline what he thought the future pattern of world economic relations should be. Briefly, what he had said was this: political freedom is bound up with freedom of individual enterprise; the pattern of international trade which promotes free individual enterprise and leaves the direction of movement of goods and services to private initiative leads to peace; government direction or control of international trade leads to war; therefore, we, upon whom the decision depends, are going to use our great economic power to set a world pattern of free-enterprise. Mr. Truman was not merely saying that the American system was the best system for the United States but that the whole world should adopt it because it alone could preserve peace and political freedom. This was not just a challenge to Socialist doctrine but to the considerable number of nations which had come to believe in or to accept as necessary some degree of government planning and control over their economies.

To the thinking European, this meant that American aid would be forthcoming—if at all—only to those countries which declared themselves willing to accept the American prescription. This impression was heightened by statements made by other American leaders to the effect that "the United States should not lend a cent to any country that socializes any of its industries." Even many of the more liberal Americans had not yet discovered that the West European Socialists were perhaps the sturdiest foes of Communism; nor did Americans as a whole realize that, to have capitalism, one must have capital; and that private capital scarcely existed in many parts of the world.

A ray of light penetrated into this gloomy picture in May, 1947, when Undersecretary of State Dean Acheson made a speech at Cleveland, Mississippi, scarcely noticed in the United States until after it had produced an audible sigh of relief in Europe. Emphasizing the staggering disparity in production between the United States and the rest of the world, Mr. Acheson outlined what he conceived to be the "requirements of reconstruction." These were: tariff reduction and greater imports; emergency financing of foreign purchases and reconstruction; concentration of American effort in areas where it would be most effective in promoting stability, freedom, liberal trade and the authority of the United Nations; reconstruction of the two great workshops—Germany and Japan—if necessary even without four-power agreement; and, finally, giving our own government power over the domestic sale, transportation and exportation of a limited list of scarce commodities.

This was the first constructive utterance on economic policy by an American high official since the defeat of Germany and Japan.*

A month later, on June 5. 1947, Secretary Marshall translated his Undersecretary's theory into practice, offering the economic assistance of the United States to "any government" (in Europe) "willing to assist in the task of recovery." The Secretary did not put forward a specific program, stating that this should be worked out by the European nations on a basis of mutual help

* The full texts of the President's speech at Baylor, on March 6, 1947, and of Acheson's address at Cleveland, on May 8, 1947, may be found respectively on pages 46-47 and 52-54 of *Put Yourself in Marshall's Place, op. cit.*

and self-help in which the United States would then participate. The key sentence in his speech, which made the proposal
seem like a reversal of the Truman Doctrine, was this:

> Our policy is directed not against any country or doctrine
> but against hunger, poverty, desperation and chaos.

Where the President had declared political and ideological
war, Secretary Marshall was now offering economic cooperation,
not just to those nations who promised to hate Communism
and to love free enterprise, but to any and all "willing to assist
in the task of recovery." This included the Soviet Union and
its satellites, provided only that they agreed to cooperate.

Until the Kremlin's archives are unlocked to the historian,
we can only guess at the reasons which prompted the Russian
rulers to reject this offer and to prevent their satellites from accepting it. One thing is certain: if the Russian purpose was to
frustrate a plan which the Kremlin may have considered merely
a more intelligent extension of the Truman Doctrine, then Mr.
Molotov made a major blunder in not accepting Mr. Marshall's
invitation. Had Russia accepted, it is most unlikely that the
Marshall Plan would ever have been approved by a Congress
aroused to suspicion and hatred of the Soviet Union by the
President. Whatever the reasons for Mr. Molotov's well-known
walk-out, it converted the Marshall Plan, which might have
ended the cold war, into a highly effective Western instrument
in its prosecution.

The sixteen nations of Western Europe lost no time in formulating their mutual aid plan. On this side of the Atlantic,
however, progress was extremely slow. The President appointed
several commissions to study European needs and to prepare
recommendations to be presented to Congress in January, 1948,
not apparently realizing that the European crisis would come to
a head long before any such leisurely schedule could be completed. The psychological impact of the Marshall promise inspired the European peoples with new hope and new energy;
they could now see their way out, but a changed psychological
climate was not enough to meet the need for immediate financial assistance. The British position was alleviated by last-
minute American agreement to the restoration of currency

controls, after a few weeks of convertibility had all but exhausted the reserves of the British Treasury. But a severe
drought followed the harsh winter, leaving Austria, France
and Italy face to face with starvation, unless interim relief
enabled them to purchase food for the winter. In the face of
these conditions, the Truman administration was almost incredibly slow to take action. The President and the Secretary
of State went to Brazil to attend an Inter-American Conference.
Not until September 3 did Undersecretary of State Robert A.
Lovett finally warn: "It is later than we think." Marshall, returning the following week, endorsed Lovett's warning, but the
President, boarding the battleship *Missouri* for a leisurely trip
home, declared that there was "nothing on the horizon to require a quick return to the United States."

Arriving in Washington, Mr. Truman announced that
France, Italy and Austria would need substantial aid to see
them through until the end of March, by which time the Marshall Plan would presumably be in effect, and that he was
asking the Congressional leaders to call their committees in
October. The *New York Times* remarked editorially:

> The Marshall Plan, temporary aid, food conservation and
> price controls cannot be more than dreams without popular
> support and understanding. These cannot be enlisted with-
> out courage, conviction and leadership which, it appears, are
> not to be had from President Truman.

It was not until late October that the President finally made
up his mind to call a special session of Congress. In his message
to the special session, Mr. Truman asked for $597,000,000 in-
terim aid and for authority to apply price controls and rationing of scarce commodities, if necessary to curb the inflationary
domestic cycle. (Only a week or so earlier, Mr. Truman had
denounced rationing and price controls as "the methods of a
police state.") Under the leadership of Senator Robert Taft, of
Ohio, Congress enacted an "Anti-Inflation Bill" which gave the
President none of the powers necessary to control inflation. Interim aid was reduced to $540,000,000, of which $18,000,000
was earmarked for Chiang Kai-shek's Nationalist regime due to
the insistent demands of the Luce publications and a lobby led

by Governor Dewey of New York and former Ambassador William C. Bullitt. On December 19, the President gave Congress the plan prepared by the sixteen nations of Western Europe, along with the recommendations of the study commissions.* The recommended compromise called for a four-year program amounting to $17,000,000,000.

While these leisurely moves were in progress in the West, the Soviet leadership was not idle. A rival "Molotov Plan" was developed to "promote the recovery of Eastern Europe." This took shape in a series of secret bilateral trade treaties between the Soviet Union and its satellites. At the United Nations Assembly, in September, Andrei Vyshinsky launched into vitriolic abuse of the Western powers and especially of the "imperialist designs" of the United States. On October 5, Moscow announced the organization of the "Cominform"—a permanent coordinating committee of the Communist parties of the United Soviet Socialist Republic, Poland, Czechoslovakia, Hungary, Rumania, Bulgaria, Jugoslavia, France and Italy. This was a revival of the old Comintern, signaling a return to an aggressive policy of fostering revolution. All these moves indicated that whereas the Kremlin had been more angered than worried by the declaration of the Truman Doctrine, it was seriously alarmed by the Marshall Plan.

In an atmosphere of mounting tension, the Council of Foreign Ministers met at London in late November to make one more half-hearted attempt to reach agreement on Germany and Austria. The conference adjourned after three futile weeks of discussion without even fixing the date for another meeting.† The world was now clearly divided into two openly hostile camps. The question was whether these two rival orbits would compete by peaceful means, each seeking to outstrip the other in reconstruction, or whether competition would assume a more dangerous form.

The failure to resolve the deadlock in Germany clearly fore-

* For the full texts of the relevant Presidential messages, the committee reports and Senator Taft's attack on the Truman proposals, see pages 66-81 of *Put Yourself in Marshall's Place, op. cit.*

† For Secretary Marshall's important pronouncement of policy of November 18 at Chicago and his report on December 19 on the failure of the London Conference, see *ibid.*, pages 81-85.

shadowed the events to come. Former President Hoover had already suggested the creation of a West German state and the making of a separate peace.* This idea was now rapidly gaining adherents and was soon to take form in action which would cause the permanent partition of Germany and a crisis over the continued maintenance of the Western sectors of Berlin.

1948 was an election year which, as usual, distracted American attention from the turbulent events abroad and rendered doubly difficult the conduct of foreign relations.

The outstanding events in Europe were: the Communist coup in Czechoslovakia (February 17); the Brussels Treaty (March 17); the London Agreement (June 2) leading to the merger of the three Western zones in Germany; the Russian blockade of Berlin and the beginning of the Airlift; the mysterious death of Andrei Zhdanov, head of the Cominform; and the sudden defection of Jugoslavia from the Soviet orbit.

The freeing of India, Burma and Ceylon; the division of India and Pakistan, followed by their dispute over Hyderabad; the emergence of Israel, and the subsequent war between Israel and the Arab states were the major developments in the Middle East.

In the Far East, 1948 marked the Indonesian struggle for independence from the stubbornly resisting Dutch; the arbitrary division of Korea at the 38th parallel; and the beginning of the rout of Chiang Kai-shek's Nationalist forces after the loss of Mukden on October 30.

In neighboring Latin America, the year was marked by a series of revolutions and military usurpations in Costa Rica, Colombia, Paraguay, Peru and Venezuela.

The Communist seizure of power in Czechoslovakia rudely awakened the Western world to the realization that the Kremlin would not rest content with tightening its hold upon its existing orbit of power but would seek to expand it wherever and whenever an opportunity might present itself. The event shook Western Europe out of preoccupation with its own af-

---

* In a letter to Congressman John Taber, dated May 26, 1947. For text see *ibid.*, pages 54-55. For a full discussion of the subsequent developments in Germany and the evolution of United States policy with respect to Germany, see *Germany—Key to Peace, op. cit.*

fairs and altered the indifferent attitude of the Truman administration, the Congress and the people, sharply increasing the tempo of policy development.

On March 17, 1948, Britain, France and the Low Countries signed a treaty of mutual military and economic assistance. On the same day, President Truman appeared before Congress to demand prompt passage of the European Recovery Plan, more funds for Greece and Turkey, $500,000,000 for Chiang Kaishek and the enactment of universal military training and peacetime selective service.

Welcoming the signature of the Brussels Treaty, the President implied that the United States would aid the signatories in case of need. As in the preceding year, it was not what Mr. Truman proposed, but the context in which he put forward his proposals that was significant. Whereas, in March, 1947, the President had been vague and contradictory in the statement of a belligerent attitude, he was now no less belligerent but very much more precise. His analysis of the crisis in world affairs was stated in four short paragraphs:

1. The situation in the world today is not primarily the result of the natural difficulties which follow a great war. It is chiefly due to the fact that one nation has not only refused to cooperate in the establishment of a just and honorable peace, but—even worse—has actively sought to prevent it.

2. The agreements we did obtain, imperfect though they were, could have furnished the basis for a just peace—if they had been kept. But they were not kept. They were consistently ignored and violated by one nation.

3. One nation has persistently obstructed the work of the United Nations.

4. The Soviet Union and its agents have destroyed the independence and democratic character of a whole series of nations in Eastern and Central Europe. It is this ruthless course of action and the clear design to extend it to the remaining free nations of Europe that have brought about the critical situation of Europe today.

President Truman had now persuaded himself and sought to persuade the nation that the Soviet Union alone had caused and was causing the critical state of world affairs. This simple and easy analysis totally ignored the basic factors outlined in the preceding chapter; it ignored the change which had taken place in the distribution and in the nature of national power as well as all the facets of a social, economic and technological revolution which had been exploited but certainly not created by the Kremlin.

The specific charges with which the President sought to buttress this devil-theory of the world crisis were by no means accurate. The basis for a just and honorable peace had been laid down in the Atlantic Charter and reaffirmed in the United Nations Declaration of January, 1942. It had been destroyed not by the Soviet Union alone but by Roosevelt, Churchill and Stalin at Teheran and Yalta. Mr. Truman contended that the agreements reached with the Soviet Union would have furnished the basis for a just and honorable peace, if they had been kept; but that Russia, and Russia alone, had violated them. Did Teheran, Yalta and Potsdam lay the foundations for a just and honorable peace? And had only Russia violated the Potsdam Agreement? As for obstructing the work of the United Nations, it was true that Russia had argued, wrangled and vetoed until everyone's patience was exhausted; but it was also true that the United States had undermined the authority of the United Nations by acting unilaterally outside of the world organization in developing its major policies both in Europe and in Asia and that the United States had flagrantly flouted a United Nations decision as to Palestine. Finally, Mr. Truman charged that Soviet destruction of "the independence and democratic character of a whole series of nations in Eastern and Central Europe" had brought about the crisis. As a matter of fact, none of these nations, except Finland, had ever been truly independent. Before the first World War all but two had not existed. Between the two wars, most of them had been members of the Little Entente, dependent for their security upon the French army. Certainly there was a vast difference between dependence upon a friendly power and subservience to a ruthlessly dictatorial overlord, but the Czechoslovakia of 1928 had been just as careful not to offend France as the Czechoslovakia of 1947 had been careful about offending Russia. As for the destruction of "democratic character," this was tragically true in the case of Czechoslovakia; but most of the other Eastern and Central European nations had never had a "democratic character" to destroy; they had been ruled by feudal squire-archies which exploited their predominantly peasant populations.

The inaccuracy and exaggeration of Mr. Truman's charges did not offset the strength of the case that might justly have been made against the Kremlin. The Kremlin *had* violated pledges, obstructed settlements, abused the United Nations and invaded the rights of neighboring peoples. The Kremlin *had* made dealing with an enormously complicated world crisis infinitely more difficult. But the Kremlin had not originally caused the crisis; it had not been a prime mover in the endless quarrels which had brought about the decline of Western Europe; it had exploited but had certainly not created the Far Eastern revolution; it had made almost no contribution to the technological and scientific advance which had kindled the smoldering discontent into flame.

The importance of this distinction between fact and exaggeration was not in any injustice done to a Soviet regime which amply deserved well-documented condemnation; the importance of Mr. Truman's failure to understand the true nature of the crisis and the exact relationship to the crisis of Soviet behavior lay in its effect upon United States policy.

The first result of accepting the scapegoat analysis was that it blinded the American policy-makers to their own past errors. Indeed, it implied that there had been few if any errors committed.

The second consequence was the adoption of an essentially negative over-all aim—the aim to stop Russia (or Communism) from making any further inroads into what now began to be called "the free world." (Many of the nations and peoples in the so-called "free world" were far from free in any true sense of the word, but, in the American vernacular, "freedom" now came to mean freedom from Soviet or Communist domination.) This negative aim of containing Soviet-Communist imperialism demanded that the United States devote its resources and energies not to creative purposes such as reconstruction and economic development, but to building a physical wall manned by physical force around the vast periphery of the Soviet orbit. Wherever Russia might attempt to push forward, the United States would be committed to exert counterpressure. American moves would be dictated by whatever moves the Kremlin might make—or by American guesses as to what those moves might be.

This negative orientation placed the United States on the defensive—a posture which is militarily unprofitable, incompatible with the American temperament, and unsuited to achieving leadership.

In addition, the policy of containment tended to make the United States the defender of the status quo, thus alienating many by no means pro-Communist peoples who sought change of one sort or another, especially in Asia and in the Arab world, where a desire to shake off colonial or semi-colonial dependence was far stronger than fear of Soviet aggression or Communist penetration.

Finally, the determination at all costs to forge a ring of steel around the Soviet periphery caused the United States to embark upon a frantic search for allies. In this search, anti-Communism and the possession of potential military power or strategic bases became the prime consideration. Apart from the democracies of the Atlantic community and the nations of the British Commonwealth, allies conforming to these requirements were most readily to be found among those nations and groups within nations which opposed all change from the existing state of affairs. Thus the policy of containment pushed the United States from the outset not only toward the support of European colonialism, which involved bases and strategic materials, but toward collaboration with feudal rules, princelings and puppets who opposed not only Communism, but any form of social change. Containment, undertaken in the name of a crusade for freedom and democracy, led to the making of alliances with outright dictators, such as Franco, and with corrupt, anti-democratic regimes such as that of Chiang Kai-shek.

So far as Asia was concerned, United States policy in 1948

consisted of little more than pouring huge sums of money into the sieve of Chiang Kai-shek's tottering Nationalist regime. In Indo-China, where the French were now bogged down in a stubborn colonial war, the United States exerted no effective influence in the direction of a more enlightened policy; as a result, Vietnamese nationalism was rapidly being captured by the Communists. In the Indonesian struggle for independence, the American position wavered between support of the Dutch and the Indonesian nationalists seeking independence.

So also in the Near East, American policy in the struggle between the Arabs and the new state of Israel vacillated between sympathy for Israel and the desire to avoid a break with the openly pro-Arab policy of Britain's foreign minister, Ernest Bevin.

One might almost say in retrospect that there was no American foreign policy except with regard to Europe. In this area, Secretary Marshall's program was energetically and ably pursued. Once Congress had passed the European Recovery Plan, no time was lost in setting up the administrative agencies in Paris and Washington. Aid began to flow and production was stimulated beyond expectations. The one great brake upon West European recovery was the demoralized state of the West German economy, but this obstacle was overcome in mid-summer by the merger of the Western zones and the introduction of the long overdue currency reform. Writing down the inflated German currency at once set off a spectacular recovery, but the consolidation of the Western zones and the introduction of the new currency into the Western sectors of Berlin produced the predictable crisis over Berlin. The blockade and counter-blockade and the dramatic Allied airlift continued to hold the Berlin position in a stalemate throughout the remainder of the year.*

In the Mediterranean area, the Italian elections resulted in the defeat of the Communists by the Christian Democratic party, led by Alcide de Gasperi and strongly supported by both American and Vatican influence. Turkey was being rapidly

---

* For a detailed account of the Russian blockade and the manner in which it was met, see Lucius D. Clay, *Decision in Germany* (Doubleday, 1950). For a shorter analysis, see *Germany—Key to Peace*, pages 58-77.

strengthened. American intervention in Greece was narrowly saved from failure by the most sensational development in Europe during the year 1948; namely, the sudden defection of Jugoslavia from the Cominform. The closing of the Jugoslav-Greek border deprived the Greek Communists of their most valuable sanctuary and wrecked their chances of gaining control.*

These gains for the Western cause were somewhat offset by the instability of France, plagued by recurring cabinet crises and by the inability of the Western powers to reach any real agreement among each other with regard to the German future, although Germany was more and more clearly becoming the focus of the struggle for the control of Europe. Yet, on the whole, the year showed a marked strengthening throughout Europe of the anti-Communist cause.

The reverse was the case as to Asia. By the end of the year all of China down to the Yangtze River was in Communist hands.

Prior to the November elections, practically everyone except Mr. Truman expected that he would be soundly defeated. At the United Nations session in Paris, both Secretary Marshall and Mr. Dulles prepared for an interregnum during which Secretary Marshall expected to be a "lame-duck" incumbent and Mr. Dulles confidently looked forward to becoming Secretary of State designate under President-elect Thomas E. Dewey. The President's vigorous campaign, however, marked by a slashing attack upon the "Republican Do-Nothing 80th Congress," gained him not only a personal triumph but recaptured for his party the control of Congress.

With his position now more secure, Mr. Truman gave additional impetus to the secret negotiations being carried on with Canada and the Brussels Treaty Powers toward the creation of a North Atlantic Defense Alliance. This project, derived from Senator Vandenberg's resolution, overwhelmingly passed the Senate on June 11, 1948, authorized the President to enter into defensive alliances consistent with the United Nations Charter and to extend military aid to nations willing to join the United

---

* Vladimir Dedijer's *Josip Broz Tito* (Simon and Schuster, 1953) reveals much of the background to the events of 1948.

States in seeking to preserve peace. (The Vandenberg Resolution marked a clear departure from the traditional policy of avoiding "entangling alliances.")

Shortly after the elections, Mr. Truman initiated a move (abandoned upon urgent cabled request from both Marshall and Dulles) to send Chief Justice Vinson to Moscow to see what might be done to end the Berlin deadlock. Neither Secretary Marshall nor Mr. Dulles were now particularly anxious to end this stalemate since it would involve talking to Moscow about German re-unification.* Both were committed to creating a West German state.

At the end of the year it was announced that ill-health necessitated Secretary Marshall's retirement and that the former Undersecretary of State, Dean Acheson, would be appointed in his place.

CHAPTER TWENTY-NINE

Truman and Acheson
(1949–1952)

MR. ACHESON successfully took the initiative in calling for the withdrawal of Dutch troops from Indonesia and the holding of free elections, but in China he inherited a position which was already out of control. During 1949 the Chinese Communists swept southward from the Yangtze valley gaining control of the entire Chinese mainland. The Nationalist armies melted away, losing their American-supplied equipment to the Communists or deserting with it. Chiang Kai-shek fled to Formosa with the remnants of his forces and established a government-in-exile. The Korean deadlock continued.

* *Germany—Key to Peace, op. cit.,* pages 70-71.

The Department of State issued a detailed White Paper, explaining what had happened in China and placing the major part of the blame upon the corruption and incompetence of the Nationalist government. This produced indignant denunciation by the pro-Chiang publicists, who not only insisted that a faulty American policy had produced the disaster but were beginning to suggest that American policy had been influenced, if not dictated, by Communists or pro-Communists in the State Department.

The one creative note struck in 1949 was President Truman's announcement, in his Inaugural Address, of a "bold, new program" of technical assistance to "the underdeveloped areas" of the world. This apparent reversion to the type of thinking which had produced the Marshall Plan produced a short-lived hope that the United States might be embarking upon a more affirmative policy. It soon developed, however, that the so-called "Point Four Program" was conceived in such narrow terms as to make it a relatively minor factor in the world situation. Congress showed little enthusiasm in following the President's lead and the administration itself made only a half-hearted effort to put through even a nominal fulfillment of the hope-inspiring promise.

Secretary Acheson's major efforts were directed to Europe. The airlift and the counter-blockade had convinced the Kremlin that the Western powers could not be forced by any means short of war to give up their hold on the Western sectors of Berlin and that a continuation of the blockade would not prevent the West from consummating its plan for the creation of a West German state. With the Berlin crisis on the way to solution, Mr. Acheson faced two major decisions: *first,* whether to continue or reverse the trend toward the formal creation of two German states; and, *second,* whether to make the proposed Atlantic Alliance into a simple declaration of solidarity with Western Europe or to stretch it into a commitment to defend Western Europe's frontiers against a possible invasion.

In dealing with the first problem, Mr. Acheson quickly abandoned any thought of an All-German settlement, proceeding to carry the trend toward formal partition beyond the point of no return. During his first months in office, Mr. Acheson energetically fostered the creation of a new Federal Republic of West Germany. After the first free elections held on German soil since 1932, this new West German state came into being in August, with its capital at Bonn and with Dr. Konrad Adenauer as its first Chancellor, heading a coalition of Right and Center parties. Moscow protested the creation of the West German state as a violation of the Potsdam Agreement and, two months later, proceeded to convert the Soviet zone into a "German People's Republic," with a government allegedly elected but actually selected and imposed by the Kremlin.*

The West was now committed to a policy of subordinating its original aim of German unification to the integration of West Germany in the Marshall Plan community. From the point of view of enabling Western Europe successfully to compete in economic progress with the Soviet orbit in the East, this was, indeed, essential. From the point of view of achieving a European peace settlement, this policy meant an indefinite postponement. There could be no lasting peace settlement with a divided Europe; there could be no re-unification of Europe without a re-unification of Germany; there could be no re-unification of Germany so long as the West based its policy upon the inclusion of two-thirds of Germany in the Western half of a divided European community.

The American policy, accepted with some misgivings by the British and with extreme reluctance by the French, pre-supposed that an eventual European peace settlement could be brought about only by making Western Europe—including Western Germany—so strong and prosperous that its power of attraction for the peoples of Eastern Europe would become irresistible. This, in turn, pre-supposed that when this point was reached, the Kremlin would listen to the demands of the Eastern peoples. In Mr. Acheson's own words, his policy was to create "situations of strength from which to negotiate." Had this policy remained one of creating only economic strength and political stability, it might conceivably have succeeded. It could not possibly succeed, if the integration of West Germany

* For a full account of the birth of the two Germanys and an analysis of the West German elections, see *Germany—Key to Peace, op. cit.,* Chapter 6.

in Western Europe should come to involve a military integration. In that case, no amount of "attraction" would cause the Kremlin to relinquish its hold upon the East.

This was where danger lurked in the projected Atlantic Alliance.

The North Atlantic Treaty, as laid before the Senate for confirmation in April, 1949, involved, in essence, nothing more than a declaration by the United States that, if any of the European signatories, or Canada, were attacked by an aggressor, the United States would consider such an act of aggression as an attack upon itself. In other words, the United States was now undertaking to create the same sort of deterrent to aggression which, had it existed in 1939, might have prevented World War II; it was putting a putative aggressor on notice that an attack against the West European signatories would involve the aggressor in war with the United States. So far, so good.

The impression prevailed in Europe that the proposed treaty meant considerably more than this. France, for example, was not interested in a promise to be avenged and once more liberated, if invaded and occupied. Premier Henri Queuille had made this explicit when he said: "Next time you would be liberating a corpse." What the Europeans wanted and expected was not only an American undertaking to fight an aggressor but an undertaking to fight such an aggressor at the frontiers of Western Europe—not merely a declaration of solidarity which might deter aggression, but a promise of protection against invasion in case the deterrent should fail to prevent an attack. The only honest answer to this perfectly natural and understandable attitude would have been: "What you are asking is an unfulfillable promise. There is no way to protect you against invasion except by preventing that invasion from being launched. This we shall try to do by declaring that war against you means war against us and by making ourselves so strong that an aggressor will hesitate to embark upon an adventure which he knows will entail fighting us as well as you."

Neither President Truman nor Mr. Acheson had made this reply. When the Treaty came before the Senate, it was not clear what the proposed commitment entailed. Mr. Acheson, testifying before the Foreign Relations Committee, made three statements from which it could be inferred that no further commitment was involved than that explicitly stated in the Treaty. He said: 1) that it was not intended to create any substantial additional European forces but merely to modernize and re-equip the existing West European divisions (of which there were about twelve); 2) that it was not intended to send any additional American divisions to Europe beyond the two already stationed in Germany; and 3) that, in no circumstances, would the United States consider remilitarizing or rearming West Germany.*

This seemed to dispose of the question. Senators Connally and Vandenberg, the Democratic and Republican leaders, publicly stated that the Treaty involved no commitment to defend the West European frontiers in the event of war.† The Treaty was ratified on that assumption. Yet, when the Military Aid Bill was presented to the Senate a few weeks later, the administration described its purpose to be that of placing the West European nations in a position to hold off invasion "until our own power could be brought to bear." ("Our own power" consisted at the time of only 10 combat-ready divisions. Russia had at least 150 divisions available.)

Neither President Truman nor Secretary Acheson have to date explained how they thought it would be possible to insure Western Europe against Russian invasion by merely modernizing and re-equipping the twelve then-existing West European divisions. The promises not to divert Western Europe from recovery to rearmament, not to send additional American troops abroad and not to rearm or remilitarize West Germany were, no doubt, given in good faith; yet all of them were broken within less than two years. The repudiation of these assurances cannot justly be attributed either to Russia's unexpected success in making an atomic bomb nor to the outbreak of war in Korea. The announcement of the first atomic explosion in the Soviet Union in September was accompanied by

* For a full account of the Committee hearings and the subsequent reversal of the assumptions upon which the Senate ratified the Treaty, see Germany— Key to Peace, op. cit., pages 80-115.

† See the New York Times, May 11, 1949.

an explicit statement by the White House that this event entailed no change in American policy. Long before the North Korean aggression, in June, 1950, plans for German rearmament were being openly discussed here and abroad.* It is difficult to see how the American government could have avoided breaking either the promises given to the Senate or the promises given or implied to Western Europe. To defend Western Europe in central Germany inevitably required augmenting both the West European and the Anglo-American forces, and this would predictably lead to the conclusion that, if West Germany was to be defended, the Germans should contribute to their own defense.

Although it was announced that the atomic explosion in Russia would involve no change in American policy, this event did, as a matter of fact, bring about the launching of an extremely important program; namely, the so-called "crash program" for the immediate development of the thermo-nuclear or hydrogen bomb. President Truman's decision to proceed at full speed with this project was reached after several months of debate within the inner councils. Several members of the Atomic Energy Commission, including its then chairman, David Lilienthal, expressed serious reservations. It was feared that concentration upon developing the new super-weapon would delay the development of atomic artillery, of guided missiles with atomic war-heads, and other tactical weapons. Among the scientists, there was a moral reluctance to develop a means of mass annihilation more terrible by far than those already threatening civilization with extinction. It was felt that, before this fateful step were undertaken, there should be further efforts to bring all weapons of mass destruction under international or supranational control. The President, however, sided with those among his advisers who felt that the United States must at all costs perfect the thermo-nuclear bomb before the Soviet Union might succeed in doing so and thus acquiring a blackmail power over the entire world. The decision to proceed was announced in January, 1950. The reasons for the decision are clear, but, from the information so far made

* *Germany—Key to Peace, op. cit.,* pages 125-133. This whole matter remains a somewhat disturbing enigma for which no explanation has been offered.

available, it is not clear why the decision was publicly announced. If the announcement was intended to open the way for a renewed attempt to negotiate with Russia, no such negotiations resulted.

In May, 1950—a month before the North Korean aggression took place—an event occurred in Europe which might have altered the whole course of the cold war. At a meeting in London the French foreign minister, Robert Schuman, disclosed to his British and American colleagues a brilliantly conceived plan for the merger of the coal and steel production of Europe under a supranational authority, designed primarily to bring France and Germany together in an economic union indissoluble by war. The plan was explicitly stated to be open to participation by any European country willing to place its coal and steel production under joint supranational control. Coal and steel being equivalent to war potential, the plan, if adopted, would make any future war among its participants well-nigh impossible.

Unhappily, three developments occurred which undermined the great political potential of this proposal.

First: the United States anxiously demanded to know whether Mr. Schuman really meant to leave the plan open to nations in the Soviet orbit; was he proposing to help win the cold war or proposing to end it? * Mr. Schuman replied that he doubted very much whether the Kremlin would, in the existing circumstances, permit any of its satellites to join but that, if it did permit any of them to do so, so much the better since this would tend to unify more of Europe and bring a greater part of its war potential under supranational control.

Second: the British Labour government brusquely declined to participate in the plan and its abstention influenced the Scandinavian countries to remain aloof. This reduction of the participants left Germany in an uncomfortably strong position among the remainder because of its perponderant coal and steel production. The Bonn government enthusiastically joined with Italy, Belgium, Holland and Luxembourg in accepting the French invitation. In Germany's case the reason was clear: the Schuman Plan provided the Bonn republic with a short

---

* James Reston in the *New York Times*, May 12, 1950.

and relatively easy road back to a position of equality among the European nations. British abstention now made the troublesome question of the Saar extremely important. If France retained the Saar, French coal and steel production would very nearly equal that of Germany but, if the Saar remained German, the balance would tilt heavily against France. In both countries the matter became a major political issue.

Third: the almost fatal blow to the Schuman Plan came in September with Mr. Acheson's demand for German rearmament. From the moment when the United States declared a German military contribution essential to Western defense, Dr. Adenauer sat in the driver's seat. Germany now had a bargaining position.*

From June onward, the year 1950 was dominated by the events in the Far East. The full background of the Korean outbreak is not yet available. Hostile critics have accused Mr. Acheson of "inviting" the invasion by his statement that Korea lay "outside the defense perimeter of the United States." It would seem more reasonable to blame the "invitation" upon the action of the American Chiefs of Staff, then headed by General Dwight D. Eisenhower, in withdrawing the occupation forces from South Korea without first placing the republic in a position to defend itself against the Russian-trained North Korean army known to have been organized before the Soviet troops were withdrawn. Actually, the original causes of the Korean conflict lay even further back in the past. The first mistake had been to leave United States troops in an untenable position on a strategically irrelevant peninsula of Asia. The second mistake was to have permitted the 38th parallel to become a political boundary between the two halves of an arbitrarily divided country. The third mistake was to agree with Russia on a date of withdrawal without making adequate preparations for the withdrawal. Instead of either insisting upon the disbandment of the North Korean army or postponing American withdrawal until at least its equivalent had been created in South Korea, the United States had half-trained and

---

* For details of Dr. Adenauer's exploitation of this position, see *Germany— Key to Peace, op. cit.,* pages 131-214.

half-equipped a South Korean army and departed.* On top of this came Mr. Acheson's ill-advised statement.

Whatever the background, it probably seemed to the Kremlin a reasonably good gamble that the North Korean Communists could overrun the whole peninsula before the United States or the United Nations would take effective counter-action. As a matter of fact, this very nearly turned out to be the case. It was only because President Truman and Secretary Acheson took immediate and courageous action, because there happened to be American troops in Japan with which action could be taken, and because Russia's boycott of the Security Council enabled prompt United Nations sanction of intervention that it was possible to prevent the accomplished fact of a Communist conquest of South Korea.

There was a close parallel between the Berlin crisis of 1948 and the Korean crisis of 1950. Each was blundered into by errors in judgment and timing difficult to defend. In both cases, prompt, courageous and gallant action prevented disaster, but in neither case did that gallant action solve the situation out of which the crisis had arisen.

Having, by the narrowest of margins, maintained a foothold at the southern tip of the Korean peninsula, the United Nations forces were gradually built up to the point at which they could take the offensive. South Korea was cleared of Communist invaders. The aggression was successfully repelled. And then— for reasons which are still obscure—someone decided to carry the war across the 38th parallel and on up to the Manchurian border. General Douglas MacArthur predicted that the war would be over by Christmas, with all of Korea in his hands. But, by Christmas, the Chinese Communists had entered the conflict and MacArthur's forces were in headlong retreat. Why this decision to invade North Korea was made and by whom— why repeated warnings of Chinese intervention were ignored— why the United States failed to take counsel with its allies—

* The reasons for this action have never been fully explained, although an interesting clue was furnished by the American chief of military mission in South Korea. Asked why we had not furnished the South Koreans with tanks and planes, he was reported to have said that "we did not dare give them offensive weapons for fear lest Syngman Rhee might try to conquer North Korea."

all these are questions to which history will have to supply the answers.

Once the front was re-stabilized at about the 38th parallel, a stalemate ensued which lasted throughout the remaining years of the Truman administration. Truce negotiations were begun in 1951 and then broken off. Casualties continued to mount. The President and his advisers had worked themselves into a position from which they could neither achieve victory nor make peace. Neither the United Nations nor the principal allies of the United States, except the Republic of South Korea, could be counted upon to back a quest of victory which would almost certainly involve full-scale war with China, if not with the Soviet Union. The Republican opposition would denounce and majority opinion in the United States could not be counted upon to back a peace at the 38th parallel.

The reason for the domestic situation lay in a state of irrational suspicion and fear for which the President himself was to a large extent responsible. As already noted, the honeymoon period immediately following the cessation of hostilities in 1945 produced not only a premature dismantling of American military power but also a careless complacency with regard to internal security. When it was belatedly recognized that a certain amount of Communist infiltration had actually taken place, the Truman administration sought to tighten up security by methods wholly incompatible with the basic principles of the free society which it was trying to defend. The loyalty order of 1947 and the procedures subsequently adopted officially reversed the established American principle that an individual shall be considered innocent unless and until proved guilty by fair trial, shifting the burden of proof upon the accused. The anti-democratic doctrine of guilt by association was taken over by the government of the United States from the notorious House Committee on Un-American Activities, which had itself adopted many of the techniques of the totalitarian police state. The Attorney General prepared a list of organizations which he labeled "subversive" and membership in any such organization—past or present—became "evidence" of an individual's doubtful loyalty. Some of these organizations were no doubt Communist fronts; others, originally innocent, had become so;

still others were wholly innocent. These distinctions mattered but little. If the Attorney General—or, for that matter, anyone else—said that such and such an organization was "subversive," then anyone who had belonged to it, no matter when or for how long, became an object of suspicion. It needed only the fall of China to the Communists and the conviction for perjury of a high State Department official (Alger Hiss) to establish the widespread suspicion that the government had been thoroughly infiltrated and that American foreign policy was being shaped by a concealed Communist fifth column in the Department of State. In the climate of suspicion and fear, created in part by laxity and the actual existence of a Communist fifth column and in part by the totalitarian methods adopted by the administration itself, it was inevitable that informers should flourish, that unsubstantiated denunciation should take the place of evidence and that unscrupulous opportunists should reap a political harvest. In many respects, the condition of the public mind resembled that which had existed during the Presidency of John Adams.

The danger arose that a free society might commit suicide in order to save itself from being murdered. The basic principles of freedom which the American people sought to defend were in greater danger from irrational American behavior than from the machinations of a Communist fifth column subservient to Moscow. The effect of this reign of suspicion and fear, if not of outright terror, upon the conduct of the nation's foreign policy was disastrous. The Truman administration began to compete with its critics by endeavoring to prove that it was more wholeheartedly anti-Communist than they. It accepted the thesis of the extremists—that any and all negotiation constituted "appeasement"—and thus worked itself into a position of complete inflexibility no less obdurate than that of the Kremlin. In Korea, this meant that a stalemated war would have to continue without hope of either victory or peace without victory. In Europe, it meant that the government of the United States became deaf not only to anything that might be said by Moscow but also to the voices of its friends.

Britain and France had supported the original American intervention in Korea but were by no means satisfied with the subsequent policy which had brought China into the conflict, nor did they agree with Washington's continued support of Chiang Kai-shek. India, which had warned against pushing up to the Manchurian border, was wholly out of sympathy with American policy. Australia and New Zealand looked askance at the emerging American plan of rearming Japan, much as the European nations distrusted the American project of rearming Germany. All of the West European nations were troubled by American insistence upon greater and faster rearmament. The Truman administration treated these misgivings as if they were natural but childish aberrations and proceeded upon its inflexible course.

In Europe, 1951 was a year of slow motion. General Eisenhower, newly appointed as Supreme Commander of the new North Atlantic Treaty Organization (NATO), flew to Europe to make a preliminary survey of the task he was about to undertake. His report de-emphasized the need of a German military contribution and stressed the greater importance of building up the forces of the NATO associates. This pleased the French, but not the Germans.

At the time when Secretary Acheson had demanded German rearmament, President Truman had promised the NATO powers an increase of the American forces in Germany. General Eisenhower's testimony was the decisive factor in obtaining Congressional assent to the sending of four additional divisions. The key sentence in his carefully reasoned exposition of American interest in West European security was this:

> While the transfer to Europe of American units is essential, our major and special contribution should be in the field of munitions and equipment.

In spite of the low priority given to their rearmament at this time, the Germans bargained skillfully to obtain concessions for the Ruhr industrialists, some of which undermined the basic principles of the Schuman Plan.* Meanwhile they eagerly formulated their own plans for armed forces.

Alarmed by these developments, the French improvised the so-called Pleven Plan for a "European Army," in which German

* *Ibid.*, pages 157-159.

contingents, limited in size and number, would be so integrated with other West European forces as to minimize the danger of resurgent German militarism. The ensuing discussion as to the extent to which the Germans would be treated as equal partners or as something less lasted throughout the rest of the year.

The Russian reaction to Mr. Acheson's demand for West German troop contingents had been an immediate, sharply-worded protest followed by a demand for a four-power conference to discuss German re-unification and a peace treaty. During the first three months of 1951, there followed a long exchange of notes between Moscow and the Western powers, leading eventually to a meeting in Paris of the deputy foreign ministers. From March 5 to June 21, the deputies held 73 futile sessions in a vain attempt to agree upon an agenda for their principals. It became increasingly clear that, while France and Britain were anxious to explore the possibilities of reaching agreement with Russia over Germany, the United States had no such desire. Behind the scenes, Dr. Adenauer was now a powerful influence against any discussion of unification. The Bonn republic, formerly the passive object of East-West negotiation, was rapidly becoming a co-maker of Western coalition policy. A four-power conference, even if inconclusive, would once more make Germany the object of negotiation; until he could be certain of exercising a dominant voice in a discussion of German re-unification, the German Chancellor was determined to prevent any such discussion from taking place.*

Before the end of the year, Chancellor Adenauer not only obtained most of the concessions he desired in order to make Germany an equal partner in the European Defense Community (European Army) but also had worked out the broad outlines of a general agreement with the Western powers which would end the occupation and restore sovereignty to the Bonn republic. In addition, he obtained an extremely favorable debt settlement. With its economy flourishing and it future position of power almost assured, the Federal Republic of Germany now found itself in a trading position such as no nation could ever

* For a more detailed account of the 1951 negotiations see *ibid.*, pages 162-164.

have hoped to achieve six years after it had wantonly broken the peace and suffered a crushing defeat.

So far as Asia was concerned, 1951 was a year of much talk and little action. The great debate over General MacArthur's recall produced a vast amount of discussion about the rights and wrongs of past policy, about General MacArthur's qualities and defects, about Russian insistence that the Chinese Communist regime be recognized and about the terms upon which a Korean peace settlement should or should not be made. Later in the year, the fluctuating hopes and disappointments of the truce negotiations at Kaesong made daily headlines. The French war in Indo-China dragged on inconclusively, draining French strength into Asia at the very moment when it was most needed as an offset to the rising power of Germany in Europe. The dispute between India and Pakistan over Kashmir defied all attempts at settlement.

Only the peace treaty with Japan, negotiated by Mr. John Foster Dulles, denoted some degree of forward motion; but whether it also denoted progress toward peace remained to be seen. Since neither Russia, the Mao regime in China nor India signed the treaty, it signified little as to future peace among the Far Eastern powers. In essence, it was a treaty between the United States and Japan, concurred in without enthusiasm by Britain and the British Dominions and signed with enthusiasm only by governments anxious to please the United States. The Japanese Treaty was, however, wholly satisfactory to the most extreme domestic critics of the administration's Far Eastern policy and, for once, Secretary Acheson received praise for his handling of the Peace Conference held at San Francisco. The United States obtained rights to station troops in Japan and Japan was encouraged to rearm, in spite of the prohibition against rearmament embodied in its American-sponsored constitution. By a somewhat tricky procedure on the part of Mr. Dulles, the Japanese government was induced to recognize the exile regime on Formosa as the government of China.

Australian and New Zealand objections to the remilitarization of Japan were overcome by means of a mutual assistance treaty which assured the two dominions of American aid in the event of attack. The policy of making a rearmed Japan into a bulwark against Red China and the European policy of making a rearmed Germany a bastion against Red Russia encountered much the same sort of resistance from the nations which had suffered most from German and Japanese aggression.

In the Near East, the uneasy truce between Israel and the Arab nations continued throughout the year, but the relative quiet of the area was disturbed by the onset of a serious crisis, beginning with an anti-British revolt in Iran and then spreading to Egypt and North Africa. Caught unprepared and without anything resembling a firm Near Eastern policy, Washington viewed with alarm the weakening of British power in an area doubly important because of its oil resources and its strategic significance; but outright support of British Near East policy—or of French policy in North Africa—could not be reconciled with professions of supporting the rights of all peoples to independence and freedom. Insofar as there was an American policy, it seemed to be aimed solely at erecting a "Middle East defense" against Soviet or Communist encroachment. This attitude overlooked the important consideration that the Near Eastern peoples were far more concerned with shaking off the European imperialism with which they were intimately familiar than with erecting a defense against whatever unfamiliar danger might be lurking across the Soviet border.

Late in 1951, the British electorate returned Sir Winston Churchill to power as head of a new Conservative government.

Early in 1952 Secretary Acheson had to overcome a sharp crisis within NATO. Although the accelerated rearmament of the West European countries, demanded by the United States, was still largely in the planning stage, the impact upon the European economies was already felt. Recovery halted and threatened to go into reverse. The Germans, confident in their bargaining position, were no longer asking but demanding that their conditions be met, if the NATO powers desired their military assistance. These conditions included a return to Germany of the Saar, full equality in the command structure of the European army and equal partnership in NATO. The French, with Britain refusing to join the European Defense Community, and with their best forces drained off into Indo-

China, were more than ever insistent upon protection against German domination of the Western defense alliance. They were discovering to their alarm that, instead of incorporating West Germany in a European Defense Community, they were about to be left more or less *tête à tête* with the Germans in a Little Europe in which Germany would be by far the strongest partner.

To solve this crisis, Mr. Acheson joined the British and French foreign ministers and Chancellor Adenauer for a conference at London and then proceeded to Lisbon for a meeting of the full NATO Council. The net result of the two meetings was an apparent smoothing out of the difficulties and the adoption of a firm program for the raising of a strong defense force. Upon his return, Mr. Acheson was hailed with such bipartisan praise as he had never yet received during his stormy career in office.*

The chief actions of the NATO Council were these:

Turkey and Greece were admitted as full-fledged members of the NATO Alliance.

The Germans were technically denied membership in NATO but were granted the equivalent by an arrangement under which the European Defense Community became a member of NATO and the North Atlantic Treaty's provisions extended to cover the European Defense Community's territory. Since West Germany was the only member of the European Defense Community not signatory to NATO, this arrangement served merely to guarantee West German territory and to give the West German government its "equal voice" in NATO decisions.

The German contribution to EDC was fixed at 12 divisions —4 armored and 8 infantry—backed by a tactical air force of 1,746 planes. This German contingent, almost exactly that which the German generals had demanded,† was to be integrated in a European army of 43 divisions and 6,000 tactical planes. The sole concession made to the French was that

---

* For the events leading up to the London and Lisbon Conferences of February, 1952, and a detailed discussion of the French and German demands, see *ibid.*, pages 180-187.

† In the so-called Petersberg Plan. *Ibid.*, page 166.

integration would take place at the army corps level, thus denying the German demand to command their own corps.

In addition, the Germans were promised the early signature
of a peace treaty, the end of occupation, a reduction in their
proposed monetary contribution to Western defense, and the
right to manufacture certain types of arms. Finally, Dr. Adenauer had his way with respect to the treatment of German war
criminals, winning an agreement to have their cases reviewed
by a board of three Germans, one American, one British and
one French representative.

Thus, less than seven years after "unconditional surrender,"
Germany had now achieved equality, the promise of sovereign
independence, the right to rearm and the function of becoming
the major bulwark of Western civilization. The force to be
contained had become the instrument of containment.

On March 10, 1952, a Soviet note to the three Western
powers put forward by far the most specific and most reasonable
proposal for German unification in the long chain of diplomatic
exchanges. Neither the substance of this proposal nor the fact
of its arrival was disclosed by Washington until after the
Western reply had been sent on March 25.*

The Russian document was in some important respects
ambiguous. It proposed unification upon what appeared to be
a basis of democratic freedom and independence, specifically
providing for a guarantee of "the rights of man and basic
freedoms, including freedom of speech, press, religious persuasion, political conviction and assembly." On the other hand,
it suggested the creation of an all-German government without
specifically agreeing to free elections. This point required
clarification.

The past obstacle of reparations was clearly removed by a
provision suggesting that there be no further limitations of
any kind on the development of Germany's "peaceful economy."

The Kremlin proposed that the new Germany should be
permitted to have such armed forces as might be necessary for

---

* For the text of the two notes, see 10th Quarterly Report of the United
States High Commissioner to Germany, Government Printing Office, pages
96-101.

its defense, that the Oder-Neisse frontier be made permanent and that Germany should not be permitted to enter into any kind of coalition or military alliance "directed against any power which took part with its armed forces in the war against Germany."

The Western reply raised four points:

1. Before there could be a peace treaty there would have to be an all-German government freely elected by the German people. Did the Soviet government agree and would it permit a United Nations Commission to investigate whether it would be possible to hold free elections in the Soviet zone? (The latter suggestion seemed somewhat absurd since, obviously, the question was not whether conditions permitting free elections existed in the Soviet zone but whether the Soviet authorities would permit them to be created.)

2. The Western powers could not accept the Oder-Neisse frontier as final. (Like Secretary Byrnes in 1946, Secretary Acheson failed to make a specific proposal for frontier revision.)

3. The Western powers considered the proposed remilitarization of the new Germany as a "step backwards," which might jeopardize the emergence of a "new era of peaceful cooperation."

4. Contradicting themselves on point 3, the Western powers insisted that the new Germany should be free "to enter into association with other countries," frankly admitting their intention to "secure the participation of Germany in a purely defensive European community."

Quite clearly, the one reason why the Russians might be willing to give up their hold on East Germany and to permit unification on a basis of Western democratic principles was to prevent West Germany from becoming a partner in the Western defense alliance. How far they would go in really permitting free elections remained to be discovered and could be discovered only if the West indicated a willingness to forego a German military participation. But this was precisely what Mr. Acheson was unwilling to consider. (French and British opinion would probably have backed an exploration of the possibilities.) The Allied reply in effect said to the Russians:

First, we want to make sure that you really mean to give us the kind of united Germany we have wanted—which means that you will agree to free elections and to a revision of the Oder-Neisse frontier. If you are willing to do that, we are willing to accept your proposal, provided that we shall then be free to do with all of Germany what you wish to prevent us from doing with respect to its Western two-thirds.

To say this was to demand unconditional surrender. Neither Russia nor the West had the power to gain control over all of Germany. Yet this was what each side sought. The Russians sought control by unification on conditions which would give their East German Communist apparatus a Trojan Horse position in a new all-German government. The West sought control by incorporating all of Germany in a Western alliance. Whereas the Russians had indicated by the very ambiguity of their proposal that they *might* be willing to grant free elections, the West flatly stated that it would *not* give up German participation in the European army.

On April 9, the Soviet government replied to the Western note, rejecting the proposal of a United Nations Commission but suggesting that all-German elections be supervised by the four occupying powers. To this, the Western powers made no reply at all until May 13, stating then that the Russian proposal would make the four powers "both judge and party" but that they would consider any other "practical and precise" suggestion. By this time Mr. Acheson had already made his plans to get the German treaties signed before the end of the month.

This final "triumph" was not achieved without considerable difficulty. The Social-Democratic opposition in Germany, led by Dr. Kurt Schumacher, openly demanded a four-power conference. Chancellor Adenauer and French Foreign Minister Schuman became embroiled in a dispute over the Saar. To cap the climax, the British Labour Party Executive called upon the British government "to take steps without further delay" for the calling of a four-power conference before signing the treaties. This rising opposition had been responsible for the mild tone of the Western reply of May 13. *The Times* (London) commented that there could "quite obviously be no German unity if the Western powers were determined to insist that a united Germany should also be a member of the European Defense Community."

Acheson remained adamant. On May 26, at Bonn, the three Western foreign ministers signed the contractual agreements which restored all but complete sovereignty to the Federal Republic of Germany. A day later, at Paris, Germany, France, Italy, Holland, Belgium and Luxembourg signed the EDC Treaty. Then, mutual guarantees were exchanged between EDC and NATO. A declaration by the United States and Britain asserted that they would regard any threat to the integrity or unity of EDC as a threat to their own nations' security. (This was the guarantee against a German break-away sought by France.) Acheson and Eden further declared that their countries would station on the Continent "such forces as they deem necessary and appropriate to contribute to the joint defense of the North Atlantic area." After the signing ceremonies, Secretary Acheson declared:

"We are standing on the threshold of a New Europe and a new World."

To all intents and purposes the foreign policy record of the Truman administration was now closed. The Senate promptly ratified the Bonn Peace Treaty and the protocol to the North Atlantic Treaty without even discussing two major implications: that the United States was morally committed to vastly greater military and economic aid to the European Defense Community than had yet been contemplated; and that American troops would remain in Europe not as a stop-gap but as a permanent guarantee against a German break-away.

The ultimate fate of the treaties now rested in the hands of the European parliaments. Mr. Acheson's sole remaining task was to press for ratification and to stall off a four-power conference with Russia until the ratifications were obtained. Only British ratification was forthcoming before President Truman's term expired and this was achieved at the expense of a wide-open split between the Conservative majority and the united Labour party opposition. During the remainder of 1952, the prospects for French and German ratification grew more and more dubious. The weak French government made no effort to bring the matter before the Assembly. Chancellor Adenauer's determined efforts to obtain *Bundestag* approval led to one postponement after another.

The hesitancy and delay were not surprising. The shot-gun marriage of France and Germany, which Secretary Acheson had so vigorously sought to bring about, entailed great risks and sacrifices for both nations, as well as for all of Europe and for the United States. Even a truncated West Germany, with its 48,000,000 inhabitants, was certain to be the dominant power in the European Defense Community, no matter what safeguards the treaties might provide; its aim would be the recapture of the East, including the territories beyond the Oder-Neisse. This might easily involve France in war, once the marriage was consummated. As for the Germans, ratification of Mr. Acheson's plan meant acceptance of the more or less permanent partition of their country, with 18,000,000 of their compatriots living under Soviet tyranny.

There were two ways by which the Germans might some day achieve the re-unification of their country: one would be by maneuvering the West into war with Russia; the other would be by betraying the West and making a deal with Russia at the expense of Poland. The first would directly bring about the war which Western policy sought to prevent; the second would not only make war inevitable but would cause it to begin with all of Europe in the hands of a new Russo-German alliance.

Making West Germany the keystone in the arch of Western defense against the Soviet Union in effect placed the future of Western Europe in German hands. This risk could have been minimized, if the Schuman Plan had been permitted to bring about a political and economic union before a military marriage had been attempted. For this, it was too late. That the Germans would eventually accept seemed clear. The final agonizing decision would have to be made by France.

As the November elections approached, it was apparent that the legacy left by the Truman administration would consist of a stalemated war in the Far East, a turbulent and unpredictable situation in the Near East and a dangerously deteriorating, half-built defense structure in Europe. The containment policy had failed because it rested upon an over-simplified and one-sided analysis of the existing crisis; because it had attempted to do an essentially political job with preponderantly military means; because it relied upon military power which did not exist and could be created only by a great, firmly united coalition; and because it had failed to provide the affirmative base of creative, common purpose which alone could unite such a coalition.

President Truman had come into office at the high tide of victory and with the nation at the summit of its power, although the bright hope of enduring peace had already been tarnished by the first signs of dissension within that great coalition upon whose unity all hope depended. President Truman left to his successor a nation torn by internal dissension, uncertain of itself and of its purpose, and a world divided into hostile camps. The Communist orbit was united under the whiplash of a ruthless dictatorship. In the face of hunger, poverty and oppression, fear of Soviet conquest or Communist penetration had not sufficed to weld the so-called free nations into a firm alliance. The anti-Soviet coalition, which President Truman had sought to bring into being, had as yet gained few adherents in Asia, Africa and the Middle East.

The dismal postwar period was not without its bright spots, even though these did not redeem the over-all failure. The Berlin airlift had provided a demonstration of both courage and ingenuity, though it did not and could not solve the problems which had brought about the Berlin blockade. The Marshall Plan, though frustrated in its original conception, saved Western Europe from economic chaos and, very likely, from Communist subversion; this remained a major achievement, even though much of the accomplishment was later undermined by diversion from recovery to rearmament. The "Point Four" idea of aid to the under-developed areas, niggardly and inadequate as its implementation turned out to be, was nevertheless at least an intellectual departure from the sterile negativism of military containment. Finally, whatever may be the judgment of history concerning the origins of the Korean war and its conduct, the decision to intervene against aggression was an act of great courage and wise statesmanship which saved the United Nations and the whole concept of collective responsibility from oblivion. However harshly history may judge the myopic vision, the inflexibility and the futility of American foreign policy in this period, it was at least a policy gallantly executed.

The fault lay not so much with one man or one party as with the nation as a whole. Republicans and Democrats alike had shared in the early postwar illusions. They were alike responsible for the premature demobilization of the nation's power and for the lack of power vested in the United Nations. They had swung together from illusionment to disenchantment, and from disenchantment into easy acceptance of a scapegoat theory and a negative policy couched in the terms of moral absolutes. Early laxity in guarding internal security, followed by carelessness in guarding the basic principles of a free society, were largely the fault of the Truman administration; but it was the Republican opposition which had stimulated and exploited the subsequent wave of self-destructive hysteria. If living costs were high, both parties shared the blame for failure to control inflation. The huge and still mounting public debt and the high level of taxation were, to be sure, caused in part by extravagance and overexpansion of the Federal bureaucracy, but primarily they were due to the demands of a foreign policy which had, in general, enjoyed bipartisan support.

To a very large extent, the cause of the failure lay in the inheritance to which Truman had fallen heir. Rather like President Andrew Johnson, Harry Truman had tried faithfully to follow in the footsteps of a great leader prevented by untimely death from completing his work of peace. But, where Lincoln's unfinished work was soundly conceived, requiring only to be executed with patience, restraint and compassion, Franklin D. Roosevelt had left an unfinished symphony, demanding a composer's gift of improvisation equal to his own. Lincoln's concluding cadences were already scored, if not yet fully orchestrated, when the assassin's bullet struck him down. Roosevelt's work ended in a cacophonous passage which only he might have been able to resolve in the full-throated chords of enduring peace.

While Roosevelt had possessed and exercised more power of leadership in making foreign policy than all but a handful of

American Presidents, his successor's freedom of action had been tightly circumscribed throughout his incumbency. Truman, by no means a weak President, began as the prisoner of Roosevelt's policies and ended as the prisoner of his own misconceptions—more accurately, as the prisoner of an intellectual and emotional paralysis for which his miseducation of the American people was largely responsible.

CHAPTER THIRTY

"Time for a Change"
(1952 –   )

THE STATE OF MIND of the American people in the autumn of 1952 left little room for calm consideration of national policy. It was by now taken for granted that the world crisis existed solely because of the Kremlin's unwillingness to help and preserve a just peace and that the one aim of American foreign policy must be to rid the world of the Soviet-Communist menace. The pressure groups affecting the making of policy all operated within this frame of reference. The devotees of Chiang Kai-shek and Syngman Rhee pressed for a policy aimed at overthrowing the Communist regime in China. The East European nationality groups urged a "policy of liberation" aimed at freeing the East European satellites from Soviet domination. The Franco lobby urged an alliance with Spain. The Jewish groups demanded aid for Israel against the Arabs and the pro-Arab groups urged aid for the Arabs against Israel, each claiming its course of action to be the only way to protect the Near East from Communism.

At the same time, many of these groups unconsciously exercised a strong influence toward dividing the very anti-Communist coalition which they desired to create. The China lobby aroused anti-British sentiment by denouncing British recognition of the Mao regime and alleged British trade with Red China. The Franco lobby fanned hostility toward France because the French objected to Franco as an ally. Most of the enthusiastic anti-Communist groups combined to arouse antagonism against India—and Indian hostility toward the United States—by fulminating against the "neutralism" of Jawaharlal Nehru. None of these pressure groups were observing George Washington's wise injunction against permitting either excessive sympathy for one nation or animosity toward another to submerge a reasoned consideration of the national interest. Few, if any, were thinking calmly of the national interest at all.

In a similar way, reasoned consideration of the national interest in domestic affairs was submerged in a nation-wide struggle between two groups, each emerging from the generally accepted anti-Communist frame of reference. On the one side were the liberal anti-Communists who believed in fighting fire with water, desiring to combat the Communist menace only with such weapons as were consistent with the maintenance of a free society. On the other side were the authoritarian anti-Communists who held that fire must be fought with fire, believing that a free society could not protect itself against totalitarian subversion without adopting some of the methods of totalitarian tyranny. Far from becoming a dangerously destructive struggle, this conflict might have served to clarify the minds of the American people, had it arisen over a clear disagreement in principle. This would have been the case, if President Truman's administration had deliberately accepted certain risks because of a firm conviction that security must be sought only by methods compatible with the maintenance of a free society. The fact was, however, that Truman's laxity had been one of naive complacency rather than principle and that, when belatedly made aware of a certain amount of Communist infiltration, Mr. Truman had at once sought to tighten up security by authoritarian methods. The manner in which the loyalty order of 1947 was carried out and revised in 1951 to make "reasonable doubt" sufficient ground for dismissal led to procedures wholly foreign to American principles of justice.

With the government of the United States taking the lead in this dangerous direction, it was inevitable that the spirit of vigilantism should infect Congress as well as broad masses of the population, and that the door should be opened to unscrupulous informers and notoriety-seeking demagogues. The fact that President Truman had first been careless of security and had then proceeded to be careless of freedom left his political opponents free to make the most out of his laxity while depriving his would-be defenders of a principle to defend. The authoritarian anti-Communists, led by the outstanding opportunist—Senator Joseph R. McCarthy of Wisconsin—thus were able to equate "Trumanism" with criminal negligence, if not with treason, while the liberal anti-Communists could fight the authoritarians effectively only if they were prepared to admit that Truman himself had betrayed the liberal principle.

Partly for reasons of partisan politics, and partly because Truman had in other respects fought courageously for principles in which the liberals believed, few were willing to face the issue with which they were confronted. Thus, the advantage was altogether on the side of the authoritarians. The political parties did not divide over the basic issue but merely over the degree to which they would accept authoritarianism in vying with each other within the accepted frame of reference. The question became quite simply one of deciding whether Joe McCarthy was "doing more good than harm, or more harm than good." When this irresponsible head-line hunter strutted across the nation's stage denouncing General George Catlett Marshall as a front for traitors, it seemed for a moment that he had overreached himself, but such was not to be the case.

General Dwight D. Eisenhower's victory over Senator Robert A. Taft in the fight for the Republican nomination gave him a mandate—if he wished so to interpret it—to break with the ultra-nationalist, ultra-conservative wing of the party. Yet General Eisenhower at once made it clear that this was not his intention, giving his endorsement indiscriminately to all Republican candidates for office, including—to the chagrin of his liberal supporters—the Wisconsin demagogue who had slandered his wartime chief. The Democratic candidate, Governor Adlai E. Stevenson, of Illinois, deprecated his opponent's action and took a strong stand against McCarthyism but refrained from facing the fact that President Truman's betrayal of the liberal principle had set the stage for McCarthy and his ilk. The basic issue as between liberal and authoritarian anti-Communism was never raised. Both candidates were men of high principle and liberal convictions who doubtless abhorred authoritarianism in every form; yet, for reasons of political expediency, the one endorsed authoritarianism's leading exponent, while the other refrained from exposing and repudiating his party's role in providing the opportunity for the unscrupulous opportunist.

Nor were any real issues raised as to foreign policy. The Republicans somewhat unscrupulously sought to make political capital out of "Truman's war" in Korea and scored heavily when their candidate promised, if elected, to seek a way to end it. European policy was scarcely mentioned, since both candidates were apparently committed to a continuation of the Truman-Acheson course, though John Foster Dulles talked about substituting a "policy of liberation" for the policy of containment. When this trial balloon raised anxiety and misgivings here and especially abroad, General Eisenhower backed away from the idea. Stevenson, during the early stages of the campaign, gave some indications that he might depart from the Truman-Acheson inflexibility and be more ready to explore the possibilities of negotiation, but failed to follow up this approach after Truman himself more or less took over the Democratic campaign.

For the most part, the battle of words centered upon domestic issues, with the Democrats saying, "You've never had it so good" and the Republicans promising more security, more prosperity and more freedom at lower cost.

General Eisenhower's overwhelming victory made it evident that he did not owe his election to the Republican Party but had, on the contrary, carried the party back into power by his personal popularity. The circumstances were such as might ordinarily be expected to give the new President an unusual degree of freedom of action, especially during his first year in office. The slender margin of Republican control in Congress would not be a limiting factor, if the Executive would promptly put forward a program commanding bipartisan liberal support.

Within a few months of his inauguration, however, it became clear that the General's course would be slowly and cautiously shaped with an eye to Republican unity, rather than bipartisan nation-wide support. This indicated that his freedom of action would be narrowly circumscribed by the necessity of conciliating the ultra-conservative, ultra-nationalist wing of the party. Barring miracles, such a procedure would probably result in a mild retrenchment of Federal activity in domestic affairs and very little, if any, change in foreign policy.

The selection of President Eisenhower's cabinet implied a swing back to *laissez-faire* doctrine and the beginning of another era of Big Business government. Actually, this was probably what the majority of Americans wanted. The country was prosperous, but the continued rise of living costs, the high level of taxation, the over-extended bureaucracy and the mounting evidence of petty but pervasive corruption during the Truman administration had caused most Americans to lose confidence in political management, much as they had lost confidence in business management in 1932. This did not necessarily mean a return to the irresponsible "Normalcy" which had resulted from a similar swing of sentiment in 1920. Big Business had, in the intervening years, acquired a more highly developed social conscience. Labor was better organized and better able to protect itself. The whole nation had learned certain valuable lessons in controlling and cushioning the business cycle which were not likely to be forgotten, even though it might temporarily be the fashion to denounce all forms of government intervention as "creeping socialism." Nevertheless, even a moderate reversion to *laissez-faire* doctrines, particularly in the field of government finance and the control of interest rates and credit facilities, might easily throw sand into the gears of an economic machine which had become unhealthily dependent upon continued high military expenditures. The success of any domestic program designed to promote greater freedom of individual enterprise would depend upon two factors in the realm of foreign policy:

1. Federal expenditures and the level of taxation could not be significantly reduced, unless a relaxation of cold-war tensions were to make it possible to cut down military expenditures. The idea that more security could be acquired for fewer dollars ("More bang for a buck!") was a dangerous illusion.

2. Given a relaxation of tensions and a reduction of military expenditure, a high level of domestic prosperity could not be sustained unless more liberal foreign trade and investment policies were to be adopted.

It appeared almost a certainty that neither of these two foreign policy preconditions would be fulfilled by an administration which shaped its program with an eye to solid Republican support. Cold-war tensions could be relaxed, if at all, only by an extremely flexible and alert policy of give and take. It was clear that any departure from the inflexible Truman-Acheson policy of attempting to force unconditional surrender upon the Communist dictators would be denounced by the majority of the Republicans in Congress—and by a considerable number, if not the majority, of Democrats—as "appeasement." This bipartisan state of mind, created by the widespread acceptance of the scapegoat theory of the world crisis, was the outstanding limiting factor inherited by the Eisenhower administration.

As for a downward revision of the tariff and the adoption of a liberal foreign investment policy divorced from cold-war considerations, it appeared highly improbable that either could be accomplished with the consent of the die-hard Republican Old Guard so firmly intrenched in the 83rd Congress.

Broadly speaking, therefore, it seemed that while the American people had expressed the feeling that it was "time for a change," the change—except for a general house-cleaning of top government personnel—was likely to be more apparent than real. Without a basic re-orientation of foreign policy based upon a re-examination of the premises, there could be no great retrenchment in domestic affairs; and a basic re-orientation of foreign policy could hardly be expected in the existing psychological frame of reference.

Before the United States could hope to achieve leadership in a crusade for human freedom, the headlong flight from freedom within the United States would have to be brought to a halt. The peoples of the non-Communist world would have to be sure of two things about the people of the United States before they would be willing to ally themselves to American aims and American policies. They would have to know: *first,* that liberal anti-Communism had definitively triumphed over the authoritarian variety; and, *second,* that anti-Communism of any sort did not constitute the sum total of American policy.

Viewing the state of mind and the political scene in the United States in 1952-1954, many Europeans pointed with dismay to the apparent similarity with the psychological and political conditions which had produced Fascist dictatorships in Italy and Germany. In both countries, they said, the establishment of anti-Communism as the single, overriding sentiment and aim had led to the destruction of democracy. Moreover, President Eisenhower's concessions to a demagogue whom he obviously despised reminded them unpleasantly of Von Hindenburg and Hitler. These misgivings could not be brushed aside as unwarranted alarmism, yet it was also important to bear in mind that Fascism (and Communism) had arisen in Europe out of widespread economic distress and a popular mood of frustration and despair. Hitler and Mussolini had not risen to power solely as exponents of authoritarian anti-Communism; they had gained much of their following by promising pie in the sky to the masses, while at the same time promising increasing privilege and power to the few; they had capitalized not only fear of Bolshevism but the distress of the many, the avarice of the few and the nationalistic resentments and ambitions of peoples which had suffered defeat and humiliation. Thus, unless a Big Business government were to take the United States back into something like Harding's "Normalcy" and another major depression, only some of the preconditions for the emergence of Fascist dictatorship would be present.

Barring a major depression or a major military defeat, the country's own history provided a parallel more likely to prove relevant. Between 1796 and 1800, the American people had pulled themselves out of a state of mind rather similar to that which existed in 1952-1954. The French Revolution and French "fifth-column" activity in the United States threatened for a time to make authoritarian anti-democracy the sum total of American policy and the acceptance of authoritarian anti-democracy the criterion of loyalty. Neither President John Adams nor his revered and beloved predecessor took any strong stand against the authoritarian tide. True, there was then a Thomas Jefferson to rally the forces of liberal democracy and no unscrupulous demagogue seeking to attain political power by exploiting the confusion of the public mind. The Timothy Pickerings and the Essex Junto were unskilled in manipulating mass emotion. Alexander Hamilton, the leading authoritarian anti-democrat, was also a constructive statesman who had rendered distinguished public service and whose authoritarianism was motivated by conviction rather than political opportunism. Anti-democracy had never been the sum total of Hamiltonian policy in the sense that anti-Communism became the sum total of American policy a century and a half later.

Undoubtedly, it was easier for reason and common sense to reassert themselves in those relatively uncomplicated days, when basic issues of principle were more readily perceived and understood. Yet, essentially, the challenge to democracy remained the same and would probably always remain the same. There was no reason to assume that a nation which had met that challenge in its youth could not, in its maturity, rise to meet it once again. The question was, rather, whether the American people would emerge triumphant over authoritarianism at home in time to play their potentially important part in the building of a world in which all men might, at long last, live out their allotted days in peace. The time factor was crucial in determining whether the United States would achieve constructive leadership or whether the words, "America Go Home!" would be scrawled on every wall in Europe, in Asia and wherever American diplomacy might seek adherents.

The world had not stood still while American diplomacy remained frozen in the cold-war pattern set by Winston Churchill in 1946. Nor had Churchill himself stood still, in spite of his advancing years. In May, 1953, after Stalin's death had brought a new Soviet regime to power, the veteran British statesman had electrified the world by a forthright declaration that the cold war had become obsolete, that the time had come to seek a tolerable basis of co-existence. The indomitable warrior recognized that war itself had become the paramount threat to Westtern civilization and that war could not be averted merely by seeking to win a race for predominant power. His words found an echo everywhere except in Washington, Taipei, Seoul and Madrid.

The handwriting was on the wall. If the United States were to avoid finding itself more and more alone with Franco, Chiang Kai-shek and Syngman Rhee—and, perhaps, for a time, with Konrad Adenauer—if the United States wished to march in the vanguard of the forces seeking peace and freedom, there was not much time left in which to develop an affirmative policy that would command the allegiance of the masses of mankind.

This, too, was not a new challenge for the American people. In their nation's youth, the American people had gained the allegiance of all men everywhere seeking freedom and the peaceful pursuit of happiness. They had achieved moral leadership by a simple declaration of their own faith and by demonstrating in action that this faith could be made the foundation of justice, of freedom and of human dignity.

The twin challenges confronting the American people at home and abroad were actually but one challenge. Effective leadership of free men throughout the world could be built only upon the example set at home.

Note

IT IS obviously too soon to attempt an evaluation of the first eighteen months of the Eisenhower administration. In general, they have witnessed a weakening rather than a strengthening of the anti-Communist coalition. Mounting dissatisfaction on the part of our Allies seems to have produced a growing tendency toward "going it alone," rather than an inclination to re-examine policies which do not command the allegiance of our friends. Whether this trend is continued or reversed would appear to depend more upon domestic politics than upon developments abroad, the crucial question being whether the administration will free itself from or continue to submit to the dictation of the ultra-nationalist intransigents in the Congress.

A Few Tentative Conclusions

THE UNITED STATES has moved through four distinct phases of foreign policy development, and it is now in a fifth phase, the outcome of which is unpredictable. In each of these stages of development, different conditions have prevailed.

In the early years of the republic, foreign policy pursued two clearly distinguishable aims: (1) the establishment of a transcontinental nation dominating the hemisphere; and (2) the expansion and protection of American trade abroad. During this period, the United States was essentially an agricultural country with a rapidly growing commercial trading interest. The American people were somewhat like a large farm family, constantly seeking to enlarge the farm, to fence it in securely and to discover and develop the means by which the farm's products might profitably be exchanged for other goods. The foreign policy of continental establishment and expansion and of overseas trade development was, on the whole, skillfully and consistently pursued. The Presidents and the men around them literally "made" foreign policy—especially Washington, Jefferson, Monroe and John Quincy Adams (the latter as Secretary of State, rather than as President). These men pursued their aims primarily by diplomacy, taking advantage of the preoccupation of the European nations with a balance-of-power struggle from which they kept the United States aloof. They were served by a small but highly competent group of observers and representatives abroad. With the exception of the declaration of war against Britain in 1812, when Congress seized the initative, the Legislative branch tended to follow the lead of the Executive, even though it frequently engaged in stormy debate.

The Jacksonian revolution changed the methods but not the aims of this first phase in United States foreign policy. The sword, rather than the pen became the instrument of transcontinental expansion. Public opinion—or public sentiment—became a more important factor in the shaping of policy, tending to push Congress ahead of the Executive in expansionist aims and projects.

In the succeeding phase, from 1848 to 1898, the United States can scarcely be said to have had a foreign policy at all. The American people were at first deeply concerned with trying to escape from fratricidal conflict, then with fighting it, and then with re-shaping their nation and with the pursuit of private profit. During this period the United States was transformed into an almost self-sufficient unit of industrial and agricultural production, delivering an increasing annual surplus for sale in foreign markets. The people were little interested in the world around them, except to the extent of wishing to expand overseas trade and to prevent any foreign encroachment upon their hemisphere preserve. Since this was a period of relative peace and stability in the world, there were few external pressures demanding the formulation of an American foreign policy, but powerful internal pressures for foreign expansion were accumulating.

What little diplomatic activity there was during this phase reflected internal conditions. Pierce and Buchanan "made" policy, but only in the sense that they were able to pursue their slave-interest imperialism on behalf of a sectional minority interest to which they themselves were subservient. Lincoln's foreign policy was conditioned and limited by the exigencies of the war to preserve the Union. During Johnson's administration, foreign policy was made by Seward, as Secretary of State, urging expansion for which the American people were not yet ready, and Charles Sumner, as chairman of the Senate Foreign Relations Committee, blocking Seward's policy, except in the case of Alaska. From 1868 to the turn of the century, not a single President or Secretary of State can be said to have shaped the rather shapeless course of the United States in world affairs.

The explosion of the accumulated internal pressures for expansion in 1898 marked the beginning of the third phase. By the annexation of the Philippines, the conversion of the Open Door Policy into a guarantee of Chinese integrity, the mediation of the Russo-Japanese War and Presidential meddling in the Moroccan crisis, the United States injected itself into the balance-of-power struggle. For the first time, its vital interests became directly involved in that previously intra-European affair; and, for the first time, the United States acquired a direct interest in the preservation of world peace; it could no longer expect to exploit Europe's wars as a neutral.

The American people, however, were very far from realizing this basic change in the relationship of their country to the rest of the world. They did not understand that from here on, if they wished to live in peace, they would have to assume a share of the burden of maintaining peace. American foreign policy continued to be little more than a pursuit of trade advantage and a jealous guardianship of hemisphere interest, until World War I temporarily drew the American people into the vortex of world affairs; from this brief involvement, they recoiled in disgust at European power politics. Yet, when Woodrow Wilson endeavored to create a world in which peace might be preserved without power politics, the people refused to follow him. The United States had become one of the great world powers, but the American people rejected both of the alternatives open to them. They declined to participate in traditional balance-of-power alliances. They rejected as well the opportunity to take part in the new experiment in collective security. For the next twenty years, the United States reverted to the isolationist illusion, garnished with neutrality legislation, disarmament treaties and formal agreements renouncing war.

The fourth phase began with the outbreak of World War II and marked the reluctant assumption by the United States of great-power responsibility. It opened with President Roosevelt's belated effort to persuade the American people that their vital interests were at stake in the outcome of the war in Europe. Pearl Harbor cut short the debate before the people had come to a decision and catapulted the United States into world leadership. Unlike World War I, the second great conflict did not eliminate the visible external threat to American security. Even before Germany and Japan were defeated, Soviet Russia loomed upon the horizon as a menace to world peace. Because of this, and because the lessons of 1919-1920 had not been forgotten, a resurgence of isolationist sentiment was delayed. By the time the pendulum reaction against foreign entanglements had set in, the United States had joined the United Nations and had become committed to the leadership of an anti-Soviet coalition.

In the as yet incomplete fifth phase, the United States has assumed leadership without, so far, understanding the changed and changing nature of the world it is trying to lead. The atomic bomb ended the long era in which war could be regarded as even a last-resort instrument of protecting the national security, yet American postwar policy has to a considerable extent been based upon premises which went up in smoke over Hiroshima. Impatience and frustration have led to a resurgence of isolationism, but only in small part of the old variety which seeks retreat from world affairs into fantasied seclusion. The latter-day isolationist reluctantly accepts the inescapability of involvement but draws the conclusion that, if the United States cannot avoid entanglement, it had better impose something like a *Pax Americana*. This neo-isolationism—an isolationism turned inside-out into a reluctant and resentful imperialism—is likely to leave the United States with fewer and fewer friends, thus accomplishing its isolation more effectively than a conscious retreat from all involvement. If the United States is increasingly cut off from the other peoples of the non-Communist world, it seems likely that the balance of power will swing over to the Communist orbit; this might make the disaster of atomic war inevitable.

On the other hand, if American internationalism takes a more mature and constructive form, resolving the past dissonance between an idealistic sense of mission and the realistic pursuit of a national interest, conceived in now obsolete power-political terms—if United States policy is re-oriented toward affirmative purposes which will unite the non-Communist world in a common crusade *for* greater freedom and more widespread justice, rather than merely *against* Communist imperialism— then the fifth phase may end in the development of creative

American leadership toward the eventual attainment of lasting peace. At present, the outcome is wholly unpredictable.

The history of these five phases reveals a number of significant trends.

It shows that, within the government, Congress has gradually assumed a more important role in the making of foreign policy as appropriations have come to play a more important part in the execution of treaties and agreements. After Lincoln, only the two Roosevelts can be said to have held the conduct of foreign relations firmly in their hands; and only Theodore Roosevelt achieved firm Executive control in time of peace. As Commander-in-Chief in war, the President can still exercise the predominant power, but it seems evident that only a very exceptional President can do so in the absence of a national emergency. The second Roosevelt was a strong and exceptionally gifted President, but even he was swayed by pressure-groups exerting their influence directly and through the Congress. The pro-Franco lobby pushed him into "non-intervention" in Spain; the pacifists pushed him into signing the Neutrality Acts; the assorted isolationist groups delayed rearmament and aid to the nations resisting Axis aggression; the inflationists pushed him into tinkering with the currency; and the silver bloc affected the nature of monetary experimentation. One of the major reasons for Franklin D. Roosevelt's effectiveness as a leader was that he knew how to balance the conflicting pressures and how to manipulate public sentiment, so that, while making many compromises and concessions, he could nevertheless steer a fairly straight course toward his objectives, once he had made up his mind what these objectives were.

It seems evident that the real power of decision over national policy, both domestic and foreign, has, over the years, shifted from the elected officials of government to an increasingly complex aggregation of pressure groups, each pursuing its own special interest without much regard for the interests of the nation as a whole. This is the empirically evolved "system" by which the American mass democracy has sought to answer the problem which tormented John C. Calhoun—the problem of protecting a sectional majority from being trampled underfoot by the national majority. The gradually and almost unconsciously developed "system" of allowing national policy to be formed by the conflicting pressures exerted by the many sectional, economic, racial, religious and nationality groups within the nation has made possible the extension of representative democracy over a sprawling, heterogeneous territory and the maintenance of national unity in a pluralistic society.

The early regional divergences of interest were, as we have seen, not easy to reconcile, but they were, at least, readily identifiable. So were the racial, religious and nationality groups which developed as the country grew, but the economic special-interest groups arising out of the industrial revolution were more complex and in many cases overlapped the older minorities. By the end of the nineteenth century, national policy was being formed chiefly as the resultant of a large number of divergent and partly unseen forces, pushing and tugging at the government in pursuit of their separate variegated interests. The result, as we have observed, was a national behavior often inconsistent and at times almost inexplicable. Nevertheless, so long as the majority of Americans belonged consciously to one special-interest group or another, the sum total of the forces exerted upon national policy did with some degree of accuracy reflect the conflicting interests of the many minorities which made up the American majority. The resulting policy represented something like a fair compromise among the disparate components of a pluralistic society. (It was not a completely fair compromise because some minorities were better armed than others with lobbying power.)

Since the beginning of the twentieth century, a number of factors have tended to distort this "system" and to alter the process of policy formation.

In the olden days, when foreign policy was literally "made" by Presidents and Secretaries of State, decisions were based upon a comparatively clear conception of the national interest and upon intelligence from abroad supplied by a small number of highly competent American diplomats. The reports of such observers as Franklin, Jefferson and the three Adamses may have taken weeks in transit, but, when they arrived, they provided a magnificent picture of background and context, as well as guidance as to the future. Nowadays, the policy-makers in

Washington must base their judgments upon a vast mass of information from abroad, supplied in part by the privately owned press and radio, in part by competent foreign service personnel, and in part by ambassadors with no experience in diplomacy, who have received their appointments as rewards for contributions or services rendered to the party in power. Much of the information so received reaches the policy-makers in unevaluated form and without context. Some of it is slanted by bias or incompetence. The most dangerously misleading reports are those rendered by jobholders intimidated by prevailing sentiment or prejudice into reporting only what they imagine their superiors wish to hear.

Modern means of communication have vastly increased the amount of information about the world available to the policy-makers; they have reduced weeks of transmittal time to hours and minutes; but they have not increased the rounded objectivity of the sum total. Moreover, most of the vast flow of information from abroad now reaches the public as fast or faster than it becomes available to the elected or appointed officials of government. Before the policy-maker has had time to digest and evaluate the most recent intelligence, much of it has been capsuled and packaged for mass consumption. Before a reasoned judgment can be formed by individuals, mass attitudes are shaped by the manner in which the latest news is presented and interpreted. Some professional analysts and commentators are highly competent and objective; some are biased; others conform to the bias of a superior or of an advertising sponsor. The modern American process of dissemination tends less to stimulate the formation of individual judgments than to foster the adoption of either-or attitudes, identification with protagonists rather than with ideas or principles, and a widespread feeling of partisan spectatorship rather than responsible participation in the formation of national policy.

The ordinary citizen does not, as a rule, communicate his immediate reactions to the White House or to his representatives in Congress, but the highly skilled and well paid lobbyists of the many and varied special-interest groups frequently utilize current events to stimulate messages from constituents which promote their interests, reinforcing such "grass roots" expressions with personal calls upon policy-makers. Thus, the Congressman is often under pressure before he has had time to form a judgment—and not under pressure from the reasoned individual opinions of his constituents but from mass attitudes fostered by special-interests. The Congressman may agree or disagree with these mass attitudes, but he ignores them at the peril of his political career.

The greater the vacuum of individual citizen opinion and interest, the more effective is the work of the lobbyist seeking to create pressure upon the policy-maker. The more alienated the public as a whole from the shaping of national policy, the more influential becomes the voice of the interested minority. It is here that the American pressure-group "system" appears to be in danger at the present time.

The machine age has been changing the United States from a nation of individual free enterprises—from a nation of independent farmers, land speculators, small businessmen and traders—into a nation of wage and salary earners. The free enterpriser has a fairly clear notion of what government policies will further or injure his particular interest and finds it relatively easy to band together with others to exert political pressure. The wage or salary earner, who owns little or no property, takes no capital risks for profit and operates below the policy-making level in the bureaucracy of Big Business or Big Government, finds it more difficult to ascertain where his political interest lies. A large part of the manual labor force has organized and become politically articulate in demanding government policies which assure fair wages, hours, and working conditions. Enlightened labor leadership has become conscious of a broader interest in national policies which will lead to more stable full employment; in time, this will involve a conscious interest in almost every aspect of national policy. But the rapidly growing, unorganized and mostly white-collar labor force—the great mass between the managerial top and the organized bottom of the Big Business pyramid—is, for the most part, temporarily alienated from the political pressure-group "system." It is true that parts of this growing segment of the population find pressure-group homes in religious, civic or other affiliations, such as veterans' organizations, but, to a large extent, they are without a conscious awareness of belonging to any special minority.

In the American society, political consciousness and a sense of possessing political power have been associated with the ownership of property and with participation in a risk-taking competition for wealth, privilege and influence. In the age of Big Business and Big Government, the social and economic status of the majority of Americans has changed from independence to dependence—from being "on one's own" to taking instructions from someone higher up in the hierarchy of production and distribution. The men and women who today find themselves without a home among the managerial elite which employs and directs them, and without a real sense of solidarity with any layer of the multiple layer-cake of the employed, must sooner or later discover a new status—not as property-owner or job-holder, but as citizen—as citizen of the community, the state, the nation and the world. Until this happens, American democracy will be in danger, because a large part of American society will remain alienated from the processes which shape national policy. So long as this is the case, the sum total of conflicting pressures will not reflect the sum total of the divergent interests of the whole American people but, rather, the conflicting interests of the purposeful minorities which successfully mobilize mass attitudes. For it is not true that the politically inert are without political influence. They vote and they contribute to the formation of mass attitudes; but they vote, as it were, by proxy, like shareholders of one of the giant corporations at an annual meeting; and their contribution to the formation of mass attitudes consists chiefly in providing the labile material for purposeful manipulation.

It would appear, then, that we are in a somewhat precarious period of transition at home as well as in a distinctly perilous period of transition in world affairs. The delay in finding our political bearings in our machine-age domestic society, hinders us from accomplishing the necessary adjustment of our foreign policy to the hydrogen age in international relations.

To a considerable extent, our domestic re-orientation is delayed because the managerial elite, which controls production, employment, distribution and the media of information, strenuously cultivates the myth of an America which no longer exists. The potency of the myth of a free enterprise America is attested by the fact that scarcely a political speech fails to speak of the man who tills his own soil and the small business-man as "the backbone of the nation." The fact is, however, that most of what we eat and the huge food surpluses we export are produced by a few giant meat-packing and food-processing en-terprises; that very few of the consumer goods we buy and practically none of the "hard" goods are produced by small businesses; and that even in retail distribution, the last refuge of the small businessman, the chain store, the mail-order house and the supermarket have become predominant. America has become, whether or not we like it, the land of Big Business, Big Government and Big Labor—the land in which at times Big Government controls Big Business and Big Labor and, at other times, is controlled by one or the other. The longer we continue the nostalgic dream of the past, the more time we shall lose in adjusting ourselves to the realities of the dangerous years in which we live.

It is perhaps natural that, in such a time, there should be a widespread tendency on the part of the ordinary citizen to feel that there is little he or she can do except to help choose "a good leader." That way lies the end of a free society.

What makes the foreign policy of a nation is, in the last analysis, the degree of political maturity of its citizens—the ex-tent to which they are and feel themselves to be citizens of the nation and of the world.

The American people have yet to develop a real sense of world citizenship, even though they have always been concerned with the world-wide promotion of political democracy. Amer-ican world-mindedness has been more of a humanitarian im-pulse to extend to the world the blessings of the American system than a readiness to accept citizenship in a world of many systems. Even this humanitarian impulse has carried overtones of unconscious ideological imperialism. We have had no wish to dominate other peoples, but we have sought to induce them to accept and adopt our concepts of political and economic organization in the sincere though naive belief that, if only they would follow our advice and example, they would soon prosper as we have prospered.

This somewhat immature and provincial world-mindedness has, throughout our history, run counter to a strong sense of nationalist isolationism which has made us not only reluctant to participate in world affairs but vigilantly jealous of permitting the world to intrude itself upon the American scene. The characteristic American dichotomy was personified in Thomas Jefferson. The world-minded philosopher, who articulated the principles of liberal democracy and asserted their universal applicability, was also no less an isolationist than George Washington and John Adams. It was Jefferson who declared that the United States must not again "be involved in the never-ending broils of Europe"—that "the European nations have a set of interests of their own in which it is our business never to engage ourselves"—and that "no spark of war kindled in other quarters of the globe should be wafted across the wide oceans which separate us from them."

The characteristic American attitude in the twentieth century has been one of willingness to intervene in world affairs when the national security has been threatened by the rise of an aggressive, expansionist power; but to intervene in the definite expectation of once more withdrawing from entanglement, once the aggressor had been defeated and the threat extinguished.

The characteristic American assumption has been that something in the nature of an automatic process is in operation by which all the world's peoples are moving toward the American concepts of liberal democracy and "free enterprise capitalism" —and that this process, when interrupted by wars, threats of aggression or civil disturbances, will somehow automatically resume when "normal conditions" have been restored.

This study indicates the need for a re-examination of these premises. It seems apparent that, in the world of today and tomorrow, the defense of our national interest will demand permanent involvement in world affairs and that we must face the imperative of abandoning the pattern of moving in and out of responsible participation in the maintenance of peace as well as in the peaceful development of the world's human and material potential. This may seem a superfluous observation in view of the multitude of alliances and commitments we have recently undertaken; but, if the Sino-Soviet Communist threat were to vanish tomorrow, it seems reasonably certain that, within a few weeks or months, there would be a resurgence of our traditional isolationist sentiment. Yet the fact is that, with or without the visible presence of a potential aggressor, the nature of the world has become such that no great nation can safely withdraw from the management of its affairs. Not only will peace be constantly threatened by the existence of fully sovereign nation-states armed with weapons of mass annihilation, but all progress will depend upon cooperation between nations in developing world resources in such a way as to keep pace with the rapidly rising population. In fact, it is not too much to say that Western civilization cannot survive—even if it is not extinguished by war—unless the *Haves* cooperate with the *Have-nots* in food production, resource development and industrialization. From this point of view, the American people have a greater responsibility than any other single people on the earth. Without their great surplus resources, the underdeveloped regions cannot be helped to develop. Unless they are developed, the end of the relatively high prosperity of Western man is already in sight.

In dealing with this changed relationship to a changed and changing world, our own history affords a few broad guides for national conduct:

It shows that our nation's influence in the world depends primarily upon the extent to which we, as a people, are dedicated to aims and aspirations common to the majority of mankind.

It demonstrates that wealth and power are actually impediments when employed for selfish nationalistic ends and without a "decent respect to the opinions of mankind," becoming assets only when employed with humility toward the attainment by all men everywhere of what all men everywhere desire.

It teaches that while the physical nature of the world changes from day to day, the deep universal longings of mankind are unchanging—that they are far older than our Declaration of Independence and not compressible into our particular definitions of justice, freedom and security. In a prosperous, Big-Business-minded nation such as ours, it is all too easy to translate the erroneous notion that "What's good for General Motors is good for the country" into the arrogant (or naive) belief that what's good for the United States is good for the world. It would seem more nearly correct to assert the opposite.

The second industrial revolution, with its infinite potential of creation and destruction, no longer leaves us a choice of joining or remaining aloof from the human race. There is no longer an antithesis between the humanitarian impulse and the instinct for survival. There is no longer a contradiction between moral pacifism and true patriotism. If we but realized it, we need no longer torture ourselves over the age-old question of choosing between what is "right" and what is expedient. The only remaining expedient for survival has become the brotherhood of man.

The teachings of Jesus Christ have now become the imperatives of survival. We have reached the ultimate threshold of which the Hebrew prophets, Micah and Isaiah, spoke when they foresaw that "It shall come to pass in the last days that . . . they shall beat their swords into plowshares and their spears into pruninghooks; nation shall not lift up sword against nation, neither shall they learn war any more."

Universal disarmament, enforced by supranational authority, and world-wide economic cooperation have become the indispensable necessities of mankind. Their attainment is difficult, not only because of the existence of cruel dictatorships which seek to enslave mankind, but because a great nation which enjoys the highest degree of freedom hesitates to convert lip-service into determined action.

The United States cannot, alone, save civilization; but, by default of affirmative leadership, it can come perilously close to insuring civilization's end.

INDEX

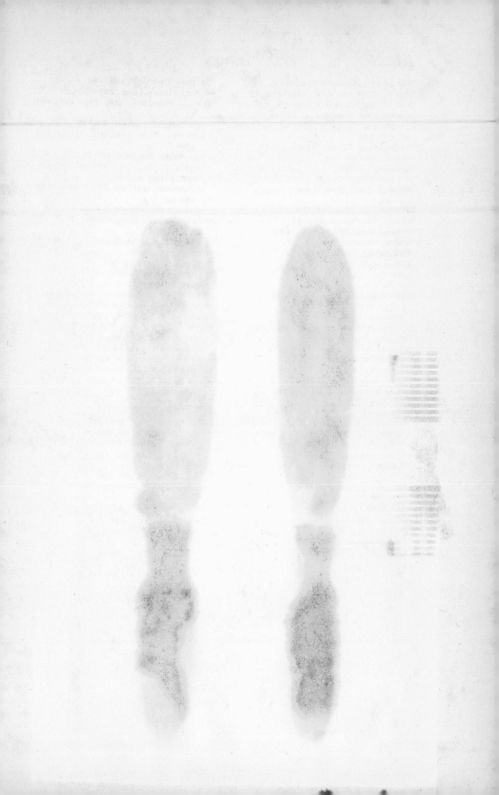

2/28/55

DATE DUE

GAYLORD   PRINTED IN U.S.A.